T0354519

JUST WHO AM I TRAINING ANYWAY

ANYWAY

A COMMON SENSE GUIDE TO TEACHING

By
Dave Slater

Order this book online at www.trafford.com
or email orders@trafford.com

Most Trafford titles are also available at major online book retailers.

Printed in the United States of America.

ISBN: 978-1-4669-0998-4 (sc)
ISBN: 978-1-4669-0996-0 (hc)
ISBN: 978-1-4669-0997-7 (e)

Library of Congress Control Number: 2011963570

Trafford rev. 01/04/2012

 www.trafford.com

North America & international
toll-free: 1 888 232 4444 (USA & Canada)
phone: 250 383 6864 ♦ fax: 812 355 4082

A COMMON HORSE SENSE GUIDE TO TEACHING 3

CONTEXT..3

PRELUDE...4

INTRODUCTION 5

PART 1   DISCOVERING THE TEACHER 8

CHAPTER 1.   THE QUESTIONS.. 9

CHAPTER 2:   UNDERSTANDING THE FUNDAMENTALS OF TEACHING.............15

CHAPTER 3:   FOUR PRIMARY TEACHING APPROACHES...........................24

CHAPTER 4:   THE STEPS FOR BECOMING A BETTER TEACHER...................42

CHAPTER 5:   LEARNING THE POWER OF PROBLEM SOLVING...................67

CHAPTER 6:   WHEN AM I WASTING MY TIME 92

PART 2   DISCOVERING THE STUDENT...103

CHAPTER 7:   UNDERSTANDING THE STUDENT.......................................104

CHAPTER 8:   EVEN A TEENAGER WILL MAKE SENSE 123

CHAPTER 9:   HOW LEARNING TAKES PLACE.......................................140

CHAPTER 10:   WHAT INFLUENCES A CHILD TO REACT.............................161

PART 3   WHAT WILL I TEACH 183

CHAPTER 11:   INSPIRING THRU BOMB PROOF CHARACTER TRAITS..............184

   FAITH TO PRAY... 190

   RESPECT..193

   SELF ESTEEM and SELF CONFIDENCE................................198

   THRIFTINESS..203

   DISCERNMENT..207

   COMMITMENT..212

   HONESTY..218

   TOLERATING THE PAINS OF INCONVENIENCE...................220

   COURAGE..228

   UNDERSTANDING THE PRINCIPLE OF PRACTICE.............231

   ENJOYMENT OF LIFE..234

PART 4   INCREASING EFFECTIVENESS... 239

CHAPTER 12:   AM I AN EFFECTIVE TEACHER.. 240

CHAPTER 13:   GOING BACK TO THE BASICS...248

CHAPTER 14:   A LESSON OF PRACTISE...271

CHAPTER 15:   GRADUATING ESCALATION OF INVOLEMENT.....................283

CHAPTER 16:   HOW TO DELIVER AN EFFECTIVE PUNISHMENT   316

CHAPTER 17:   NOW IS NOT TIME TO QUIT...341

CHAPTER 18:   PUTTING IT ALL TOGETHER 369

PART 5   THE ULTIMATE TEACHERS 393

CHAPTER 19:   RECEIVING GUIDANCE FROM THE ULTIMATE TEACHERS........394

INDEX...408

PRELUDE

I have made it a point in my life to never be afraid to undertake something new. As result, I will take great pains to learn. I teach this to my students. In this book I have shared my real life experiences; they make me what I am. They give me the wisdom to draw on.

INTRODUCTION

I graduated from Weber High School in '73 and thought of myself as an ineligible candidate for the Vietnam Draft, due to a medical disability. By this year in the war, the draft was no longer being called up and none of my classmates were inducted. In those two years following school, I had been working very physical labor as a farmhand; I muscled up and never did I have any ill effects from my disability. I also further matured somewhat in my thinking and now viewed myself as a fully capable being, not one encumbered with a limiting deformity. I voluntarily enlisted to fulfill what I then thought as my civic duty to serve my country for six years as a member of the United States Armed Forces. When going through my pre-enlistment physical I simply didn't draw attention to my back defect and the doctors didn't find it. I applied myself to my fullest while enlisted, and as a result, did extremely well.

Since that time I have taken on my quest for knowledge as a yearning student, and then later progressed to pass on knowledge as a skilled master teacher. I am the father of five children whom have grownup and matured into responsible adults. I am proud of their accomplishments. I am also, at present, the pleased grandfather of nine grandchildren. After the Army I went back into agriculture and supported my family as a farmer and rancher for twenty-six years.

As my children left the nest and moved from home, I signed on as a Wilderness Therapy Guide. For six years I dealt with problem kids, ages thirteen to thirty-two. The clients were troubled adolescents whose parents hadn't yet given up. With aspiration, their folks were reaching-out for help. These youths showed up in the program with problems of addictions and developed behavioral issues as they tried to defensively cope with their painful life experiences. Many had histories of failure to apply themselves. My duties required that I spend with these students, twenty-four hours a day, eight days at a stretch, every other week.

All clients received a weekly session with a licensed clinical therapist who kept in touch with their parents throughout the youth's sixty-plus-or-minus-day stay.   Search polices and remote location eliminated the infiltration of non-regulated substances; any previously prescribed drugs were administered under the strictest practices. Challenged with the implementation of positive values and self-awareness, they were daily held to a standard that required investment into improving their lives, both physically and behaviorally, Personal accountability was always upheld, while, environment and time eagerly gave consequences for poor choices. During their duration out in the wilderness, without the modern luxuries of life as distractions, these kids learned how to make wiser decisions in order to better problem solve. To graduate they had to learn to make and keep goals. They had to develop healthy relationships with their guides and group of peers.

Daily, all back-packed their camps about the upper sonoran wilds while being subjected to finding water and dealing with whatever nature threw their way. They were worked with therapeutically until they learned alternative steps to control inappropriate behaviors, to stay clean, and to be prepared to succeed in future schooling. The physical exercise, roughing it, and survival atmosphere mentally awoke their awareness. They gained an appreciation of what they had back home. They recognized a gain of more control in their lives by working with their parents' desires, instead of fighting against them.

I saw hundreds of troubled clients during those years and realized that the reason these youth needed help wasn't theirs alone. Most lacked consistency from their parents. Some had parents who chose not to be engaged in their lives beyond providing for entitled material wants.

Many parents didn't understand how to raise their levels of involvement in order to act as effective child trainers. These well meaning parents wanted to do right by their children, but they lacked the knowledge and skills to demand that their kids act responsibly and compliantly. So busily engaged in meeting their children's desires, most parents hadn't learned to properly say "NO." They had conditioned their kids to continue using a demanding childish mindset, which obtained every want through the manipulation of others. They retained little control. In their desires to be good parents many avoided confrontations. They had allowed their kids to train them into succumbing and permitting resistive, obnoxious or abusive behaviors instead of becoming the type of parent that their child's behavior required.

During graduations, parents would come and spend a day and a night with their recently changed children. It was easy to recognize why some of the youths had behaved as they did, after viewing their parents' coping skills. I gained the insight that parents hold much of the blame for the childhood behavioral problems they allow their kids to develop.

My credentials include: I have helped my wife raise our kids. Of course, I have made many mistakes. But in them, I have learned as well. Working with youth who have been sent to wilderness programs in hope that they can once again get their lives in order, I have seen the results of mistakes which so many other parents have made. For years I have trained horses and seen the commonality with training these fine animals and in the training of youth. *Both can become learning students in the hands of a capable trainer.* I have had the opportunity to use these ideas presented in my book and seen them perform wonders in the wilderness, at home, and in a horse assisted therapy program which I have developed. I strive to utilize the principles taught within this book in my daily dealings with others.

All potential students basically want the same things out of life.
They can be reached as individuals when their needs and wants are understood and enhanced in proper ways.

I claim the "Common Sense" to have learned from observation, exposure, and implementation. I have discovered knowledge and offer to you, the explorers of this book, the same opportunity.

Read, learn, and then enjoy your new skills which you will develop.

PART 1

DISCOVERING THE TEACHER

CHAPTER 1: **THE QUESTIONS**

"**Y**ou're late! Just where have you been?" she bombarded. Her words delivered the instant the door opened; a peeved anger resonated through her voice.

"We went to the Dairy Freeze after leaving Cindy's. I didn't think you'd—"

"So yah thought you'd sneak in again, did yah?"

In attempt to explain herself, the trapped daughter started again. "Mom, I'd—" only to be chopped short once more by her irritated mother.

"I've waited up two hours just to catch you, *young lady*!"

"Why can't you just ask me how it went," flashed back Sue in retaliation, "without jumping down my throat?"

"WE NEED TO TALK NOW!" shouted mom.

"Not when you're acting like such a jerk!" Sue's countenance flipped flopped one-eighty degrees triggered by mother's lead. Her retort started at the shrieking level of mom's, and then increased further to about 100 decibels. Simultaneously she thrust out her tongue, shook her hands, and waved her fore-arms side to side, all the while teetering at her trunk. Theatrically she purposely mimicked mom's freak-out. With that, she turned flamboyantly and started marching towards her room.

"Don't talk to me like that!" screeched mother. "Wait 'till I tell your father about this; he'll ground you for a month!" Yet Sue, without looking back, was still continuing up the stairs. "Did you hear what I said, young lady?"

"Yah, like that'll be the day!" hollered down the freshly aroused she-devil. "I am tired and I am going to bed. I don't have time to deal with your anger", she shouted back with mirroring vengeance. Sue jeered back over her shoulder for one last scowl. Her extravagant melodramatic display only succeeded to distract her pounding accent, causing her to snag a high-healed sandal on the carpeted stairs. She stumbled to catch herself, but missed quick placement on her now out-of-sequence bare foot. Sharply she stubbed her toe, causing a cry out of pain, "OH," she yipped.

Mom cringed slightly at the teen's misfortune, but quickly passed on offering sympathy. Allowing only her own justification of anger, "*She desired that!*" Mom reveled.

Discounting her throbbing toe and abandoned sandal, the youth forced her defiant march up the last flight. Stomping down the hall, she threw open her bedroom door, burst in, and then slammed it closed, so-as-to drive home to mom the message: **"YOU ARE NOT IN CHARGE."**

"That girl has got me so worked up," thought mom. "I should have just smacked her right then and there; maybe then I'd get some respect. It sure would have made me feel a whole lot better."

"Damn kid," she thought climbing in bed. Stealing a look at her alarm clock; it was 12:45a.m. "Now, I won't be able to sleep a wink." Fuming she thought of how tired she'd be at work tomorrow.

Lying in bed, the remembrance of the evening's disaster was keeping her awake. The clock showed 2:53. Over two hours had passed and Mom still continued to fret over the earlier incident, but fading was the personal anger she felt over the ill effects from Sue's lack of respect. Replacing it was a mind full of so many questions.

"Maybe, I should just forget about it and leave her to learn responsibility on her own? That sure would be a whole lot easier." Thoughts continued to bombard her as stinging hail driven in a stiff wind.

"Looking back at last night, I wonder what would have hap-pened if I hadn't jumped all over her? What if I'd just given her a hug, or at least given her the benefit of doubt as to why she was late again ...at least until she could explain?" Mom's chance for sleep was now long gone. "She's only fifteen; and not yet an adult. How could I have been so rough on her? ... **Poor kid**"

The correct answers were just not there. More thoughts raced through her mind, each one leading to others. Each thought directing a mini role-play. Which was right? What effect would the different approaches make on Sue, if played out?

"It seems that for the past two years every time I confront Sue, we end up in a fight. I just want Sue to be more respectful and to see the error of her ways." Mom continued to question herself further, "*I am doing this for her own good, aren't I?*"

"Although Sue never minds what I say, I still think she's basically a good kid. She does get along with her father, but why wouldn't she? He acts more like her friend than a dad ... she has no reasons to fight and or to have any problems with him!"

"Why, that man hardly ever disciplines her. It is though all he is interested in is having a good time and doesn't want to spoil it by creating any problems. ... Stirring up problems, now that's something he leaves to me. I surely remember his two greatest quotes, '*I am not the one with the problem. If you have a problem with it, then you do something about it.*' Or he would say, '*That's your problem, not mine!*' "

Throughout her night of lost sleep and mind numbing questions, one thing was starting to stick in her mind. It seemed to not go away; her tired brain kept coming back to it again and again. She forced this thought in order to give a relief to the night's difficulties: "*Basically, with Sue, I have a problem.*" It was an effort to give clarity to her questioning mind, and it did offer an ease and a relief to lump all the turmoil of the past months together.

"*Yes, that's it; basically, I have a problem,*" she mused as she sought slumber. "*Now ... sleep might come.*" With this new defined solemn, almost did a peace overtake her.

Suddenly, without warning she was once more jolted back into consciousness and into vivid recollection! "What's that again; did I say, '*I have a problem?*' I sure don't like where this is going." Again the questioning started. She summonsed her energy to dismiss that weak moment's thought by forcing a new fixation on: "I am not the one with the problem, Sue is. She makes me so mad sometimes!"

Once more back to her mind came her previous thought, like a pesky fly that is swatted away; it still keeps returning to circle around for another bussing. "And that word *"Basically"*, it sure sounds a lot like, **"Basics"**. Wasn't "Basics" the very word which Greg Taylor was using the other day?" Now mom was not just thinking, but actually carrying a conversation on with herself.

"Yes, I do remember it was "basics", or rather it was, "Back to the Basics" which he was using while referring to my horse. I had been having difficulties with my pretty palomino, problem horse. Greg saw and then offered a helping suggestion."

"My Problem Horse", sort of reminds me of my daughter. It won't mind and it tries to get away with things. Sometimes it even seems to fight with me when I try to control it. Often I have to force it to rein, just like Sue." Mom's thoughts were now beginning to channel together, giving her force and momentum.

"Now I remember exactly what he did say, 'In order to get that horse to settle down, you are going to have to go back to the basics.' Greg should know; he spends a lot of time training his horses. His daughters show them in competitions and do very well. Of course his daughters behave very well themselves, also. When they come over and visit with Sue, they are so polite. I don't think I have ever heard any of them talking about fighting with their parents. Yes, his daughters are well trained like his horses. … So unlike mine!"

"I recall last fall, the new horse he got for his oldest daughter; it was a big spoiled pet. Still, he bragged, 'I paid six thousand dollars for that blood line.' Mom continued to focus in on her neighbor and his horse, "In just four months that bay acted like a totally new animal. It developed a different attitude; it was willing, supple, and submissive to his daughters. That horse, after his training, didn't fight with them nor was it spoiled and demanding; it even seemed to look toward experiencing new things."

"I just want to teach Sue the right things to do," mom again switched her thoughts back to her daughter and allowed herself the luxury of dwelling on that thought for a while. Then appearing as a

wild stallion breaking out of a corral and heading back to the hills racing for his freedom while gathering speed and desire the closer it got, here was her new thought racing through her mind: ***Doing the correct things for the right reasons.*** All was starting to make sense.

"Last night sure didn't turn out the way I'd have wanted," she again saw a new replay of the previous night's scene in her mind; only this time it was starting to have a different ending. ... *"Yes that's it! That's the answer!"* In order for my involvement with Sue to go a new direction and have a different ending, we must have a new beginning— *I think I've found where to start.*

A plan was starting to form in mother's mind, "Tomorrow I'll go over and talk more to Greg; I believe that there may be something to that phrase, "Back to the Basics," his horse sure benefited. I am beginning to understanding his success with his daughters also."

Have you ever found yourself in the dilemma of Sue's mom, of having more questions than answers regarding how to handle others? If so, this book is for you.

You are now taking the time to read, and also, attempting to gain knowledge about a chosen subject. You are currently approaching a teachable state. Let me, in this book, share with you some of my experiences that have helped me see the correlation between training a horse and teaching children. In fact, you will see the similarities with all other forms of teaching and interaction with others. As you ponder and understand this guide, you will begin thinking, **"Now that makes sense; it's so easy."**

Just read and follow the guidelines and you too will have a new beginning in your quest to becoming more effective as an imparter of knowledge. You will realize how and why learning takes place. You will see yourself not only as a parent, but also a skilled child trainer when you implement the ideas that you'll learn. New tips will enter with force into your mind as your inspiration process awakens more fully.

You will develop a new relationship with your charges when you are committed to train and enlighten. You will get more results. Sit back, find some quiet place and allow yourself, like Sue's mom, to enter into the Common Horse Sense Guide to Teaching.

CHAPTER 2:

UNDERSTANDING THE FUNDAMENTALS OF TEACHING

Teaching is like the public demonstration of an artist's talent: many display in exhibition of their mastery; others strive to inspire and enhance another's understandings.

In order for you the reader, *acquiring knowledge as a student*, and I the author, *arousing you from my role as a trainer*, to get anywhere in our goal of you becoming a better imparter of knowledge, we first need to establish a foundation from which to work. We should come together on common ground. You should become aware of the terms and generalities used in this book, so that we may communicate in the same language.

Parents, adults, supervisors, even friends who find themselves with something to pass-on are all possible teachers. All have the potential to impart of their understandings.

Whenever you have any sort of interaction with a child, you are taking on the role of teacher and educator of the lessons of life. This book will help you recognize what lessons your children are learning. It will give you the power to deal with problematic behaviors. The answers are found in this common sense book to the question, "What is the most valuable role I can take to prepare them for life?"

And for you, who find yourself in the position as a supervisor or a trainer to employees or other charges, this book also addresses:

"How can I expand my skills in order to better facilitate my charge's improvement?" All who attempt to educate others can benefit.

The design of this book is to enable any form of teacher to combine a horse sense used in the training of horses, together with a newly awakened common sense approach towards teaching, and use both in the teaching of the willing student, or in effectively dealing with the problematic child. This wisdom will inspire all to improve and become more effective as educators, thereby meeting the needs and wants of their students. This book will empower you as a parent, employer, professional teacher, or even simply as an experienced traveler who has passed through some of life's paths to use the best timing and methods to impart some of your knowledge to others.

Foundational Definitions

A **Guide** is: 1} one who directs a motion through a strange place. 2} one who guides by example. 3} one who makes others aware of the forthcoming, by the sharing of information and experiences, or by the directing of the paths they should follow.

An **Instructor** is: an imparter of knowledge in a systematic order designed to accomplish a specific task.

A **Master** is: one who has displayed by his actions an advanced competence.

A **Mentor** is: a trusted counselor who has common interests with his pupil.

A **Parent** is: 1} biologically one who begets offspring. 2} one who takes on the role of being a primary provider and caregiver to his or her children.

In today's society parents have implied jurisdiction, and so, they are therefore deemed in charge of and have the responsibility for their own children, unless proven to be incapable of meeting the child's basic physical and mental needs. As a parent it is necessary to take on all the roles of a teacher in order to fulfill that primary role.

A **Supervisor** is: 1} one who oversees or directs a project. 2} one who directs or oversees other persons or charges in their involvement in a set activity.

A **Trainer** is: 1} a director of growth. 2} **one who changes a behavior through his interaction**. With his assisting of a charge to develop new skills, by the use of offering a discipline or a reward, a trainer will affect a charge in order to get a predetermined outcome.

All of the previous can be lumped into the definition of a Teacher.

The definition of a **Teacher** is: 1} any imparter of knowledge and wisdom. 2} one who shows, instructs, or presents new ideas. A teacher is any experienced being wishing to impart some understanding to another.

A **Charge** is: a person, or animal that is in the care of, under the responsibility of, or the recipient of the obligations of another.

A **Child** is: 1} a student to new ideas; a youth to new experiences and training. 2} any living body which is capable of learning. A child is moldable like an unhardened piece of clay which can be shaped by anyone, but reaches its highest potential when it is willing and pliable and can be sculptured by one possessing the right talents. A child certainly can be any progressive adult, if he is teachable and moldable. —By learning, he too is making headway toward his highest potential. {**Because this book relates to both equine and all manner of students, the word "child" can encompasses any dependents, or charges of a teacher.**}

In the instructions of this book often the words *child, student, pupil, charge, youth, learner,* or *apprentice* are used inter-changeably as they all can be associated with someone who is lacking in the experiences of life. They all can be associated with someone or something that has the capacity, or is willing to learn. To assist your learning, you will be exposed to the repetition of ideas. It is by repeated exposure that learning is solidified to one's thought process. When the student can recall a thought, or implement an idea as his own, then he is on the road to becoming a master.

Out-of-Control Behavior is the purposeful action of a body to deal with an unwanted situation without using compliance, respect, or an acceptable problem solving skill. It is not a behavior problem in which the displayer doesn't have a choice in what they are doing. It is a defense reaction used to cope with an unwanted feeling. The thing about an unwanted behavior that is truly out-of-control is the teacher's inability to change it unless he assertively confronts it.

A **Reward** is the offering of a gratification which is received either in the present, or the future; it is presented to a participant after their service or attainment. The obtaining of a reward encompasses much more than just someone else having to buy a behavior, or having to dig into their emotional savings account to pay compensation for a service. It is any type of physical or emotional gain recognized or received.

Common Sense says: **A reward is relevant.**
 It's a reward to get rest when working.
 When just resting, it is a reward to become productive.

In the reading of this book you will learn the skills to become a better teacher. You will gain the appropriate knowledge to be able to affect a change in another person. Enjoy the down to earth, Common Sense philosophies of the author. They will help you increase your effectiveness when dealing with children, horses, and the like by utilizing their wants and needs for learning or change.

You, from the skills in this book, can develop into a wise and skilled master sculptor. Having the abilities to mold as clay your pupils and charges, you will look at each teaching situation as a chance to bring out more of a finished image. You will enlarge your understandings of things such as:

Common Sense: **The trainer has no way of triumph, except to exhibit a greater force than his pupil. This force can be in the form of wisdom, the exhibit of love, or the taking of control.**

Common Sense: **In order to teach, I must have someone striving to learn; otherwise I am just sharpening my own skills.**

Common Sense: **Being an effective teacher requires that I teach for the correct reasons, use the right timing, and offer to my pupils recognized incentives.**

Common Sense: **Learning can only take place as the student engages and puts forth effort.**

Common Sense: **The amount of growth gained will be in direct proportion to the amount of efficient effort one gives.**

Common Sense: **Both parents and teachers increase their effectiveness when they share their wisdom out of love, when their motivations for interaction are for the benefit of their charges, and when they stand ready to administer the wise relief of pain.**

Common Sense: **Those involved in the teaching business such as teachers, trainers, supervisors, and instructors should have as their goal: to assist their charges to be self-sufficient.** There will be a time when the pupil must stand on his own without others there to guide and help him along.

-   The Starting Point:

The primary question that should be asked of self, before embarking down any teaching path is: **"Why must I teach?"**

To obtain an introspective answer, consider first the two motivational extremes of, *"Why one is motivated to teach."* They are either:
"Selfless"   **I do it for them.**   Or,
"Selfish"   **I do it for me**.

I do it for them: I help my charges benefit from my experiences by teaching the skills I know now; but wish I had known before. My hope is the new information will benefit to my pupils.

If I teach for the purpose of helping my charges, I will adapt my approach to come across as compassionate, caring, concerned, or possibly tough and ready to be engaged. I will change my approach and methods as-soon-as I see that there is a better way. Since I am using a selfless teaching approach, I do not seek my own gratifications. My agenda is for them to benefit, and not for me to fulfill a hidden personal motive. As result, my pupils will then sense my purpose and feel that it is them who are important to me.

Because of service based involvement, this teacher will be viewed as a meaningful role model, regardless of technical knowledge.

I do it for me: I act with a core purpose of having my expectations met. I only interact that I may seek some form of personal gain or ease of obligation; I act to fulfill some self-centered desire for gratification which I believe will come as result of my teaching. *This could be the fulfillment I receive from assisting others, or from rescuing them from their difficulties. It may only appear my egotistic thought: "I have done my best." My self-claimed purpose might be as innocent as saving them from the agony of having to learn everything firsthand.*

To identify why you are teaching, you must consider:
"Which of my expectations are being met?
"Is my primary goal to serve the needs of my students?"

Or in exact opposite, "Is my serving of others the result of my quest for gratification and selfish desires? Are my desires to be effective foremost geared around gaining more for myself?" If so, then I won't necessarily be looking for ways to change or improve in order to best serve the desires and needs of my students. While engaging with another selfishly, I'll only seek for improvement and efficiency, so that I might further benefit.

Can you pin-point: Why you are teaching?

Perhaps as you intro-spec your desires to teach so that others might improve, you also recognize that you stand to benefit as well. There is often a mixing of the two extremes, a middle path:

As I teach others, both they and I benefit: This is the teacher who is teaching to impart knowledge to his charges out of his love and concern for them, and at the same time he may be personally realizing a financial benefit, a social improvement, or a sense of fulfillment to his own joy. He may come across as a caring professional wanting the most for his charges, eager to sacrifice his own needs and comforts in order to provide for others. At the same time, he requires of his charges a payment for his efforts. In this, the healthiest relationship between the teacher and pupil, the teacher by recognizing his gains has the continued desire to improve his efficiency and helpfulness to his charges, and the students receive maximum gains from the efforts and involvements of this caring teacher who does whatever it takes to best serve their needs.

Acting in this realm of teaching, the teacher should consider both causes. The teacher's desires are not the dictating factor of his involvement, neither is the overwhelming desire to help his charge. It is the wise combination of the two, with the uppermost importance placed on the student being given his best chance for improvement.

Fundamental differences between masculine and feminine roles:
References to masculine and feminine teaching roles are used to describe the teaching approaches presented in this book. These

approaches are merely called after the gender they typically resemble.

To be most effective as a teacher, it is necessary to adopt parts of both roles.

A *Masculine Role* receives its self definition by its experiences. Being masculine means the user is more likely to have the inter-driving force to build, problem solve, and to battle. A masculine approach has the user looking at life as a challenge to be overcome.

In a family, the Father's Role is to protect and provide an environment for a home where he directs his children toward opportunities, so that they may be challenged to reach their highest potentials.

The masculine, Loving Father Approach is all about having one's charges exposed to the things in life which might challenge them. This approach is to see that they are given the opportunity for those experiences.

A *Feminine Role* receives its self definition by its concern for others. It is defined by an inter-driving force to show caring. The user affects the lives of those around her by providing care, service, and compassion. While in this feminine role of the Nurturing Parent [Good Mother] Approach, the user gives the necessary things to her children to make their experience in life easier and helps them through situations which may cause grief or sufferings.

A Mother's Role in the family is for the nurturing of her charges. She performs her objectives of serving her children with their safety foremost.

The feminine, Nurturing Parent Approach is all about saving charges from things that could hinder them. It is about giving service to one's charges, and seeing that their feelings are not damaged.

Common Sense: **It would be impossible for a child to reach their highest potential without exposure to both the Masculine and Feminine Roles.**

Sole parents that find themselves with the responsibilities of a child will have to take on attributes of both roles to best serve their family. **To be given the freedom to expand, the child must be challenged, nurtured and protected.**

You have analyzed your motives why you feel compelled to teach. Now it is important to further pick an approach to use in this imparting of your knowledge. You will use one or more of the next chapter's approaches every time that you teach. As you become more aware of them, you have an increased ability to choose wisely.

Understanding your motivations and teaching approaches will assist you in making decisions of how much effort and involvement to put forth. You will realize, first comes the defining and refining of yourself, and then you can assist others. You will learn how to adjust your approach, refine your skills, and where to turn in order to receive assistance in best serving your pupils. You will learn how to stay more involved and free-thinking in dealing with your child's needs. As you gain more understanding and enlightenment, you will have the ability to become more effective.

The next chapter offers to you an awakening of self-awareness. Understanding its options constitutes a beginning place from which all encounters with others start.

Discover what type of teacher you are.

Understand further why you feel a need to teach.

CHAPTER 3:

FOUR PRIMARY TEACHING APPROACHES:

The Passing

As a battle wise warrior,
with a grey furrowed brow,
I pass a wandering youth
who's eager to find how.

Shall I speak to the youth,
my life's treasures to share?
Offer to the lad directions,
who perhaps wouldn't care?

Do I instruct how to sharpen,
thus a strong sword he can wield?
Teach him correctly to advance
and when it's proper to yield?

Perhaps I'll offer drink and a rest,
next shield bright sun off his eyes?
Do I laugh whilst he laughs,
and then cry when he cries?

Or jump on his strong shoulders
to be carried back to my home;
then bribe him thus to tarry
so I won't be left as alone?

Is it easier to recite, "See yah?"
Perhaps wave a lukewarm, "Hi?"
Dread I've only time to look away,
and hope he, too, passes me by.

Red Hawk

Each of the four Teaching Approaches is found in this poem. They depict the different motivating purposes which direct a person's involvement to be a teacher and to engage with another. They open the possibilities for teaching to happen and for learning to occur. The would-be teacher already possesses and knows the information that he could use to help this needy child. His choice is whether or not he shares it, and, if so, what approach he will use should he decide to assist the young traveler?

Teaching Approaches:

1. LOVING FATHER APPROACH

The definitive goal of the Loving Father is to raise the potential of his charges. This is done by his involvement in their lives. Just as belief in a God has this Supreme Being designing for his subjects to experience a fullness of joy, so does a teacher coming from this approach want for his charges to likewise be the best they can be. This teacher also experiences a greater personal happiness by providing an opportunity for his pupils to obtain more of their potentials. The Loving Father style teacher encourages a successful accomplishment of challenges.

Using the Loving Father Approach will at times seem hard on a youngster. A master at using this approach will size up any situation by how much gain it offers the youth. His motive is to assist the child progress. He knows that in order to grow and get better at any task one must increase in ability. This gain encompasses the enduring of pain. If in the rigors of action a little injury happens, "Oh well, such is life." The teacher who uses this approach, but does not fully understand it, may feel the urge to coerce his pupils into the performing of tasks. He believes that after the hardships of a task diminish and fade, then the gains received will outweigh any previous sufferings. Even when wrongly executing this approach, his motives are still that his charges will become better because of their forced upon experiences.

To benefit his children, a masculine father would shoot them from a cannon barrel, if he thought it would do them some good.

This masculine father means well, and he's so proud when his child does "manly things." He hasn't yet realized that in order for a child to get maximum gain they must perform willingly. A child must retain its freedom of choice. The previous statement should be revised to show a freedom of choice to carry out great things rather than a child forced against their will. It then would read:

To benefit his children, a father should help them understand their advantages in being shot from a cannon, then when they are ready, assist them into the barrel and light the fuse.

Father's Duty

A Father's Duty is to provide a safe environment for his charges, wherein, they may have the opportunities to work towards reaching their highest potentials. A masculine father will defend his children if he thinks that they are out matched or are in harm's way.

Introspection: *As one's motives become defined as being those of a loving father, a self revealing question should be asked. Am I protecting my own interests or are my concerns chiefly for my children?*

A man by nature seems to be at his best whenever he is combating some kind of challenge. Even though he will send home his pay as a means of providing for the support of his family, the father who is distanced from his kin must still question his motives. The soldier going off to war, or even the busy father who must work demanding hours away from home should ask himself, "Am I going off to battle as a means of hiding from my family responsibilities, or do I feel that by my leaving it is going to assist me in providing for my families' needs and to further help me to keep them safe?"

A generation ago, by leaving a father was also distancing himself from his family and the chance to interact with them. The same thing applied to the father who chose to work away from home or allowed himself to continue on a schedule which resulted in his not being home with his children. By his distancing he was losing many an opportunity to be involved in his children's lives.

I knew a Captain in the National Guard who in this modern time of the internet would e-mail each of his children several times a week just to keep involved in their lives. He daily corresponded, offered counsel, and kept them in his prayers. After he came home from Iraq, he mentioned that this period of separation brought him more closely involved in his children's lives than prior to his deployment. Before, he was at home and could have daily spent time with them, yet he felt he was too busy. *{Really he knows now that before he was too selfish and didn't understand the ramifications of solely pursuing his own interests.}* This soldier showed me that while physically living with his family or apart, it was always his choice whether or not to distance himself from his children, wife, and family responsibilities.

2. NURTURING PARENT—GOOD MOTHER APPROACH:

The Nurturing Parent takes care of her children; she protects them from harm, stress and injury. She treats her children with compassion, and is quick to forgive their shortcomings. She will sacrifice her wants and needs in order to aid her charges. She uplifts them by raising their self-esteem. She will view any situation from the perspective of, "Is it safe for my child, and are they being stressed in any way?" Because of her desires to assist, it is easy for her to stay as the foremost influence in her young child's life.

Most of the higher forms of life in the animal kingdom have a *single parent* raising their young. Oh daddy might be around, but usually he is too busy pursuing his own interests to be of any help. If driven by his instincts, he may even offer a form of behind-the-scenes defense and protection for his children as he guards his own wellbeing. With a disengaged sire, most of the burdens associated with the training of the offspring fall mainly on the mother. Periodically there are visits from good old dad, where he tries to impress others for personal gains and desires. In many of such cases the female endeavors to protect or keep apart her young from her self-serving mate as she recognizes this non-nurturing male's primal desires may not always be best for them.

Common Sense: **A Nurturing Mother receives her joy from the giving of service and from the return of affection.**

My wife is an example of a Nurturing Mother. She makes it a point to give praises to her children. In our home you could daily hear her say, "You are cute as a boot." Interpreted this meant: "You are indeed good looking, a good person, and/or should feel proud of your own worth." Dana would take occasion daily in some form or other to build up each of her children's confidence. In addition, she would give the kids praise for any real effort they did at attempting to solve problems, rewarding with, "You are so smart." I can't ever remember her ever tearing down one of her children. If they made mistakes, she would discredit the actions and not the individuals. She has always seemed to focus most energy on the ones that might be struggling. After such a mom, it turned out that my children grew up and became gorgeous like unto their mother.

Going overboard toward the Good Mother end of this approach, is the parent that strives to keep a charge's dependence. A socialistic government is a good example of keeping its people as dependants. The needs of the people are provided for under the pretense to help make life easier for them. In this society it is believed that this well-meaning government must intervene in the providing for its subjects because they can't properly provide or make wise enough decisions alone. Hence the government must step in where its people are lacking. The general consensus is: *This extreme intervention is a welcome thing. The governing body is doing a better job than the people could if left on their own.* But, in doing so, it is also taking away from their freedoms and choices to learn, struggle, or fail, and then ultimately rise up from their setbacks to overcome their own deficiencies. Likewise is a teacher who goes overboard in encouraging her pupils to remain dependent; her charges are not being allowed to grow up. This displayer of well-meaning is mainly serving her selfish interests by fulfilling her gratifications of service and power in her greediness of remaining the foremost benefactor of her charges' lives.

An over-nurturing parent feels that if her child experiences failures or rejections, it would be experiencing pains or hardships unnecessarily. Any child left to endure pain is going against her very core mind-set. She feels it her duty to bail her child out of any difficulties. She acts on her instinct to nurture, and doesn't fully process that failure is the very thing that will force the child to get stronger and to improve. She will intervene in her child's learning process to shield them from the disapproval of others. She means well, but is too afraid to see her child struggle.

Do you interact as a teacher from either the positive or the negative of either of these approaches? Are you acting so much from an extreme side of either that you're actually limiting your own effectiveness and hindering your child?

3. SELF ENTITLED APPROACH:

In its simplest form this approach is nothing more than the Loving Father gone astray or an over-nurturing parent. These teachers mean well and still may feel that they have the betterment of their charges as a purpose of their interactions. Yet, they are still employing a predominantly selfish mindset. They may not even realize that they are using their charges as a method of obtaining personal gains or as a means of fulfilling personal desires. In such cases as these teachers re-evaluate their techniques, they will realize there is a better adjustment that can be made that will best help their charges to be inspired to improve.

Let us look at the full blown Self Entitled Approach Teacher. This guy has as a primary objective to profit personally from the efforts of others. He selfishly seeks to, *"Gain from Another's Pain."* To do this he entices others in the belief that they will benefit personally if they participate in his plan.

The following are examples of persons being subjected to a Self Entitled Approach:

- A salaried or paid employee who works to receive income from an employer.
- In faith for a new look, the poor sap who spends money on a diet plan which, in fact, doesn't work.
- As a consumer, you have been taken in by companies selling cigarettes or other harmful materials under the disguise these items are harmless and desirable.
- A child being told to shut-up or else. *The primary reason for it is the selfish relief of the caregiver.*
- You need this class, so you have to endure a teacher who is just in it for the personal benefits. He refuses to make his material interesting and appealing to his students.
- Being the subject of intimidation from a person of influence, who uses his power to get your forced compliance in the direction of his advantage.

The Self Entitled Teacher does not get a lasting compliance from an unwilling charge. His effectiveness will only be as long as he retains the ability to force his charge to behave, or he continues to have the means to offer enticing benefits to the reluctant. When the benefits received are no longer appealing or the power of the teacher is found lacking, then the charge will question remaining involved.

In some cases as underlings, we find ourselves subjected to the entitlement of others through no choice of our own. We find that we are subjected to a forcing, or we become caught up in an overpowering form of control, in which we have no envisioned escape. This superior entity may have the ability to force us to comply, but when its power is not from our choice, then we will be engaged within its envisioned outcome only to the **elimination of our own obligations of compliance.** Without our consent, when we feel forced to do something for another, we will put forth as small an effort as we think can be gotten away with. It will be our goal to remain in motion under the radar of detection.

{We will compromise the level of our compliance: Like choosing to go at our comfortable pace, which may be sixty-eight in a sixty-five

mile-an-hour zone, because we know that we will not be stopped and ticketed unless we are going faster than four miles beyond the speed limit.}

The opposite of being subjected unwillingly to another's self-entitlement is doing something which we, as receiving pupils, choose to do because we recognize the **gains** offered.*{see: page: 124}* We chose to relinquish some of our personal freedoms in order to be more supposedly assured that we will benefit. Perhaps we feel that if we allow ourselves to be subjected to someone or some entity, then this becomes our best choice. We feel they can better take care of us than we may be able to when left solely on our own. Or we believe that we can afford to pay their asking price, in order to receive of their services, knowledge, or of the great implied things they offer. We allow ourselves to be governed by another, as a trade-off, in order to get something we want.

Since the purpose of all Self Entitled Teachers' involvement is the collection of returns from their efforts, they require that we give them a gratuity for their services. They don't work for free. When the payment that they require is too much for us to bear, or we quit believing that the benefits they offer are worth the pains that they demand, we will seek to abandon our present involvement. Our participation in the future will be greatly reduced as they lose their controlling appeal.

Common Sense Lesson: The Controlled Diet and Exercise Program

Most diet and exercise plans end up being forgotten and abandoned because at some point the sufferer, whose stomach is screaming for nourishment as he works up a sweaty body, has come to the realization that the personal benefit of his last horridly long hour of personal torture counteracts only the calories of the simple and tasty muffin which he ate out of starvation from doing the program in the first place. The once important goal of slimming down has lost its momentum when the dieter has decided, "The gain just ain't worth the pain!" The disenchanted will abandon his pursuit of getting in shape, and he still has to pay for his exercise equipment and program, the contract demands it.

To be effective, a diet and exercise plan must have the cooperation of the dieter ... right?   .... {"Not necessarily."}

If a diet-trainer was involved, he could have success as an entitled teacher without the willing cooperation of his pupil. The trainer could **force** his student to comply by taking away all choice in the matter. Then the results of the diet and exercise program would've more assuredly happened and perhaps in a shorter length of time. The trainer could have taken away Fatty's means of transportation and forced him to hoof it wherever he goes. The coach could then sit back and watch the calories come off and Gordo's muscles tone up, as well. The resourceful trainer could have controlled the food. He could have locked the fridge and left nothing within grasp for a hungry body to munch on except a prescribed amount of healthy foods. These amusingly effective, yet harsh controls, could have forced success without really having the cooperation of the dieter. In addition, the trainer could use intimidations, bribes, and other controlling means of limiting the freedom and choices of his charge.

Without the charge's full cooperation is it possible for the trainer to force his students to comply, lose weight and get in shape?

"*Yes.*" Think of all the unwilling horses which are taken out of their corrals to be given a workout, some against their will, or the many animals that have finished their portions of rationed feed only to stand and look longingly at the hay stack for hours on end. Just as it is possible to starve or force a horse into losing weight against their will, to the intent they become fit for our use, it is also possible to force another person against their will and we benefit from their sufferings. This entitled personal trainer could succeed with his manipulations and see some results in the fulfillment of his goals without the willing cooperation of his charges. But just how effective, in being a trainer, is he who has only forced cooperation? ... Is there a lasting change that has occurred?

Is this a bad method of teaching?

... It all depends on the motives of the teacher. If using coercion in conjunction with well-meaning as a tool of persuasion and the teacher is also including love and encouragement for the purpose that his compelled charge will discover the benefits of its new found position and therefore want to duplicate, once more, this gain, then he is not using Self Entitlement. He is actually using the Loving Father Approach. However, if he is using his powers to follow his own curriculum of forcing compliance for the purpose of ultimately proving his abilities bring results, then in this mind set he is indeed using self-entitlement. It is the motive of the teacher which determines if an approach is good or bad.

Common Sense: **It is not so much what you teach that matters most, but why do you? The same information could be shared by any teaching approach. However, the lessons learned by one's students will differ according to the instructor's motivations.**

Go ahead, be brave and test your motives.

Ask yourself:

- Is the thing I do the performance of an obligation?
- Do I feel that I have to act in order to meet some imposed pressure or desire?
- Before I offer to teach or assist another, do I stop and mull over, "Does this approach assist me into becoming better-off?"
  {If I answer yes, then I have my reward in the relief or the personal gains which I feel; I am performing or acting as a self entitled person.}
- "Or, is the thing I do an offering to help others along? Are my intentions that others receive gains and experience growth?"
  {If so, then for now, I am acting self-less.}

We are indeed teaching from the entitled approach when we find ourselves is a situation where we benefit from the pain of others, either from their labors or we find our egos are stroked from their participation in our lessons. It is time to revise your reasons for teaching if you would correct another or have the need to hurt and belittle them just for your own selfish purpose. As you undertake to teach or to change another, be sure your motives are for their benefit, and not just for your own personal gain in having them be of some service unto you.

A master teacher taught, "Do unto others as you would have them do unto you. {see: St. Luke 6:31, Mathew 7: 12} This master teacher taught what has become to be known as the Golden Rule.

The Golden Rule is the opposite of a purely entitled mindset. In it you don't look constantly for ways to change people; you accept and show love for them as they are. You never ask someone to do something that you are unwilling to do, or at least pay fairly in order to have it done. As they learn to recognize your fairness and embrace the love that you show them, they will grow in their desires to please you. They will seek your assistance when they falter. As you treat others with equity, they will have more of a desire to respond likewise back to you.

It is Good Business

If you are an employer or a supervisor in the business world, you are entitled to receive a fair day's work for a fair price. You must benefit from the labors of others, otherwise why would you have a hireling? However, deal with them as you would want to be treated if the tables were turned. Be reasonable in exchange for their services. Analyze the benefits you offer; make sure they are of equal value to the employee, and not just a lopsided gain on your part where you're seeking to get as much as possible while offering a payment smaller than expected. This thinking is not of God; it is just plain entitlement. The employer who is wise enough to treat his employees fairly inspires them to be more loyal and productive. When he pays reasonably, he can hold them to a standard of excellence where he can benefit additionally by their desire to increase productivity.

In addition to paying fairly, make opportunity to be with your charges. It is in the taking of a break or a pause from the normal everyday stress of production time, when you freely praise and build your charge up, that you build a rapport. Then with both working in rapport {a relationship of harmony and unity } toward a common goal of safety, quality and productivity, the supervisor may, less intrusively, offer suggestions and critique. The worker will accept these offers as tools for his improvement, and not view them as criticism levied by a supervisor hell-bent on tearing him down. **Let the employee see you enjoy spending time with them.**

{This makes a huge difference; try it.}

4. INDIFFERENT TRAVELER APPROACH:

This reluctant teacher's goal is just to be left alone and not to get involved. Choosing to remain aloof is a natural impulse. This individual feels his wants and wishes are so important that he is selfish with his time. By adopting the Indifferent Traveler Approach, this person misses the opportunity to comfort, to nurture, to impart knowledge, and to help others. The harsh but truthful rationalization that causes one to not get involved is the feeling that, *"Presently others just aren't important enough to me."* As this thought kicks in, it denies its author any benefits that may have been his, had he chosen to share with others. He may even rationalize that he does care for them, but he presently chooses to fulfill his own agenda. Stuck in this approach, there is no chance for growth for either a potential teacher, or a would-be student.

It is by our nature, as humans, that we first take care of and serve ourselves. Whereas our choosing to remain uncaring and uninterested may have indeed brought us closer to fulfilling a personal goal, we have also sent the message to our co-travelers, that we are not so concerned for them. This goes against the true motives of a Loving Father and a Nurturing Mother whose goal is to help others reach their maximum potential. No unengaged teacher ever helped another by taking an Indifferent Approach.

The following are self-rationalizations that an indifferent traveler uses either as selfish thoughts, or as he vocalizes his unwillingness to justify his reasons for choosing to not get involved.

- I don't care.
- I don't know how to help.
- Oh, they'll be ok; I don't need to get involved.
- I'm too tired.

- I don't have time for that now.   *{And probably never will later.}*
- I don't want to be bothered with any more problems.
- Figure it out for yourself; that's how I had to find out about life.
- I choose to just let things work out by themselves.

Now read again the previous justifications for a-could-be teacher who is set on remaining unconcerned and purposely uncaring. Read them again, not as selfish excuses offered to avoid dealing with another person. View them as a teacher using reflective words for a different purpose: The self-less purpose of helping the child. See them as being given by a fully engaged and concerned master teacher who is vocalizing these justifications in order to place ownership of a problem back on the unwilling child.

Can you see? The engaged teacher could be showing these very rationalizations to the child as to why he can't possibility help. But in this case the same wimpy excuses, when used for the right reasons, would become a means of helping the child to gain self-empowerment by forcing the belief: **If something is wanted done, then they are obliged to do it themselves.** The student must begin action, or no action as taking place. The same excuses for not helping could actually be used for the purpose of teaching accountability. This opposite purpose teacher would really be quite involved in the lives of his charges. He would be showing his love by allowing the gain of others. He supports the statement: **"It is not so much what you teach that matters most, but why do you?"**
...Of course at a later occasion, after the child has made effort, this master teacher would approach the child and inquire, "How'd you do?" He would help the child process and possibly adjust his performances, once the child is willing to listen.

Common Sense: **Do not become detached so far that when a student does willingly search for answers, rather than just wait for entitlements, you as a teacher will not be there for his assistance.**

Remember, every time we come in close proximity with another we are teaching something. Even in the most happenstance passing we are still influencing others. If we withdraw and do not expand our opportunities to engage, then we will be viewed as remaining aloof. Therefore, if we do nothing, the singular lesson we may be teaching is that we don't care one iota. To beat the natural desire to remain an indifferent traveler, it is helpful to have additional skills at our command to complement our intent to show an increased level of involvement upon the passing of a potential student.

Common Sense Lesson: The Programmed Response.

Military etiquette demands as two personnel cross paths within a close proximity of each other, one being of lesser rank, that the lesser initiate a personal exchange.

- Whenever meeting an enlisted of higher rank, the lesser initiates an exchange by acknowledging verbally the senior's rank and throwing in a timely greeting.
- A verbal salutation, "Attention!" is announced when indoors to inform others of the approach of a ranking officer; the lesser personnel snaps to the position of attention while waiting for the officer to past.
- When out-of-doors, the expected performance is an acknowledgment of the senior's commission where the lesser gives a salute with a verbal greeting as both continue on their ways.

These exchanges are expected. For the lower ranking personnel to perform is not a matter of personal choice; it is a required policy. Only the wording of the greeting is left up to personal style. Typically it is, "Good Morning Sir," or similar, depending on the time of day.

- In response, the higher ranking officer when saluted is required to come back with a rehearsed reply and a counter-salute.

It is easy to see which of the two are acting beyond their obligation to follow military etiquette. They will be using more than a programmed shallow response. Very noticeable is when either genuinely initiates a true attempt of engagement with the other.

While serving, I noticed that when one or the other expands beyond these minimal required interactions, it would usually uplift or inspire the second by suddenly establishing a common bond. If only a bare minimal exchange happens, then it condones a personal unwillingness to engage, teach, or learn from the other. It was refreshing, as an enlisted man, to receive more than the minimal required acknowledgement from the officers who by virtue of rank were granted a teacher status. Even if they only asked, "How are you doing?" while their body language and inflection expressed a real show of interest, it would make my day.

Likewise, for all those in or out of the military who have been granted teacher status, whether sought after or not, as they decide or decline to step out of their "Indifferent Traveler Approach," they transmit similar messages which resound every time they are in close proximity with a fellow passerby. At every passing, it is the choice of each individual, whether to convey to the other of their importance or of their meager triviality.

Perhaps the most bang for your buck way is to say, "I care about you," is with name acknowledgement. I once witnessed an inspirational speaker by the name of Bruce Crankshaw who taught twenty-five youth for about thirty minutes. I felt his passion. He kept interacting with them by making light as he struggled to learn every name by the end of his speech. He succeeded in all but four or five. He developed his topic of discussion around so he had to ask direct questions of each of the youth. That moment has long passed, and I can't recall the subject of his talk, but I will never forget the excitement of those kids, nor the emotion and personal interest he showed in interacting with each of them by name. They devoured his every inflection, anticipating a personal recognition.

Common Sense: **In every encounter with another, a message of awareness is sent.**

Here are more ideas on how you can prevail over becoming an unconcerned passerby and initiate contact with another person. They are arranged according to the level of interest you are likely to convey. At each encounter, the recipients may respond back to you by likewise showing their inclination for further contact. If they express no desire for further involvement, then it was still a success; you at least demonstrated your level of awareness of how important they were to you:

Greeting Levels of a Passing Interaction:

Lowest level : **No Contact, Gesture or Sign of Acknowledgement.**

"You might, just as well, be on the moon. There is no way any interest is wanted," just keep moving on without any effort of engagement and this message is being sent. You justifiably pretend that maybe they don't see you, or you try to make like you don't see them.

"*Yea, right.*" Whether true or not, in this encounter the message was sent and received: **No involvement is wanted!**

Low level: **Establish Eye Contact.**

Be assertive yet personal enough to look the other person in the eyes. The failure to make eye contact is a sign of indifference. As you make eye contact, you are sending the message that you at least acknowledge their existence as a living being. If they fail to return your eye contact, they are in turn sending the message that they judge you as not important enough to get involved with at this time.

Mid level: **Offer a Genuine Facial Expression.**

It has never ceased to amaze me how much analogical communication can be obtained from a person's facial expressions. To lift another out of a dispassionate mode a smile is sometimes all that is needed, but it must be done with a personal eye contact.

A horse is also a huge giveaway of his desires and intents for interaction. Out for the world to read are his eyes, ears, and over-all facial expressions. They tell a story about his intentions and moods. Much less giveaways are the intricacies of a human mind and the subtleties of communicating what one means to equal the expressions displayed by one's face. It would take a huge book to describe in detail how to read a face. It suffices now to say that when passing by and wishing to engage, offer a genuine smile. With it comes the other facial expressions and body language to additionally show that you are sociable and welcome further interaction. {*I have never been able to read a welcome in a fish's face; their faces are dull and uninviting.*} In this mid level you convey more than a fish. The other person will be able read much about you by the look in your face.

Moderate level: **Display of Sarcasm.**

Example: "Oh aren't we looking pouty today?"

The message sent by making a joke or a comment at the other's expense is that, "Although it is necessary to have association with you, I still am upholding my own superiority." If the other person has reason to hold a grudge, then you just fueled it big-time. Their comeback will not be welcoming, and it will be designed to meet the same inappropriate level as was yours. It may even go beyond in an attempt to make you pay for your ways. Sarcasm will only work at breaking the ice if it is either really funny, or they have the ability to be truthful about themselves. A deeper communication is sent.

High level: **Verbal Declaration or Acknowledgement.**

Example: "Good morning." or "Boy, it sure is hot today, isn't it Steve?"

Here you are verbally inviting the other person to engage with you, one-on-one and on common grounds. You are making an open invitation for further engagement. You establish a higher level of rapport and solicit a personal response when you address the other by name.

Highest level: **Ask a Sincere Question of Concern.**

Example: "Tell me, Joe, how are you doing with that deadline?"

This is the highest level of engagement where you are abandoning your own wants because you care for the other person. You establish yourself, at that moment in time, with the sole agenda of doing nothing else except trying to find out what is going on in the other's life. As you show concerns in something that has been troubling them, they have very little choice but to engage back with you.

{It is common nature for one to reciprocate when they think that another is truly interested in what they may say.} People usually respond when others show concern and offer compassion or help. In this level of greeting you must show that you are truly listening, not merely asking, "What's up?", and then going on with what you were previously doing without pausing to show a genuine interest. Properly preformed with an agenda to understand enough so that you might assist, you utilize refined listening skills and you present yourself in a position to engage with their life.

With the right "Passing Interaction," you act as a guide leading a fellow traveler into further engagement. When you move out of your comfort zone and attempt to interact on the highest level, you are giving priority to another's needs. By your displaying the tone of your wanted involvement, you are now left subject only to the other's perceptions and desires. Not-withstanding their willingness to engage, they can to be led into further interactions.

You decide how to interact with others, as governed, by your agenda of doing something for another's benefit or for yours. With your awareness comes the power to evaluate and regulate your actions and control the progress of your students. It is by your actions that the student begins to interpret your level of concern.

Having contemplated, with each interaction, the all important first step to becoming an effective teacher; you can accurately answer, "*For what purpose do I feel the need to teach?*"

CHAPTER 4:

THE STEPS FOR BECOMING A BETTER TEACHER

FIRST: "Why do I feel a need to teach"?

This was addressed in the previous chapter, and should be pondered in your thought process every time you undertake to educate. **You alone decide. Your decision affects the response of your pupils.**

SECOND: **"What will I teach?"** ...

The previous recognition of your purpose for teaching is half the battle. From your enlightenment the next step blooms:

"What on earth will I teach?"

... *Answer*: **That depends on what the student needs to know!**

Now just who determines that? Is it you as the teacher, or is it the student? To help with your decision, first let's examine the difference between a need and a want.

A **Want** is a desire—a feeling of a failure to possess. It is a wish to be fulfilled. A child will recognize that he has wants, and will be able to, at least momentarily, pinpoint what his desires may be. Wants will vary. They will be like shade in the summer and sun in the winter, constantly changing in priority and direction throughout the day. Any person will seek different wants as he re-defines his desires. A want will change depending on the present mood or whims of the dreamer.

A **Need** is the lack of something useful or necessary. The person in need may not always be able to recognize their own lacking. As a caregiver, it is hopeful that your experience will help you into being able to see that another is in need of assistance when in their complacency or lesser skill level they can not. A person will in no way recognize a need if they don't know that there is a problem or they can't identify a shortcoming.

If one thinks that, *"All is well,"* then to that individual there is no problem. A more experienced person can notice a difficulty, and then desire for an improvement. "This is where the teacher comes in; he helps his pupils become aware of what they need to know."

Side note If I am aiming to change something in my own life, I would first have to realize what it was that I really wanted. I would have to train myself to learn to dream again. With that controlled dreaming I will re-define my wants. My clear wants would help me to identify what my needs are in order to accomplish my dream. Before I can elect to aspire to any change, I must be able to imagine an improved end result.

… As a teacher, I will be that experienced person who helps a student to understand his opportunities to improve. I will help guide him to see new horizons. I will train him towards progression. As I do my best to increase my own wisdom and insight, I will also inspire the same quest for knowledge and improvement in others; I will teach that they may learn to dream.

Common Sense: **I will learn the value of a prod into action.**

Learning to dream is done by setting down and taking the time to envision a wanted outcome. Start the process out by saying to yourself, "In my perfect world, things would be like this: _____." Then fill in the blank. See in your mind's eye what the end results would look like. Allow yourself the time and the freedom to go through many different role plays of emotions and dreamed successes. You begin to realize what gains and self fulfillments would be yours when your imagined outcome {*your wants*} become a reality. This will be the power that keeps you on track during the many side trips and corrections that will have to be made. By remembering the happiness and envisioning the improvements that are possible in your life, you will be able to use this driving power to self prod yourself along.

When used correctly, spurs are not to inflict pain on an animal, but are used as another means of prodding it into action. As a horse trainer I fully endorse the use of spurs. They help to keep the animal motivated. As spurs keep the attention of a horse by giving it an extra stimulation and reminding it to keep making corrections and progress, your dreams of the possible perfect outcome will be the reminder you can use to prod yourself along. Furthermore, when teaching another, I will strive to show that they may develop the power to prod themselves into action by their dreams as well.

*   *   *

Common Horse Sense: Using Prompts
When teaching {starting} a colt to learn how to respond to a rider, it is advisable to use all the available prompts. Exaggerate clues when first beginning, such as over-leaning or shifting your weight to alert the horse of an up-coming suggestion. If you haven't spent the time teaching the beginning animal to properly yield, you will have to rein with an increase of boldness until the colt gets the picture; even a slap on the rump may be needed. The use of spurs is recommended, but not where you throw your heels back hard. Using a shock attempt to gouge a hole in the side of your animal will only awaken its response of fear or anger. The excessively spurred beginner will retaliate in repercussion equally as shocking back to you. Use spurs only as a prod into action, as stimulation to your beginner to change its course of action or direction. Use additional resources as needed. The colt must learn to move to pressure, so that it may begin to see what possibilities can be his.

*   *   *

If it is my goal to teach another person some lesson, in order to help them solve a problem, I would have to determine first, "Is this a difficulty which they realize needs to be changed? Or is it a problem that I have? ... Is it a situation where I am the only one uncomfortable and consequently want them to change so I feel better?" Just because I am uneasy and eager to affect a change in others, doesn't mean they see a shortcoming. I would have to ask myself, "What does this student really need to know," then add the words, "to be able to beat this problem I see?"

To effectively teach change to others they must also recognize the need for an improvement.

Here's help in understanding that principle:

Common Sense Lesson: Potty Training

During the first years of a child's life, when and where a toddler chose to relieve his bodily wastes was not a problem to be dealt with yet. While the child was very young, this was not something in your power to do anything about. Whenever the child went, you cleaned it up … end of discussion.

At sometime, as the child approaches 2½ to 3½ years-old, a parent starts to have an issue with all those stinky diapers. He starts to worry about the social ramifications of his child not being potty trained. In other words, "The child going in his pants starts to become a problem for the parent." It was something that the parent had accepted before; but now things need to change. Currently the stinky diapers are an issue according to the thinking of the adult, but are not yet a source of concern for the youth.

The question, *"How will I create a way for this to become something my child wants to change?"* is currently on the mind of the new parent.

See how it works? To solve this problem, you the parent must become a master teacher and create a situation where the child also wants to solve your problem. **It must become his problem as well. Only if it is a problem for the child, will he want to correct it.**

Common Sense: **To effectively teach, concentrate on what your pupil wants.** If it be that you teach to fulfill a personal agenda, then you must guide or change what your student desires.

What a child wants in life is **the relief of pain**, and to have **control over his own life.** He wants them in that order. To get the kid to buy into the idea that still going in one's diaper is a problem, the guide starts on a path to make junior uncomfortable with soiled pants. Pointing out the stink or the yucky will begin to make the child uncomfortable and aware that things need to improve. The instructor trains the child to know of the possibilities of relief from this discomfort. The child is guided to recognize the freedom of being dry and not being subjected to the scorn and humiliation from still doing things as a baby.

The master teacher helps the child discover added self esteem and the new positive self image, as-well-as, the joys of no more discomfort {pain} from the mess. He leads the child into discovering more relief of pain and more control of freedom than he currently has.

If the child was able to rationalize, he might realize that the uncomfortable feeling of being wet or the burning discomfort of having a crusty poopie stuck to his hindie could be avoided by a timely trip to the potty. The caregivers' work is done as-soon-as a child with this ability to rationalize is taught how to go to the potty. Big people don't go in their pants. The child sees big people as having control, so he will seek to do the things those big people do. This child will soon realize: "I go to the potty, so I am a big people. I have control." Having more control over their lives is a powerful motivation for kids.

The trainer will have to attempt to use a different approach for the kid who just doesn't care to act big. One such approach involves candy, or any other wanted treasure the child may crave. Candy brings the relief of pain, especially if you are feeling poorly because you can't get it. Getting some sort of treat can be used as a reward or a bribe. Offering it for a job well done helps the child want to do whatever it takes to get the sweet gratification. If it takes going to the potty to get the delight, then so be it.

Be consistent and firm when they miss the proper timing and still want the goodie for their intentions. In the early weeks of training, there will be the occasional mishap where the child is so involved in other adventures that the potty thing seems too much of a bother to address. To give the candy anyway would be a bribe, this teaches them that they only have to want to go potty; it teaches them to make a fuss in order to get a bribe or a payoff. **A bribe is**

something that is given to get an end result. It could backfire as-soon-as its pleasure or its value is gone. Let them know that for now they have missed their chance of payment, and they still have the power to earn it in the future. **A reward is something that is given because a progress toward the end result was obtained.** If they have a mishap, then they get no payment of bribe or reward; they must try again.

Especially with youth, the thoughts of a reward or a bribe go a long ways toward encouraging the kid to do some expected thing in order to earn the "dangling carrot." If the expected end result was compromised, then the payment of a reward should similarly reflect the less than desired outcome. How many parents have experienced the infamous dry run where the child will seek praise or a reward for going through the motions of going potty, when in fact they didn't do their duty? The children's trainer ought to create an environment where the kid is willing to work for a goal, so keep them thinking that in order to receive it they must perform as expected.

A **goal** is more than a wish for something to happen; it goes beyond a want. A goal necessitates an end result, and a plan to obtain it. There must be work towards the implementation of that plan, and an assessment process to map progress and determine if the correct end result was reached. A **common goal** is where both the trainer and the student are willing to work toward the same end result, even though their reasons may differ.

When using becoming potty trained as the end result, an experienced teacher will create a learning environment where his student desires to follow a plan to reach this common goal. In the beginning a candy is offered as an incentive to go potty. The child soon realizes that if he goes potty, then he gets a reward, a candy or a kickback. So, it will soon become his desire to go through the motions of going potty. It will become his goal just as it is the goal of his trainer. Be happy when he is striving to do the right thing, even though it may be for the wrong reasons. **If he is, in fact, making**

progress toward the correct thing, then you must reward for the slightest try.

The wise teacher will point out additional gains besides getting candy. He'll tap into the child's desire for acceptance. With the child's first attempts for success, his trainer will exclaim, "You're so big sitting on the potty. Just like a big boy." Such praise is offered with a thrown-in great bright smile. Later he may add, "You're not like a baby that wets himself," the trainer will reference the undesirable behavior as he exaggerates the shaking of his head "NO" while wearing a huge painted frown. When the child finally goes, clapping for the child also works, plus directing the child to tell others of his positive potty experience to get their praises. Together all can clap in unison and voice additional admiration for the positive conquests of the potty goer. The child is now the Big Kahunna; he is The Man! Who wouldn't want to continue doing whatever it took to keep getting such tributes?

In addition, throughout the day, be sure to point out to the child that you are dry, and ask him if he is also? You are training him to recognize between dry and wet; he is learning the difference between being comfortable and being miserable. When you help him to check, ask if he needs to go to the potty now? It takes his experiencing the quiet impacts in his own life when he goes potty to be able to recognize some of his non-eulogized gains.

... Be patient, not all children learn the same way. Sometimes wanting to go potty doesn't come until the child develops more maturity.

As going to the potty becomes more of a routine than a chore, you can raise the expected level of effort in order to get a reward. This is called to **refine**. It is the process of creating the environment where the child wants to do the right thing and is striving to continue to improve his skills. During refinement, a reward is not offered with every slight effort that the child is doing, the trainer merely acknowledges these tries, and then rewards noticeably with every extra improved attempt which the child performs.

Finally there is the age proven method of creating the desire in the child to go potty to avoid a perceived pain. This may be done to avoid someone's verbal scorn or a prevention of physical pain, as in a spanking. Now don't get all modern on me, telling me how wrong it is to spank a kid. People have been spanking their children since recorded time began. Why the Bible itself says, "He that spareth his rod hated his son: but he that loveth him chasteneth him betimes." {Proverbs 13: 24}   It also says, "The rod and the reproof give wisdom: but a child left to himself bringeth his mother to shame." {Proverbs 29: 15}

I don't go for any form of beatings or spankings that the parent may inflict as a way of gaining revenge or that are done for the purpose of inflicting pain. I only condone spanking as a form of getting the child's attention, in consequence of the child's chosen poor behavior. There is no better chance to teach a lesson then after you have his attention, for then he is open minded to listen. When he is aware that a failure to do a task will result in a discipline, he becomes willing to perform that task to avoid a perceived pain. If you discipline a child, afterwards show an increase of love, so that the child doesn't think of you as an enemy and therefore carries a grudge. A perceived **pain** may also be anything that the child views as being uncomfortable; they learn to perform the task, because they want to avoid being miserable.

THIRD: Ask yourself, **"Am I skilled enough to possess the right knowledge, to help my charges?"**

Or question, **"If I don't personally posses the right stuff, then where can I go to obtain it?"**

*   *   *

Common Horse Sense: **Too Much Pressure**

Dillon is a fifteen-year-old neighborhood boy; he is a gentle giant of a lad, standing at six-foot and three-inches tall, and weighing buck-naked on a good day before breakfast, a mere two hundred and seventy pounds. This lesson is his discovery about how to sit a small horse.

His mount was now in fact fighting, but only in an effort to relieve her pain. She wasn't acting in meanness or defiance.

Previously she was trained to be very light mouthed, so much so that in the past even the smallest child could control her. She would move out when her reins were touched and was prone to turn quickly at the slightest signal. Her soft-mouth reining preferences, and his uneasiness and great strength, all gave an interesting challenge for Dillon.

Today, her resistance started when this inexperienced rider slogged aboard, he immediately un-centered her balance of gravity by swinging up from too far on the outside of this small animal, and then throwing himself up and beyond the saddle's center. As she fought to correct herself by staggering sideways to regain balance, he gave a quick jerk back on the reins pulling her head back to the side and causing her to topple. She was struggling against his control in an effort to eliminate the hurt he was putting on her.

Before he had plopped on today, he had nothing to rely on except his past experience which constituted of a couple of rides done over four years ago with him nearly one hundred and fifty pounds lighter and with much less strength. His previous greenhorn's familiarity had conditioned him to just pull back as a signal to stop whenever his horse started to move and he wasn't ready for it. Today, answering to survival instincts as he unbalanced her, he reacted by jerking back hard. She was just trying to regain her footing. Implanted in his head was the thought: "*He had to get her to mind.*" Responding to his infliction of pain, she continued to do the very thing he was trying to prevent. She kept moving, and he kept pulling back. In the ruckus, she was taking him down with her. He didn't know what to do. He wasn't purposely being aggressive, and he knew that things weren't going right. He also knew that everything he did now was getting a more disastrous reaction from his mount. In his predicament he realized another thing also; he knew that he didn't have the skills necessary to teach or control his horse, so he yelled—"**HELP!**"

I was standing but thirty-five feet away and watched his mount nearly squash him. She by some acrobatic maneuver caught her plummet and landed on one of her front knees, her hind-end was curled underneath, and she was resting on Dillon's lower leg. In the midst of his tugging, she managed to climb back up with her heavy load. Both were still off balance. Her movements were only an effort to upright herself and take back her head. Still Dillon was yanking back on the reins. My first reaction was to defuse the reset bomb, ready to go off. I commanded, "Just sit still for a minute, until she gets used to your weight!"

At the time I couldn't see that he was pulling much too sharply and with too much pressure on this light mouthed horse. As soon as he quit pulling her to stop, she corrected her stance, ceased fighting the bit, and simultaneously quit doing the jig. As he ceased, she now had no need to continue fighting against the pain. She settled down at once.

"Now don't move anything, but your hands; ask her to yield her head from side to side," I said. He attempted so by bringing her head back with a hard tug. She again started fighting against the solid shank bit with a tight chain chin strap. "Hold on there," I said, having moved in closer to them now. Giving this situation all my attention, I wondered why such an easy horse for other kids to ride was suddenly acting out of character. It was easy to see what was causing the fuss. I instructed, "She has a far too aggressive bit in her mouth and it must be changed now before you can do anything with her. She is fighting against the hurt you are inflicting with that bit. She will never yield unless we change a few things."

Dillon was part of a group of kids that had come over to ride six of my horses that night, and as part of the confusion I had not properly overseen the choice of her head set. This horse certainly didn't need a harsh bit with a tight chin strap. A hackamore was placed on her, and he again tried to get her to yield her head to the side. Yet again she winced as he pulled too aggressively, putting a hurt on the bridge of her nose. I could hear her labor to draw in air, and see the fire in her eyes as she resisted his pressure. Even with that second non-bit-beginning headset, she was still being hurt in the hands of an unskilled rider.

"**You are pulling back way too sharply!**" I said. "Let's give you an even lighter bridle and teach you not to use more that two ounces of pressure, she will respond better to that. **You have been hurting her.**"

Dillon was ready to get off and give up, and I am sure his horse was too. He agreed to attempt just one more time. I could see the fear in his eyes, and the promise of additional defiance in this previously gentle horse's demeanor.

Relief did come in the form of a third change of bits, a light training snaffle without any leverage bars. Time was spent teaching the giant of a boy how to rein gently. The horse responded to his new touch now without fighting. Both were working together, not fighting against each other, all because he was smart enough to know that he didn't have enough knowledge to deal with his charge alone. So he asked for help. In his dilemma he knew he didn't possess the right stuff.

*   *   *

FOURTH Question: **"What is the most effective technique I could be using?"**

You can now understand why you want to teach. You also know that to get a child to want to learn, you must be able to offer a gain that they will see as desirable. You have assessed your own abilities and will seek help if you are lacking. That leaves your next step as deciding on what technique will be most effective for you. Let's practice putting it together and see how it all works.

Common Sense Lesson: Using an Effective Technique.

The instructor's immediate objective: To teach a child how to paddle a canoe.

What are the most probable methods that can be used to teach a student how to paddle a canoe? Let's look at them arranged according to the Four Teaching Approaches. Using the metaphor of canoeing, these methods can be explained as different techniques which may facilitate whatever approach the teacher takes. The key factor in deciding which Teaching Technique to use is to understand them as different options, sort of like adjectives to modify the approach. You learn to develop the skill to select the one which best serves your style.

1. Using the *Loving Father Approach*: The instructor/parent decides that it is time in a student's life that the proper art of canoeing is learned; he feels that it will be an increase in the potential of the child, or perhaps the instructor just feels that the enjoyment felt by properly performing this task will be a positive beneficial experience for his pupil. This tutor arranges for his student to have an opportunity to paddle a canoe because he thinks it will be good for this child.

A well meaning teacher, who's coming from this Loving Father Approach, may resort to being sneaky. This is where the canoe paddling experience is sprung onto the child. The naive youth may be tricked into sitting in the canoe; believing that a more experienced escort will do all the work, and then suddenly it is announced that it's now his turn to paddle. Or Junior is manipulated into padding under the pretense that it will please the instructor, or in quest to satisfy a private curiosity; maybe even out of fear if he doesn't paddle then some unwanted social pressure is sure to follow. Either reason used in getting the child to just start paddling will work; the **Sneaky Technique** encompasses all the tricks.

Remember the objective is to teach the child the proper ways to help them become better paddlers. This teacher is under the illusion that although he may have to trick or dupe his students into paddling at first, if the experience is positive for them, they, in turn, will actually like it; they will want to enhance their schooling by asking questions on proper procedures and by wanting to practice. The dilemma is: if the child was coerced into paddling, it will remain desirable only as long as it continues to be fun. After the fun is gone, the student will tire.

If the factor for compliance was a threat, in hopes that the student would participate and afterwards see the benefit of new knowledge, the teaching method meets the criteria of being sneaky. And it additionally uses the compliance demanded of a dictator. However, when the tyrant's threat is no longer feared, to achieve a desired change a student must now be driven by gratification, or he will surely tire.

Using the "**Adventurer Technique**" this teacher spends whatever it takes to talk the child into the fact that it will be a profitable experience. He tries to get the child to embrace the new experience as an adventurer willing to conquer and overcome. This technique presents to the child the feeling that it is still a personal choice and promises an increase of personal satisfaction with freedom. Getting to the other side of the lake faster will be theirs if they just start paddling. So the child starts with all the anticipated adventure and grandeur of Louis and Clark. He feels he's conquering non-chartered waters and fame and fortune will soon be his. But if this is the extent of the teacher's involvement, if the child receives no more help and guidance than the desire for personal exhilaration, the thrill will not prevail forever. Soon the child will tire.

The **Engaged Parent Technique:** The parent remains occupied with the child throughout the canoeing experience. They both enjoy the benefits. This parent stays ready to offer assistance, support, and instructions on proper canoeing skills as the child becomes willing and ready. In addition, this instructor is there to have fun himself and to relish in any advancement made by his pupil. Both child and parent experience a growing experience; even though together they both may tire physically, the memories can not be worn out.

Managerial Technique: The teacher/parent, while wanting the best opportunity for his child, is also aware of his own lacking agenda or proficiency in the art of paddling a canoe. He will arrange for the child to receive training by someone whom he views is as more an expert. This may be an effective way of teaching canoeing, but doesn't enhance the parent-child relationship much if the parent opts to not keep involved during the canoeing experience and is satisfied in merely employing someone else as the instructor. The child learns canoeing, but the parent misses out on showing just how much he cares. It is the newly employed trainer who gets to spend the time with the child. The lesson learned by the child is, "My parent has more important things to do than to spend time with me." Soon both the parent and the child will tire of this method, as they grow increasingly apart in interests.

2. An instructor utilizing the ***Nurturing Parent Approach*** will try to see that her child receives instructions on canoeing. However, she will also be very protective that this child is not unduly stressed or burdened. Within her direction, any learning while being subjected to this technique must always remain an emotionally positive experience.

Because her main objective is to save the child from any hardships, this well-meaning instructor, who is thinking she is operating with-in the guidelines of a *Good Mother Approach*, may go too far and adopt an **Overly Protective Technique** to teaching canoeing. Here she seeks to save the child from any difficulties by injecting the belief: they needn't have to paddle if they do not want to. Paddling a canoe may be far too difficult and taxing for her children. So why should they be burdened? There are different alternatives rather than their child having to do the hard work. *'Others more accomplished will provide a ride; all the child needs to do is help, if it wants.'* She injects the mentality: *'The child will become a victim if made to feel uncomfortable; the poor dear should be able to sit back and partake in their free ride.'* Limited with that criterion, soon others will be tired of paddling all that dead weight around the lake, and the child will tire of not being productive.

3. The ***Self Entitled Approach*** has the teacher instructing his students for the purpose of meeting personal objectives and goals. This teacher is in it mostly for himself. He could utilize the **Victim's Technique,** where he persuades a pupil into paddling in order to selfishly lighten the teacher's personal load. The instructor makes known an injury or an impairment in his abilities which prevents him from paddling with the efficiency he would like; therefore, the child needs to help. If the child buys this, then it is an easier ride for the teacher. Employing the child's sense of duty or honor to do all the work, an extremely resourceful teacher gets his tired carcass hauled around the lake.

The teacher operating from a *Loving Father Approach* may combine it with a Sneaky Technique, by presenting himself as needing help. The student is tricked into being exposed to the chance to learn, grow, and experience. This instructor may feel that this was the best way he could engage the efforts of this student. The Victim's Technique could be used from a selfless standpoint of helping the pupil improve, or as a means of obtaining a selfish entitlement for the teacher. If the instructor's only reason for teaching is the latter and he believes the more efficient the student becomes the easier of a ride he gets, then he has to offer some form of payment to get the canoe, his cargo and himself paddled around.

A reward, a bribe, or an emotional incentive that is offered as a payment will work only as long as the child feels those benefits outweigh the effort, pain, and sufferings they perceive themselves as having to endure. If the offering is weak, they will not paddle. You, as a teacher, are on your own "up a creek without a paddler," as soon as the child realizes that he is the one doing all the work and you are getting all the gains.

Since there is no pain involved for the child if the roles were reversed and you were doing all the work, they would remain content watching you do all the paddling. They wouldn't feel obligated to help or to offer any form of payment if they somehow felt entitled themselves. Be careful that you don't teach entitlement to a child, it is very easy to do and would be perfectly acceptable to a lazy individual. As an instructor, spend the time to instill in your pupils that success in mastering a task is sometimes its own best reward. Teach that achievement is a worthy payment, and certainly is the most lasting and powerful one.

The improper use of the **Critic Technique**:

All you really need to remember, in order to motivate the child into wanting to keep paddling for you, is to constantly be pointing out to him all the things that you see him doing wrong. You keep showing criticism. Keep reminding him of all his errors and faults. Be critical of his efforts. Do keep insisting he always continue working at improvement and forget to offer a rest or an earned reward. Be sure to show an abundant amount of lack of patience and understanding if the child fails to perform to your expectations. Do this, and before you can even really get a good start, both the teacher and the student will tire.

It is easier to tear down what you have not built up. The only proper use of the Critic Technique is that you tear down another's efforts, so that they and you may have a chance to rebuild better the next time. If you stay engaged with them and offer assistance, then this can also become a positive teaching technique.

4. *Indifferent Traveler Approach*:

In this approach there is no technique, beyond the purposeful actions of the potential, yet unwilling, teacher to remain unbothered and not be intruded upon. The key objective of this could-be teacher is to be left alone.

An **Unengaged Technique** is most likely employed by this indifferent teacher. The unengaged will retain his selfish purpose for not teaching, but in reality all he conveys to the child is lack of concern and feelings. He teaches he doesn't want to be bothered beyond his own initiations and comfort levels. This technique is to offer no assistance or very little at best. Let the kid get in the canoe himself, and then let nature take its course. After the solo experience the Indifferent Traveler will not engage in sharing the child's passions, or help him to strengthen a weakness. Nor will the reluctant instructor revel at any success junior obtained thru trial and error. A very ineffective way of teaching, but used by many of slugs for parents as they rationalize, *"There will always be someone else out there that will take up my slack."* The teacher using an unengaged technique has little effect on outcomes or results. He merrily continues to go on his way, leaving the student alone exhibit stamina or to get bored and tired.

Side note **The only redeeming quality of the Un-engaged Technique is when it is used as a facade. In false disguise, it is employed by a well meaning instructor to force students to act and do things on their own. This educator has the child's best interests at heart by choosing this style of remaining unengaged—thinking at this time it's the best thing for the child. Eventually he/she will process with the child the happenings, in attempt, to help guide them into discovering for themselves any**

valuable lessons. The purpose for using this technique was to create a better timing for the child to learn ...after the fact. Used this way it's not selfish.

In all cases, regardless of the technique of the instructor it won't take long for a child to tire and to realize that he wants help. His efforts are not propelling the canoe with the force and precision that is demonstrated by a more accomplished canoeist. If the technique and style of the teacher was effectively chosen, it will inspire the student to want to know the most proficient way. It is when the child is seeking to improve itself, that's the optimum time to show how to propel the canoe with more efficiency to make the experience more a pleasure. Teach him to work together with the other canoeist instead of against them so that forward momentum is not compromised. Teach the proper way to bank or pivot. Teach to paddle in a figure "J" if paddling alone. Using patience a master teacher could even get the child to pay attention while demonstrating the proper techniques such as reaching forward to pull against the water on the first half of a stroke and pushing against the water's resistance on the second half. The instructor has been given an opportunity to teach once the child becomes tired of being inefficient.

The first objective can now be fulfilled as the child permits himself to learn. Finally he can see the advantage to a different way. He will notice his improved stroke become a more efficient propellant to his vessel, whereas before he may have thought he knew it all or needed no outside help, or simply couldn't be bothered to learn.

To improve your abilities of imparting a lesson, ask yourself before starting to teach, "What is my most effective way to get this lesson across?" Review the purpose of the desired lesson in your mind. Envision the preferred outcome and steps you'll have to do, in order, to achieve it. Treat it as a challenge to be overcome and use the problem solving steps in Chapter Five. The extra time spent dealing and going over your lessons where you pre-solve it and rehearse in your mind the principles you wish to convey will prepare you for the real event.

In the few examples of techniques shown previously, they all shared a common objective: "Giving the student the experience of canoeing." It is easy to see that some are more effective in motivating the student to want to learn than others. They are chosen by a teacher to enhance his approach. They support his motives as to his purpose of teaching in the first place.

Let's examine four other examples of teaching techniques:

The **Dictator Technique**— Demanding compliance

"Rats, I missed the bus! Now what do I do? Oh boy, I sure have a problem." These thoughts were rushing through my head. Do I wake my mother and tell her that because of my error, my problem has just become hers? Do I insist that she needs to help me cause I require a ride to school?" Quickly these thoughts vanished as I snapped back into reality. If my older fourteen-year-old sister and my younger twelve-year-old brother both made it on the bus, there was no excuse for me.

She had previously told all us kids of the consequences of missing the bus: "If you miss the bus, then you walk to school."

In my mind there was no room for further thought; off I trotted. Even though I missed the bus I wanted no part of compounding my problems by either crying for help or choosing not to go to school.

The bus usually picked us up at 7:15a.m. getting us there around 7:40, after making six additional stops. I choose to jog. Walking never crossed my mind for to do so would've certainly ensured that I would arrive late and further compound my error. I trotted off and arrived at school five minutes before bell ran at 8:00a.m. I was sweaty yes, but, never-the-less, on time. There would be no repercussions. I paid my penalty for my error; what's more I had finished my first long distance run. I wasn't worst off for the experience, why in fact I was feeling great. I had a problem, and then I overcame it. "**Cool.**"

The real question to consider was why did Mom choose such a teaching technique?

She was born in the beginnings of the Great Depression, and so for survival her folks taught her to be frugal, to stand on her own "two hind feet", and to always do her best. She expected these same things out of her children. Part of her belief was, once a child got old enough to be responsible, they are expected to get themselves up in the mornings, finish their share of the families' chores and to walk everywhere or ride their bicycle anywhere they wished to go. It was taboo to ask an adult for a ride, unless they had reason to go also. As for waiting for someone to pick you up, you didn't. You were expected to start walking for home as soon as you were through with your event, and *never* was an adult asked to wait for a child. You were either there waiting at the appointed time and place for a pre-arranged mercy ride, or you were already hoofing toward home. It was not permitted to lollygag after an event in the hopes that someone else would offer a ride.

Her teaching approach was that of the *Loving Father* type, in that, she wanted her children to reach their highest potentials ... but combined with this approach was the technique of a demanding dictator. You had better do things her way, by gum. She was always looking for the lesson to be taught, and never deviated in expecting a very high level of conformance. She was very weak on the offering of rewards, leaving the children to glean their own gains by osmotic absorption, like unto a refined adult who understands and acts just because something needs to be done. Her desires that the child be the best they could be were commendable, but her technique was lacking sensitivity and was self-entitled.

She was a nurturing mother in the sense that we always had food to eat, and we were invited to partake if our chores were done and we had helped prepare it or cleaned up after. Physical wounds were looked after, but never unduly babied, for she was an old-school type nurse. The showing of compassion was few and far between. Emotions displays were not coddled; they were talked about and addressed head on. She allowed no anger or self-pity. We were invited to participate in whatever she had as long as we upheld her imposed standards.

I believed as I grew up, she looked at kids mostly as challenges to be overcome, not assets to be enjoyed. Her opinions were valued, but rarely sought after. As a youth, subjected to her teaching techniques, I thought she was just being mean.

I now believe she was well meaning in her desire to train her kids to become responsible adults. But she didn't stop there. She understood that in order for a value to become a trait it must be practiced, so she demanded that we be responsible as kids also.

As a self-interest seeking youth, hardly ever did I want to spend time with her as a form of enjoyment. I don't remember her taking the time to be much interested in what I was doing or seeking to be my friend. I distanced myself from her as much as possible. Who wants to be criticized and lorded over? Who wants to be kept busy doing make-work tasks, and very rarely ever given a reward, or hardly ever praised for a job well done? It was expected that you gave your best efforts; she demanded it. Yet as a typical youth, I longed for a break from her trying to correct me.

I do give her all the praise for teaching her children, and especially me, to have a good work ethics. She taught us to do our best, be honorable, and to have faith in God. She taught us to be accountable for our choices and actions. I respect her immensely, for she stayed true to her values. As the years have passed, she has developed much more compassion. Now I really enjoy talking with her, for in my maturity, I understand her past techniques.   In addition, no longer is she in the same teaching style. She now is a mother with a more laid-back agenda. To this great mother, who raised me, I owe my success in life; to her I give credit for my own strong points and many of my character traits. Her motives were always to train her charges to meet a higher potential. A lot of my style in teaching has come from her.

Being the Teacher --- Verses Being a Friend.

A teacher's motive in doing what he does and soliciting interaction with others is that he is trying to impart knowledge into the life of another. We have discussed why he feels so inclined. We will continue to discuss the reasons behind his approaches and styles and how it affects the desires of his pupils to retain this information and elect to change. Anyone who is engaged in imparting any type of knowledge for another's enhancement is a form of a teacher.

A friend's motive for doing what he does and being with another person is not to take on the traditional role of a teacher who imparts knowledge. A friend acts out of a common interest. He shares experiences out of affection or esteem; he helps his buddies along. A buddy wants to be with the other person because he is getting something out of their relationship; he is getting enjoyment and wants that for them, as well. A true friend doesn't have an ulterior motive for being with another beyond common enjoyment.

It is ok to be entitled when being a friend, for you are also seeking a satisfying experience. A friend doesn't criticize; he only accepts differences. His agenda isn't to force a change, or to punish, or express a demand, or to apply a pressure on his companion to learn as does a teacher. If needed, he will out of love feel obligated to help a fellow friend, because he cares for them. When the friend crosses the line to effect change in another, he then becomes a teacher.

As a teacher, if your pupil would rather be with a peer {someone with a shared interest} don't be surprised. They turn to their pals for help—not always because they feel the peer has more knowledge than anyone else. What they feel that the friend is more in touch with their lives. In contrast, the average adolescent is much more influenced by the pressure of their peers than by the distant demands of their parents or teachers. The influence of their peers is right then, any repercussions are immediate.

In your role as a teacher to take a break from always needing to instruct, step aside from your personal program of always trying to effect change. You don't have to structure all your involvement so another's life can become better. Just be yourself and enjoy the moment; be there with the child. It will build rapport and give the student a much needed break from always being under pressure to perform or to retain knowledge. Some of the most memorable times I ever had as a student were when a teacher finally stopped trying to shove knowledge down my throat. They, with me, just experienced a moment. As a teacher, you still shape lives for the good as you uphold high character traits and act as a friend; you will be sharing a relationship even though you might not constantly be in the stereotype teaching mode.

The **Friendship Technique:** Being there with the Child.

My own father could represent the icon of being there with his boys in order to participate in experiences. ...as long as it was hunting or fishing. He took my brother and me with him as soon as we were able to keep up. We went to every type of public hunting or fishing season; we never missed the "Opening Day." And we again participated with him at least once during the remainder of each season. We had great times and I wouldn't trade them for the world.

I remember only a few times of him taking us aside and helping us through an emotion or of him helping us to discover other possible ways of doing things that were more effective. I guess he was fulfilling his role of being a parent as best he knew how. He was spending time with his boys as a friend and hoping that this was enough. He was a great companion and fulfilled his role as the families' provider, but he left to my mother most of the responsibilities of teaching about life.

* * *Side note: * * * **In looking back at my own role as a father, as my children were growing up, I too often used this same approach, thinking that in the limited times I spent with my children they would be able to absorb knowledge. As I sought ways to be there with my kids, it was easier with my boys. Unfortunately I usually made it be on my terms. There were a lot of things that I didn't fully understand about teaching.**

The **Fellow Traveler Technique:** Both the teacher and student are learning together.

As a teacher, there will be the time that you struggle to remain in that role, especially when you have to share knowledge on something that you know little or nothing about; you may even have to read and figure it out in front of the students. As you do, your role has just changed for that moment; you are now also a fellow student joined in a common purpose. If you don't know the task at hand before you embarked to teach it, then you are also merely a fellow traveler …possibly a friend with the same common interest who is seeking to gain knowledge. Don't be surprised if your charge might understand the task sooner than you; in which case if you will reward {give praise and acknowledgement}, then you are still being a teacher.

The **Guide Technique:** Showing an alternative way.

As a five year member to the wilderness staff for "Red Cliff Ascent", we were instructed that our teaching role with the clients was to be specific. We were not just there to watch someone's child while we forced them to make changes for the good. We weren't there to punish problem kids for past behaviors or for poor present responses. Our role was also not to be their friends, nor to focus on seeing that they had a great time in order that they feel good about themselves. We were not encouraged to seek to support their feelings or past efforts. Our role was to be their guide. We were to present alternative decision making to the youth; to train them to see that for every choice that they made, a consequence would follow.

We taught them that no man is an island, and they not only affect themselves, but their choices also have an effect on others. We were there to keep them safe in an outdoors wilderness environment, and to help them realize that by proper choices they will have an easier journey down life's paths.

We were there with those kids in an environment far away from what they were used to. We were to be like unto a GPS {Personal Guidance System}. We taught them how to use the signals they receive every day to find a true path through life.

Teaching as a GPS

High above and reflecting downward, giving all the opportunity to tune in, are satellites. It is their function to keep rotating around the earth, so that they may send information back. This information can be accessed when the need arises, whenever someone tunes in correctly. The ever-present excepted values and social choices daily influencing a young learning mind have similarities to these satellites; they just keep sending information to any who tunes in.

The GPS accepts the signals of those satellites. It converts the signals to data that can be used to map destination and location. Using this data, the GPS can be programmed to show projected time of arrival and points of interest to the user. When used right, the GPS gives an unwavering path to follow.

A guide acts as a GPS, helping the students use information which they are receiving. He doesn't always dictate choices but does engage with them to ensure they have the educated opportunity to sort out their options. The teacher, as a guide, helps his pupils to learn problem solving techniques, as-well-as to define and sort out personal values. He assists student to obtain the skills necessary to follow the finer details of each trip and helps the inexperienced to mark locations he wishes them to visit and discover; he alerts them to know what their alternatives may be. All throughout life there are many unusable signals; some, if followed, will confuse and mislead a young mind.

The student has to either trust and use some sort of guide, or to rely on his own instincts to direct him through his journeys. Instincts are only as good as the judgment one possesses. There are many side trips and much time is lost exploring various paths that others have chosen, and then lost their ways. Armed with proper values and problem solving skills, obtained through an engagement of a guide or through the school of hard knocks, the student then has the power to use the signals he receives constantly from worldly sources and to make his best decisions in his travels through life. He can, after learning how to assess where he is at any given time, make necessary adjustments to keep on track with his destinations. He can use his learned personal values to refine and adjust his efforts in obtaining his goals. The guide has the ability to help his student discover how to obtain their goals.

As the teacher chooses his approach to teaching, he uses a chosen technique that depicts his inner desires and purposes. These techniques become additional factors that support the motives of the teacher. The students then learn by what their teacher is portraying, in addition to what they hear him say.

All teachers have as a purpose: the design to affect the lives of their pupils. A wise teacher takes his pupils at their present level of development, and then provides instruction, information, and opportunity for improvement; he empowers them to make their lives better.

It is crucial in a student's development that they learn to problem solve. As they are plagued by set-backs, they can identify where they are lacking and what is not wanted, and then discover how to make it better. Admit it, in your life you have also been plagued by a few setbacks. Were they always handled in the most efficient manner? Would you have liked to have done things different?

Read in the next chapter how to empower yourself and others. Learn how to make those problems go away.

CHAPTER 5:

LEARNING THE POWER OF PROBLEM SOLVING

Common Sense: **You can't keep doing the same things and expect different result, this is insanity. Something needs to change.**

So what do you change?

Let's start with a system for figuring out just what that is.

What is a problem?

A problem is a difficulty that creates perplexity or distress. Simply wishing for a problem to go away requires no effort and produces no results. If all you do is just keep wishing, then by default you are agreeing to accept things as they are. There has to be an **effort** toward a transformation. You may even deceive yourself and say, "I chose to do nothing, so no more problems."

"Yea, right!"

It is still there and you still have to deal with it. All you are doing with your denial is succeeding to put it off for a while. You only fool yourself; the problem although momentarily forgotten or dismissed still remains.

Yet, let's don't dismiss the act of wishing for something to go away. It does have some value. It tends to settle our minds temporarily. In fact it is enjoyable. It insulates the author from having to go through any of the troubles of problem solving. It gives a false sense of power and gratification with dreams of how wonderful things could be if troubles were to fade away.

… Case in point: How often have you wished you had just won the lottery, and had at your disposal Ten Million Dollars {$10,000,000}, of which you could spend on anything you wanted. Dreaming of how you would use that money can be momentarily soothing and even exciting. Or, how many times have you wished for a better life, so that you could have the same opportunities as the hero has in a book or a movie? In so, don't you momentarily find increased pleasure? Alone, wishing produces no lasting gains, but it does give us a temporary sense of power and fulfillment by providing an escape from having to do the hard work first.

You can take this power in wishing and teach a student to use it in conjunction with other steps to really solve problems instead of just enduring discomforts, or postponing any confrontations. As a teacher, you have already used a portion of these steps to problem solve when you acted on your need to teach another. You recognized a potential, and then shared it with others in an effort to start their perpetual empowerment. Teach your charges more than just the idea of problem solving; educate them how to use the steps that will lead to conquering problems. You will be teaching them to do more than to wish or dream of a want; they will be learning to improve and to effect changes in their own lives.

Common Sense: **If as the result of your behavior you're not happy, change your actions; you don't have to feel this way.**

Common Sense: **We get complacent about what we do time and time again. In order to improve we need new goals and challenges to meet.**

STEPS TO PROBLEM SOLVING

Steps to Problem Solving	Goal Achievement
1. Identify the difficulty.	**A**. *Wish for a better end result.*
2. Isolate the cause.	
3. Define a solution... Find the solution by treating the problem as a goal, and implementing the steps to goal achievement.	**B**. *In your mind, see yourself as if the end results have already happened.*
	C. *Make a plan to acquire the end results.*
	D. *Implement the plan.*
	E. *Evaluate and re-adjust as necessary to reach your goal.*

Step 1: **Identify the difficulty.**
"There aren't any clean dishes to make supper with."

What is the difficulty that leaves you wanting for things to be better? Be specific in determining what it is that you want to change. What exactly is the action, done by someone or something, which you want to be different? You must be able recognize what it is that you don't like.

To identify the trouble think, "What is it that I am not happy with?" ... Don't go overboard, keep it as basic as you can and try to only address one issue at a time. Only after you have figured out the "What" do you now have a problem that can be addressed and changed. You have no chance of solving something that you can not identify correctly.

Step 2: **Isolate the cause.**
"The dishes are still in the sink, dirty from last night."

In problem solving, it is necessary to not only identify **WHAT** is annoying or uncomfortable, but also to isolate its probable cause. Figure out **WHY** it is happening in the first place. Analyze the circumstances around why the problem is occurring. Answers will begin to form to your understanding as you review the cause {better yet, your perceived cause} of the problem. Is this a task that might require talking to individuals who have enough experience to help you see clearly why something is amiss? *Why is your problem happening?* Once both the "WHATS and the WHYS" are understood, then there exists a real enemy to combat and to conquer. The only missing question is how to deal with it correctly?

The truthfulness of your perception will be tested in the future as you attempt to define a solution and implement your most logical plan of attack against your new found enemy.

Common Sense: **If a difficulty is caused by a need for change from another and you can't dismiss it, then it is still your problem until you as a trainer become involved enough to guide them toward transformation.** {see: Chapter 15}

Step 3: **Define a solution.** This is the "HOW" to fix your problem.
"The dishes must be done."

So far you have been able to come up with what you didn't like, and the probable cause making it occur. That's great for now you have isolated your problem. You are on your way to being able to fix it.

Now follow the steps to "Goal Achievement" in order to get your best results. You take that isolated problem and its causes, and start wishing for a better ending or solution. You start seeing yourself as though the end result has already happened; you foresee the enemy as being overcome, and your problem as already fixed. By seeing the end result as already happened, it is easier to figure out what steps to do in order to make it so.

A. Wish for a better end result.
" I wish Johnny would take responsibility for his mess."

This is what you would experience if there was no dilemma, or if your problem didn't exist. The better end result is where things are great and your dreams come true. Start wishing purposefully in order to determine your desires in regard to your problem. ...Do you want things to change? ...Are you willing to consider doing things different? ...Have you decided what you really want?

Don't cheat yourself; this wishing part is sometimes the most fun. When you have come up with what you want to happen which brings you the most joy in regard to your problem, "STOP!" You have just envisioned a possible positive feature instead of a dilemma. Make a mental note; this is your hoped for end result. You will never accomplish your goal by merely just wishing, but you will often during the goal obtaining process want to refer back to this wish in order to again renew the pleasures of hope and obtain the power to ascend.

B. In your mind, envision the end result as already happened.
"I am not overwhelmed. There is not mess. Johnny has taken respons-ibility."

By reviewing in your mind this second step in goal setting, you will come closer yet to understanding and refining your **wants** {Wishes to be fulfilled or obtained.} and in determining your **needs.** {The lack of things necessary for the obtaining of your desired end result.} Here you will be contemplating all the aspects of your wanted change. Your objective is to figure-out if it is worth your efforts. When you can see your end results, and they bring you the fulfillment of the dream you wanted, you'll get an emotional peace of mind. Have fun with this step also. Do remember, this peace will not last, but it will be yours whenever you permit a mental re-visitation of your envisioned successful end results. **Allow yourself to review the gratifications that are possible. When you do, *you'll be inspired to obtain them.***
"I feel great, the dishes are done; no one feels they've been taken advantage of."

It is OK if you indulge yourself a little in your envisioning, for later during the process of doing the actual work, you may get discouraged and falter. But by remembering those gratifications, you can again receive the self-encouragement and drive to continue to persevere. So far, you haven't started to get anything to happen, only reviewed and examined various possibilities. Focus more on the one that gets closest to fulfilling your wishes and dreams by providing your perfect end results. This could be the solution to your problem, if you can meet the needs it requires.

Do you have what you need in order obtain your end results?
"I will feel taken advantage of if I clean up the mess myself. I am afraid of the confrontation I will have with Johnny. I could use advice."

Consider this question carefully, because, now the preparation starts. You must determine whether or not you have the skills to combat this problem by yourself. Can you follow thru and defeat it as you presently are? If you are lacking, now is the time to acquire more tools and gain in knowledge. You solicit information, help, and direction as needed.

Asking for Help:

Common Sense: **Real men don't need to ask for help.**

How many real men do you see asking for directions? Any man worth his salt would rather drive around for fifteen minutes, or longer, than take two minutes and ask for help.

"HEY, MEN, it makes no difference where the instructions come from to get to a destination. ... **Why do we resist asking for help? Why do we choose to keep our foolish pride and go without assistance, thinking, *'Just give me a little longer and I will get it figured out?'* We should be wise to learn from the women. Ask for help! ... *Well ... not right off, only after we have exhausted all our other options. Like really, what kind of man would ask for help without being desperate first?* "

Isn't the nature of a man to battle and conquer? ...You decide. You can remain ever-so mule-headed and preserve your pride by insisting on graduating from the School of Hard Knocks or take advantage of all your options so that you can get on to really getting things done the right way, instead of stumbling onto which way to head.

Go ahead and role play in your mind different solutions to your problem. See, before you actually start on the task, which of them brings you the end result that you want. If your ability is such that you can't define the end results of your role play or possibly picture a solution to your emotional, physical, or mechanical problem, then you need help. As mentioned, go out and get skilled, or find someone that already possess the knowledge and ask for their advice. Read, train yourself, and prepare before you actually start on the mechanics of your solution.

C. Make a plan to acquire the end results.
"This morning, I will tell Johnny to clean up his mess."

With the preparations coming together in a continuing reality, use all your resources to come up with steps for your most correctly perceived solution. Formulate a plan based on how to best address the issue. A simple plan should include: what to do, and when to do it. If necessary, prepare a list of the steps for your plan in an order to facilitate its completion.

A more complex plan which includes utilizing the actions of others to help solve your problem ought to allow for the reflecting of your feelings. You have got to assertively inform others of your desires in order to enlist their help.

You inform others of your emotional state.

- Be sure to abstractly state the incentive for your feelings by rehearsing, **"Why this is so,"** not your views as to why things happened as they did it. It isn't helpful to focus blame.
- You express your hopes for the future.

Your expressed hopeful expectations include: **Who will do what...** *Formulate self-expectations as part of your plan of action, and rehearse to others your expectations of their involvement toward your envisioned solution.*

"I feel overwhelmed when I see the dirty dishes left. Johnny, these are dishes you and your friends used last night. It is my hope to use those in our next meal. Will you please clean up the mess so I may fix our next meal?"

You obtain immediate inspiring power as you inform others of your desires and as you declare ways, in which, you hope for them to support you. As others are aware of your feelings and hopes, they are better empowered to know how to assist you. Both can now more efficiently work toward a solution. You start to see your envisioned results happen. Why go it alone?

It's time to start the work of implementation when you have either exhausted your resources to prepare, or because of your acquired skills you have come up with a logical plan that most likely will produce the desired outcome.

D. Implement the plan. This is where success starts to happen.

*"**You inform Johnny how you feel. He may still not have enough guilt to start on the daunting task of cleaning up alone. Instead of focusing on the unproductive task of heaping more shame on the kid and forcing his hand, You start on the on the dishes. You ask, without intimidation, "Would you help me?" He might want to help, because it was the mess left after his party**."*

Only as you start implementing your plan, is it possible to notice any actual results. You begin to become engaged in performing the labor that really effects what you wanted to change; all else to this point, although necessary, has really been speculations and wishes. Up to now, your dreaming has inspired your commitment toward action; you may have even awakened an interest in others toward solving your dilemma. As yet, your efforts have only been acts of strengthening and mere preparations. That you may have felt some of the emotions of a finished end result during the wishing and dreaming steps may be true, but those emotions were not reality based. They were quickly fleeting feelings based on perceived possible realities which didn't last. Now you must do the deed, perform the task, and labor at whatever it takes to fix the problem. If you kept your list that was made during the prep period, refer back to it to keep on track. Or … if you are content to he-man your way through performing the "do's" in order to reach the end results, that's your choice. But, you may have to stop your momentum in order to again determine what it was you were going to do next, especially if multiple or dependent steps are required. As you begin doing, then you will witness results happen. It is then that others will also feel obligated to fulfill your hopes and expectations of them. To require that others start meeting your expectations, before you have shown that you are willingly engaged in the process of change, is a hope that the young and the immature cling to.

As you become lost in your work to fulfill a solution, remember to periodically reward yourself with a review of your preferred envisioned end results. Picture them again. You deserve the emotional up-lift. You can get an increase of desire to finish the work as you indulge again in an additional mental fulfillment of your dreams.

"I wish the dishes were done, and Johnny was helping me clean up the mess"

Continue to be open-minded; often as you work along at implementing your plans, it is easy to see that your preparations and present expenditures of energy are not turning out as you thought they should. Often we find it difficult admitting that our efforts are falling short. It is easy to be so engaged and caught up in the emotional aspect of winning that we think, "All we must do is to keep doing and our problems will be overwhelmed and solved." When implementing a plan to fix a concern, if it can be seen that it is not working as intended, make necessary adjustments.

"Johnny still hasn't shown any desire to help. The dishes are getting done, yet my feelings of being taken advantage of are not going away."

E. Evaluate and re-adjust as necessary to reach your goal

"Am I getting the results that I had envisioned?" If the answer is no, then now it is ok to **get mad**! You can use this emotion to help you win.

Utilize Your Emotion: Listen to yourself as you get peeved at an outcome, either from the incompetence of others, or as result of your own inefficiencies.

What do you say? ... Try growling. Vocalize some form of "Errr," as you force a vibration up from deep within your throat. Expel it through clenched teeth. Stop reading for a moment and try it.

Growl to exhibit your emotional irritation!

Go ahead say, "Errr" ...

That's it. Now once more say it again with more meaning and commitment.

"ERRR!!!"

Can you feel your emotions come to life? Add to it a raised upper-lip and perhaps a squinted crazed eye. Use this awakening of emotions and this guttural growl as a reminder of what to do if results don't match with your dreams. You simply summon up your passion, get mad, and break into your best "E.R.R.R." When you are striving to reach a goal, and you don't like results you got, then you must **Evaluate**, **Re-adjust**, **Refine**, and **Repeat** until you get it right. Use these actions to get back on track.

"***Things didn't go as planned. So changes must be made***":

"*Again address the problem accordingly that the envisioned end results might happen*: ...*Let Johnny know how you feel*. ...*Command for his help so you can let go*. ...*Create an opportunity for both to work together on the mess*."

The Changing of Others

Common Sense: **As a parent, it is my responsibility to help my kids learn problem solving skills.**

If no instruction is given, then the child is left to come up with a solution on his own. He is abandoned with nothing but limited personal perspectives. Without proper training, his solutions will be whatever brings to him some immediate gratification.

As a teacher, it is ever my hope that, after a child receives any of my lessons, he will give a feed-back similar to, "NOW, I GET IT!" as he catapults toward change. But this rarely happens." *I must be patient in my expectation of another's change.*

"Do I understand the principles which I wish another to grasp? "

Think for a moment just how my efficiency as a teacher would be compromised if I hypocritically expected another to honor a principle which I could not. I cannot be drowning myself and simultaneously offer much help to another. In order to teach others how to combat a difficulty, it is necessary that I have acquired a level beyond where they struggle from. I must be able to reach back and float them to an improved position. I must possess an attribute before I can most effectively teach that trait to others.

To empower my students with problem solving skills, first I acquire them myself. Now, as I see another struggling, I am in a better position to help direct them to a higher end result. Mostly I'll help them to understand that they should keep working on their wanted end result. It is sadly true that some relief will be theirs when they presently cease trying to figure things out, especially if they were being uncomfortably perplexed. When they abandon the hard task of trying to find a workable solution, a brief relief does give an immediate gratification; it offers a temporary freedom of not being bothered. This **quitting allows an instant liberation of pain**. Yet these abandonments of a possible ultimate triumph also leave a lasting emptiness of personal doubt and frustration which a successful solution could have filled. To give-up leaves the child with less personal power and in a lower state of self-respect. Many non-tempered youth will quit whenever their efforts don't produce the right gratifications. They let their feelings of discouragement trick them into quitting. Because I am taking on the role as mentor, I will help them to understand the principle of perseverance.

Perseverance is not the mastery of an undertaking; it is an honest effort to keep improving toward an end solution, despite setbacks.

Common Sense: **Some difficult problems need to be addressed many times in order to get the envisioned end results.**

It is only by evaluating and adjusting do different results emerge. **Change does not always take place immediately.**

{Teachers and Parents that was for you, Read with me again the last Common Sense statement.}

"SOME DIFFICULT PROBLEMS NEED TO BE ADDRESSED MANY TIMES IN ORDER TO GET THE ENVISIONED END RESULTS."

It isn't possible to always get what you wanted on the first, or the tenth try … especially when working to effect change in others. You may feel compelled to take the poor results that you did get and re-treat them as new problems. But, before you decide to start over in a new re-addressing of your old problem as a new difficulty, remember to again refer back to your original purpose as a teacher. It was: "To assist your charges into reaching their potentials." If your charge became closer to that purpose during your previous attempts, despite that fact that all things are not the greatest, then the results were indeed positive. Any positive progression means you are making headway toward your end results—so relax and count your efforts as a partial success.

Perhaps you offer your best side forward in the attempt to smooth a shaky relationship, yet you end up getting a response back that you feel doesn't match up with your efforts. Do you now quit trying under a justifying pretense which confirms that your method or plan didn't work? Are your thoughts dwelling on, *"That previous attempt was a dumb idea, and that person doesn't appreciate the things I do for them?"* If so, you are acting entitled, you're expecting to receive something back for your efforts, which the other person feels you haven't earned. It takes great effort to rebuild a collapsed relationship, a mere moment can tear one down.

If in your attempt to solve a problem you get a result which wasn't worse than what you were getting before, at least there is an inkling of hope. Re-kindle your courage to hang on. You did have some success in the form of: things at least didn't deteriorate.   Stop, before you again retry and rejoice for that which did transpire. Can you pick out any small improvements that you may further build on? Can you see—your faith was not in vain?

Common Sense: **Often the obtained results will fall short of your expectations. So what is stopping you? In order to win you can start again.**

* * *

Common Horse Sense: Success through Repetition
     If the end results are not what you wanted as a trainer, then you still have a problem. Either the horse hasn't learned its lessons correctly, or you need to adjust and refine your methods of training because your expectations were not conveyed clear enough. Even

when your lessons are taught correctly, the horse may today understand a principle and give a correct programmed response to stimulation, then tomorrow act as if it hasn't a clue. Because the horse is a living, breathing, decision making being, it is capable of not always doing what it's been taught. Perhaps it's distracted, or a personal preference takes over, or the beast simply can't remember what is expected of it. Worst case scenario is: it's acting out in defiance against being controlled by another. This is when repetition and practice helps to embed into its non-pliable mind the correct reactions. **"Sometimes the only way you obtain success in your desires is by patiently repeating the correct steps again and again."**

Refinement: A horse needs many times to go back to the basics of his training in order to refine his responses; he needs to be given this opportunity to practice. The wise horse trainer recognizes that with every repeat an improvement could be possible by giving an opportunity to re-adjust techniques until thing become right.

*   *   *

Common Sense: **"That which we persist in doing becomes easier, not that the nature of the task changes, but our ability to perform increases."**
    …We learn by doing, as we do our ability increases.
    The previous common quoted phrases make a lot of sense. *But how do our abilities increase?*
    Our strength increases after the repetitive working of muscles, from utilizing a healthy body that is capable of rejuvenating and rebuilding itself during rest periods. After using our body to its fatiguing point, our cells rebuild during rest cycles stronger then before. With persistent exercise and rest **we have the ability to give more effort.** Likewise by repeated use we also can experience an increase to our thought process.
    Solution solving increases as we practice because we are able to evaluate and refine. By making a conscience effort to improve, we assess ourselves and become aware of our short comings. We can consciously choose to do differently the next time. It is with a series of performing, evaluating, and then following with self correction that our abilities get more proficient. **We continue with the capacity**

to do more with less effort. So we now are freer to make even more refined changes and adjustments that will, in turn, lead into a polished end product. Better results will happen as we persist.

As you continue in reading this book, it will help you evaluate, refine, and if necessary go back to the basics to re-train yourself, and your charges. You will find more strength and have an ability to do more, as you endeavor … again.

Common Sense Lesson: I Always Do It the Same Way.

There is a task that hopefully each of us does once to twice a day, and we will probably continue to do it every day for the rest of our lives. As result of all this practicing and performing, we should be so proficient that we waste not a second on repetitiveness or inefficiency. We should be such masters at it that we couldn't conceive a pittance of thought toward improvement. Yet, I would wager that if we were asked, "Could a better job be done?" Most of us would have to answer, "Yes." … *The task is: Brushing our teeth.*

In many occasions in our lives we have personally undertaken to change or improve our approach to this subject. Often we have been pleased at our new implementations; we make headways at being more proficient. But why is it still, when we believe we are in a dire hurry, do we choose to go back to a sloppy and less than masterful performance?

Over the space of a lifetime, how often do we brush our teeth? *The amount could exceed 26,000 to 50,000 brushings depending on whether or not we do it more than once a day, and if we live into our seventies.* We should ask ourselves, "Are we happy with the present job we're doing? Are we spending a full three minutes each time on the task which includes going up and down on each individual tooth, both front and back? After so much practice we should never have to get our teeth cleaned, nor should we have cavities because we are doing such proficient jobs … right? If not, then we should strive to refine and adjust.

Refinement and adjustments are a constant ongoing process of life. To accept we have no room for either would be to have mastered a task to its utmost level, or it shouts, "We are in a state of personal denial."

Only the mediocre are content to not seek improvement. They have accepted their present station, without resolve.

Wise is the individual performing a task which needs to be repeated because the first attempt was not to his satisfaction. It is he who makes every effort to improve and refine his methods to become ever increasingly proficient. He is not content to be satisfied with the status quo. He learns from his mistakes and sees ways to improve in his effectiveness through an ever increasing under-standing of his own duty. He increases his knowledge of the expected end results.

When dealing with others, it is your responsibility to FIRST see that your methods and understandings are in the process of refinement, then you can work on the improvement of others.

Common Sense: **For sure-fired success, act as if your end results have already happened. Take on and acknowledge the attributes that you are wishing to develop.**

As part of the problem solving process, and as stated in the second step of goal achievement, treat yourself and others as if the end results have already happened. If your goal is to affect the lives of others, then act accordingly as if you were a person of confidence. Supporting your desired end results as already true will connect yourself and others into becoming as such.

For example: If you want **honesty** from others, then just let them feel that you **trust** them. They will want to retain the gratifications and personal achievement which they feel from you as you're displaying confidence in them. Help them to do just this, by pointing out any rewards that are theirs now and the others which could be theirs in the future, if they do what it takes to keep hold of your trust.

Don't spend a lot of time dwelling on, "*What if they take advantage of me?*" You are in the business of affecting for the good the lives of others, aren't you? Or are you just protecting your interests and looking out for number one? Go ahead and show faith in them; only the most brazened will willingly jeopardize a trust. However, in such a case where they shamelessly misuse your trust, again it is your choice to help them to do whatever is necessary to regain your lost confidence. To assist them, you recommit to become involved with them on a higher level. Or, you may choose the easier path and give-up. You may even become indifferent and abandon them so-that you are not hurt again. The choice is yours depending on your motives. *Whose interest are you trying to serve?*

Throughout your involvement with your charges, always give them reason to continue to trust you. Being the recipient of your honesty will promote them into wanting to display this trait as well. Even if your intentions were honorable, if ever you felt it was necessary to mislead another in order to obtain a desired outcome, then as soon as possible own up to your deceitful practices. Even though they might not agree with your methods, they will at least be given the opportunity to understand your motives; they will appreciate your honesty. You will keep their continued trust.

Likewise, for any positive trait you desire to develop in others, if you want your best chance at affecting their lives, then role-model to them. Let them recognize the benefits by witnessing your proper usage. You show the positive side in action, so they will aspire to obtain it.

Common Sense Lesson: Treat Others How You Would Like Them to Become.

She always supported him as the final decision maker. She never talked cross at him, or aggressively voiced an unsupportive comment. Almost constantly, she strove to make his short hours in the house be as pleasant as possible. She treated him as if he were king by waiting on his domestic needs while constantly showing him love and respect. Never did I hear her complain as to their meager existence as farm workers. After he lost their farm, she still supported and encouraged him; never throwing blame at him. She knew that he had done everything within his capability to make it

A COMMON HORSE SENSE GUIDE TO TEACHING   83

work. She trusted that somehow he would continue to make the correct choices and remain their provider.

He, in return, made comments in her presence to other people of how lovely and beautiful she was. So genuine was he in his praising of her attributes, no one could not be in the same room with them without feeling that she was indeed a most elegant queen. He overlooked the fact that she was a large as a heifer, never making comments to the negative or comparing her with another's physical beauty. He was always appreciative of the help and support that she gave. He always marveled that someone as-grand-as she could indeed be happy with him.

Both had a high regard and admiration for their spouse, and in return the other lived up to that standard. Each gave the same respect and admiration back which they received. I, as an impressionable young adult, could see the great relationship my Aunt and Uncle had. I thought of them both as the utmost persons I wanted to aspire towards and become like. I realized, "That's how I wanted my future marriage to be ... with both spouses treating the other with uppermost respect, love and honor, and getting in return the same treatment." I will never be so dishonest as to claim that I have succeeded completely in my marriage of thirty-seven years, but that is my goal, and as I realize my shortcomings, I am working still towards that end result.

As a trainer, you have already been utilizing some of your problem solving skills; you have been working at changing what you don't like and turning it into something that you do. When you've encountered a past problem, recall how you followed some or all of those steps in-order to solve it. Sometimes you may have skipped a part and still had success, nevertheless, knowing the whole process will help you on perplexing issues. When you become empowered and understand correct principles, then you have the ability to teach and train others to use them also. Their and your problems will become curable as you address them step-by-step.

Don't give up

Remember this last, but not least, important principle of problem solving. It hasn't been listed as a separate step because it needs to be incorporated with each step along the way. It is: **"Don't give up."** By predicting positive outcomes, then going out and doing the steps to make it so, good results can be obtained. Predicting failure or that something negative might occur permits one's rationalization process to think it a good idea to just give up. Why not? Things most likely won't work out anyway—especially to someone who quits when the going gets rough. Having a defeatist outlook stimulates the looking for reasons and things which support pessimistic theories. There is an inner force within each of us to make it so. Remember to get mad ... {E.R.R.R} if things don't work out. Only then do you have a chance to effect unwanted out-come.

Avoid Negativism.

Yes, it is to your advantage to have a substitute plan if your first attempt to effect change in others is not successful. But, when you start to summons up alternative measures by questioning people's responses before they happen; when you choose to spend time on *"But what if?"* ... in order to prepare for a negative experience, then you put yourself on the defensive and could get into a mind set that will defeat yourself and others by disallowing success before it can transpire. Always allow more than a fair opportunity for others to change and develop, and then give them a chance again. They may be on the verge of metamorphosis and a little more positive support will make all the difference. Negativism does not inspire others. Only after multiple disappointments should you set into play your substitute plan. Keep in the mindset of still helping others, not under the pretense of having to revise because they're failures.

*   *   *

Common Horse Sense: Don't give up; get back on.

For months I had been working with the fourteen thru seventeen year-old boys in my scouting group to get them ready for an upcoming three-day horse ride. It was now just a month away and preparations were an uphill battle. Not that the boys didn't want to go, they wanted to have a fun time; what they didn't want was to put any effort into the getting ready.

On a Wednesday night while I was waiting for these boys to appear for a prearranged practice horse ride, I was working with a young horse to refine its slow canter. I had, in that hour prior to their 7:00p.m. appointment, three boys drop over to tell me they weren't going to show up tonight. Their excuses were all very lame.

One said, "I don't want to get dirty."

Another remarked, "I can't come because I am going to cook dinner tonight for my family. Sorry."

A third stated, "Tonight, I just want to stay home."

Dismissing any hope of the other boys actually showing up to ride, I continued cantering my inexperienced horse in my round pen. It had been raining and hailing in the two hours previous—also a reason that I supposed the boys possibly didn't want to ride tonight; they were afraid they might get wet or become uncomfortable.

Suddenly the least expected boy appeared. He stood and watched me ride for a couple of minutes before my horse slipped and went down in the wet corral. She fell down on her side, squashing my leg under her. I rolled off the saddle giving her chance to stand-up and get off my trapped leg. "That hurt," I said, as I got up. I shook off my own pain, and then rubbed her to reassure everything was ok. I knew she meant no ill; she had just slipped. I got back on and started to trot.

"You'll heal. All pain goes away ... some just faster than others," he chivied with a huge smile plastered on his face.

"Yah, it just takes longer to go away the older you get." I delivered back with a grimace.

Tyler had showed up. He was a bit surprised to find that he was the only boy who did come to ride. Since one boy to teach is a great honor, I got off my horse and commenced working with him. We worked on the proper way to approach an animal, and how to tie a rope with a bowline knot around a horse's neck. We practiced saddling and his getting his horse to lower its head so he could put on the bridle. Each step was a new experience. He learned fast and was willing. He then climbed in the saddle and we spent time on his learning to get this horse to yield her neck to the side, prior to actually moving, so she would respond to his control and be supple. He was nervous and out of place on the animal, but as the experience continued he grew more at ease.

I always tell a kid that he can possibly end up on the ground. I made it also a point for which I prepared Tyler by going over the following: "The horse can startle, and any rider can lose his balance. It happens so fast. You must be ready, especially when you move into a situation that is different for the horse. Learn to recognize when your mount is nervous by the signs she gives you. These signs are: blowing through her nose, raising her head up, her ears coming upright, and a choppy nervous walk or demeanor." I cautioned, "Be prepared for her to do this whenever you move into a tight or strange place. As you notice these signs, move you hands into a two handed-double rein position; take up the slack of the reins and hold them low at the base of her neck, that way you'll be able to keep her in control, if she bolts. Also, I added, "This grip will help you to keep your balance."   *{I might add now, after the fact, I was going way too fast in this teaching. My objective was to give him a riding experience that very night. Time, I thought, was of the essence.}*

About thirty minutes into a short trail ride, Tyler was doing great. On our way home we crossed a broken down fence which had a wire lying on the ground. My horse was inexperienced, so I thought, "What a good chance to teach her to cross a wire." I lower my own hands to be ready, in case she reacted negatively. She went over beautifully. A couple of seconds later, I heard two hooves hitting the ground hard behind me, and saw out of the corner of my eye Tyler being propelled down onto the ground. His horse had stopped hard after two quick nervous side steps. Yet, he kept on moving. He had lost his balance as he tried to rein her, or stop her, or something? She, an experienced horse, had spooked at the single low lying wire.

"I am done riding," were his words as he hit the ground. Then spitting dirt out of his mouth, he added, "No matter what you say!"

There he sat hunched over, his arms rapping his legs. He remained in his sitting fetal position, next to a sage brush, for a minute or two.

"*Great,*" I thought after realizing that he wasn't really hurt, just startled, "*What do I say to help him get over this?*" His horse was just standing there a few feet away. I was still, at this point, sitting on mine, watching, seeking to give Tyler every opportunity to rise to the occasion and get back on.

"No, I just can't do it," he said, trying to justifying himself in his own mind, and presumably also to me. His horse faded away slightly from his half-hearted effort to hold her while he made a very weak attempt of getting on. "I'll just walk home," he remarked as he aborted. He stepped back from his horse, and looked at me for rescue.

I got off my horse and walked over to his while saying, **"You know it isn't the great fall that a guy goes through. It's what he does once he gets back up that makes the man."**

With that I held her mane and rein, and climbed up on. My reassuring confidence eased her. She waited patiently for my clue as to her next move. "See, she's ok, I believe that it scared her as much as it did you." I looked right into Tyler's eyes while putting a reassuring hand on his shoulder. "And, you forgot what I showed you about hand placements. When anything looks out of the ordinary, move your hands back to double reining. At the same time hold the reins close to her neck and low, that way you can keep your balance and your control." I demonstrated the reining moves again and brought her head around each side several times to establish her submission. Then I climbed off.

That kid said nothing, but moved toward his waiting mount which I held from moving to give him a little more confidence. He climbed up, and I did the same on mine. I was careful to ride right along side of him, this time. After two minutes at a slow walk, he remarked with doubt, trying to defend his actions again in his own mind, "I can't do this thing anymore. I am going to get off."

Let me tell you some of his history. —for about two years, he has been involved in my scouting group. In each instance where he has been in a situation that required effort on his part, such as following through with a commitment, he'd fall short unless pushed or pulled by someone else. As he would accept an assignment that would take some preparation, or that would require of him to go out of his comfort zone, he'd, without fail, not follow through with it. In each of the beginning planning stages, he'd be willing to participate and would actively make plans to go on an outing ... even up to the night before. Yet on the day of the event he'd not want to go. To get him to go and he'd have to be picked up at his house and be fussed over or he wouldn't participate. Whenever he could be persuaded into going, he would spend the first half of the outing struggling to distance from the goings on by purposefully moving outside of the action zone, or by vanishing without a trace to be off alone, instead of becoming involved with the leaders or the other boys. He acted as if he was locked in a depressive and self-pity mode. Then later he'd join in the activities and have the time of his life. He seemed to require others making a big effort over him, before he would allow himself to get involved. "That's why I was so taken back when he showed up alone to ride horses tonight."

More history: His family suffers from depression. One brother, one sister, his Mom and his Dad choose not to put themselves into challenging situations, and then they feel disappointed in themselves because of this choice. Some of them have withdrawn from society, and then taken months or years to again rejoin it. In their self-protective modes, they feel they've let themselves and others down, yet they still continue to not push or challenge themselves.

"You know," I said, "all throughout life there will be things that we don't want to do, even things that make us scared. As we act, despite our scared feelings, and push ourselves into continuing to endeavor, even though we are still afraid, we become stronger for it."

Here I was telling this to the same boy who at fifteen-years old and standing in at five-foot and eight-inches tall was totally afraid, and then latter so proud of himself, when I challenged him, one month prior, to go on a bike ride with me down a small hill. He had never pedaled over a mile from his house, and had never, even in his dreams, thought that he would be able to ride his bike down that hill. He was so very proud of himself after doing it; like the satisfaction that comes after a hard race when a difficult physical challenge has been overcome. In this bike ride, he experienced the kind of adventure for himself which causes a feeling to swell inside by just remembering the experience. It was a source of great pride for him to re-tell anyone who would listen. Today with these horses, we were again standing in the makings of such another event.

My mind was searching for a wisdom-filled comeback; I knew that I had been given an opportunity to help teach this kid something he was not learning at home. He was in a "Cave of Darkness," and looking for a little light to follow. {see: page: 149}

I continued, "You will have things in school that you will not want to do; you will have responsibilities that scare you. You may find yourself hiding from or not wanting to finish paying off a debt ,latter on in life. And even as a parent, you will at times not know what decisions to do with your family. You will get scared, and not want to continue because of all the bad things which you imagine might happen. Just do the best you can, and that means keeping your balance when you anticipate things can go wrong. Be prepared for them, and don't give up as they happen. As you do, you'll get stronger and gain the skills that will help you stay on for the hard things in life."

Pausing for emphasis, I continued as I let go a little more, "Ya know Tyler, what goes around comes around." The beginnings of a smirk formed on my face. "I know from what you said to me earlier today that you can take a little pain and get over it. Be aware that life is full of little setbacks that a true man will face, and then decide to triumph over to finish what he started."

With those words, that kid stayed on, and then thanked me fifteen minutes latter as we finished the ride. While we put the horses away, he kept talking about his adventure. He couldn't believe he had endured such an awesome thing. Of course he was nervous and scared, and was not completely comfortable with what had happened, but he had chosen to grow, and stayed on. He was, once more, so stoked, so beamy proud of himself. As he headed for home I could hear him yell over his boney shoulder, "Now I can tell my friends that I was bucked-off, and then got back on!" He was hurrying to boast his grand adventure.

"Yes you can, Tyler, yes you can," I yelled back as I watched him increase in speed and jump a sage brush while giving a little kick of glee, like he had sunk the winning basket just as the buzzer goes off in a high school state tournament.

*   *   *

A good place for you to teach practical problem solving to others is found in developing a commonly shared goal. Use a shared common interest and let them witness your wishing and dreaming, followed by the carrying out of organized steps to obtain a wanted outcome. You show them the power that can be theirs as they learn to surmount and conquer their troubles. In unity, both tackle the same problem. They will see your correct process in action and gather insight on how they can solve problems on their own, so that no longer does a hardship need to be merely accepted and endured. In your common goal, let your student express his wishes along with yours. Be very supportive of his ideas, don't discredit them, but lead him into the understanding of their pertinence. If modification is necessary, then together discuss where to compromise. When their dreams are far from an obtainable reality, guide them to see that they and you can re-adjust, and then re-do in order to exchange any unrealistic thoughts into reachable goals. By doing so, you keep the interest of your student to stay joined with you.

As you join together beware. It may be your dreams that are unrealistic in the way that you have chosen to obtain them. Be sure to keep an open mind and share with your pupil any reasons which cause you to re-adjust your thinking, that they may see the process of using wisdom for themselves.

Let them know that it is OK to try and fall short of the intended mark, and that a mere failure is nothing more than an invite to try again, one more time ... but, now with added knowledge and new experience.

"It is better to make a mistake with the full force of your being than to timidly avoid mistakes with the trembling spirit." Pp. 126 WAY OF THE PEACEFUL WARRIOR by Dan Millman Published by New World Books

As well, let them see that you stand with them in their attempts to redo and again overcome their difficulties. A shared goal is the best way for multiple persons to solve a problem and all still think that they have retained some control.

Learning how, then teaching others to properly problem solve brings change. Treating others as you would like them to become, inspires them. By not giving up at set backs and then having the personal resolve to re-adjust and refine efforts, envisioned results are obtained.

CHAPTER 6:

WHEN AM I WASTING MY TIME

Common Sense: **The use of proper timing is the key in determining when to teach.**

If an instructor is just giving out information to be received by anyone that may be listening, it is nothing more than a lecture. Who of us hasn't forced ourselves to sit and endure the time moving slowly at a *tick...tick...tick* as an instructor proceeds, his voice seemingly locked in monotone suspension, his lips moving methodically just a-spewin' words out of his mouth, and him going on-and-on impervious to others' feelings while seemingly not really caring about the mental suffering of his pupils; he doesn't attempt to make his subject interesting or in any shape or fashion appealing, and in no way or in no how is he energetic, nor does he choose to show any passion at all, and we are stuck there being forced to endure without a means of escape? Truly we didn't want to be there, and so will in about twenty–four hours only remember about one-fourth of what was said. Without some sort of implementation or purposeful wanting to retain the information, {such as note taking or reviewing the information over in our minds} within the next twenty-four hours we will again have forgotten all but 25% of the fractional amount that we did recall on the first day after the horribly boring ordeal. We continue losing; recalling only about 25% of what was remembered on the day before. We just keep on forgetting any non-pertinent information. Truly it is a very ineffective way to teach, by lecturing. For we who have been stuck having to undergo this boring lecture the timing for learning was not right.

Timing is critical to learning. It will never be better than when the student wishes to learn. No matter for what reason, if the student is seeking to gain information, any chance of his retaining something and thereby learning are greatly improved. He will hang on to more, if it is applicable to his needs. In order for learning to take place the student has to be putting forth effort, preferably to the same level or more so than his teacher. Effort is spent by the student as he asks questions, uses association; pays enough attention to make a personal note, or practices the concepts. Your possibilities to teach always include making yourself available, and then deciding on your purpose and which style you use in teaching. By teaching when the student is engaged and wants to learn, your information will also be presented at a time when they are prepared to put forth the effort to give you their attention.

Getting a Charge's Attention

How is it that when both involved in the same event, at the same time and place, one student will be bored and get nothing out of it, and another will think it was the best presentation ever? The answer is attention level. One is for whatever reason paying attention; he is engaged. The other, although present, is letting his mind wander at this moment; he is not really experiencing the need to learn. When your presentation of the subject is not enough to hold onto the wanderer, what you need is an **Attention Getter**. With this tool, you generate a diversion to the current mind set of the un-interested student; you create a situation where you can't miss.

*   *   *

Common Horse Sense: Getting a horse's attention.

For a lesson to be effective at all, the trainee must be paying attention by keeping his mind channeled on what the trainer is trying to do. With each failure of the horse to perform, the trainer ought to question, "Why isn't interest being shown? Does the horse have the slightest idea what is being asked? Or is it being resistive or obnoxious and purposely displaying poor behavior? In any case, the trainer should not let the inappropriate responses continue. A good wake up call is used as a horse misbehaves or ignores his trainer. When mounted, a slight bump or a tap of pressure on the reins should bring back the attention of most previously trained, but temporarily side-tracked animals. Getting the attention of a knowingly disobedient horse is all together a different matter …

…**Case in point:** The other day while trimming hooves of a fresh horse, possibly it was only the third time in her six-year-old life, she allowed me to trim the first front hoof before she let me know that she'd had enough. She started by pulling her foot away, once, twice, and on the third attempt, I smacked her with the rasp and raised my voice to let her know that I didn't approve of her behavior. Receiving the wake up, she then stood still. She had been not paying attention to her role as the subservient. She had out of boredom and defiance pulled away.

After the reprimand, she did allow me to finish that foot, yet she was still giving signs of fixing to explode. She apparently still didn't appreciate her role, and was hell-bent on educating me that she was in control and didn't want to be bothered. So, as I started rasping the next hoof she quickly pulled it away, causing me to falter in balance. To un-equivocally establish her defiance, she popped me in the left thigh.

It was now time to get her attention in order to teach her the lesson, *"I want you to stand quietly, while I trim your hooves!"* For me to just get angry and to lash-out impulsively wouldn't have been wise, I would have caused further damage where she could have advanced her defiance. If I was to effectively educate her, I must first get prepared and then couple that with the right timing.

In her present state of mind it was impossible for her to learn; she was not receptive in any way. She was being entitled, and her mind needed to change. Prior to trimming another hoof, I needed a change in her behavior, and before I could get that, I needed to alter the way I had her tied to the hitching rail.

I neck-tied her with nylon rope and took the working end through her halter, under her jaw. This I tied securely to the hitching rail. There was no way she was going anywhere. "Yes, to all you humane horse enthusiasts, I do know that a cotton rope will not burn and is less rough on an animal that is intent on pulling away." She and I have gone through this before; I know she has the strength and can get a resistance-to-all mentality. Once, she wigged-out and pulled apart two three-quarter inch ropes, one right after the other. Today, I wanted to deeply impress: **Her fighting against being handled was not something she wanted to continue to do!**

It took a few minutes to get her and myself ready to what I was sure would happen next. She stood defiantly still to my cautious preparations. I was sure to move slow and non-threatening until all ropes were in place; I knew she was still into fighting mode against her feet being handled further. Once everything was ready, I abandoned moving non-threatening around her and assertively positioned myself under her back leg. She pulled it away hard to teach a lesson of her own. She was stating, *"Don't mess with me!"*

Now I came alive and kicked up my action. I wanted to show her that I wasn't going to allow her to get away with her defiance any longer. The time had come to drop my passiveness and do what needed to be done, even if it made her uncomfortable.

She flung back hard to get away. The freshly tied 5/8 inch nylon rope held fast. I gave her pressure to keep moving, with the jerking and waving of my arms, while forcefully displaying an angered look in my eyes. She became crazed pulling against her neck and halter tie. She was fighting again all restraints. Having broken lesser ropes before, in her escalated livid mindset she was even more determined to keep pulling back. She was determined to do again what had worked before.

First lesson to teach: She needed to respect being tied. By me stimulating her to keep moving each time she pulled back, and then letting up as she choose to stand still, she learned that being calm didn't hurt and that fighting against this rope did.

After awhile, she offered no more resistance, so I, once more, climbed back under her. Even as I did, I knew she was still not through being obnoxious. She had learned to be submissive only to the hurting rope. It was my purpose to make sure she realized, without a doubt in her horsey mind, she was causing her own grief and consequences. She allowed me to get set in position, and again kicked when I started rasping. But, she didn't pull back against being tied by that biting rope. She was now more selective in her defiance; she only moved and kicked with her hind feet.

It was now time for the big guns! During the neck re-tying break, I had gotten on and in position for battle, my gloves and a half-inch cotton rope. I fastened that cotton rope around her pastern, under her fetlock. The working end of the rope continued on back through a solid fastened ring some eight feet behind, then doubled back toward her. It was left lying slackly on the ground next to where I would be rasping. Being setup in this position, this non-burning rope would act like a pulley to tighten and stretch her leg out should I pull on the working end. I had prepared for war, yet still gave her another chance to conform.

With the new kick, I grabbed onto the end of the rope and tugged with all my might. Her kicking leg was held locked, three feet off the ground, in extension some seventy degrees behind her. I continued holding on and pulling the rope to give an even-more uncomfortable feeling to the stretching.

She escalated her defiance, and started into a kicking spree. As much as possible, she kicked her hind leg with vengeance. Since I had prepared, her kicking now gave her no relief. It only caused her more grief. Using the pain caused by her rebelliousness, I proceeded to go back to a form of "The Basics" and taught her by imposing pressure, and then releasing that pressure. I was currently teaching her that it was better to stand still than kick against her tied leg. She would get no relief whenever she chose to fight against the restraint.

Throughout this difficult learning process of her letting go of a past behavior, the neck-tied rope continued to remain loose. Although she continued in defiance, she was choosing not to purposely injure herself ...she had learned that previous lesson well.

When she tired of thrashing about and took a break from her defiant wigging-out, I loosened the back leg rope a bit, and simultaneously placed a hand on her somewhat less uncomfortable, but still extended leg. {It was now time to teach her that she would get not relief it she chose to fight against me.} My touch caused her to start up again, so on came more pressure and discomfort as I once-again forced an extension to her rebellious limb. In vain through exhaustion, she tried her past proven behavior of fighting against control. It wasn't working now. As she fought against me, to her discomfort came reminders that the more she fought the more pain she felt.

In addition, during my preparations for the anticipated fight, I had hobbled her front legs. She discovered she must curb her defiant kicking in-order to keep her balance; otherwise she was going down. She quickly became very aware of this. She was still nervous to my touch and wanting to kick out, but also knowing that it produced only additional pain, unwanted discomfort, and lost of balance. Because I had her attention, she was now open to my teachings. She didn't like the discomfort of having her leg controlled by another, and was hunting for what would eliminate it. Other lashings-out against my hand on her leg brought discomfort and unsteadiness back again. When she wearied and quit, she quickly got a relief of pain. During her resting, I again touched her leg. If she endured it without lashing out, no more pain happened. As she refrained from fighting, she received an additional loosening of her hid leg and the added stability of balance.

Soon she got the picture. The less she resisted, the freer she became. She learned to stand and be still. No real harm came to her as she allowed this man to handle her feet; it only came back when she kicked-out. As she tired of her unproductive show of force and permitted me to handle her foot once more, I completely freed up her leg and finished trimming that hoof. The next two hooves went smoothly without incident. In order to teach this previously unwilling student, my attention getter needed to become more deviant than she.

* * *

Common Sense Lesson: Using an Attention Getter on a Pupil.

An old Sheepherder, by the name of Frank Firm, shared with me a lesson in my early parenthood that has stayed with me these many years. He repeated it often whenever he saw someone making a mistake that could have been avoided if they were just paying more attention to what they were doing. I title it as he did:

"What That Kid Needs"

He would start out by saying, "What that kid needs is an attention getter." He would stop right there in mid-sentence and not continue speaking until you had given him your undivided attention. Only your undivided interest would egg him on to continue. When he was sure you were listening he would add, "Just use a four-foot, two-by-four and an empty bucket and you can get the attention of any youngster. With the two-by-four, CRACK OPEN their noggin. Next fill the empty bucket with common sense and just pour it right in. Then they'll soak it up."

Now I am not condoning the beating with a board, but I am testifying as to the effectiveness of using a good attention getter, they work every time. …This one sure got yours!

For a distracted pupil, the use of proper timing will help to get their attention. In fact, a wise educator will create it. He will manufacture a need to know by putting his students in a situation where their attention is being given when and because they feel it is vital to receive more information. The master teacher will have his students hungry to devour more of what he has. He may be funny, or he may be sharing information in an extremely interesting way so it captures the interest of his pupils. The master could be even sharing the very information that is currently on the mind of the student wanting to obtain. In each case, the discourse is presented such a way that the student's attention has been captured and held in unison with the teacher's information.   {Such as a cleverly done commercial on the TV which takes a new idea and presents it with skill by motivating any listener to sit up and take notice. The idea presented wasn't remotely close to what the listeners were previously thinking about.}

With the student wanting to undertake new ways and willing to learn new things, a common ground is shared between the educator and the learner. By creating the need to know in the student, the teacher can freely impart his knowledge. The timing is accurate because his pupil is hungry and willing to receive.

I have found the best asset one can have in trying to teach a new skill is: when the students, whom really want to do something by themselves can't; they fall short. They, forced by their own desire to succeed, intuitively turn to one who supposedly knows more. In that scenario learning takes place fast and effective. The teacher has a willing audience that is paying attention and will quickly practice or put into play what they learn.

Contrast those willing students to the conniving youth who also seeks help, but doesn't have as his objective to learn. His is the objective to just get a task done. He weaves a web of trickery. Be careful that you are not caught-up. He will depict the impression of asking for help, but he is indeed asking for more. He is seeking to get you to do his task for him, or to allow his lesser participation in order to eliminate his own obligation. Some manipulators are very good at this skill, having mastered it to an art of perfection.

If you are obliged to help a student by showing him how to do something, and you are in question of his motives, simply just stop doing it. ...See what happens? The youth that isn't really paying attention won't even realize your pause; he won't even notice that you quit. It is being counter-productive as a teacher to continue doing for this child. In fact by continuing you are only showing your readiness to be manipulated.

A common excuse by a manipulative student when pleading for help is: "I can't do it as near as good as you." or "You need to show me how, so I can see it done right." To check if this student is not being lazy and is truly engaged in seeing that his task gets done correctly, do their task noticeably wrong. He will question you. This creates the opportunity for growth by him supposedly teaching you the right way. You created for him a chance to help himself by his becoming more involved in helping someone else. You out manipulated him.

If you want to really be more effective at teaching a skill or lesson, then help your pupils to become so empowered that they endeavor to solve their own problem. Don't solve it for them. However poorly done, once they have had the self esteem building experience of doing the task themselves, then you may point out a more effective way to assist the child. But, only after you have taken a minute to relish with them in their accomplishments as such may be. Fight the notion to point out helps and hints in order to assist the child, until they have had a measure of success on their own. Be discreet when introducing a possible new suggestion, it is better if they feel it was somewhat their idea also. Your inopportune inter-ference may not be appreciated if your do not acknowledge what effort they have so far invested.

A student, after attempting and coming up short himself, is much more committed to learn if he can recall or witness another person effortlessly, without smugness, mastering the same task. He becomes more teachable and is much more receptive to seeing new ideas and methods from a humble, yet skillful, teacher. You, let him know that he, with perseverance, can also master the same.

Be ready as a teacher; your students at anytime may suddenly have the need to know. It is an amazing phenomenon to watch a sluggish mind wake-up and become alive. They may ask you, as if for the first time, the same thing that you have told them a thousand times before. Only now for some reason they need to know; they've been aroused. Tell them again. This may be the first genuine instance where they really wanted to know; they now are truly listening. This is a great opportunity to teach.

"So when are you being a good teacher?"

...When you teach a student to solve his own problem in order to get what he needs. An up-front way to do this is to let the student know that you will not do for them, and you still expect them to function on their own. Your role is to merely guide them in the proper direction. This will work as long as he can still see a benefit for being left on his own, and that you are still there if needed. Using this approach you will soon be out of a job as the student learns and has success. You will no longer be needed to teach until the next time the student finds himself lacking.

...The best teacher empowers the student to do as much as he can possibly do, and then the teacher does likewise by filling in the gaps. Together, both accept joint responsibility and both perform by changing when shortcomings are realized.

Teach to make things different.

So many of us wish things would have been different. Maybe we wish we'd developed better skills in certain areas ... perhaps obtained more schooling, or learned to speak publicly with greater fluency, or even have developed different habits, talents, and values. Possibly we could have saved more of our income earlier on, so now the power of compound interest would be working for us in a large retirement account, instead of the burden of consumer debt with its compound interest working against our struggles to pay it off. With children, we may teach more than where we currently are by showing them where we would like to be ... if we had developed a different perspective or additional skills earlier on in life. We should help them prepare for what they may not even have thought about yet; we introduce into a student's mind new ideas and perspectives.

You are a teacher ...

Anytime you ask another person to do something, you are using a teaching approach. With every interaction you are displaying your motives by the techniques you use. You are a teacher of some sort every time you come in contact with another person. You are either showing how much you care by engaging, where you are trying to divulge something that you think might be of benefit, or you are teaching them you don't care a bit. All persons are teachers when they can aid another's life by sharing information, experiences, or are helping to direct another towards a path to follow. Anyone who feels some sort of responsibility to assist another, and then acts on it is a teacher.

When you realize that you can make a difference in someone's life, that's when you should teach. This could be as you pass a perplexed stranger looking for the Spaghetti-Os in the supermarket. Or, see a fellow co-worker struggling with a task at work which you understand, or even when you want help a partner see a different point of view. As you learn to work with and guide a pupils' willingness to learn, your attempts to teach change to others becomes much more effective.

In the up-coming Part Two, you will see that everyone could be a student, when they are in the position that they might benefit from another's knowledge or insight. Join with me as I share more Common Sense Lessons to what we should be teaching. The wisdom of the next section is vital to enhance your understanding as a teacher and a trainer. You will discovery what makes a child and a horse behave as they do.

PART 2

DISCOVERING THE STUDENT

CHAPTER 7:

UNDERSTANDING THE STUDENT

IT is helpful to have an awareness of what a student wants and how they think. Since a student is a child of knowledge, we will discuss how the learning process starts in a baby, and how it continues to grow in a youngster. This information will help you make more educated decisions when faced with a chance to teach and effect another's life.

A **Student** is: 1} any being who is in the process of, or is capable of learning. 2} a charge who is being trained.

To **Learn** is: 1} to gain knowledge or understanding of or skill in by study, instruction, or experience. 2} to come to realize, or come to know. 3} to acquire a behavioral tendency. {Weber's New Collegiate Dictionary}

As you can see by its definition, to learn is an action. It is not an action of those who teach, but of those students who discover knowledge. It takes place with a student as he tries to get gain. {see: Chapter 8: *page: 123*} If the pupil is not in the mode to attempt to gain by his actions, then no learning will take place. The teacher is merely wasting his time, while the pupil remains only an object which happens to be in the presence of a lecturing teacher. To learn, the student should be willing to put forth effort, endeavoring harder than the teacher, for it is he that is in the position to gain.

Common Sense: **"The more effort you put into learning—that you'll do."**

Properties of a Willing Student

1. Eager to do more than just try:
The willing have a higher level of commitment.

The willing student strives to achieve, aspire, or excel; they make effort to master or to improve, they don't just simply try.

For a person to say, *"I will try,"* is to leave an option to do nothing or to do just as little of effort as allowable in order to get a teacher off his back. When asked for an accounting of past efforts, the student who knowingly gave a poor performance will attempt to justify with the flimsy rejoinder, *"But I tried."* For anyone to say *"I will try,"* is almost always a statement that they are not striving to improve; they are content that their mediocre efforts are or will be good enough, they have a poor level of commitment.

Three Levels of Commitment:

I. Even though it is not a flat denial or a refusal of any responsibility, it is still a poor response and commits the giver to nothing special, but to give some effort, if it is convenient. When presented with any task, to be passive enough to only commit to, **"I'll try,"** shows only a small level of agreement that too often is matched with an equally small level of effort. I'll try is the lowest level of commitment.

II. A better response in fulfilling a task, although it still gives room for failure, is to say, **"Ok, I will do the best that my ability and situation allows."** Go ahead and except a challenge to say this, the next time someone asks you to perform. You will be amazed to see how effective it is in getting them off your back. It commits you, the giver, into putting forth effort until a hardship shuts you down. It challenges you only to be proud of mediocrity.

Most people will accept this as an honest answer, they expect nothing more. They also have failed before. With your promise of personal commitment on this level, you will aspire to put forth only a good effort.

Common Sense: **A willing student more than just tries. He strives to improve. Only the champion has the spirit to excel.**

III. The best response to give which also locks you into the highest level of commitment and gives no room for failure, is to say, *"Yes, I will do that."* There are no excuses; you go and do. You display that you have the guts to perform hard work. The severity of the task is not as important as your pledge to accomplish it. With this highest level of commitment, if after your best ability has been given, but still the task is not satisfactory, you will be inspired to re-commit, refine, and re-adjust. You will seek help in order to obtain additional skills and knowledge, so that your job is fulfilled. If needed you will go far above what is expected of you in order to succeed.

Common Sense: **It is effort that turns our failings to strengths. In accordance with our commitment, we must role up our sleeves and commence to work. Inspiration comes from wise teachers, and the strength to endure comes from God.**

Think of the achievements that can now be accomplished with inspiration from exemplary mentors and with the strength given us by God. There is no failure when we are committed to succeed, only set-backs to be over-come.

2. | Teachable: |

A willing student is teachable.

I will use the following example of picking a pup to explain.

* * *

Common Horse Sense: Teachable like a good puppy.

When picking a future dog from a litter of puppies, if it's important to get one that'll have the easiest time learning to mind, or be most eager to work, or even exhibit the greatest potential to be taught tricks. Be sure to pick a puppy that is teachable and not full of self-pity.

The best method for choosing a pup of potential is to spend time with the litter; you develop rapport. The first object is to get them to where they like you. Puppy-play with them, then push them away and give them a choice to come back to you. As most pups are trustful and loving, this shouldn't take too long. Pick from pups that are old enough to wean, by this stage they have developed personality traits, from which you can make your best decision.

Pick the one or two that you like most, and then make them believe they made a mistake by you scolding them and raising your voice. Give them a meaningful spank or a swat. Be sure you make them individually believe their behavior is not what you wanted, and you're ticked about it. Don't be so sensitive that you worry about the effects on the puppies; their mother does this all the time.

If you can't scold a pup, then you are defiantly too soft hearted and will struggle when it comes time to train it. The pup which doesn't hold a grudge and will come back for more after you have disciplined it, also, displays signs it'll be teachable to new lessons. It is showing its willingness to learn or to make up for any bad behavior. A little tough-love gives the pup an opportunity to make adjustments.

In retrospect, if it hides or cowards away this pup will be a weenie full of self-pity. It will be inclined to remain so. It is a **Cry Baby** who will not foremost be willing to please its master. It will more than likely choose to remain afraid, and not venture out of its comfort zone in order to undertake something new for fear of making a mistake.

It is important that you don't focus on what it looks like, or what you imagine it to become. Pick the pup that will come back again after it has been scolded. It is this pup which will be the most trainable.

* * *

Unlike a puppy, you can't discard a student simply because they will not come back to you after you have scolded them. The fact remains; you will have a harder time teaching a student who is wallowing in self-pity after being called out for a mistake. You will certainly have more difficulty teaching students who aren't putting themselves in the fore-front to learn and improve. You have got to increase your level of involvement with these types of students, so that you can get them into the mode to be teachable.

3. **Expresses a desire to push against force:**

Other than gifts received from a charitable benefactor, every gain in this life comes as result of overcoming some sort of opposing force against it. Like an eager to run horse, a keen student is willing to except the challenges of defeating forces that are before him. He pushes himself to overcome obstacles, and seeks to experience gains of his own. {see: Chapter 8}

A natural impulse of an eager horse and an adolescent student is to have a measure of control of their lives; they have a need to win at something. A successful sports coach understands how to channel this natural desire to prevail; he adds to it skill and knowledge and soon he produces a winner. As a teacher, your success is seen when you apply some sort of power against your students which awakens and stimulates them. Any benefits that a student receives, as result of his expressing his need to win, translate into him feeling that he is still in control and it will further stimulate him into repeating the same behavior. So why not learn, to your benefit, how to use your student's **natural instinct** to push against a force? If you can utilize their desire to win; if you can enhance their desire to prevail against a pressure and you channel this energy towards getting results, then you both win.

Understand that to triumph is a natural desire of the keen student as he pushes against another's control. It can be further understood by analyzing a horse's actions in the following Common Horse Sense instructions: "Accepting a Challenge" and "Nothing to Fight Against." Your job as a teacher is to further awaken these desires using them to guide and train your students.

* * *

Common Horse Sense: Accepting a Challenge.

A horse will run faster if it's in contest against something. In order to coax the winning efforts out of a race horse, a jockey will sit high on the back of a horse, near its withers, so as to not interfere in the moments of its stretching body. Having an understanding of the principle of pushing against force, the jockey will load the horse's bit with a resistance; he gives a slight pulling back. In conventional thinking isn't this the same action required when a horse is asked to stop? The only difference is the stimulation that the jockey gives is a constant pressure which his mount feels and by instinct moves into this resistance or into the bit. The moving into the bit is a push against the controlled pressure of the jockey. The result of this interaction is the horse running faster; it is meeting a challenge to be overcome. There is almost a competition between the jockey and the mount; each putting resistance against the other, and each fighting harder because of it. If the jockey would release, it would disarm his mount's desire to push into pressure and as result the horse would run slower.

A character trait of a race horse is accepting the challenge to be in control; it gets pleasure and gratification from competition. The same animal that will push against his jockey's bit will also run faster against opponents than it will alone. It is gratified by the excitement of **competition.** It accepts challenge, because it is gaining control when fighting an opponent. It has heart to keep it up. Without a challenge, why try hard?

* * *

A gung-ho student in choosing to keep up or by trying to do more than the other guy is also accepting a challenge. And because his actions are going in the direction wanted by the trainer, he is said to be competitive and his efforts reflect a good thing.

A **rebellious** pupil has this same need to win as the competitive one. The difference is that he is thought of as being disobedient if his actions lead in a direction which is away from the one desired by his trainer. The rebellious is only doing just as the his counter-part, increasing his efforts when he feels the forces against him have amplified; he likewise is pushing against a force, however it is perceived that he is doing a bad thing.

*   *   *

Common Horse Sense: Nothing to Fight Against.

A horse by instinct will react to a pressure more so when it is applied, than when it's released. A **pressure** translates into some sort of discomfort which he will be trying to eliminate. The greater the pressure, the more effort he will place into trying to relieve it. His instinctive response will not be based from reasoning, but mostly from a flight or a fight reaction in an effort to obtain some relief. He wants to have control in his life, so bases his reactions in attempting to regain it.

The skilled equine trainer will use his charge's desire in order to get it to do just what he wishes and wants. For his purpose, he uses its desire to push against a challenge. However, when he sees that his charge is moving in the direction that is not wanted, does he still keep amplifying this present stimulation and continue in putting more and more pressure against the horse?

"NO! What he does do is quit making the animal go faster." He understands that as a horse will react to a pressure and give resistance harder because of it, the animal will quit pushing, even relax and stop forward movement, when the pressure is diminished.

The horse trainer develops a desired proper response from an animal by a noticeable change of stimulations. He places an opposing second pressure against the animal that will now cause it to react with a different response. And when it does correctly, he offers a reward for the new actions; he gives the horse a slight rest.

By receiving a rest repeatedly for its response, the horse grows to realize the movements of his action that produced his relief. It will want to perform again the same way. It will want again that same relief and lessening of another's control. The horse doesn't understand that the trainer is controlling him. The animal thinks that it the one controlling the felt pressure.

Don't confuse this *relief of pressure* as being the same as never applying a pressure towards obtaining a change in a currently unwanted behavior. Failure to create a pressure which will inspire a change is an injustice; it is a lack of parenting or a shortcoming of a teacher which doesn't promote improvement. A purposeful immediate *release of pressure* given in reward for a new behavior offers further gratifications that have a horse wanting to keep up his new course of action. All can win. The horse, because it is now getting something that it will recognizes as welcome, and the trainer because he got the reaction he was after. For all to win, first a pressure to deviate from an unwanted behavior must be applied.

* * *

Common Sense: **As a trainer of horses, children, or any others, it is vital to understand pressure. It is possible that you may force your charge into compliance where the charge goes along because it is the path of least discomfort. But, for it to express a willing change of defiant behavior, you must train yourself to know when to offer a release, so that the opponent is disarmed. This leaves nothing left to resist against, therefore the fight is over. {see: Chapter 13: Going Back to the Basics}**

A word about the difference in a **relief of pressure** versus a **release of pressure:**

The **relief of pressure** is the trainer still remaining in control, yet backing off a little. It is offered to get the charge to diminish its resistance. To the receiver it's a felt lessening of control which is responded to by the natural instinct to give back a reduction of opposition.

The **release of pressure** is a felt discontinuation of controlling pressure. It is offered in the form of a reward for a correct performance. It disarms the recipient from having to reciprocate in retaliation.

A child likewise has many of these same desires as a horse; they also want to be in control of their lives. This feeling of control means that they expect to experience their desires, instead of what others are forcing upon them.

As a teacher, or trainer it will be necessary on occasion to control a child's behavior when he acts out, goes astray, or he uses his desires for freedom wrongly. To entice the child to continue with his inappropriate behavior, all we have to do is keep putting the same pressure on him.

Do we, as educators, keep our charges fighting against us and the lessons we wish to impart by applying a constant non-diminishing pressure?

Just as the jockey, when we wish our charges to cease in their display of inappropriate behavior, our first task is to stop applying the same continued pressure or resistance against them. Once we masterfully exercise control and relinquish our need to keep forcing, and then offer to our student a slight relief of pressure, they acknowledge this new lessening and diminish their opposing resistance. We can obtain more control by diminishing or shifting our stimulus against others.

When we require a different response out of our charges we vary their stimulation. We alter pressure on our child to get him to modify his course of action. And then when the child responds correctly to any degree, we offer a new release. It is for a desired behavior that you are able to release your control. This release of pressure represents to the charge a freedom from the control of others. If the same altered stimulative pressure is ever felt once more, he will again want to repeat his new actions which he thinks delivered his freedom.

If the child accepts your offered release, then he is disarmed; the contention is now over. The child is getting a rest because you got, to a degree, the response that you wanted. By offering a release of pressure, you are teaching your pupil how they may get gains for certain behaviors. The child is pleased, because at the moment he is free from another's control. He feels that he won a small victory, and you are controlling the child to give that response once more.

It is so important that you are releasing for the right reasons, and not just because you are fed-up with the current actions of the unquenchably disobedient child.

Offer a release of pressure only for the correct responses. *****If you give-in to a child who is throwing a tantrum, then you're motivating him to throw a fit again. *****

To deal with a child that is displaying a temper, you distance them from the trigger which is stimulating their flight or fight sequence. Offer a relief of pressure. You impose a separation; remove them from the source of their rage. Offer an incentive towards a change of direction, so that you may, as soon as possible, reward when proper behavior is shown. You may have to be creative in your releases as you point out something that they were doing correctly. Make sure they know for which proper behavior they are receiving some liberty. Your objective is that they receive some benefit for another behavior, other than their explosion of anger.

{They are very much the same, when it comes to behavior issues and learning, the child and horse. If you understand one it will help you in your efforts to train the other.}

4. **Wants improvement:**

A willing student can be inspired to reach up and obtain his greater potential:

Jesus understood this principle of pushing against a force in order to get gain. He taught this lesson to his disciples in the parable of the "Three Servants and the Talents":

A rich man, prior to his extended journey, gave talents to his servants. These talents represented an opportunity to improve and grow as individuals; they were sums of money. On his return he asked an accounting from these three servants. Two had accepted this opportunity to improve and had doubled their worth. Their lord praised their efforts and called them, "Good and faithful servants ... well done. "The third servant didn't except the challenge to excel, probably out of fear. He remained unchanged by the new opportunity and did only a bare minimum to get by. For him the answer of what to do with the opportunity to improve and learn was dealt with by his burying the money, so that he wouldn't lose it. He wanted to have it available in the same unchanged condition on the return of his lord. His lord called him, "A wicked and slothful servant," and cast him out of his presence. {see: St. Matthew: 25:14-30}

Each man made an accounting according to their willingness to learn. All were given the opportunity to push against their own fears and to gain by their own efforts. The larger the opportunity given them, the greater their chance of improvement or failure.

Two of them excelled by increasing the total amount of their talents; they gained their lord more money. They overcame the temptations to let well enough be by putting forth efforts to obtain additional gains, first for their lord and then for themselves. They didn't give up in striving to increase their potentials. When a challenge was presented before them, they rose to meet it. They gained the title of being trustworthy and dependable by verifying the belief which their lord must have had in them. After all, weren't they given the most responsibility to start with? For themselves, they gained more confidence and ability to overcome additional fears in the future. Conquering a fear now, leads to the opportunity of more gains in the future; it results in more power over one's own life.

The skeptic might ask, *"Didn't they take a chance investing the funds of their lord?"* Yes, but he was their lord; they must have had some understanding as to what he would expect them do with the money and possibly had been taught how to do it. They could have minimized their risks and chosen wisely where to invest by using wisdom in picking options. Truly they did have some risks and fears, for wasn't that why the third chose not take a chance? He was ultimately wrong with his complacency. His lord didn't return and say, "Thank you for not losing my money." The lord's message was clear, "You have lost an opportunity to improve yourself; you should have overcome your fears and not been so lazy."

Never give up reaching your highest potential! You have the potential to reach your objectives; the choice is yours either to give-up and quit, or to endure. The willing have made it their choice to continue to persevere. As a parent, I thank God that all my five kids have learned to not give up, it is the most valuable lesson that I can teach.

5. **Committed to achieve:**

A good student should be willing to Cowboy Up. This means getting back on until you have conquered your greatest potential; there is no excuse for failures. Just get on, and do what is expected of you; "Get'er done!" **Cowboy Up.**

* * *

Common Horse Sense: Cowboy Up

The late Nineteenth Century cowboy signed on to do a job, and that he did. His pay was poor and often collected only once or twice a year. His personal comforts were not a consideration if there was work to be done. He agreed to accept the responsibility to ride a range or a circuit, in which he was not expected to be seen or heard from until properly relieved. Sometimes he was left alone for months at a stretch. He stood single-handedly against nature, the elements, and other problems of the day. If supplies ran out he made do until more could be obtained. During these solitary months when a water source went dry or a boundary needed to be re-enforced, he was left to his self-reliance to come up with a solution in order to fix it. If a problem with a cow or calf, his horse, or even his health occurred, it was his skills and knowledge which came to the rescue—not his cowering or dependence on someone else. When he got bucked off, it was nothing special; he simply tried again until he got it right. A personal injury or set-back didn't signal that he was through, but rather alerted him to the fact that he might have to find another way to finish his tasks. He honed his abilities, and then did what was expected of him. With this cowboy, time was not of an essence, foremost in his mind was performing and finishing honorably.

The Twentieth Century phrase, "Cowboy Up," receives its meaning after the old range riders of yesteryear. It has come to mean, "Quit, your crying and whining, and expecting someone to save you. You go it alone. You have to fulfill your responsibilities; no matter what hindrance you encounter."

The willing, knowledge yearning student should adopt the "Cowboy Up" mentality in his approach to life. Since a teacher is a student as he explores new ideas and learns new skills, he can, regardless of peril, setback, or personal difficulties, also learn to *"Get'er done!"* when he takes on a cowboy's commitment not to fail.

* * *

I hope understanding a willing student has been helpful. Of-course you know that every student is not willing, but they can be. That becomes one of your objectives as an engaged teacher; treat them as if they already are. It will help to inspire some to become as such. Give responsibilities, like the lord in the parable of the five talents in order to encourage a student to accept being accountable. An opportunity is presented, followed by them being given a chance to perform it. They are held to a standard which inspires improvement. A teacher first makes sure his pupils understand correct principles, and then he leaves to allow them to test their willingness by performing with that knowledge.

Common Sense: **Let them learn. Don't always feel a need to micro-manage. Allow others to grow that they may learn to responsibly take care of themselves. Be there to give advice, but don't do it for them. Sometimes you are giving the best chance for another's improvement by just walking away and letting them have their chance to succeed, fail, or break-even.**

{Teacher, that means that often you must step back and allow the student to do, so that he sees his efforts equal to, or as surpassing yours.}

Common Sense Lesson:
To Allow Others to Grow, I Walked Away

As a trainer of youth, it was my goal to give as real an experience to my Varsity Scout Groups as possible; I yearly offered them a manly adventure to fend for their selves. I was willing to be that engaged with the boys to give them a change to grow and develop; for some it was the chance of a lifetime. Out on the trail, each boy's experience and success was a direct correlation with their attitudes, the preparation they put into getting ready, and their abilities to cope with challenges of a personal nature. ... Thrown in also were the dealings with their mounts. Together, we spent days in getting them and their animals ready. I wanted each group of boys to expand their self-reliance and to have the time of their lives.

During one such trip, a three day one-hundred mile horseback trip through the untamed Beaver Mountains in Utah, each meal was pre-assigned out to a father-son team. They were to provide, carry and prepare a meal for the rest of the fifteen hungry horsemen. I, with my two sons, had agreed to provide a feast of not small proportions on the second evening.

As that afternoon arrived appetites were soaring because the group wasn't being satisfied with the previously scant portions that had been carried in by saddle bags and served by the other teams. To bolster up anticipations, all throughout the day I wasn't being shy in touting the up-coming meal's promising proportions. I even had my own sons joining in. They hadn't, as of yet, experienced the slightest bit of worry about the details of our assignment; they hadn't a clue what we were going to eat, or what their role in the fixings would be. They probably thought, "Dad will come up with something, and we'll just help him as directed."

When questioned about what we would eat, my only response to the hungered was, "It will be provided, and you are sure to get full with the magnificent eating."

We arrived a little early to Big Flats, the pre-arrange place of our second evening's camp and our feast. There was still one hour before the appointed time, in which oblivious to the boys, two volunteers would meet us there with the fixings of this promised glorious meal. I had the hard task of engaging the boys into caring for their mounts before they set down to recuperate from the exceptionally hard last two days. Mostly they wanted to just exist and wait for someone to feed and take care of them. Finally, because of a combination of guilt, bribery, and duty, all did what was expected of them. They washed and picketed out their horses, as well as, set up camp and the preparations for their own comfort during the night. This was the second night and they knew their duties, even though some had to be reminded that in order to use their horses the next day, the animals had to be taken care of tonight. Of course there was the expected discussion on the subject which mostly included reminding them to the fact that their mommies were not present to take care of them. And that they were on their way to becoming men; therefore they needed to be responsible. Camp needs to be set up, and they are to pitch-in to do it.

"Where was the food, and why aren't you starting to prepare it?" On this, I was questioned multiple times. I guess they were worried that they weren't going to be taken care of. To be honest, I was starting to get a little bit worried myself, for by now, the volunteers were one hour late.

All I could say was, "Keep setting up camp and getting ready for night-fall; the meal would be provided." I had now dropped the part of it being so wonderful, for my own doubt was starting to creep in. *"What if it didn't come at all?"*

"So, why didn't you just shoot one of the many deer that were seen in the meadow as we arrived a little earlier?" a hungry youth questioned as he impatiently waited, still seeing no meal or even the preparations for such.

"Cause that would be poaching. This is a scout camp and we don't want to break the law; but that certainly wouldn't be a bad idea, if it was the correct season," I still hadn't told them of my idea for the meal. I wanted it to be an experience on top of a surprise.

The camp was finally set up and the horses were taken care of. Nothing more was on the trail riders' minds than to just lay there and catch a nap while they continued to wait for the Slater Gang to wrestle them up some grub, the highly promised, yet undelivered, meal of no small proportion. I am sure that they each harbored the secret thought, "How lucky they were not to have to be a part of the preparation tonight. They had done or would do their assigned meal, so why do they need to be bothered now when it was someone else's turn and they are so very tired? Now it will be just great to just catch up on some much needed rest and wait for a meal that still wasn't being produced."

"Holy cow, those volunteers were now two hours late!" my thoughts were starting to haunt me. I was becoming ever concerned. Going to bed hungry wasn't what I wanted to present as an adventure.

At last, I heard the familiar rattling of my, loaned to them for the task, pickup's livestock racks. I was elated, for now I could distinguish the burning fire of my doubts and continue to put my plan into action. The volunteers with our meal were approaching.

It was the time to let the others in on my scheme. I started into my pre-thought speech, "You boys for the last two days have pre-formed like real men, not whining … well … maybe just a little." I paused to check out a few of the guilty, whom when met with my glance conjured up agreeing smiles. "Anyway, it's time to Cowboy-up again. You boys need to prepare the mutton meal for yourselves and the leaders tonight. They have been doing so much for you; it is high time that you guys did a little something special for them."

I was careful to include in this speech, three vital parts.
> First: I was rewarding them for their past efforts.
> Second: Telling them that they could have done better.
> Third: I was inspiring them for the new task at hand.

I then singled out my two sons, "Cheston, and Daniel, you will need to take charge. Get the rest of the boys to lend a hand. The other leaders and I are not going to help tonight. In fact, I am going fishing." With that I forced myself to start to walk away. Before I left, I thanked the volunteers for bringing up the meal. To satisfy my curiosity as to why they were two hours late, I had to ask?

"We had problems … that blasted sheep jumped out of our grasp and took off before we could get her loaded into the truck." They fessed-up in their defense. "We spent over an hour trying to re-catch and load her."

"She kicked me in the jewels!" one poor unlucky sap exclaimed.

I hadn't thought just how retrieving a sheep out of a corral and loading it into a near-by truck could have been so difficult for novices who had never seen or actually done it themselves. One capable man could have straddle-ridden her to the awaiting truck and lifted her inside like a three-wire hay bale. He would have cradled her by grabbing a hind quarter with one arm and a front shoulder with the other, and then rolled her up onto his thighs. He could have popped her up and inside the open livestock rack with the combined strength of a lifted knee and a reverse front curl of both arms. This is such a familiar and simple thing for a singular experienced live-stockman. It would've been hilarious to watch two guys simultaneously struggling against themselves and fighting a sheep. The retelling of the escapade helped to defuse the anxiety of the suppertime's wait. Together all enjoyed a good man-laugh at the greenhorn sheep wrangling antics.

"Thanks, you guys certainly must have had a great adventure chasing her down. Great job on getting her re-caught and loaded. I and the boys thank you for your efforts. It wasn't pleasant thinking that we might have been going to bed hungry," again, I started to walk away.

"But the sheep is not dead yet. She's still alive!" one doubting boy blurted out.

"We wanted this experience of riding through the mountains on horseback to be as real as possible; on your own with your trusty mount, going through the elements, and killing yourself some fresh meat when you wanted to eat. We didn't want to poach, so there is an 'almost deer' in the back of that truck," I was on a roll. "No one is going to do it for you, if you want to eat, then go for it. Think of it as another great-big challenge." I watched their faces turn serious, "Oh, and be aware that there is only forty-five minutes of dusk before it gets pitch dark, it is a cloudy night so better hurry."

It was one of the hardest things I had done; I was walking away while leaving ten tired boys to kill and gut a sheep, and then to prepare her and the rest of the meal out there in the woods. They would have no table, sink, or proper utensils other than what was in their personal gear. And no adult help. I knew that I could trust my own two sons into stepping up to the challenge; at so many other instances they had proven themselves before. What I was after was to offer another chance at growing up to the kids that expected to be provided for. These were the ones that were still stuck in a dependent or a self-entitled mode, who were content to just to wait for someone else to take care of them rather than do for themselves. I wanted to give these boys the taste of being self-reliant, or an experience as close as possible to it. If they didn't step up to the task, then all would go to bed hungry. I was prepared for that. I also hoped that the others leaders wouldn't cave-in and try to do for the boys.

As I sat there on the lakeshore, I had plenty of time to reflect on how I had to distance myself from the goings on or I'd have surely caved-in. I was too weak to just watch and not get involved. If I had stayed there and watched their struggles, soon I would have been answering questions, or showing some better and more efficient way to do things. I would have meant well and done it in the name of helping the boys of course, but soon I would have been right in the middle of the preparations and robbing them of their chance to personally grow further and to experience an additional taste of self-reliance. I forced myself to stay out of camp; there was no way that I was going back and risk being a savior by bailing them out.

More than once the thought came to me that I was abandoning them in a time of need, but then as I reviewed my real purpose, I was strengthened to stick to my principles, "No, I wasn't going to do it. This horse-riding trip was for them to live a pure manly experience; they needed the challenge and the growth."

They did it. They didn't let me down, but more importantly they didn't let themselves down either. It was long past dark, but two hours later as I returned from supposedly fishing, all was well. All had eaten their fills except one father-and-son team. This team had chosen to go to bed still hungry after sharing together one can of Beanie-Weenies from the emergency cache of their own saddlebags. For these types there is always the supermarket or a restaurant where they can be properly served in style. But for my sons and those who helped, they gained from a taste of being self-reliant.

They further learned to Cowboy-up and they received the personal growth that comes from doing what needs to be done, despite excuses and personal preferences. I was so proud!

I have since heard my son Daniel, rehearse the challenges he faced that evening: With their dull pocketknives, they had to kill and skin the sheep, plus prepare the rest of the meal. They, Daniel and his brother Cheston, experienced a further challenge trying to engage the rest of the boys into helping to prepare her, into gathering firewood, and making enough coals so that the fire would be ready when the Dutch Ovens were placed on it. They couldn't afford to waste much time as dark was looming and they were so hungry. That experience is one of his most highly valued feats; his Dad just left him and his brother to do the whole meal, and only some of the other boys helped. He knew that if he didn't take charge, it wasn't going to get done. The hardest part to bear was most of the boys were just standing there, reluctant to help, and waiting to be served.

As a teacher, learn to release the pressure; don't micro-manage. Be there to give advice, but not too close; that way you let others grow. You care enough to walk away and allow others some liberty to perform, for this is how you see if your charge really understands the principles you're teaching. It will challenge them to achieve. It is not the purpose of a teacher to rescue a child from all distress or frustrations during their plight through life, only to make aware optional ways and skills. When presented with a challenge, a person's reactions or emotions are his choice and therefore his responsibility. As a teacher, you only need to be there to offer more knowledge and insight, to help the child perform with proper behavior, and to assist him should it be for his future advantage that you do.

In the next chapters of this book we will discover, "What a child really wants," and "When and how they learn." It will help you further in your stratagems as an imparter of knowledge.

CHAPTER 8:

EVEN A TEENAGER WILL MAKE SENSE

Common Sense: **What a child wants is to have power over his life, to be independent, and to make his own choices.** His choices of actions are based on progressive understandings, and are set into motion for the purpose of helping retain this freedom.

Don't assume this means the child wants to be responsible for all aspects of his life; he only wants the control or freedoms to have his desires met. To say it in a well known verse, according to the child's thinking, **"It is all about me."**

A child wants to have things, feel good, and answer only to his own bidding; he wants this power. To him a bad choice is one that doesn't give immediate gratification. So he experiments with different responses until he comes up with ones which yield his desired outcomes. In maintain his perceived freedom of retaining control, he acts against whatever doesn't go his way. Even though future imposed resistive actions may lead to his eventual loss of personal control and freedom, he justifies himself that as-for-now the present sensations of power are enough. **He will make irrational choices, in order to meet his wants.** Knowing no more then a fool, he willing gives up his future freedoms, for some immediate pleasures now. His desire for instant gratification, is greater than his wisdom.

"A child wants to win!"

Knowing why a juvenile would possibly want to learn will help an educator become a more effective teacher. The successful teacher understands that the primary driving forces that influences why a child does as he does: **TO WIN.** The juvenile's wants are also based on his being a winner. His guard against remaining a loser is answerable to private choices and desires. If by his current actions his desires are not being met, then a student will seek to learn additional behavior in order to obtain them.

The driving forces that cause learning are:
1. Seeking a relief of pain.
2. A yearning for an improvement of life; using personal choices.
3. The desire for gratification. By means of:
   A. Sensations
   B. Acceptance
   C. Material increase

These driving forces are the *"gains"* to be had from learning. They are the benefits one gets that keeps them willing to play the game. With an acquisition of winning benefits come peace-of-mind, happiness, thrills, pleasures, and or elation. All of which are elements of **Joy.**

So, why does a child really want to learn?

To fulfill his Pursuit of Joy.

Joy is felt as we experience gains. It is the commonality of all the driving forces from wanting to learn. Yet true lasting **JOY** is obtainable only as we maximize our highest potentials.

Now you know the secret of being a great teacher. You help your pupils recognize their gains through your involvement. It is that easy!

There is no magic "**HOCUS POCUS**" to perform, or additional things to do than that. There are only different ways to express your involvement and various offers {rewards} which you may present as gains to be obtained.

About Gains:

It is not the way they obtain gains that attracts and holds a child willing; so much as it is the gains themselves. Most important are the benefits which they can taste, feel, hear, or measure. Children will gravitate to the easiest fulfillment of their desires. If a young child sees another gaining from a particular method, then they are inclined to experiment and try that process also. Whether or not it works for them will determine if the child continues to repeat that technique or searches for a new one which will yield his wants.

As a caregiver, you can't give the child all possible gains they crave. In order for gains to be truly esteemed as most valuable, they ought to be earned by the recipients, not just be givens. The learner needs to put forth the effort to get his gains, and as his teacher, you merely help to steer him to know how.

Now you understand the secret of being a great teacher; first decide to, and then become the best teacher you can. Next, help the child to get winning gains. ... Read on and your insights will expand. You will obtain more wisdom from a different exposure to knowledge. The use of that knowledge is equivalent to power. And towards power is where people gravitate. **You can be a force of power to help others.**

Wow! That's the desired goal of any educator, and one must be willing to work to get it. So let's continue working at becoming master educators by examining, in a little more depth, each of these driving forces that cause a child to want to learn.

1. Seeking a relief of pain.

Pain is a discomfort, it manifests either in the form of a bodily sensation or an emotional uneasiness. A new babe, with no tools of environmental control or learned coping mechanisms, neither tries to minimize nor prevent pain. It simply lets its emotions flow; it reacts. Crying is a perfect example of reacting to discomfort.

A progressive child, in order to get relief from a discomfort, learns different reactions to his pain. *He continually searches for something that seems to make his pain more bearable.*

Another reaction to pain is fear. Fear is an apprehensive emotion caused by a real threat or a perceived danger. Which matters not; both can be intensely real in the mind of a child. If fear is present, it affects responsive actions. Avoidance to what is feared is a learned preventive defense causing a distancing from whatever appears to be the cause of discomfort. Running away from, inflicting self harm to the ploy of gaining control, falling victim to deep anxiety, and refusing to deal assertively with fears are forms of taking flight and avoidance; they inhibit the very actions needed to conquer a pain.

The overly aggressive will meet his fears with any combination of forceful displays involving blaming, threats, resistance, or shows of violence. He tries to intimidate his fears instead of figuring a way to eliminate them. Without an increase of knowledge and experience, a child's mind is not open to new assertive coping alternatives designed to ultimately do away with his pain. He is only left, governed by fear, to the masking of his pain in order to produce some relief.

Some of the chief ways that are used to produce some relief from the felt discomfort of a pain:

- **Covering the feelings of a pain, by not dwelling on them.**
- **Refusing to succumb to the effects of pain.**
- **The use of reality altering means.**
- **Enhancing the pain with an emotion.**

Above are reactions that one develops to help endure a pain.

They are only ways of seeking relief from a discomfort.

Below is the only successful method to **eliminate a pain.**

Recognize the source of the pain, and then take the necessary steps to conquer it.

The ineffective manners, in which we choose to react or deal-with pains, are mostly the same ineffective techniques used whenever we choose to escape a fear. By using ways which only give some relief, pain's sting is still there. Many people become so adaptive at controlling their various grievances that they never actually get around to any elimination from their lives. They believe that their current ineffectiveness is the best choice they can do. They simply learn to live with their physical sufferings and emotional pains.

Still, this is better than the misguided soul who feels that life isn't fair whenever things aren't easy, and so he strives to eliminate or avoid all of his unwanted challenges.—By this, he experiences little growth.

As the child develops and his thinking further evolves, he realizes that life is full of challenges to overcome. He learns to tolerate his struggles as he awaits the gains. Eventually he gets to a point where he finally understands that without pain there is no chance to improve or get stronger.   ...{**Best case scenario: With added strength, commitment, and the proper knowledge he could develop additional skills to where he could conquer his challenges while eliminating most of his pain.**}

We will examine each of these ways to deal with pain:

Covering the feelings of pain, by not dwelling on them:

We do possess much ability to control our own thoughts. ... Not always can we prevent a thought from creeping into our minds, but we can decide whether or not we stay and dwell on it. When we feel a pain we wish to go away, we can cover it up with another thought and focus on that instead. As we give the new thought priority, then the previous pain seems to diminish.

"IF YOU DON"T THINK ABOUT IT; IT WILL GO AWAY."

Not that is does go away, but your mind can really only dwell on one thing at a time.   We control our thoughts by covering up the unwanted ones.

Sleep is an excellent way to cover a pain. It erases all when our mind is a rest. It also gives us a chance to re-evaluate in the morning when we are thinking clearer. Things often loose their sense of urgency after a good sleep.

Replacing an unwanted pain with a sought after feeling, also helps to cover the undesirable. Substituting instead with an up-lifting song or a fond memory will prevent a pain from taking over. Being so caught up in other events of the moment will diminish the need to focus on an unwanted pain. What others tricks have you developed to fool your mind into not dwelling on its present distress?

Refusing to succumb to the effects of pain:

"Arrr-Matey, tis a manly thing do ye"

Oh don't we make ourselves proud when we refuse to show weakness toward pain? This is the most unwise of all the controlling methods. A pain is there for a reason, it is there to tell us that something is not right; we have been hurt. To not succumb is to put ourselves at risk of prolonging our injuries. If we refuse to give in, then we must be willing to except this possibility. On the other hand, recognizing the fatigue of the tired or the weakness of the worn-out is also a predecessor to an increase of strength. Since it is a necessary evil in becoming toned and well polished, then to endure it is most manly. To those hoping to increase in their physical and mental abilities, some challenging discomfort is regularly sought after.

"For we blokes 'ave more important matters to be u-doing than to be a snivel'en."

To not succumb to a pain is a tad bit risky, but oh so manly! What pride we take when we learn ways of enduring with our pains. Not every fellow can, you know.

{It's a sign that it isn't important enough at that moment to dwell on. We purposely don't want to fixate on it, because we're more focused on showing: it can't control us. Locked in this manly mindset, our time is not to be wasted in the wimpy reaction of being overcome with a mere pain or inconvenience.}

The use of reality altering means:

We can numb our minds so our reality is distorted and clouded. We can indulge to the point where we are not in touch with the truth; we just don't care anymore. The falsehood of purposely setting ourselves up to endure a second discomfort, in order to force our mind not to dwell on the first, is a poor way of coping with things which we think are beyond our realm of changing: as in the over usage of drugs and alcohol. Although we may alter our minds temporarily, afterwards without additional means of becoming high there is sure to come a discomfort with an emotional let-down. Playing games, movies, and TV also alter us as to true reality. They place us in a false realism; they give us quick entertainment where we find our real-life pains don't matter any more. Rationalizing the truth, when done often enough or dwelled on hard enough, has the same effect to distort our realities.

When we become so dependent to the regular use of reality altering means, as a method of coping or of escaping, our usage supports the elution that we are gaining some control over our lives. Because we become comfortable in this self medication, we avoid confronting the actual cause of our pain. We set ourselves in danger of becoming an addict to these soothing false realities.

Enhancing the pain with an emotion:

Utilizing the expansive energy of a pain to fuel anger, jealousy, desire, disappointment, and envy are a few of the ways emotion can be used wrongly to cope. One can go overboard in trying to cover up their original loss.

How often have you witnessed a person experience a hindrance, then react by "wigging-out"? This person becomes so driven by emotion, that he or she dismisses the discomfort of their original setback. Caught-up in the rage of the moment, emotion controls reaction. They experience an arousal of their nervous system which manifests itself as an increase of heart-rate, a quickening of breath, and an influx of adrenaline which stimulate a fight response.

Unchecked, they react overly aggressive, emotionally out of control. Their design is to defend themselves and take back their loss.

Additionally, I am sure that you can recall witnessing a sports game or a movie where the character experiences a should-be debilitating injury of some sort. The soon-to-be champion, goes through a mental changing process, and then is able to use his newly aroused pain as catalysis to be combined in a past emotion long buried in a grave of denial. A compound is formed, from which the oppressed is then able to conquer the original source of his long festering emotions: The meek ex-fighter, when seeing his love get hurt, becomes mad and his put-aside abilities miraculously increase. Now he can defeat a previously overwhelming foe. Emotion guides him towards victory. With the awakening of an emotions within this bigger-than-life character, also is stimulated a similarly sensitive swelling within us. We secretly wish we could energize our emotions to defeat our enemies as well. If only we allowed our pain to just enlarge as this hero's, then too, victory could be ours! **{Within some, this twisted coping mechanism is their best norm of operation.}**

Such a triumph would be wrongfully ours if it were obtained by only allowing our emotions to increase. **{In reality, whenever rational behavior and thinking are thrown aside, rarely is anything solved except damage to self or surroundings as one aggressively, and perhaps abusively, acts in opposition.}**

A healthier outlook is for us to step back and realize that it wasn't the emotion that caused our hero his victory. It was that he felt a re-commitment to follow through and achieve his goal. The key was his using a dormant potential. The only thing that the emotion really accomplished was to remind him that indeed he had a problem to deal with, and then he assertively did.

Don't be content to just endure your discomforts, or even to seek for their brief relief; for a lasting solution, strive to overcome them.

The healthy, yet not without risk, thing that a pain should fuel is the inter-desire to act wisely towards its elimination.

Recognize the source of the pain, and then take the necessary steps to conquer it. Be prepared to change course when more productive paths are recognized: *Sources of pain can be from*:

Anger	Grief
Anguish	Jealousy
Anxiety	Loneliness
Depression	Physical Discomfort
Discouragement	Punishment
Fear	Unfamiliarity

Many of the previous pains are from the disheartening feelings of our emotions. It is not the job of a teacher, a caregiver, or any other second person to have to make them right for us. They are our responsibility and we alone are accountable for their effects. When we start taking responsibly for them, then we can take the steps to control and ultimately eliminate them. After the honest acknowledgement of our pains, a competent counselor can help us recognize the healthy steps we could take to cope with our pains. But it is up to the afflicted individual to do it.

We must overcome our pain; otherwise we are just covering or postponing it by prioritizing something else instead. We are never really free while we are under pain's influence. Only by admitting we have a discomfort, and then wanting to do something real about it will we be so inclined to learn the proper steps to combat its source. We may not have it in our power to be able to eliminate all the sources of our pains, yet we can learn constructive ways of dealing with them.

We use the same techniques to combat pain as we do to solve a problem. {*see: pages: 69-76*} For a pain is a problem that can be addressed, changed, eliminimated, or just endured. Through the elimination of pain comes the highest personal increase of freedom.

2. A desire for the improvement of life; using personal choices:

Earlier on in life we probably had parents and teachers as our role models, until it was noticed that these real every day people were not in control over all the aspects of their lives. We then started looking elsewhere for our heroes.

A developing child, or for that matter an adult looking to improve his life will copy or emulate different role models whose certain character traits seem to be yielding them an ease of life. The learner sees them as having the power, control, and freedoms which he desires. Be they a ballplayer, a princess, or a celebrity, a child will sees his role models and want to have the same things as he perceives they enjoy, i.e. the wealth, fame, and praise of man. It is a natural instinct to follow or want to be as those with power.

Since the young mind still hasn't learned where true power comes from, he may start reacting like an aggressive parent, an enraged peer, or an entitled role model. He may begin using what he sees working for others. He learns to make use of anger, a loud voice, or other variations of emotional outbursts that will make those around him aware of and experience in his pain.

"Now where did he get that from?" If the questioning individual could step back and see things more clearly, then they would recognize these unwanted traits as something the child was learning from the negative example of others; possibly from members of his own family, or even from them, the questioner? The child exercising his choice of copying those traits in order to establish control in his life, also.

I suck...

In a learner's quest to obtain knowledge and personal control, he will at times come to the realization that his methods of doing things are lacking in effectiveness. *"He figures out that he sucks. He sees others getting what they want. They are enjoying benefits and he is out-maneuvered—left as the rut piglet still sucking hind teat. His ways stink. He is being held back in his chance of experiencing fullness and pleasure."* As stated before in timing, whenever he dislikes his present course enough to want to effect change, this is the very moment when this learner is most likely to want to hear, see, and experience new ideas. He is now ready to be taught more proficient methods. He starts an effort to obtain improvement to his life. A child who can see another's way of doing things as superior to his own will want to learn that new way. —**Be it a socially accepted behavior or one that is questionable**. A self-gratification is felt by the learner as he develops these new skills and talents, replacing his own lacking methods. ... But, let it be his choice to make.

3. The desire for gratification.   By means of:

A. Sensations

When a child's delight is aroused above a normal state of being, by any stimulus, the child will seek to maintain that gratification. They will make efforts to maintain that desired acute awareness to their senses of taste, smell, and feelings. It is the teacher's duty to train when, where, and how to safely obtain these sensations of happiness and joy. He teaches what is proper, lawful and socially excepted. A child has to be taught in order to keep his desires and indulgences in check.

When the youth seeks gratification from the use of drugs or other mind altering sources, then there is cause for concern. First, the youth often lacks the wisdom to be prudent; he could be harmed. And second, the use of these sources only produces a short lived blockage of reality, yielding at best only a temporary feeling of happiness. When it is the child's purpose to cover his reality by the seeking of chemically enhanced sensations, or when he "uses" in his design to escape from combating displeasure or pain, then help is needed from other sources to expose him to alternative ways of doing things. No lasting gains can be had by mind altering substances.

Emotions create sensations. If the sensations are positive the child will want to learn ways of regularly feeling this effect. If an event produces an unwanted feeling, then he will seek to learn ways to distance himself from it happening again.

B. Seeking Acceptance.

*   *   *

Common Horse Sense: Acceptance is being part of the herd.

The horse is a herd animal. They chose to live together with other horses for protection in numbers and for companionship. Depriving a horse of companionship is a method of training that quickly gets it to want to join with the trainer to fulfill its needs of acceptance. The horse can be schooled and manipulated into going against its wants of being free by using its stronger desire to be part of a herd. So great is the need to belong to some sort of a group that if it is isolated, to be accepted it will seek to join even a tormenter.

*   *   *

Being accepted gives one the feeling of belonging. It allows the comforting gratification that one is not alone. Like a horse, a child will also do things that alone they might not do, if they think that action will get them accepted by others. **Peer pressure** is a real factor in the lives of adolescents. A child will learn and push himself beyond previous comfort level in the hopes to get praise, admirations, love, and acceptance from others.

The seeking of self-gratification through being accepted can be witnessed in the now too common choice of kids playing video games. The purpose of these games is not designed as a form of relaxation. It is to entertain its players with the sensation of winning at competition, in which they must beat themselves, overcome the odds, or defeat the nonhuman programs of the game. Great expense is put into making these games as real or as humanlike as possible. The more real the game seems the more gratification, sensations and emotions the players will feel. Some games even go so far as to praise the participants with a human like voice aiming to enhance the experience.

These video games are well made tools to alter a person's perceptions of reality. No wonder more and more youth are having trouble coping with the problems and stresses of the real world; they are fulfilling their needs of gratification by interaction with programmed computers, and non-personal machines. They are trading their time that could be spent with thinking, feeling, and personally interacting with often non-predictable animals or humans. The temporary satisfaction felt in tech games leads them to rationalize, "If I am winning, then I must be OK; for a winner is always accepted." To a self-gratification seeking youth these experiences, with their easily manipulated imposters, seem real enough. The techies get their much needed self-fulfillment from this exposure of non-reality.

Players who win at tech games experience the same types of emotional gains that can be obtained when finding solutions to real problems and winning at life's challenges. They are fulfilling a fundamental want, but only a temporary sensation, as their quickly passing self-high is felt. This high would be much longer lasting if experienced while overcoming and mastering interactions with real humans and animals by accomplishing meaningful real-life goals. With these accomplishments they could be enhancing their lives instead of wasting them on less consequential things. Limit your child's choice of video games.

Best is the reward that can be earned by the mastery of real life experiences. As a caregiver and as one who is wise to the true reality stealing abilities of these time traps, help the child limit his usage. Encourage interaction that is real, not fabricated. Should they perform well in school or in the home setting, you could allow, as a limited reward, some supervised time with these entertaining impostors; many crave this quick gratification. What a child needs are teachers who are willing to help them learn how to set proper goals down here in reality in order to receive true gains; to be socially healthily they should learn to recognize and seek after more productive and lasting forms of gratification.

C. Material increase:

Only the most naïve would dispute that with the increase of material wealth, we also get some gratification. If a material increase is desired, then the wise child is willing to learn new skills and knowledge in order to obtain it. The purpose of increasing in wealth is the obtaining of more assets. Once obtained the newness wears off and the previously sought after material becomes more of an everyday possession. The pleasure we once felt diminishes. For a while in order to once again experience the same contentment, we again recall the benefits that we received from obtaining the coveted items. We re-think, "How nice our new toys are." Only so long will this work and soon we will find ourselves longing for an additional increase of material goods. To satisfy our yearnings we have got to have more!

Money and possessions only give temporary pleasure and enjoyment. We are driven to learn more, so that we can earn more. There will never be enough, and we'll never be content for long if obtaining personal gratification from a material increase is all that we seek.

Obtaining gains takes effort:

The lazy one wishes for gain without effort,

many an opportunity passes him by—

Trapped in shadows from success of a brother,

muses, "If I had his great luck, then I'd try."

Red Hawk

Common Sense: **The lazy individual wishes to receive without putting forth much effort on his part.**

The lazy is still stuck in the thinking of a child; he still thinks that others owe him, and he can receive without putting forth sufficient effort in his own behalf. He focuses on the good fortune of others, as if it was coming to them from just being lucky. He rationalizes: their success is the result of them falling into the right opportunities, instead of them having to earn their gains through hard work.

Beware… setting and then fulfilling a real goal takes much more effort than the flicking of a handle or the pushing of a button. When the only present gains felt are emotional and physical discomforts, the growing unwanted thought of staying with a slow to be realized goal will discourage most novices. The lazy or un-tempered are just not up to enduring many trials in order to get stronger or to put themselves into the position to receive future benefits. **Patience** is a virtue, but not for the weak.

A child can learn to endure with patience thru long suffering when he recognizes that lasting benefits follow hard work. Before this life altering transformation can take place, the child in each one of us cries out for life without difficulties. It doesn't want to have to endure the hardships of pain or hard work. Only by being forced to endure adversity can one gain this character trait. Of course this lesson must be taught slowly to a youth, at first, by ever increasing his requirements to get rewards. As he matures, he realizes that others also have to work to get their desires; rarely is a gain obtained without some type of goal combined with concentrated effort.

Common Sense: **A good teacher makes all the difference in the world. He shows new methods, plus he increases the efficiency of his struggling learners by inspiring and reinforcing their desires to endure. From the witnessing of patience and longsuffering, a child learns to endure in order to receive.**

The Pursuit of Joy

To a child, "**What is Joy?**"…

… It is relief of pain.

… Gratification through the pursuit of pleasures.

… The improvement of life.

{*In the mind of a child, he doesn't need to be taught or told what Joy is, he already knows. It is what he wants. And it is varies, dependent on his present mood.*

… SO CAUTION, TEACHERS AND PARENTS BEWARE! If you know what's good for you, then you'd better not go and mess that up.

Even that unhappy teenager has forces which drive his actions. He is motivated to retain his freedom and follow after his present interpretations of Joy. Often as an authority figure, you represent someone who is mostly trying to take that away. In order to get him to join with you without him having to be forced, you must somehow promote his feeling that your very purpose for doing is to offer an improvement to his life. This opportunity is not that you are hell-bent on enhancing his life in spite of him; it's that you're so engaged in helping him that you're conscious of his wants also. You want for him to obtain Joy, yet you have a different way for him to get it. To solicit an adolescent's eager cooperation, he needs to be liberated from the presumption that your purpose is to hamper his freedoms and progressions.

As you perform your interactions with him from an approach of helping, be sure to do so in a way that the freedom retaining mind will recognize something beneficial from your interactions. … If you can't pull this off, where he still recognizes some freedom, then you will be destined to wait until his maturity catches up with his wants, or your abilities improve.

To an adult, "What is Joy?"…   **Why it is a progressive developing quest—**

Earlier on in life, when possessing or thinking with only a slightly evolved adolescent mind, Joy was to be had in various quantities obtained from an arousal of one's senses. It was presumably equal to the success, the amount of money, or the tastiness of an indulgence. It was additionally felt in the degree of fame, the value of a car, and or any fulfillment of sex that one could acquired.

With experience and years, the adult mind develops into understanding that lasting happiness is not just obtained with personal advantages which can be lost or discarded; it is to be had from becoming the best person one can be.

In the continuing pursuit of Joy, one eventually finds that it is not his gains or material increase that gives lasting elation; it is what he may do in the service of others. To totally maximize his Joy, he must be anxiously engaged in the helping of others to also experience ultimate happiness.

—A fullness of Joy is neither a frame of mind, nor a possession; it is the purpose for existence.

CHAPTER 9:

HOW LEARNING TAKES PLACE

Common Sense: **To learn is to acquire knowledge and under-standing. It is only measured by its ability to be recalled and only useful to the obtainer by implementation.**

* * *

Common Horse Sense: First instincts and desires.

In the first few minutes of a newborn colt's life he is unaware of the world. Driven by his first instincts, the natural urge to stand, walk and then nurse, this new-born is oblivious to outside influences. Even pain does not fully register, only the desire to get his belly filled. He is aware only of things revolving around him. In his innocence, all things are for his fulfillment. Only as the colt starts becoming aware of more of the world, does it react to additional stimulations.

The expectations of its owner are high, as he sizes up this baby. Bloodlines, size, conformation, coloring, and anticipated proper training, all support the hopes that this new born will grow up to be all that is envisioned. Why not? After all, nothing so far has happened to diminish this possibility.

* * *

Stop for a moment to answer these questions:
- What was the most important thing to this baby?
- Does this new baby have any fears?
- Is this a bad baby?

Think back the last time you saw a new born. It was so cute and so full of potential. Gazing at an infant it is so easy to see it's perfect, in that, it isn't governed by fear, nor has it developed any bad traits. Soon it will be so eager to progress in learning. It will develop fear as it sees this emotion displayed in others, and apprehension as it tries to avoid being uncomfortable. Only if it fails to measure up to the expectations of its owner/caregiver will it be labeled as "bad". The lessons of learning this baby encounters, in any form, will effect its future actions. Its chosen teachers will affect its desires for learning; they will influence its choice of actions; they will influence its potential to turn out "good" or to turn out "bad".

Two year old behavior

Early in his life, an infant has claim on its parents for its wants. Alone it can provide nothing beyond using a built-in instinct to cry; this is its best reaction to pain. Way before an infant has reached one year old, it has learned to act-out thereby manipulating its benefactors into providing for its desires. What started out as a reaction to pain develops into a conditioning, as this child learns that when it cries others will respond. Do to this conditioning the child develops its behaviors: *"When I'm uncomfortable, I'll cry, 'cause I know no other way to engage others into making things all better."*

As a youngster starts to develop, it continues the belief that the world does, in fact, revolve around it. Therefore, when it wants, it soon figures out how to take. By watching and learning, it develops additional ways of manipulating others into providing for its wants. In the beginning, with no sense of what is right or wrong, it was responsive to its wants by using whatever means possible in order to obtain them.

Sometime around when their child is the age of two, most parents are finally realizing that it is no longer as cute or as acceptable for it to remain undisciplined. They are starting to tire of the uncontrolled behavior their child is showing. i.e. The taking of what it wants by their manipulation.

> *When a manipulative two year old behavior is no longer acceptable, the teacher might have to introduce some form of pain compliance to get the child to behave a different way.*

Around three, a child is starting to get old enough to begin to rationalize his thoughts, and if taught correctly he will start to realize that his choices of actions have consequences. With each action the child learns to expect some sort of increase, or accepts some type of loss. In other words he is beginning to recognize some minuscule accountability for his behavior. A trainer helps the child to further recognize these consequences. If wanting an ever-increasing improved level of behavior from their children, parents will continue to progressively revise training, so that additional accountability is recognized.

Common Sense Lesson: A Missed Chance to Train.
I watched one of my daughters struggle with her two-year-old in a hotel's hallway. The child was being typical, and when he was not restrained with another's grasp, he felt the need to express his freedom. Given the chance, off he goes on an excited run down the hallway leaving mother in his dust.

Jennifer raised her voice, "Hayden, come back," her command was only met with the youngster kicking it into a faster gear and continuing to flee. He realized, he was beyond mother's grasp and was experiencing his freedom.

"Come back!" Her tone had increased in its volume.

I detected almost a laugh from the child. He showed no type of acknowledgement depicting any form of compliant response.

"I'll spank," she exclaimed. There was still nothing, but the child defying the resistance of his diaper, gravity, and his mother's commands as his short legs scampered energetically down the corridor. "OK, now you are going to get a spanking!"

Still nothing from the escapee.

So mom was forced to do the very thing that she was avoiding doing in the first place; she was forced to make a scene with her child in a busy hotel hall with other people watching. She had to go running after the child in order to retrieve him. Upon reaching her young son she grabbed his arm. He flung and thrashed around on the end of her hand like a fish at the end of a hook-and-line the first moment that it is lifted out of the water into the hostile environment of the air. She did not give a spanking, only used her larger size to hold him by an arm and keep him from further running off as he continued to flip and flop.

Once outside the door way, Jennifer, feeling a relief to have that scene over with, released her grip on her catch and he bolted off to the next distraction, a close-by parked motorcycle. He started to climb up on it. She had to grab his arm again in order to control her son who's now kicking and screaming that he wants to go for a ride.

* * Side note: * * * I watched the whole goings on, while wanting to intervene and tell her that she should carry through with her threats of discipline. That, as she failed to carry out her demanding for Hayden to come back, together with her threatening of a spanking, a lesson was being taught to her son. He was being schooled to not be afraid of Mommy or even to mind her, but to keep on doing whatever he wanted and nothing would happen. Telling a child to behave, or threatening them with a punishment, even offering a reward, comes with the responsibility for her to carry it out. I did nothing, partly because I didn't want to add to my daughter's embarrassment, and partly because I had seen her in the past discipline her son. I thought that something was still coming. I at least should have talked to her, after the fact, when she was not dwelling in the emotions of the event. I missed my chance to teach, and to show that I cared. I chose to do nothing and hoped that things would work out for the best by themselves. I was a perfect example of an indifferent traveler.

Behavior is Learned

Common Sense: **Your behavior is the sum of your real or imagined experience. It is by thought or conditioning, your choice of how you act out. Only from additional learning do you have a choice in new behavioral actions.**

A **good teacher** will provide additional learning and experiences for his pupils to discover various behavioral choices. He will share ideas, stories, and problem solving techniques; he'll by example be a model for his charges.

"From where do you want your charges learning proper behavior, if not from you?" Children need to be exposed to new experiences so they can develop an expanded choice of options.

A **better teacher** will help his pupils to see that always they have a choice of actions, and according to that choice, different out-comes are possible. He will be an engaged guide that leads them from a poor choice towards a more correct one. If this isn't enough, then he will become a trainer, and will force change to their behaviors.

The **best teacher** will even help his pupils to process events that happened during the time of day when they were not together. He will become fully engaged to care enough to ask of their day and of their thoughts. First he listens, and then rewards for any proper choices made. This master teacher will help them see optional endings and results by teaching of the pros and cons. He possesses the abilities of the lesser teachers, and goes beyond forcing control. He enables the learning minds to see they have the power to control outcomes in their own lives by using educated behavioral choices.

Behavior is affected by, but not limited to our present emotions.

An **Emotion** is a sensation that is brought on by a course of events and one's feelings about them. The event itself is not the emotion, but it's how we are affected by it which leads to our present mental state of affairs. Although we may not be able to control how we feel about what is happening, we do have the choice of whether or not to act out on our feelings and let our emotions rule. We can use a healthy rationalization process of looking at options, then picking one that produces the outcome which we desire. When we choose to let a poor course of action be dictated by our present sensations, we are not skilled enough. We, at times, may need help in realizing that we don't have to be subjective to our emotions, that always do they retain the ability to choose what our behavior will be, despite what present sensations we are presumably experiencing.

The engaged teacher will help his charges realize that they needn't be a slave to their emotions. He will teach: **A spectrum of feelings can come and go, yet one who possesses self-control will remain in command of how he chooses to deal with his feelings.**

Common Sense: **Emotions are the key to remembering an experience.**

The greater the level of emotion that can be tied to a learning process the less likely one is to forget it. The specific details of the event might be forgotten and the skill that was observed might fade into the un-retrievable realms of the mind, but the emotion will long endure as a powerful stimulant. Combine a strong emotion, one that will not soon be forgotten, with the dreams of mastering a task and its pending rewards. *Walla!* You have just created a powerful inspiring and lasting experience.

Common Sense Lesson: Observing the Learning Progression.

I recall the privilege I once had of playing a game of "Hi Ho! Cherry-O" with my wife and two granddaughters, ages three and seven. As we played, I watched in delight as Macie engaged in the activity. Counting and speaking were not her skills, but she did understand basic commands and questions. Whitney, on the other hand, could read on a second grade level and was competitive for a school girl. During the process of the game I witnessed progressions of learning involving the two girls.

The object of the game is to pick all the plastic cherries off your tree and put them in a bucket. First one done with all their cherries is the winner. Beware of the dog and a bird, they will cause you to lose picked cherries or spill the bucket, then you have to replace all the picked cherries back on the tree and spin a number to again take more off.

Although, Macie didn't have a clue as to the difference between the figures giving permission to take off two cherries or three, she was elated to play. As the game progressed, she soon grasped the idea was to pick cherries and place them in her bucket. At first Grandma and Grandpa praised her for efforts in which she would take off any number. "Yeah, Macie! You picked off a cherry. Clap... clap... clap." She was ever-so gratified; she had shear delight from something that caused her grandparents to heap upon her these glorious praises.

The feelings of delight were not felt by both girls at Macie's first pickings, for there set older sister patiently waiting her turn while plagued with her tree still full. She couldn't allow her sibling to receive unearned praise! *Imagine, for just picking cherries out of turn, lavished rewards were being obtained.* Whitney wasn't jubilant watching this traitor getting praises for just copying a motion.

At Whitney's insistence, younger sister must be held to a higher standard. "She was playing a game with rules wasn't she?"

So the younger was held to a standard to only take off the correct amount. "Ok Macie, it's your turn. Now just take just two off. One ... now another ... twoooooo ... that's enough. Good job." Both grand-parents were once more busily heaping on praises, "Clap ... clap... clap." To Whitney's dismay there goes the unequal praises from others, again. No one was clapping as Whitney would take off cherries.

After her turn, little Macie didn't possess the patience to wait for three whole people to take theirs before she could again take hers. In her mind wasn't this a game of gathering cherries for praises? And wasn't she making the choices to participate in the very thing that was presently improving her life? After scanning and finding the clappers preoccupied, she would commence, with pudgy hands, clapping for herself as she picked more out-of-turn fruit. She was exercising her choice to improve her life. If others wouldn't give what she wanted, then she would seek it herself. Of course this was so cute that unrestrained clasps came forth from her grandparents. And again came the dreaded, "Yeah, Macie!"

"How could they do it," Whitney thought? She couldn't stand it any longer; here she was trying to play the game fairly in order to get earned gratification and praise from others, and there was little sister raking in all the glory for cheating. Surely in her seven year old mind she rationalized these ideas, "I too want others' praise. Little sister seems to be getting all the attention and great interactions from cheating." A light glistened in her young mind, "I see that cheating earns praises. So, I will cheat myself. Yea, I'll go for it." But, an old haunting thought struggled back into her remembrance, "Wasn't my father just talking to me about the negative aspects of cheating? I know the answer; I'll just be sneaky. I won't be accused 'cus no one will see. I'll win, so that people will think I'm wonderful, also." Slyly she sneaks off a few cherries. Her object was to win, to feel gratification, acceptance, and praise.

As soon as the snuck cherries came off, she hears, "Whitney, what are you doing cheating?" Dad had been over-looking the goings on.

"Oh rats, busted—"

In the above example the three-year-old was just following a natural progression to learn. She was copying others in order to get gain, improve her life, and feel personal gratification with its Joy.

The seven-year-old also was going after the same things. Her ability to rationalize was greater than the younger child; her methods in obtaining the same desires were more complex. She held herself on a higher level of expectation, and so should the care giving adults in her life.

* * * Side note: * * *   It is when care-giving adults keep allowing the child to pursuit the same self-interests and to use the approaches that were acceptable in their youth that the older child gets on the wrong track as they continue to act as unconstrained two-year-olds. They think that the world revolves around them and they are not accountable for their actions; they remain resistant in taking any responsibility for their needs.

In the wilderness therapy program where I spent years as a senior instructor, we received as clients, adolescents who were often still stuck in a two-year-old self-entitled mindset. Their parents had failed to teach and hold them accountable to be responsible for their own actions. Mom and/or Dad must have thought that is was more important to be their friend instead of being a trainer who forced lessons of accountability. They had failed to teach with the skills necessary to force their children to grow up. At the point we received these kids as clients, many still retained out-of-control behavioral problems which were barely tolerative back when they were still young two-year-olds, and now certainly unacceptable as they'd become teenagers.

To get our clients into a teachable state, where we could begin to effectively guide them into change, we took all entitlements away, other than the necessary chance for food and shelter. We expected them to start doing things that led toward receiving their wants by other means instead of their previously developed patterns of trying to manipulate others into giving in to their acting out. From day one, we taught they were the ones who were going to be held responsible for their choices, not their parents, or other caregivers. Gone were the days of them manipulating others, whom supposedly cared, to yield in desperation. They lost the power to force others into providing to them all their wants. At home, their parents had given plenty of reasons for them to keep continuing their socially out-of-control behaviors. It was now over. In order that they get the help which they required, it was our obligation to effect their change.

By the structure of our program, we were with these kids twenty-four-seven. This is a luxury few parents and other teachers have, so we had the time to impose our teachings. We also had the time to wait until the youths practiced new skills. We started with laying a new foundation with us in the role of guides and teachers, not fun-loving friends or easily influenced parents. Soon the clients realized that their past behavior wouldn't work out in the wilderness, that the staff couldn't be manipulated, and that nature was a cruel teacher who couldn't care less. They gave up on their two-year-old antics and started experimenting with acting responsible and learning to do things for themselves to make their stays more pleasant. They learned that triumph comes from preparing to succeed. They started learning new skills and receiving the gains that come from new applied knowledge. As result, they started growing as individuals into responsible young adults. One of the powerful factors of a wilderness therapeutic program is that it allows the responsible clients their earned comforts while the rebellious continue to make life difficult for themselves.

When is the best occasion for a child to learn?

Common Sense: When a child learns most readily is very simple: **It is when he wants to have answers.**

Teachers take heed—

The golden opportunity to share knowledge is not always present.

—As a teacher, if you are present when they crave knowledge, then you will be granted the privilege to impart.

Remember that what *a child wants* is to have *his desires met*. And what *a teacher or parent wants* is to also have *his expectations met*. When both of these wants, the child's and the adult's, come together working on the same problem, then a joining in a **Common Goal** takes place. This is a healthily relationship were both the child and his trainer are after the same end results. Both now are engaged in craving a solution for the problem, because they individually see the end results as serving their own hopes. It becomes the ambition of both to see this goal thru.

Common Sense Lesson: Cave of Darkness

Imagine yourself as a youngster out with a group of class-mates on a field trip taking a tour deep in the bowels of a cave. You are part of a group walking along a lit path following a guide who is explaining about various formations and telling the history of when the cave was first explored.

As usual there are the intent learners in the front where they can hear the guide; they keep tight together as a group. You, however, are different. You have no desire to spend a whole day listening to some old codger talk about boring *"stalagnights and stalagtights."* You came to have some fun! To entertain yourself, you have drifted to the rear not really following the pack. With a group of buddies you are playing along behind the main body of students. While your fun-loving troupe is involved in a game of "Hide and Go Seek," in and around those *"stalag-thingies"*, you are filled with the undeniable urge to relief yourself. You have to go bad, super-duper bad. You know that no one is around at your present position; your game-mates are separated at the time so no one will see you go, but most importantly it doesn't matter anyway. It's too late to wait. *"I'll catch-up in just a minute,"* is your driving thought.

While you are so separated by choice in a secluded chasm of the cave and doing your "thing" a horribly misfortunate occurrence happens. It takes longer than you thought, and the clean-up is messy. Your short supply of emergency toilet paper is now gone. There is no way you are going to draw attention to yourself in this embarrassing position! You can verily hear the others ahead still listening to the tour guide. A slight panic mode is starting to set in as you realize that you are being left behind with your huge personal problem. You got to hurry. In order, to catch-up with the rest of the group, you are forced to take off and use your socks.

"Still it's not enough ... stupid game of "Hide 'n Go Seek" anyway!" Your anger is starting to set in, first at others, "Why didn't my friends find me?" And then at you, "Sometimes I do things that are so dumb. Why did I eat four bean breakfast burritos, what was I thinking?"

No time to waste as catch-up is crucial. Survival demands that despite the mess that can't be completely taken care of now, you pull up you pants and hurry toward where you can still hear the others. It's only a faint distant sound. Again trouble, a fork in the cave! Now there's more than one choice of possible ways the others could have gone? Picking the one which you think a sound is coming from, you start to run forward. After a while you realize that you should have caught up with them. No one is around. **"Where are they?"** Its past time to yell for help—you momentarily stop running and with your loudest voice yell, **"Hey, wait for me!"** But, as you listen for a comforting reply, it's hopelessly impossible to hear over your loud labored breathing.

"I must hold my breath to be able to hear better," you try again. Still nothing, no response! You sense, ***"I'm in a bad way."*** Again you hold your breath until your lungs burn, "Phew," your spent air escapes like a untied balloon, even though you were fighting with all your might to hold it in. *"With all my problems now I can't even breathe and help myself at the same time!"* You are exasperated. Another yell, and once more you try holding your breath to hear. Nothing works. *"Now, they're probably so far away and too engaged in what is going on in their group, that they can't hear my cries?"*

You bet yourself that they don't even realize you're separated, and will not until the tour is finished and the traditional head count is made. Earlier you were so indecisive, you changed your mind so often about coming before you entered into the cave that the leaders will, if they do count at all, think you went back to the cars with the six others whom where too afraid to go in. It will be dark outside soon. *"Now isn't that a scary thought?"* After the main-body walks back to the cars and takes another head count and they finally realize that you are in fact not anywhere to be found, then it will be too dark to search.

A new thought enters, "I can't count on Joe and Mike to save me by telling the leaders I am still in the cave; those two are too scatter-brained and so easily side-tracked that they will only be thinking about getting back to the cars and filling their own hungry bellies."

"Why do I pick such lame friends?"

"'Thump-ump, thump-ump, thump-ump', there goes that heart again. **AHHH!** I can't hear over my own beating, stupid heart!" Your thoughts are becoming irrational.

"I must go back to that fork in the cave and try the other direction." Panic is setting in.

As you hurry back the same way you came in order to the get again to that choice of paths, then it really happens. The by-far worst thing in the world—yes even worse than the one that literally started all this mess in the first place, the lights in the cave go out. It really doesn't matter why they go out: generator failure, the tour finally ended and the guide turned them out and left, or an act of God; all the same. "BINK" and in your cave it becomes dark. "Pitch black" there is no illumination at all.

"I must help myself." With your mind just barely working, you make your way by feeling along the cave walls and stumbling blindly across the floor. The passage way opens wider, and you think that possibly you are at the remembered fork.

"I'll have to try that other passage, possibly the sound was coming from there, I am not sure, but I have to try … or was I just hearing things? I don't know anymore. I can't find an ember of light for guidance. I can't see a thing."

"H- E- L- P!" Now you know that you are doomed.

The daunting experience of finding oneself in a totally dark cave, or any other place void of light or knowledge, is totally humbling. The disoriented child doesn't know where to go or how to act. He's stumped; he even questions his own ability to react. He realizes that he's helpless and is unable to gain more knowledge of what to do on his own. Now comes his questioning of what is real. He no longer has a clue as to what is effective. He has questioned his own abilities and found them as lacking. In this state of bewilderment, either real or contrived, he will relish even the smallest degree of light or additional knowledge. In the dark, at this time, in order to help himself he must not shut down. He must become submissive to learning and willingly enters into a truly teachable state, otherwise there in no way out.

In any cave of darkness with all anticipation of hope gone, the individual becomes despondent and gives up; they quit trying. The only way to reach one who has shut down is to cause them to abandon these inner feelings and look outside themselves for help. When an individual is full of self-inflicted pity, they have no desire to receive help or even to help themselves; they become sickened with an infestation of **Cry Baby Syndrome.** In order to reach them the teacher must create a diversion so as to cause the "Cry Baby" to forget their own troubles and to look at someone else.

In direct contrast, if any faith in something beyond their present conundrum is still present and their aspirations are still yet alive, they in a childlike state will undertake anything or follow any source of light or direction when it is recognized. If a light, representative of a higher power, does become present and a solution starts to be realized, then the child will begin to help himself by moving toward it. With this hope of advancement, he will start building again his confidence.

With a power of confidence again felt, it is less important for them to continue making an effort to change. Gone now are most of their compelling desires to listen to new ideas, or to continue unquestionably following others. For with self-confidence, a child's teachable state is reduced. However ineffective his ways may be, he is still most governed by his needs to feel in control of his own life. So, unless the child can continue to recognize that even more personal gains are obtainable in the following of instructions and directions of others, he no longer has the compelling desire to be submissive unto a higher power. His receptiveness toward learning has been reduced.

A wise educator will have as his goal, to touch the non-seeking mind. He knows that it is often necessary to wait for the proper time to teach in order to be maximum effective. For when the youth is having success doing things his own way, he will feel little benefit from the wisdom of others, because he is not open to new ideas and methods at that moment. It is mostly when things aren't going smooth, does another approach seem worthy of a child's effort or consideration. Since it is not possible to always be there when the need for knowledge is expressed, an inspiring educator will present his lessons repeatedly in the hopes that they become deep-rooted into the child's memory to be recalled latter if needed. Because of the many past exposures, these lessons can be recalled if the child had taken any initiative to learn them.

Still even more effective, than waiting and being there just as a child becomes desperate enough to seek for assistance, is for the shrewd educator to create a situation where his would-be pupils are willing seeking answers. He affects when they want to have what else is being offering, thereby; the educator is controlling when they want to learn.

Common Sense: **Don't wait; Create.**

Only rarely does a golden opportunity come up and grab you. It mostly occurs when you are chasing after it in hopes for a catch. Oh what elation fills a teacher's mind when a student seeks for help to solve a problem they've been having. This is what every self-less teacher desires. Not so much that the student needs help, but that the student wants to improve and is willingly seeking more knowledge. This great opportunity happens when the kid finally wants help; the willing seeker wants to learn from you.

But, as a teacher is this "great opportunity" also the proper timing for your schedule and other obligations? Is it sometimes an inconvenience for you to stop what you were doing and now help this seeker? ... You will get few opportunities if you set the parameter that they must conform to your schedule and likings.

Create an adjustment of what you want. Remember it is your job as a teacher to expose your pupils to knowledge, and there's one that needs more. He seeks what you can offer, so stop what you're doing and catch him before he gets away. Make effort to create the time; utilize that valuable opportunity to teach when it is offered.

We all have an agenda, and perhaps there is no way at this moment you can squeeze in another thing. Right now, you're forced to postpone giving further instructions because you are previously occupied. {**That others are preoccupied is understandable to you and possibly other busy adults; it is a socially accepted part of growing up and dealing with others.**} But is it for a youth who needs to know now? For this impatient soul, your assistance is the most important thing on their minds ... despite your needs.

Take note that: the lessons you teach are limited to a student's perception of your response. Even in the busiest times, you can have the assistance-seeker still wanting to know, or you can turn him off and against further involvement. You should do more than just ignore them and send the acknowledgment: "That at this moment, you could care less." The end result which your pupil is waiting for is that you interact with him from the highest level of engagement, where you are showing a priority to his needs. This takes time, of which you may not have then. At the very least, interact with him at the second level of interaction. Offer at least a smile and eye contact. These cost nothing. With so little as this, they will retain their desire for your assistance. Don't just ignore them, even when you are horribly pre-occupied.

As you force yourself to give some satisfaction of your involvement, in order to keep them still wanting your latter input, you create a new opportunity to teach. *see: pages: 39-41*

Possible ways where you can set-up a new opportunity are:

"Could I address this in fifteen minutes? Or, *"I'll get back with you in one minute, OK?"* Either, could be your suggestive response, just as long as you make them aware that you are still very interested in helping. You haven't just stated or implied that you are too busy and left them hanging on as to their next move. And to further inject that you are concerned with assisting, you haven't demanded that they meet your schedule; you have politely asked for their approval. You have offered, "Could they alter their expectations slightly?" Instead of coldly demanding that they servilely accommodate your time frame!

Their response back will either communicate, *"Sure, I'll wait,"* in which case it was a success, for you succeeded in teaching that they were important. Or it will be a display their disappointment by some form of them communicating, *"I'll figure it out alone, if you're too busy to help."* Or, after the fact, *"I really needed your help, and you let me down."*

Don't dismay, you as a teacher have shown that you care, and that they are important; their response back to you will be from the level of maturity and unselfishness that they are used to acting from. You are not responsible for their attitude, or their behavioral response. So when met with a manipulating response, repeat again that, "They are important to you and you wish to help." Also you frankly, without emotion, re-state, "So I will get back to you at the latter time indicated," and then end the communication.

In fulfilling your promise of reconnecting, either at a specified time or as-soon-as possible, {the latter being a weaker commitment and showing a much lower level of wanting to adjust your schedule in order to offer help} be sure to initiate as you do get back with them, *"How did you address your concern since we last talked?"* ... *"Do you still have a problem?"* ... *"What is still your biggest concern?"* With these questions you quickly show interest in them. Or you ask, *"How might I have helped, that things would have gone different?"* You show your present willingness to re-engage at the highest level of involvement.

"How can I help?" will suffice if you are getting back in a quick timely fashion. It is in their response, you will see a possible common goal you can join with. They will be more inclined to consider your differing views offered from the genuine perspective of helping, than to respond favorably to your egocentric declarations of their shortcomings.

For getting down to the nitty-gritty in your inquisitions of a student's efforts use, *"So, what do you think that you did right?"* Listen to their response and recognize any efforts. Focus on rewarding for the proper ones. You want to create a teaching moment where perhaps things will improve, so always before you pick apart and offer any suggestions, be sure to state, *"Johnny, you're awesome! Thanks for waiting, even though that is not what you wanted."* Validate some or all of his performance.

Now, you may add, *"Johnny, did you know that possibly you could've done a better job if ...?"* You are showing that you care and appreciate his efforts. You are, again, asking Johnny to consider a possible improvement. You have re-engaged and solicited the opportunity to teach, once more.

Many teachers are trapped in the premonition that their being available for help is also fulfilling their obligation to teach. *"I am here. All you need to do is just ask for my help,"* is their self justification for believing they are indeed good teachers. Nevertheless, the diffi-cultly of the process which they subject their students into enduring to finally be able to obtain an audience stifles most attempts. They do indeed put all the responsibility of any contact back on the shoulders of the student. They are not actively soliciting opportunities to assist; their true motives are other than helping students improve. They are mostly hoping that the student will discover solutions without having to be bothers. Being this teacher is not your best presentation; you can do better than that.

A great teacher offers things of interest, intrigue, humor, and new pertinent information. He creates in his students the quest for fulfillment. Because of the way this teacher is exposing them to knowledge, students now have a desire to gain more information. They feel a yearning need to know what the master can impart. He skillfully controls the environment, the timing, and the pupil's attention, as-well-as the giving rewards to his students' advantage such as a great story, or a side splitting properly timed joke. The skilled orator will share a thought promoting experience which reveals to the budding mind that they also possess the very skills which, if nurtured, will enable them to see a solution long before the answers are revealed. What self esteem becomes theirs as the observers recognize a dilemma before it becomes the object of discussion. Introduce to the students that they possess skills; this inspires them to want pay more attention. In addition to properly presenting his information to make it appealing to his students, this educator makes it a point to periodically join with his charges, taking the burden of initiating contact onto himself.

A wise educator will create a need to know by putting the student in a situation where it is vital to have more information, similar to being all alone in a cave of darkness. Then he gives them a chance to get enlightened. When the student is willing to undertake new ways and learn new things, a commonality can be nurtured and established between the educator and the student as they enhance the student's life. The teacher can freely impart his knowledge and the student is hungry and willing to receive it.

Why doesn't my child learn?

What of the parent who does go the extra mile? Who goes out of his way to give opportunity, yet still feels, *"My child is never willing to learn from me?"* How many parents have had these thoughts? *"That kid is never at that point where he is willing to do as I show him. He thinks he knows best."* As parents, eager to teach, many stand ready and willing to respond their child's plea for assistance which never comes. They have shown time and time again the proper ways, but to no avail; the kid never seem to get it to the point where they show a desire to learn what the parent has to show. Now and then, as parents or teachers in desperation at our wits end, we feel, *"This student will not learn, and least of all not from me."*

This promotes a questioning of, *"**Why is this so**?"*

Nowadays we live in a world of so much information. Every minute of the day, someone is willing to show a potential student how to do something. Think of the millions of lessons that a child is exposed to on the television and at school. If retention and ability were possible from just being shown a skill or from being presented an idea, then we would all be champion figure skaters. We would be able to recall the knowledge from everyone we have ever listened to or from all the words that we have ever read. This is not so, a child of learning is much more selective than that; in fact a child does not learn from being shown at all.

A teacher reveals information either through his actions or his words by showing an awareness which he has obtained. The teacher may show much, but it is not through being shown that a child learns; it is through a **personal discovery**.

To **discover** is to become aware of something not previously known. It is that act of grasping for oneself an idea or vision, and then recognizing and personalizing its potential. This is the factor that causes learning for the individual, as one comes to the realization of the information and experiences to which he is being subjected. An awakening of understanding must take place. True learning occurs as one experiences a **personal discovery.** He becomes aware of something new and therefore wants to implement it into his life. He realizes that, "Hey, now I know how to get this to work for me!" Without scheduling its implementation, any new knowledge only becomes more information that probably will be filed in the hidden realms of the mind to be forgotten or discarded as other demands take precedence.

Common Sense Lesson: How to Blow One's Own Nose

Understanding how a person learns through discovery can be easily seen as one recalls how a youngster learns how to blow his nose. A concerned mentor will attempt to teach a snotty-nose toddler that it is possible for him to force mucus into a tissue or a hanky. Junior doesn't have to forever endure the hassles of having his nose wiped by someone else, or endure the socially shunned ramifications of snot running down his face. He can discover how to help himself.

At first, the well meaning teacher will say, "*Blow*," and the child will do just that. Junior will blow air out of his mouth, following the instructions given him. The youth hasn't a clue how to blow through his nose. So, his teacher will demonstrate the proper technique in effort to show him. The mentor will correct the child in the attempt to help him understand. He will demonstrate and hope that the child will learn by example. He will find amusing the youth's attempts. Just how many tries to finally get it right will depend on the youth's ability and the skills of the teacher; mostly it's dependent on the child's willingness.

If either quits before success is obtained, then the learning process will not happen.

Eventually, the youth does it right. The kid has taken the information and discovered how to implement it for his benefit. He has learned how to make it work. This is when the mentor can have joy with the child whom finally learns. The child has heard and seen an idea, then discovered how to utilize it. He recognizes its benefits. He has learned how to blow his nose. {The new challenge is to just get him to do it ... that's another story.}

The frustration that a teacher feels when he thinks his pupil will not learn is either from the fact that the child hasn't discovered for himself the principle, or chooses to keep doing what has worked in the past because he can't recognize the benefits of a change. Don't give up as a mentor; keep showing your pupils. They finally discover a principle when their desires of willingness, their experiences, and their abilities come together. Then it can be said, "They have learned." To stave off any frustration felt, expedite the learning process by developing new skills and techniques. These will enhance your abilities to properly show new lessons with the right timing. Always utilize all available helps.

CHAPTER 10:

WHAT INFLUENCES A CHILD TO REACT

What a child learns is from the results of his experiences and the lessons taught by the different teachers he has been associated with. Stored in his mind are these many lessons based on his ability to remember and his understandings. He exercises his freedom of choice by his implementation of what he believes he knows. Stimulating his choice is not the truth, {what is really happening to the child.} but his perception of it, ever changing as rivers of thought in his mind. These thoughts are formed and refined as result of his interpretation of the lessons he's been exposed to. He's discovered how to react to them. As a teacher you are a key influence in persuading his yearning to discover. You can sway many of his desires of gratification. You can compel him to problem solve. Be aware, you also influence his perceptions of fear.

Spooks and Perceived Fears

*   *   *

Common Horse Sense: A student's apprehension is influenced by his mentor's display of fear or confidence.

I have observed that the concerns which control kids are very much introduced and perpetuated by the displayed fears of their mentors. As our grandchildren, ages: one through seven, come and visit their Grandmother and me, we will make a routine stop out to see the horses. If occasion permits they will sit on the horses and take a little ride. Their degree of fear and interaction to the horses varies. In the beginning without experiences of their own to draw on, they were left to react according to the lessons or the reactions they see being displayed by their teaching examples.

Our youngest daughter, Lara, has never shown an interest in riding horses. She has the displayed reactions of her mother, a fear of involvement. Like her mother, she has never developed an understanding of a horse, or the ability to ride beyond sitting the saddle of a stable horse. This fear has developed not founded on any personal misfortune on Lara's part, but as results of her focusing on the few negative mishaps that she remembers seeing. Over the years she has chosen to focus on the negative memories instead of the productive and pleasant ones. Her fear is now displayed to her child by body language and deflections of her voice. She now is overly cautious and protective of her own son.

In sequence to his mother's fears, whenever Kaysen, my second grandson, is coerced into interaction with the horses, fear will quickly take control as he witnesses his mother's display. He will cry and kick and act as though an evil demon from the depths of Hades has again surfaced. This display of **freaking-out** then causes the interaction with the horses to end. Again, these reactive displays are not the result of any personal mishap or his viewing of negative behavior problems from the animals. His fears are **spooks**. {A fear, oft times, of nothing real.} They are reactions in the mind of my grandson to his perception of reality, as taught by Lara, his mentor.

Two other grandchildren, Whitney and Macie, love the horses and cry when they don't get a chance to ride or spend enough time with them. Their father, Cheston, my oldest son, spent much time with them as a youth. In the course of his experiences on the ranch during his growing up years, he's had a number of mishaps with the beasts, some included mustangs which were less predictable. This son has realized, through personal experiences, the need for respect of animals. He coveys no fear of horses while around them. He dutifully teaches his children to safely respect the large beasts; they are at ease as they want to and do spend time with equine.

Jet, my one-year-old grandson, is encouraged to attempt new things by both his parents. His father, Daniel, has seen mishaps and also experienced good times on and around horses. He conveys a healthily lesson to his son to enjoy them, and not be governed by a fear of what could happen … but has not. Jet is encouraged to try, and has a great time. This little guy doesn't have any negative lessons to base any perceptions on, and has developed no fear of the animals.

A fourth child of mine, Jennifer, will through her body language and voice deflections exhibit a moderate degree of fear and caution. She has never fallen or experienced mishaps of her own, but has seen others lose control mostly through their own inabilities. As a result when she is with her son, Hayden, he will show a perceived fear. His **perception of reality** is based not on his experiences, but on what he witnesses in his mentors. When he is in the presence of a mentor that is displaying the apprehension of fear, he is triggered toward unwarranted worries. When his mother is not present, he will be calm and at ease. His reactions vary according to what he sees in others. He fluctuates from enjoying himself when he is alone with me, to turning fearful in the presents of his grandmother, or cautious and apprehensive with his mother present.

Because of a mentor's own fears, a distorted perception of reality is transmitted to his pupils. This leads them to also having the inability to address or to confront a problem realistically; it promotes faulty thinking.

* * *

Common Horse Sense: To flee or not to flee? That is the question.

Stretching its neck outwards to keep as much distance as possible, the horse advances gingerly watching all the body language of the human for any sudden movement that would signal danger. Cautiously stepping forward in an attempt to touch its nose to that hand, it elects to stay as far away as possible until it makes a thorough investigation. The reluctant animal is poised to put distance between him and the potential trouble, if any sort of discomfort is perceived. Its senses are peaked, tensed and ready to flee. Only the tips of its nose hairs will make contact. A sniff is all that can be allowed before lighting quick it executes a whorl off to the side, and the fearful horse is away at a safe distance where it will assess whether there is a need for further interaction or just more flight.

As you present a potential danger into the personal private space of a reluctant horse, whether by suddenly approaching without warning; exposing an object, or presenting any interaction which could be interpreted as a threat, you ought to train yourself to an awareness of the body language of your horse. {Or for that matter any other type of student.} You can not control its actions, but you can control the reasons for them. Just before its self-defense mechanism kicks in and it pulls back or whorls away, if you, as the source of the perceived pain, will take a step back and retract the threatening gesture or the advancing perceived jeopardy, this will take away the perception of danger and promote a de-escalation of your student's fears by allowing the animal to relax off his guard. Learn when to not come on so strong that you cause a negative reaction.

You introduce and then pause for a moment, this allows the animal a chance to get ready for the different stimulus; you are diminishing the potential of it reacting out of the perception of a sudden danger. You train yourself to not present any new task without first giving the horse a warning, thereby alerting the animal to be aware, *"A change is coming."* When introducing something different, you can control whether or not they flee by paying close attention to their signs of stress. Ease-up and don't put any more pressure on them than they can bear. ...

It's a master who can pull this off.

* * *

Common Sense: **Just as a fear can be a reaction to something real, it can also be from things imagined. What a child responds to may not be real or always based on reality, but it is based on what their perceptions of reality may be.**

"**Spooks**" are the real or perceived fears which frighten a horse. They cause the animal to come alive into a state of alarm or arousal in an effort to deal with the unexpected surprise. With the appearance of a spook, a calm horse will leap off to the side or suddenly erupt into frenzy, because it is trying to distance itself from what it thinks is a real danger. It could be as simple as seeing a shadow, a flittering bird, or an unanticipated movement of a piece of trash, even perhaps a strange sound that isn't familiar. Even the presenting of a saddle blanket, which it has worn many times before, can cause a spook if the horse is overly nervous or hasn't been handled for some time. To cure them it is necessary to subject this student to a repeated exposure of their spooks in a non-threatening way, all the while, having them feel the calming confidence of their trainer. Rarely will one exposure or session of de-sensitizing eliminate spooks forever; the animal may again perceive the danger at any time. But repeated exposures and de-sensitizing will assist towards the lessening of the frequency.

"**Freaking-out**" is a learned reaction of inadequacy, based on one's lack of another course of action. It can be witnessed as kicking, screaming, becoming angry, or any number of other violent displays of uncontrolled behavior. This display of emotion is so out-of-control that often it leads to the breaking of objects or to injury as the perpetrator looses his ability to use rational thinking. When enacting a freak-out, its author has a desire to do something in retaliation to the emotions he's feeling, but the passion of the moment so overwhelms his being that it catapults him into frenzy. He is propelled forward; abandoned and now out of question is his ability to use a rational response. Freaking-out is not a shutting down, but rather is an attempt in trying to do something about a predicament; it is a purposeful stab at dealing with it. This harmful display can be overcome and discarded as the perpetrator learns alternative behavioral responses. In dealing with a charge that freaks out, a guide has to lead them toward an acceptable alternative reaction. A trainer calmly rewards preferred responses and allows the overly-reactive student no mileage in getting what they wish for by their unwanted conduct. In time with proper help, freaking-out can be viewed as not needed and replaced with knowledge of new actions in the pursuit of self-enhancing gains.

As a trainer, it is by **de-sensitizing** your charges that they will turn from their inter-defense mechanism to take flight and seek distance from the cause of their discomforts. After many non-intrusive exposures from the source of their fears, the weary will come to the realization that the situation didn't move beyond its original cause of alarm. The source of fear didn't escalate into a producer of actual pain, only an empty perceived threat. The inexperienced youth's perception starts to change as they sense that they haven't really been hurt too severe; hence, no need to freak-out or take flight for they have the ability to endure this present inconvenience.

Teach a child a different reactive alternative to help them handle, without flight, a perceived danger. This will help them to gain confidence. An individual who distorts reality needs help in realizing that although their fears may be based on some truth, they are also compounding and making their anxiety larger and more important than it needs to be. They need help realizing that fear doesn't have the power to govern them; they still have a choice of how they will combat it. As they learn new alternative responses to cope with a dilemma, the less they will focus on their fears. In addition, the freer they become to not be hurled into trepidation's subjection, and they experience an increase in their own power.

Therapeutic treatment presents aids to help modify how a person sees and reacts. It helps to empower a person to take action instead of being governed by a reaction. By pre-rehearsing effective alternative actions the person is able to cope with their own perceived fears and realities and is thereby left with more power of choice.

* * *

Common Horse Sense: Training a wild mustang colt.

As a wild mustang, part of the Panacca, Nevada Herd, she was running free for three years before she was rounded up and caught by order of the Bureau of Land Management {BLM} and placed into the "Adopt-a-Mustang Program". Before I got her, she had been green broke, and then not touched for eleven months. I remember the words of her previous owner, "Ride her in the corral all you want. But if you want her, you'll have to pay for this mustang before you take her out." The reason of his words soon became apparent; she was still wild at heart. If she was not contained in a small enclosure, I couldn't get near her.

Even to catch this mare in a corral, I had to use the Flag Method. This consisted of keeping her running from me by waving a flag on a short pole. After she had tired, showing the signs of heaving sides, sweat and fatigue, then I let off pressure. Each time she would allow me closer to her before she would again flee away. I could see the fear in her eyes and the urge just bolt for good, but the confines of the six-foot iron pipe corral made that not possible. Never a trust built up, only a reluctant acceptance as she realized that it s was futile to keep running where she couldn't obtain liberty. She did seem to listen and was slightly reassured at my calming voice droning, "You're ok." By repeating it many times over and over again when she was standing at a halt, it acted to further desensitize her against my presence. Even still, it took an hour before she allowed me close enough to where I could put a rope and halter on her without her running off. But even at that, she would stiffen in terror as she was handled or rode. There was no question in my mind that if I ever lost her, only entrapment followed by a repeat of the Flag Method with an extended time for her desensitization would ever allow me close to her again.

She had a beautiful paint month-old filly at her side. Since I was in the market to buy a mustang after being convinced previously of their low maintenance and self awareness for survival, I felt like I was getting two for the price of one; so I purchased her with her foal to use in rounding up of my cattle.

Four years latter I had sold all my cattle after a two-year-drought and the continued expensive prospects of having to feed hay instead of pasturing. Now having no use for the mustang mare, and also needing to seek additional employment to supplement my insane habit of trying to pay the never stopping bills, I turned her loose in a mile long field with my other horses, which included an Arabian stallion.

The next year she gave me a horse colt, which grew up not being handled or even touched until he was one and a half. Herself given no further human interaction, she raised him to flee from danger with the survival tendencies of her once wild life. She, being his teacher and mentor, ingrained in him that if trouble presented itself, even in the smallest degree, then the thing to do was instantly distance from it. She successfully schooled him on using a flight response for protection from any perception of pain or imagined fear.

Realizing in order to train her colt, it must first be separated from its mustang mentor that it might be accessible without mom's influence; I trapped and moved it, to be alone in a small pen located next to two other experienced horses. My agenda was first to expose him, whom was later named Charlie, to human interactions, and then to was to teach him to lead. I chose the Monty Robert's method of "Joining Up."

{This training method consists of separating an animal in a round pen where it's not possible to distance too far from any perception of pain, or danger. Should your pupil resist your interactions, it is forced away, to feel isolated even further. Because of a natural instinct to be part of a herd, it will eventually give in and surrender into "joining up" with the only thing available —you. In this environment void of places to hide and isolated from all other distractions, the equine trainer pushes away the terrlfied animal whenever it doesn't stand still for him or if it tries to leave his presence. He simulates a lead mare as she scolds a young colt for its improper behavior. Only does she allow the colt back into her graces, which means back joining the herd, when it has shown the proper signs of repentance such as an ear cocked toward her, looking in her direction instead of for a path of flight, and/or licking and chewing. With the colt in this repentant and submissive state, as it expresses its desire to get back into the graces of the lead mare, then further herd interaction takes place. By instinct, even when pushed away, a horse can't bear to not be part of a herd. It will give up

fleeing from danger, and makes the attempt to join obediently with even a scolding mentor.

As the trainer, as you approach the colt, if he tries to flee out of fear, then he is pushed even further away to the point where he realizes that it is you forcing him, not him exercising his freedom of will. He is continued to be held at a distance until he becomes repentant and tries to join up again by giving the proper signs. He is allowed to join again with you as long as he doesn't misbehave.

During this time of his being with you, it is your responsibility to make it worth his while. The idea is to teach the colt to stay near the trainer. He discovers not to flee, that no real harm will come to him if he just stays by the trainer.

In the course of future training whenever the colt misbehaves, it is pushed away into exile, until it becomes submissive once more, only then it is allowed to re-join. Quickly the learning animal realizes that is better to endure whatever the trainer is doing, instead of again earning chastisement and once more being forced out from its comfort zone away from the herd. This new awakening allows it to do new things with conditional acceptance. It learns that compelled compliance will bring less trouble than to flee away and invoke the disproval of the trainer.}

Although I had read Monty's book, and had successfully trained other horses with his ideas, I had not as yet caught the vision of *rewarding longer then you work.

Charlie, after being given only three sessions of working with the flag method of training; would allow me near him in his compelled submissive state. He learned to lead and even to quit trembling when I touched him all over his body. A saddle was placed on him and he learned to accept this too. I was on my way. I had a young horse, less than two, which was taken from a feral state and now was carrying a saddle. All I had to do was to wait for this promising colt to get older, and then I would start riding.

To my dismay, like many teaching opportunities, the available window of training was only short lived; soon I was out of time and had to go back to my supplemental job of teaching troubled youth in a wilderness environment. My shifts often consisted of being away from home for up to two weeks at a time. As result, Charlie was left alone in his pen and not worked with again for five months. The desire was there, but reality demanded my interests elsewhere, for it was the spring, and summer was looming. My schedule was more than full. When I was not out with the youth program, I was busy trying to take care of my ranch, putting up hay, watering, and tending to my other non-relenting duties. The training of this young horse was put on hold until the late fall when things slowed down a might. My wife fed him for me during my absence, and during this period he developed bad habits based on his fears.

Like I said before, he had learned to accept human interaction only after he was in a submissive state; when he could see no advantage to flee. Each day, as Charlie was fed during this extended period of non-training, he would see a human as someone whom had forced him to submit. And when he resisted, the human had used more force, pushing him to the point of exhaustion. Humans were not good things; they were a bit scary. The very act of such a being walking past his pen would cause him to flinch a little. As the days of non-interacting continued, this drawing back grew in intensity. The truth is it escalated, fed by his imagination into a spook-reaction each time a human got near him. With repeated exposures to these questionable beings and not having any new or added experiences of resolve or reassurance to relate with, his perception of fear escalated. As feed was tossed into his pen, or when a person walked by he would flee away with conviction and fright to get what he thought was a relief.

I didn't like what was happening to this young horse, but knew that unless I had the time, thirty minutes to one hour a day to work with him, he wasn't going to get any better. I now had a horse that was worse than when I took him from his mother. Because of his perceptions, he was truly afraid and would flee at the slightest human interactions. He became dreadfully afraid of humans. I realized that in order to catch him, or just get close again, I must invest a great deal of time.

The corrective training method I choose to use was one I had learned many years before. Since I wouldn't have a large amount of time to work with him until fall, I elected to put it off until I was back off a shift from the desert and things on the farm would slow down enough that I might squeeze it in. Then I would de-sensitize him from his fears of fleeing away from scary humans. My idea would work. I had done it before.

{Fifteen years ago, I had struggled to catch a flighty gelding. It was in a large pen with three other horses. That gelding would not let anyone near him and made a great game of running around and through any non-squeeze gate system, avoiding any attempt towards his capture. Of course his other padlock mates joined in following his defiant lead. It was equally impossible to lay hold on any of the other horses, unless they could be cut off and separated from the negative behavior of that rascal.

In frustration, I remarked to Dave Jenson the horse's owner, whom also was an older much experienced sheepherder, "I'd like to shoot that gelding; he can't be caught without great hassle. He's influencing the others also."

His answer was so simple I thought myself in a presence of a master. "Just dump the water trough, and then go back every day and stand by that empty container. Don't chase him or try to catch him, in time the horse will come to you."

"How long," I said, thinking about the heat and how cruel this all sounded? I was visualizing four horses experiencing the pains and slow death from dehydration.

"As long as it takes. ... About three days, if he's really stubborn, then it'll be longer," said the old master.

This method worked sure enough; the other gentler horses came to me right off, after the first, full summer, day of thirst. I allowed them to water, but stepped in front of the stubborn white gelding to block him off. He was trying to sneak in behind them to steal a drink without me having the opportunity to touch him. I shooed him away by stepping in front of him with my hand extended as a touch gesture. I was sure he under-stood what I was asking him to allow. I was only asking that he allowed me to catch him before he had his drink. And as he didn't the first two days, I didn't advance on him. I just merely stood, for a moment, waiting for him to come to me, just as the other three. He chose not to come in close, so I turned the water trough over again until the next day.

Each day the others drank their fills and permitted me to handle them; he was left thirsty. On the fourth day he was parched enough to then play my game. He became my best friend as he approached me, then stood still so I could catch and handled him prior to his drinking. Unfortunately this same four-day-ordeal had to be repeated again each time the gelding went any length of days between being caught. It was easier to just not use him, and of course this also meant the other three, as they would run away also—not in show of defiance as that gelding, but more in instinct to stay with their herd leader.

My revenge came nearly two months later when one day out in the field stood three horses and lay one white gelding. I remember my thoughts as I approached that dead animal, his legs stiffened outwards. *"Well, look who finally got easy to catch. Go ahead and run away now."* His other pasture-mates were still standing close, hovering over their fallen leader. They came up to me, so as to ask, "What happened?" Their flight was now gone.

In preparation to drag him to his grave, I walked up and slipped a rope around that rigid carcass with its swelling sun-ripening belly, I remarked to my former nemeses, "Oh you want to stay? What a good horse!" I sneered sarcastically. There would be no more running away from me this time. No, I wasn't sad, nor did I really care what he had died from. My problem was over. I knew that now, not having that leader and teacher of bad habits, the others would be easier to catch and use. ...And they were.}

So in accordance with my previous plan, Charlie was denied water. The first twenty four hours I did nothing; I made no attempt to make contact. I just let him go thirsty. On the second day, as I approached to lead him to water, he still would have no part of me, and moved quickly to the outside of the pen. I left, and he went dry. On the third day, as I filled a water trough fifty feet away from his pen. I purposely held the hose high to make the water splash into it; the noise of the running water definitely pricked his ears. He kept his eyes focused on the quenching liquid. I gave him the opportunity to be caught once more.

Charlie stood his ground and didn't turn quickly away as he had done before; he needing something from me. I could see the apprehension in his eyes, as he focused on me, and then the tantalizing drink. He only moved away slightly when I entered his pen with the rope. I drew nearer. He started showing a fear and a need to distance from me; I made a point to approach cautiously, watching for his nervousness to further escalate. Just before he bolted, I backed up one step. My purpose was to take away the need to flee. He was free now to except this thought, "This man must not be a threat or a danger because he is moving away, and boy am I thirsty." Using this method, I approached him slowly using calm words and no aggressive movements. Charlie allowed me to put a lead rope on him, and then he nervously followed me outside of his pen to where his relief was waiting. Keep in mind this was only the fourth time in his two-year-old life that he was handled. He tensely swallowed his fill while I stood near. I made no other approach, only stood by him as he drank then returned him to his dry pen and to his private empty water trough until the next day.

For the next four weeks, when I was home, I daily caught Charlie, who only on the first two days chose to give signs of needing to walk from me. Quickly he had learned to stand patiently waiting for me to take him to water. I started to touch him as he drank on the fourth day. He calmed towards handling, after a few more days he would drink without terrifying fear shinning through his eyes. He learned to quit flinching as I walked by, or threw him his feed. He even looked forward to me catching him for other interactions. We developed a common bond together. He was getting something other than discomfort out of our relationship. I was now a good-guy; no longer a scary spook.

What Charlie started to receive was a reward. Oh yes, part was the water that quenched his thirst, but in addition, he started to realize that he was not going to be hurt. He found as an incentive for his good behavior, a soft handling and a chance to be accepted in a herd—my herd. His reality was changing as he could see that humans were not all about work, they presented a reward also. Man creatures were not always about pain, and in fact if cooperated with, they represent companionship.

*   *   *

Common Horse Sense: A horse's behavioral reaction is influenced as it observes the body language of its handler.

"You will love the trail rides Sam. They give you a freedom unlike anything else," his sister promised. "You will bond and become one with the horse and nature," she continued to tempt her brother, offering him to share in same experiences she had found during the past year, as she discovered the world of riding horses in the Southern Utah Mountains.

Soon images of superbly riding through the hillsides filled his young mind. Dreaming of his black cape billowing freely in rhythm to the expansions and contractions of his powerful mount, he envisioned himself as a skilled rider on an obedient horse. Both man and beast acting as one, they shared a common destination, and a common goal. Each enhanced the other. These grandeurs inspired Sam, "Yes, I want to learn to ride." So he showed up in response to the prompting of his sister with these visions of grandeur enchanting his mind, "Oh... to be like Zorro and his faithful steed."

The sun was getting busy along its journey, the temperature was promising, both supporting a glorious day. From the world of point and click electronic devices to this of touching, smelling, and personal exposure he entered. This was true reality; in it lingered the hung-over moon still not yet vanished from the western skies. It was the gentle breeze carrying the unique aroma of horse manure, and it was real interactions with live persons and impulsive animals. It was not made up for someone's viewing pleasure to simulate life; it was genuine, a whole new experience for this young video playing dreamer.

"First brush off the winter coat before it gets all over you and the tack ... besides the horse loves to get off that hot long hair. Start here, brush the withers, the sides, and the rump," I said, keeping an eye on this new would-be equestrian. It was late winter/early spring and the overgrown coats still clung to the fresh horses; they were rested and full of energy from a deep winter's break. Fifteen minutes later he was still slowly brushing on the same side as if in a trance; going through the motions, yet getting nothing done.

"You can move to another spot on her back," I said. I made a mental point to become more intent and watch Sam more closely. During the next ten minutes, his horse still hadn't moved a step, and neither had he. He was meaninglessly stuck in the same repetitive motions, neither moving his feet nor reaching for a non-brushed spot. The delight-filled face of a dreamer had been replaced by the stupor of the shell shocked. "Try brushing her rump and other side," I offered, trying again to sever his daze. He successfully took a five-minute brushing job and turned it in to a fifty-minute unfinished ordeal. He allowed his fear to bud and blossom within. He gradually became so nervous to move around the animal that he was starting to convey his fear and apprehension to it.

What started out as a cool and collected horse was now being energized by Sam's fears and distrust. When it came time to bridle his horse, he stood at arm's length and recoiled back every time the horse would so much as twitch or shift its head slightly. Fifteen tries, plus or minus, that poor mare had to endure Sam's attempts to put the bridle on. Half a dozen times I showed the proper way to get her to lower her head. Then I demonstrated the correct procedure of placing on the bridle and taking it off. However, Sam fumbled and fidgeted so much he was causing the animal to move her head at his improper tugging and choppy movements. It had started out as my goal to empower Sam by allowing him to bridle her by himself; but, I relented and finally abandoned this goal and did it myself after seeing the damage he was doing. He acted as if she was a coiled rattlesnake poised to strike—if she so much as switched, he would jerk back in retaliation. Soon his exaggerated movements of flight became her reaction to him as well. His saddling and riding attempts were much the same. He had this horse so confused she didn't know what to expect. Yet still he wanted to continue.

"Whoa, whoa, stop!" were his out cries, as she shifted weight or inappropriately moved to his mounted requests. Or should I say, as she reacted to his miss-attempts at requesting her compliance. At each step in the process of training this youth, I would show him, by example, the proper techniques, and the mare would respond to my requests with compliance. Sam needed to be talked through each task again and again. Each time he would acknowledge that he understood and then in his attempts to saddle, rein, or control his horse be so inconsistent and panicky with his exaggerated actions of ambivalence that his horse would follow his lead and react with fear and confusion. Only after many repeated attempts would he force himself to fumble into somewhat performing the task. Since his interactions with her were all interlaced with displays of fear and inconsistencies, he never did get his mount to be yielding or submissive. Counting the brushing, and tack redo's, the many minutes of just staring blankly into space, together with the many other attempts to obtain the riding experience, this poor mare endured a four-hour process with Sam. In desperation to indeed give him the full experience he had hoped for, I broke my own rule:

Do not let a student outside the corral until they can execute the basics of stop, start; balance, and reining at different speeds with some degree of proficiency.

I finally let Sam and his *currently-compliant* mount outside of the corral. Because of my many past experiences with this animal, I thought it would just follow, with a trailing mentality, behind the other three. What could go wrong, hadn't she endured Sam already for so long without any grave incident?

While outside the corral, but still in the yard, to further practice Sam was asked to take again his mare through the routine of getting her to remain subtle and yielding by the bending of her neck, also known as the flexing of her pole. {This is her moving the first vertebrae joint just after axis of the head.} I was to be occupied preparing the other animals to depart so I would not be able to devote all my attention and energy on this duo, as I had been. After again being shown how to do it properly, he agreed but didn't do it after I left his side. He chose to do no meaningful practice on his own. He had practiced numerous times in the corral, yet without someone pushing and encouraging his every move, he just sat on his mount hoping she would be still, and awaiting for my next involvement. I guess to his thinking there was no sense creating problems for himself;

After his four-hour-training marathon, I knew he wasn't quite ready. But still, I wrongly permitted Sam to ride along in order to let him to have a good experience. And because of what happened next, I have since adopted a new and improved rule:

Do not allow someone to ride outside the confines of the corral until they are able to ride on their own. They must practice the basics, with no one else forcing them to do so, until correct performance become second nature. Their horse must be submissive, not reactive to being forced.

The other horses were ready now. So out through the yard gate and onto the trail the first five animals left. Sam wanted to follow, but was having a slight difficulty in getting his horse to move. Since outside of the corral, she had just been taught a new lesson by Sam's choice to do nothing. She learned if she stood still and didn't move, then her rider would give no confusing signals. After enjoying this harmony, there were those feelings of fear and confusion again, as Sam struggled to get her to move once more. Finally he jerked her hard into action, and she sprung toward the yard gate to follow the others. Her walk was a faster pace than he was expecting. Of course Sam, having just demanded action and then getting it, was startled by her immediate movement and seemly burst of speed. So he in beginner's retaliation immediately tried to shut her down by yanking her to stop, yet his body was riding her to go. He was not in control and was simultaneously losing his balance. He demanded; she was leaving.

She had endured four hours of tension while waiting for a rider to make up his mind and give her a proper signal she could recognize and respond to. He had given that signal, and she was responding to his request to the best of her ability and compliance. Just as she moved forward, not wanting to be left behind, here come more confusing signals again by someone for whom she has no respect. Perplexed by his fears and over reactions, this poor animal saw her chance to be free. After a few steps of the horse-verses-rider struggle, she left the yard gate on a buck. Springing on her back legs, she arched beautifully, then planted her front legs beneath her squarely. While still vertical, she followed through with her hind end extended fully in an upwards reach. She was in true rodeo fashion. The whole ordeal had been too much for her.

This would be Zorro experienced his wanted billowing alright, but only with his arms and lips as he flailed through the air. Like a baby bird trying its wings on its first flight. Up, up he launched only to peak and plummet down challenging his arms and legs as though he were treading water for a purchase of solid ground. He hit hard, and quickly crawled out of her way. She gave an extra buck for good measure making sure her tormentor was indeed dismounted. The riding fantasy was now ended.

"I don't want to ever ride again!" he blubbered, as he sat crying in the fetal position.

I had previously thought myself a fair hand at reading a horse's mind; but I sure missed seeing that one coming. I watched the horse come to a quick stop, then start licking and chewing. Now, she was through; no meanness left. Hours of confusion and frustration had been released. "She is done," I said, "There will be no more problems."

"**I will never ride again!**" he bluntly stated seeing how he was getting no mileage out of his whimpering shutdown. He was not hurt, but was left feeling that he had lost control over his life. To his understanding he had done what he thought was the right thing. His experience was a bad one, and he had no desire to repeat it again. He was truly in flight response to the unknown and little understood. His actions were saying, as he sat in the dirt watching what I would do, "I am content in my own abilities and efforts, and have no further desire to experience that type of lack-of-control again!" Sam hasn't ridden since. He now is not teachable in the matter, because his goal of riding has changed. He has no further desire to develop or to improve, or to again put himself in the same uncomfortable situation.

His horse was standing riderless only twenty feet away; she was showing repentance. She was still teachable. That mare just wanted something she could rely on. I got on her back to give her some consistency; she responded beautifully. She finished the ride with another youth rider; they had not a moment's trouble.

The next day I joked with Sam and thanked him, ***"For riding the devil out of that horse."*** He couldn't believe that the horse didn't give any more trouble.

"She was nervous and emotional following your leading example; come try again, and you will do better," I said, leaving the invitation open for his return.

"No chance."

We still continued to be friends, but he didn't take me up on this offer, until three years latter.

{*Lesson Learned*: *A horse can be calmed or riled by the emotions and actions of its handler, it will mirror accordingly.*}

* * *Side note:* * *   **Never again have I allowed a youth outside the corral, until they could control a horse by getting it to yield and respond supplely, not by reining it by force to where the animal is reacting out of pain.**

Common Horse Sense: Never walk behind a horse.

"Don't get behind that horse. You could get kicked!"

How many times have you heard a well meaning person, who is assuming the role of a knowledgeable teacher, make that statement?

Nothing could be more damaging to a pupil than when we, who are in a position to be emulated, seek to discourage an action by making a statement that's founded by our own fears and lack of understanding.

When you make such a statement, don't you feel great in your effort to be so protective? Coming from the Good Mother Teaching Mode, you have pointed out a danger, and the students are avoiding it. They are blindly following you. All is well now, isn't it? Obedient and rational thinking pupils, without any personal experience to draw on, will take the teacher at her word and not get behind the horse; they are into self-preservation and therefore will make sure to avoid the potential of injury from a source which they have no control over. The initial warning of caution was effective, yet lacking.

Some students are so in-tune to self-preservation that their minds work overtime and enlarge the statement, "You could get kicked," into a perceived understanding of, ***"Get too near that horse and you will get kicked."*** This influences their future intimacies with the animals. They now are too afraid to approach the equine monsters in order to lead, ride, or share any experiences with them. At the very least, they will show fear and flightiness in their body language causing their own feelings of anxiety to transfer to and escalate an already apprehensive horse.

The lesson: to be aware of a horse's hooves has indeed been taught. But, has it been taught in the most effective way?

What will happen when this child sees the exact opposite happen? What happens when this child sees someone else standing near the rear end of horse and they are not being kicked? Does this send a message to the youth that what they heard from their teacher is totally wrong? They can't deny what they see: There is a person who is not being kicked by that horse. Now, is it okay for them to approach the animal anywhere, because this animal doesn't kick? This message will confuse the child in his understanding of the principles in approaching and getting behind a horse.

Let's go back and start over once more. The primary reason the protective teacher made the statement, 'Don't get behind that horse, you could get kicked,' she was aiming to prevent the child from getting hurt. She was in the Nurturing Parent Approach, but also, being too overly nurturing.

In an alternative, what if she had included in her concern for the child's safety, a Loving Father Approach, combined with an increased engagement? Consider the difference:

"Stop! Don't run up behind that horse. It doesn't know what you're going to do. You could make it afraid. You may get hurt as it tries to get out of your way," the behavioral educator certainly now has the student's attention. This allows for optional behavioral teaching, instead of just a commanding a restriction of freedom.

"Be aware, and approach a horse in such a way that it knows your intentions. Watch me I will demonstrate the safe way to get near a horse." The concerned teacher now raises her own level of participation in the teaching process and shows the proper way to approach a horse. She shows that in order for the horse to not be frightened or suddenly startled, it might be necessary for the approaching child to stop and allow the horse a chance to realize there is no threat. The "scary child" may even need to take a step backwards before continuing on into the horse.

The children's trainer instructs her students to always make the horse aware of their presence before approaching. She shows that, one must stay in close to minimize the affects of a conceivably flying hoof. She shows them that it is possible to move safely around the animals, and that they ought to keep a hand on its rump—in physical contact with a **calm horse,** before attempting to walk behind it. The informed teacher states, "A horse is just as capable of biting or striking from its front side, as it is from its rear. Use the same cautions on all sides."

It is okay for her to make the statement: "Beware of working around a horse, when another animal is in close proximity. This is where most horses kick, not aiming to get the person who is next to them, but striking out against the presence of another rival." Continuing to elaborate, she can include, "Most horses are governed by a pecking order; some will strive to enforce it by kicking and biting or defending themselves, as they feel threatened." By so stating the truth, she as just isolated the problem of acting out as something that all horses can do, and it is possible for an alert and aware person to be safe around them.   .

"Now it is your turn to do it safely," says the trainer, as she watches and gives critic to the students who demonstrate an understanding of these principles. As they come to discover and develop some skills in these matters they will feel a sense of power when around the animals; they will see themselves as safe, alert, and knowledgeable. The learning mind will now watch others in their intimacy with horses in effort to pick up more efficient ways of performing these new lessons. Now, all the concerned teacher needs to say when she views a potentially dangerous situation is, "Are you being safe?" If her student needs a reminder or a refresher, the teacher again demonstrates until she is sure that the child understands.

Evaluating any situation with a horse and discovering ways to execute safely will now be on the mind of the student, instead of being governed by fear, which prevents many interactions.

*   *   *

Common Sense: *Fear's apprehension allows mostly for the presumption of ways to get hurt.*

PART 3:

WHAT WILL I TEACH

CHAPTER 11:

INSPIRING THRU BOMB PROOF CHARACTER TRAITS

"**A** frog can never teach his tadpoles how to be butterflies, because it is beyond him to know how. However, he could teach them how to be the best frogs in the pond ...

Common Sense: **Despite his best intentions, one can only teach what he knows or understands."**

To comprehend these statements, consider this recap of a teacher's efforts as told in the following lesson:

Common Sense Lesson: Can a Chicken Teach a Duck to Swim

"They dance so beautiful don't they, mommy?" she gazed mesmerized as the images on the TV screen dazzled her dream filled eyes with enchanting movements. There to her astound were dancers toned and polished with years of sacrifice and experience coming alive in the eyes and mind of this five-year-old.

"Yes they do ... just like you and your beautiful mother," she remarked sarcastically; although not without truth, for she was indeed a gorgeous figure of a woman, in her early thirties, she was a real knock-out in any setting. She, as a form of playing with her third daughter Lara, often danced around the living room to engage her fifth child into confidence building interaction.

"Teach me to dance just like them," replied the eager youth.

In her daughter's eyes, mother was as beautiful and graceful as the dancers on the television; she could twirl and bow with an elegance. Dancing with mom was one of her daughter's favorite pastimes. Lara was getting old enough to realize her own skills were lacking. Dana displayed no particular talent in dancing, but to her little girl, her play-dancing never failed to conjure up the feelings of admiration. Soon her daughter would also notice Mom's dancing deficiencies.

"Would you like to take dance lessons?" Mother replied. For sometime now, she had witnessed the desire in her daughter to perform. In preparation to assist this child, she previously had checked information out about dance classes for young girls. She had been trying to find an opportunity to present this gift to her daughter. She was an engaged parent that wanted to see her children increase their potentials; this time it meant going elsewhere to enlist the abilities and skills of others. "You will have to practice every day," she informed. In her mind, she knew those were wasted words; practicing is what her daughter wanted most.

"Yes I do. When do I start?" the willing student replied while leaping for joy.

Twelve years latter, it was a glorious day for me as I sat next to my wife. We watched the Canyon View High School's re-enactment of the musical "Grease." Lara had landed the leading role of Sandy, and was doing a great job singing and dancing before the audience. It made a Dad's heart swell.

She had turned into a talented young woman, a beautiful blonde, full of self-esteem and very popular in her school. Lara also was a Varsity Cheerleader. In addition, not only did she have dancing and singing abilities, she also had a scholar's mind. Her priorities remained conservative as she later gave up glittering stardom to further pursue and obtain a Leadership Scholarship at Southern Utah University.

Throughout the years, Dana had supported and helped all her children. She gave generously of her coveted free-time to see that each one had the same opportunity to support their desires to expand and improve themselves. She had given them each a choice of a musical instrument, sports, or dancing to help them develop and experiment with their adolescent creative desires. Each time, she demanded that if they decided to start one, then they would be expected to stay at it for a year. They must give an honest effort to learn in return for what help and support they would need. There were occasions when one of the children wanted to quit before their year commitment, and she would remind them of their agreement and require them to honor their part. She never demanded excellence just that they practice and work at improving. She expanded her role of a Nurturing Parent by showing support and also expecting that Lara and her other children grow as individuals.

I, on the other hand, rarely had the time or the opportunity to attend and support physically many of my children's activities. I did attend at special occasions, but most of my involvement was in the Scouting Program for eight years, with my sons.

It was not as though I was totally un-involved as a father, for in their growing up, I required my children to help out at the farm. I was under the dilution that the harder one worked the more character and beneficial opportunities one obtained. On the farm they learned good work ethics, and how to put in an honest hard productive day. The nature of the daily work offered many opportunities with dilemmas. They were years ahead in their maturity when compared to other kids, in their abilities to problem solve. I also believed in them earning a fair wage for their many hours of labor; they were taught how to save half of what they got. I could have been better as a father in my additional support of their non-farm interests. I was under the fantasy that time spent working would latter turn into family assets. Reality was that as a crop would fail or succeed only to be rendered valueless in a supply and demand market, I was obligated to continue operating for years out of the demanding obligation to my farming and ranching profession only to be able to pay the bills. Such frivolities as spending non-production time with my children, why that I could seldom squeeze it in.

Today was different. I stopped my personal agenda to support my daughter.

That day, in the High School Auditorium, I was grateful for many things. I was proud of my daughter; she had taken a desire, set goals to obtain it, then worked hard and fulfilled her dream. Now, she was benefiting in the rewards. She had truly learned to "swim" as a graceful duck moving effortlessly on a dawn lit pond. I was proud of my wife, whom with little ability to dance, "*she as a chicken*," had managed to see that her daughter had been taught how to "*swim.*" I was also grateful that God, in his wisdom, had designed creation so that it takes both a male and female to produce offspring. I was thankful that He endorses marriage: a unity that provides an opportunity for children to receive a balance of instruction and parenting from two parents working together to stretch and to nurture the developing minds of their children.

Can a chicken teach a duck to swim? No! When it comes the point of actually showing by example, forget it. Chickens certainly don't swim. It's an ugly sight as they flap and flounder in the water, making progress only by the shear panic motion of their flightless wings as they lift themselves up and down in an effort to fly—their legs ever running but never able to leave the water's grasp. Some things just weren't meant to be.

As a hen cackles her announcements to the world of her newly laid egg, so can a teacher of youth encourage and announce the benefits for her ducklings, to learn to swim. She can see that they have opportunity to be trained. She can cluck for her ducklings to follow as she leads them to the pond where a wise master duck can go over lessons of swimming. She can stand on the shore and encourage and support. She can participate in their enthusiasm, voice her concern over their difficulties, and praise them for positive advances. She can offer the support, which they need. With her involvement, she enhances their opportunity to swim.

Common Sense: **Become the one who influences others to succeed. While it is great to be able to do all things, it is not necessary. Use the ability of other to help you. If you need help as a teacher, go out and get it.**

Keep in mind: It is not a necessary requirement for parents to do all the teaching of their children by themselves. Getting others to help with teaching responsibly is commonly used, as in the case of utilizing the school systems. At school is where parents entrust others to help them in teaching advanced lessons to their children. The same is with a boss who hires a specialist to teach a skill he himself doesn't possess or hasn't the time nor opportunity to offer instructions to his charges. This is a very effective method, as long as the **primary responsible educator** still makes checkups on the progress of his charges by asking questions and clarifying any foreign values they may pick up.

Parents, who continue to show interest in the progress of their charges, even though others are doing the actual instructing of the lessons, will teach that their pupils are important and not being shuffled away because of mere convenience. Their students are being referred to a more knowledgeable instructor to supple-ment their learning progression.

{Notice the phrase "**primary responsible educator.**" When a student leaves the classroom of a paid educator, that instructor's responsibility to impart knowledge ceases— the parent's never does. The parent still has the primary responsibility to teach his children; he never is relieved of this.}

Can an educator teach a skill he doesn't posses? *You betcha!* He can know that he is lacking in understanding of the subject, but still can guide his students towards obtaining the proper knowledge. He can encourage, support, and seek out master teachers who do have the knowledge and the ability, while he remains involved enough to praise for positive advances. He can continue to oversee his charges progress and be there for their concerns.

Teachers, to be effective we don't have to be able to do everything, but we do have to know how to assist our charges into obtaining empowering objectives. Our pupils will see our love, interest, and assistance in helping them meet their goals ... while we show that we care.

Common Sense: **When endeavoring to teach, our role is to first train ourselves; we enhance our characters and our abilities, and then offer that guidance to others.**

The term, **"Don't wait ... create,"** also applies towards self improvement. What good does it do us to wait for things to miraculously improve, or for others to help us, when we have not given our best efforts? We get nowhere in problem solving if we do not go into the steps of actually doing the work and making things happen. Do not wait around for **wisdom** to fall upon you as the rain from heaven which unless caught and stored properly is only a source of temporary relief. Actively look for ways to develop your abilities. In fact, diligently seek to create opportunities for that improvement. Using work and study, gather the waters of knowledge and understanding into wells and reservoirs to be later drawn upon.
When we turn down an opportunity to practice, from the stand point of thinking that it offers no chance for added growth, we are presuming that we posses a mastery in-which we can not improve. ... *Have we reached such a plateau in our lives?*
Would that we still be as children having an unfulfilled capacity of knowledge and improvement. During our formative years this was our inquisitive self-centered quest. Even as adults, we still have the individual obligation to work towards self-improvement and **refinement.** The benefits from progression will be ours much faster, when we are actively creating opportunities to improve instead of complacently waiting for them to find us. As a bonus, our competence increases, and so does our useable resources to help others.

Teach Values and Character Traits

A **Value** is: something of quality that is desirable. It is also an attribute that we esteem worthy enough to develop. It may be necessary to practice and struggle many times as we undertake to incorporate any esteemed value. When a value is learned then reviewed over and over again, it becomes ingrained into our character. A value, through usage, becomes an unconscious response; a positive Character Trait.

Character Traits are the distinguishing qualities we posses. They define us as individuals. They can be either of a positive, or of a negative nature. Negative traits lessen our value as individuals; they demean us and others. Positive character traits increase and build up our worth to ourselves and to others.

*   *   *

Common Horse Sense: A Bomb Proof Horse

Every person, who has ever looked for that special horse with whom can be entrusted the inconsistencies of children, will recognize the phrase, "**Bomb Proof.**" This is the old mount that has nothing to prove to the world. He has had enough experience that he is totally predicable, and so it is presumed that he will not under any circumstances act out in fear or anger. This old gentleman will remain easy going, no matter who is riding him; he has proven himself to possess character traits of value.

*   *   *

A teacher attempts to instill into his pupils worthy values as foundations for their characters which they may develop into worthwhile "Character Traits." He would that they didn't depart from these traits, that they become dependable, develop integrity, and prove their earned trust just like that old bomb proof horse. Some of the values that lead to bomb proof character traits can be more easily understood as you read these common sense trainings, I have experienced in my life.

Common Sense Lesson: Having the Faith to Pray

Having been taught of my mother and father to have faith in a God, I, likewise, taught my own children the same. On one occasion, my two sons, ages eleven and nine went with me to take a load of hogs up north, in order, to try to establish a market in Logan. It was a seven hundred mile round trip. It was before cell phones in Southern Utah, so when I pulled off the freeway to catch up on a much needed nap, we were pretty much on our own. It was 2:00a.m. We found ourselves stranded on a dark deserted ranch turnoff when our borrowed truck wouldn't restart. I conveyed to my young sons our predicament. They immediately had the answer, "We should say a prayer and ask for God to help us get the truck started."

The grave situation had me thinking, "I needed to get outside and look under the hood and try to figure out why this previously running truck wasn't starting. Right now was not the right timing to ask for God's help. How could I ask for help with a problem I hadn't yet figured out? I certainly wasn't in the mood to comfort two little boys by going along with their whims of pure trusting faith without doing what I could for myself first. I was confident that most likely I could solve my dilemma on my own."

My thoughts were centered around, "*I am going to do better than just exhibiting a child's plea for assistance. This is going to be such a great teaching opportunity for me to show my sons, how to solve their problems.*" I will teach them: "*Do what you can first; if you are still lacking in resources and abilities, only then should you ask for God's help. I would teach: When asking it is even better if you can be specific. State the exact problem and the reasons that you need help. Don't just blindly cry a general plea for assistance. Yes, this dilemma would turn out OK. I would properly teach my two sons about prayer.*" Yet, as I shut the cab door, I offer those boys only my wisdom filled reply, "God only helps those who help themselves."

Upon examination, I concluded as my fears were confirmed, "*This truck had a dead battery.*" I had hoped for something easy like corrosively dirty terminals. So before anything else, I first performed a road-side pocketknife surgery. I twisted off the battery clamps, scraped them clean, and pounded them back on. It was a simple, past proven, technique to again establish a connection on a capable, but neglected, battery. No avail, this battery was still dead. We were indeed in trouble. No one was going to stop way out here in the dark. I was out of things to do within my ability, so now it was time to show the boys how to pray. We will probably be spending hours just waiting for it to become light enough, after which, I was going to have to hike back to the freeway and try to flag someone down in the morning for a jump. We were not easily going to be on our way.

Just as I was going to get back in the truck to teach my lesson of when it is proper to pray, I saw up the road, about three hundred yards, a pickup pull from out of nowhere and stop. Realizing that this might be my only chance for assistance until morning, I sprinted off to ask for help. I had to hurry before it left. By the time I got there, the driver had turned off his lights —my guess to also catch a nap. I rapped on the window from out of the darkness.

"Could you help me and give a jump? My truck won't start."

"Where are you? I don't even see an outfit," came a reply from within the dark cab.

"Down the road a little, you can't see my truck; the battery is dead." Soon with his assistance, the problem truck was jumped and he drove off, apparently not sleepy anymore.

I was definitely, now, going to further teach my boys the lesson of doing all you can to help yourselves. "Yes sirree," I would say, "Most things can be solved without bothering God." What a great lesson I would be able to show them; I had done it all myself, and requesting God's help, this time, hadn't been needed. ... I felt like a Man!

As I climbed into the truck, I said, "See all I had to do was to find the problem, then run and ask that guy for a jump.

"Dad, that guy came there because we said a prayer; we prayed for help without you, as soon as you left to go outside," my innocent and faithful teachers informed.

I was taken back. "Thanks for praying," was the only reply that I could say. I was stuck on this thought; *"I was wrong, and they in their childlike faith had been right. God had answered their prayer." Who was I anyway for actually thinking I had done anything on my own?*

As I develop more wisdom, I realize that everyone should be able to cling to a self-sustaining power. In order to have hope, we must have faith in something greater than ourselves. It defines us as having the potential to improve, and the humility to be teachable.

·

Having faith does enable a person to believe that there is always a loving Father out there who cares about them and is willing to help. With that assurance, one may add the personal discipline to go out and do whatever is necessary to become better than before. We are not alone. I haven't failed since to give God the credit. And I make more effort to teach my children of God's love for them. I also acknowledge to them that it is not a weakness to identify where help might come from, and always is God a source. As a teacher, edify your children about God's Love. He will be a comfort and will help them throughout their lives.

Common Sense Lesson: Exhibit Respect

Destined to spend nearly all of the waking day alone, just after her honey-moon, while stuck forty miles from the nearest oiled road, I sentenced my previously suburban sweet heart with hours of boredom living on a desert homestead north of Delta, Utah. What a shock! It didn't take long for her to realize that as a farmer I wasn't going to spend the hours on end with her as she had experienced when we dated. She needed something to share her time with. So we got a baby. Well almost, what we got was a puppy to keep her company. She named her new companion Phil, after the town of Fillmore, through which we traveled bi-monthly. He grew up thinking he was a kid; Dana seemed to credit him with humanlike attributes. She now wasn't so lonely spending much time with her kid, Phil.

Phil was a good timing happy Australian Shepherd. Not a mean bone in his body. He loved doing doggy things: playing fetch, riding in the back of his pickup truck, and playing catch with his ball. He would engage in direct conversation by listening and responding with his facial expressions to the point it seemed that he understood the very essence of what was being said. But even with her new buddy, the solitude had its effect on Dana. We had to move closer to town in order to keep her sanity. I obtained a job at a dairy, she and I moved closer to neighbors; our son, Phil came cheerfully along to his new home.

Four months after the move, I showed up with a kitten, Dana despised it. She had no use for a "kiss-up cat" and would get jealous as I would hold Pussy on my lap and stroke the feline in rhythm to her content purring. Being young, I thought it was amusing to provoke my wife's jealousy, and so would purposely antagonize her with my showing of affection to the cat.

Phil on the other hand, liked the new addition; he was elated. To him was like being given a new toy. Answering to some doggish instinct, he would hold her down, and place his mouth completely over her head, and poor Pussy just had to bare it. {Not much to do otherwise when a body nine times your weight decides that it is going to play with you.} Phil wasn't intentionally trying to hurt her. … He was just playing. Twice, Dana despite her abhorring of the cat was moved with compassion and saved the poor little creature when Phil got to playing too rough with his Pussy.

Not long after the first mauling, Phil was again playing with his recently healed cat toy. This day, what Dana could see, through the window, was her dog playing ball. He was tossing it up into the air and running to catch it, only to repeat this over and over again. A strange sound was coming from the outside; soon it evolved into the moans of the dying. That crazy dog wasn't playing catch with his ball, after all. He was using poor Pussy!

That evening, I came home to a rescued kitten hunkered in the corner; she had been drenched wet from saliva, and was now limp and mauled to a frazzle. She had received no nurturing for her ailments, only a slight humanitarian rescue from her tormentor, and then abandoned.

As for the dog, it was too late to punish the scoundrel; he wouldn't have understood. The only good that could have become of it would've been to make me feel better. Instead, I devised a plan to teach Phil to respect cats: It consisted of catching a wild cat and tricking it into teaching Phil the much-needed lesson on treating others with respect. I was sure that it would successfully impress upon this dog that indeed cats are a force to be reckoned with. In my mind, if Phil learned to respect any cat, then he would also learn to respect Pussy. He would learn to play nice, or leave her alone.

Scratching out a living, where I worked, were a number of feral cats. They were seen daily hunting mice in the haystacks, so I took some tuna and a couple of gunny sacks with me the next day. With patience and tasty tuna I was able to entice a hungry cat close enough to catch it. It wasn't as wild as I thought. It soon emptied the can. I carried the now docile, soon to be master teacher of respect, back home in my arms.

"Ok, let the dog in," I signaled to my wife, as I sat on the edge of the couch holding the black cat by its middle in my outstretched hands. I had decided to let the disrespectful dog and his soon to be Sensei do battle in the house. Who wants to run the risk on the cat quickly leaping to freedom up a tree, or over the fence, and ruin a chance for good entertainment and a much needed lesson? "Boy this is going to be great," I was priming my wife to excite her. She and I were going to see a show; we were going to watch a dog get what he deserves by the paws of a feral cat.

Phil came in and right away goes over to the neat game, "Looks as if we are going to play with a new cat." I could see it in his eyes as I read his body language. He said, "Can I play too?"

Together, nose to nose, I let the black cat and Phil touch; I was still holding the feline in my outstretch grasp. The cat was indifferent; I guess having one's belly full of tuna does that. Phil was still showing excitement. He continued giving the expectant impression, "Sure looks fun. What do you want me to do?" He looked for guidance to signal his next move. His countenance added, "Go ahead! Let's get started in with this new game of yours; after all, you're the one who's holding the cat." Long he stood focused in anticipation, still wagging his tail. But beyond that nothing was happening, the cat didn't hiss, or act mean, and it certainly didn't command any respect. Their touching of the noses was nothing like the touch of the gloves that a referee asks for while he explains the rules just before a boxing match, these two weren't going to start sparing on their owns. I needed to escalate the situation or they could wind up being best friends.

So I barked loudly as they still touched noses, **"WOOF!"**

Game on ...

I still can't believe what happen next, the black cat, like a limber gymnast, twisted inside my clutches and started climbing up my face. She had spooked and escalated into flight mode. Her forepaws embedded into my upper checks, her lower claws into my under jaw. So fast did all this happen, I had not time to react. The movements of the cat sent the dog into action, he shifted in closer, poised tense, waiting for it to dare to move again.

"If that cat makes another move and the dog joins in, I am going to get a whooping," I thought, "I must do something quick."

I tightened my grip and tried to remove her from her perch. **"WRONG MOVE,"** shot through my face, as she responded by further sinking her claws. The harder I pulled her out and away, the further her sharp razors imbedded in. The cat looked frantic side to side knowing that the dog was still there in her face, and also realizing she was stuck because she couldn't with-draw her own claws from their soft fleshy purchase. She knew for all indications, she was going to get a whooping. Her reaction, grab in deeper.

"D...A...N...A!" I yelled in attempt to awake her from spectator's horror and into action. She had observed the goings on and therefore had moved back in awe, not wanting to also get involved in this mess.

"First grab the dog's collar, drag him to the door and kick him outside," I barked. This done, she reluctantly returned.

"I need you to help me get these claws unstuck." I ordered.

"You just keep a hold of that cat; don't let him get me!" she commanded back."

As if I could do anything else but?

At my instructions she picked each claw independently out of my flesh; I was occupied holding the cat still around her mid section, in order to keep her from trying to spring away and tearing my face further in the process. Dana had to press in the middle on the back of each paw, one at a time, to obtain a forced retraction. Having freed the cat's paws out of my face, she then refused to take it for fear of her own safety. So I, my face smarting like the dickens and oozing with blood from multiple puncher wounds, was left to deposit the feline outside. I threw it outside never to be seen from again.

As for "Poor Pussy," somehow Phil must have learned to leave cats alone, for little cat was never mauled again. I guess I must have been a pretty good teacher, huh? One thing was for sure, there was one dog that learned respect for cats that evening … **me**.

* * * Side note:* * * **When Phil was dragged outside, he came right over to the window and finished watching the proceedings. I still remember the look on that dog's face, "Learning to respect cats is such fun; cats make great playmates."**

Respect is treating another as you would want to be treated yourself. It is the reverence one gives another person or thing as he leaves it alone and doesn't molest it, belittle it, or try to cause a change to it solely for his own purpose or gain. It is not a value based on causing another's avoidance, as in their reaction to a fear. It is a value based on having an honor and admiration of an object. Showing respect is: Granting the same decency that we would want to be given ourselves.

So often I have heard from non-conforming youths, who were acting from a gang mentality, the phrase: *"You need to show me some respect!"* Their thinking on the subject is not entirely correct, because in order to get the esteem that one expects, it is up to them to earn the other's honor and admiration by personally performing acts of quality and value. Obtaining another's respect should not be confused with earning of another's fear thru intimidation. In order to obtain respect, a requestor is obliged to act accordingly, it cannot be commanded; the burden is on them.

We should give a reverence freely to others. We should not expect others to show it toward us until we have earned it. Whenever others commit acts, of which we can not condone, we can abhor the act, but still we should value the individual. Aren't we are all the creations of God?

Common Sense Lesson:

I Offered Them an Increase in Self Esteem

While I was working as a wilderness guide, over the years the company's policy was revised. Now, it was a requirement to get the kid's permission. I must obtain their supporting vote-of-approval in order to do an especially demanding hike. In order to realize just how hard that was: imagine a group of five to nine out-of-control kids all thrown together with their inabilities, the average group consisted of some who haven't as yet refined any form of personal sacrifice, and some who were individually lacking in personal values, all were suffering from a general lack of self esteem caused by having been tiptoed around by parents whom were too afraid to confront their own fear that their behavioral deficient children would dislike them or would react in an eruption of inappropriate conduct since their kids hadn't been held to any standard of excellence; it was of these kids from which I was asking unanimous permission to take them into a week of abnormal hardship and challenge. {*Phew, what a sentence!*}

I'll say that again, but easier to repeat and understand.

"Think how hard it was to ask a group of reluctant losers to become winners?"

Despite these obstacles, as an instructor for a wilderness therapeutic company, I had an undisputed amount of successes. My groups were very often willing to push themselves in attempt to beat previous record setting times.

How can you get a person who has a recent history of very rarely following through with a goal, or of hardly ever personally committing to do more work, to do just that? ... *The Answer:* They need to be awakened to the powers of having self esteem.

I developed a plan to give these reluctant kids, an opportunity to do a "Three Peak Hike Challenge", so that they might experience a rise in their individual regard by traveling forty-plus miles with full packs in as little as time possible. Not a terribly hard task, but throw into the same week that they still had to do all their Self-Awareness Phase Work as normal. In-fact for the right to do this Three Peak Week, they had to do an above normal amount of phase work. Time would be of the essence, so no extra could be had. Therefore, sleep would be reduced to a scanty minimum. In addition to the mileage, the hike also involved scaling three different mountain peaks, ranging from 8200 feet to 9700 feet. I developed, in order to awaken the kids into agreeing to do the hike, the art of coercion to a refined level. Once I had one or two willing students, they would do most of the convincing work involving the reluctant ones for me. They talked and encouraged each other into challenging themselves.

"How was it pulled-off again and again?"

I used the following methods to transform the losers into winners: {**Highlighted are a few of the key words to help you understand the process.**}

To start off, while using the **Loving Father Approach** to teaching, I would get a general feeling for the group's desire to challenge themselves. This would then govern my next moves.

If it was a **fear**, that was holding them back; I would be open and truthful in my answers to educate and let them in on what to expect during their challenge. Most fear goes away when confronted with knowledge of how it may be beaten. I would be sure to display self-confidence in my own abilities, and display my faith that the kids had more ability than they gave themselves credit for.

If, as a whole, the group's failure to perform was out of **Laziness,** it was met with the knowledge that if they refused to step up to the challenge willingly, then they would be compelled to do almost the same efforts without any of the rewards. {**Of coarse with this threatening tyrant style of forcing, I stimulated very few into action. It mostly helped to solidify their resistance.**} They were used to authority figures giving open ended threats that were never backed up.

I did eventually sway them by remaining firm in my powers of dictatorship. I waited until after the students completed a small, yet successful, compelled hike. They were still thinking that they would never willing consent to a self-inflicted major trek. Then, I could talk plainly using **praise** and **compliments**; letting them know that they also had the ability to do an even larger compelled hike. I pointed out to them: To remain reluctant on a large hike will take more effort, on their parts, than if they were to do it submissively while trying to enjoy the moment. So, why not go along willingly and receive an offered incentive?

*"Yes, this was indirect use of a **bribe**!"* **Presenting a bribe that may be obtained, as a substitute for a punishment which must be endured. It does work.**

I, with confidence and concern for their well beings, pointed out to them that it became easier, **even possibly fun**, when they set a goal to raise their own potentials, instead of waiting to be forced.

I pointed out the hardships that would be experienced and **helped them see that by pains they grow**. I also educated them as to what **gains** physically and emotionally that would be theirs, after they endured the hike. They were, in turn, quick to realize the increase of **respect** which they thought others would give them as their families, caregivers, and friends heard of their accomplishments.

Always, I looked for and **created opportunities** to build their characters. The company offered a food **reward** for a Three Peak Week, but I expanded this offer to help them realize a more lasting **gratification**: *Knowledge that they had the ability to rise and overcome a challenge.* I so wanted all my students to develop an increase in their **self confidence**. The finishing of their hard week could bring to them such. They were then led to understand that if they could overcome their current great test in the Utah Desert, then they could also learn set goals and rise up to meet any challenges which they might face at home or in the future. This **knowledge** led to an increasing of **self esteem**. The self esteem gave them a boost of **power,** which enhanced their desires for **freedom** thru healthy, positive, and challenging means. All was preformed with the correct **timing,** from the stand point of always helping the students increase their potentials, using **compassion** when needed and showing a genuine concern for them instead of compelling them into fulfilling my selfish agenda. They pushed themselves thinking it was their choice.

My students were able to experience and get a taste of this principle:

In order to obtain self-esteem and feel good about myself, I must learn to respect and be proud about who I am and what I can do. Self esteem is more than someone telling you how good you are, it is the admiration you hold for yourself, as you look in your heart and examine your inter-soul.

If it is your belief, you can succeed.

Common Sense: **Teach to your students: Winners aren't content to coast. They will not be satisfied to glide along with the ease of gravity. Let others be content to coast when the going gets easy. A winner uses a period of ease to enhance his speed so that he is still being challenged.**

So often, many individuals who are full of self-esteem, yet still inexperienced, will feel they have the muscle to charge up a hill in order to get more quickly to the top. They upon reaching a false zenith will be out of energy as they view that more additional effort is needed. They are the very ones that will want to quit when things suddenly turn out harder than they expected. They lack the wisdom to conserve some strength in case there is more climbing beyond their anticipated horizon. They may luck out and sometimes finished first, but they are not the definitive winners.

In the mind of the experienced winner is the prayer, as they find themselves lacking, **"God give me strength to slow down just long enough to catch my breath; that I will not just coast, and when I can see the end, may I still have the reserve to push myself further if need be. May I not be content until I have given my all, and then added, even more."**

A winner will not quit or burn out before they reach the finish. If you are truthful, you will recognize that there is always additional room for improvement, and your high level of self esteem will demands that a job is done right. That's a commendable character trait. But it's only a predecessor to the champion who never quits improving. A winner is driven by a passion to excel, and as he does he finishes first. Yet, it's the champion who tries to better his last performance.

Common Sense Lesson: **Self Confidence** to Tackle Any Challenge.
"There isn't any type of problem that you should be afraid to fix. Look at it, analyze it, and you can make it work. Perhaps you may run out of ideas, or you might have to stop half-way thru and go out and obtain more skill and knowledge; you may even have to ask for advice and assistance, but in the end if you apply yourself you can solve any problem." **Mervin Preston**

These words have always had a favorite place in my heart. They were the most important lesson he taught me. I was just eighteen, and was started on a career as a farmer and stockman. My Uncle Merv was my mentor. In a world of the early seventies, solid state was just coming available; many electronics were still open boards with tubes and transistors. The computer had not been introduced publicly. Car manufactures had just started using parts with slightly more sophistication than mechanical switches, levers, open air carburetors and points. My uncle was a wiz at being able to fix anything by using his common sense; he wasn't afraid to take anything apart or to tackle any challenge. I, being an impressionable youth could see the power that he possessed. I felt he was in control of his destiny, and I wanted to be like him. It was inspiring to be around him, for his positive attitude was contagious as he seemed to always go out of his way to energize others. He spent over two years helping me develop my own talents and traits. I have tried all my life to emulate his strong character.

Teach your children the same way. They will learn most quickly if you, as their mentor, adopt influential values into your character. They can more easily envision in themselves possible traits as they witness them in you. We all have someone that we know who just seems so confident and able, all the time. It isn't that these confident people never come up short or that they haven't experienced a lack of success; they just have learned to keep on trying until they get things right. They have dismissed the damning affects of personal doubt which steal away opportunity. They don't let their failures and disappointments bring them down. Show your charges your self confidence that they may develop it for themselves.

Common Sense: **About Money**

> You have heard, **"Money can not buy happiness."**
> Now hear that, **"Without money you can't buy a thing."**

It is a fact of life, once we leave the nurturing care of others, we must provide for our own needs. Everything we wish to possess must to be traded for, grown, stolen, or purchased with an exchange of time and effort. Money is the standard that represents the symbol of time and of its worth to others. As the desire or usefulness of any product expands its worth to others, the ability to exchange it for more benefits also increases; we can ask for more money. **To take responsibility for our wants, we must either demand from others, or exchange for something else of value.**

Common Sense Lesson: Thriftiness: In order to have the luxury to spend later, learn to save now.
A good rule of thumb to live by is: save 10% of your gross monthly earning in an interest earning investment. This sum is to be managed, but not spent, until your retirement. With the average yearly interest earnings of a mutual fund bringing around 10% yearly you could easily built up a good nest egg.

This principle is hard to teach to a youth, for he requires money to purchase the items he wants at the present. And now, that he finally landed a job, the furthest thing from a young adult's mind is saving for retirement. "My lands, the kid just started working and now you are going to ask him to think about stopping?

It may be a good thing if you could get junior to spend a little time with Grandpa; have the young-un asked him how quickly the years go by. Have the kid ask the old duffer how big-a-pile he wished he'd of saved and rat holed in his early earning years. Have him tell the young spender, what things to squander money on. Let the wise and experienced share his knowledge of things which increase in value. Go ahead; it will make the old geezer happy that his grandkid thought enough to ask for his advice. Who knows; the old timer may even still have a few things he could teach you, as well.

Teach your child the potential of earning compound interest and the wisdom of starting early. Let's say an outgoing eighteen-year-old lands a job and starts making $10.50 per hour. He wisely starts putting ten percent of his gross, which is $168.00 {one hundred and sixty-eight dollars} a month into a tax deferred IRA as soon as he receives his first paycheck. Then over the years as his salary increases he finds himself making, at age thirty, $15.00 per hour. He now adds an additional $72.00 for a new total now of two hundred and forty dollars a month into his IRA. For ease of figuring assume this is the wage always earned. He keeps this saving up until he retires at age sixty-five. With an average yearly interest earned of 10%, he would now have a total of over $2,100,000 dollars built up in his IRA. Not a small some of money for such a sacrifice.

On the other hand, if a thirty-year-old with no other savings, started putting ten percent of his gross monthly income, $240 {two hundred and forty dollars} it's the same amount his more thrifty counter-part is also putting in. If he also puts it into the same type of account, he would only have at age sixty five, $880,000 dollars. This is less than half as much as the earlier and wiser saver would have accumulated. By choosing to spend all his income instead of saving for the first twelve years, this less frugal thirty-year-old only increased his purchasing ability, from age eighteen to thirty, by $24,000 dollars total. By the age of sixty-five, his failure to save early would net him a loss of interest earning potential that would be close to $1,200,000. A potential million dollar loss for the later saver; $10,500 dollars a month less retirement income for the rest of his life!

If the younger saver left his nest egg in an IRA or a 401K account which continued to earn an average of 10% annually, and he only used the earned interest at his retirement, he could enjoy over $18,000 a month to pay taxes and live on. Now which is best, to put off saving until later and only have a potential $8,000 a month. Or use willpower, scrimp a little, and force oneself to save early, and then have the possibility to have $18,000 a month? Although now, having $8,000 monthly does seems like a desirable income, it will only be a modest amount in thirty years. You help the youth to figure this out!

"Mutual funds have had for the last twenty years an average annual increase of 10%, despite the occasional years of economic depression. Account balances will vary greatly according to the actual interest earned. All things considered, if invested the same way, the earlier saver would have at his disposal much more than what his later counterpart will have accrued."

A common disease that has been allowed to enter into the minds of many people in these last two generations is the unbridled desires of accumulation. We have become a throw away society; we purposely purchase items that are disposable in the justification that they are cheap, and we can always get another. No longer do we subject ourselves to repair and mend; it is so easy just to buy {charge against our futures} a new one. We have lost much of the thrifty mentality of our forefathers who lived in an era before supermarkets. They survived just fine before the ease of internet ordering. Being thrifty is using what we have, not wasting, and keeping our items in repair so they'll last longer. It is saving for a rainy day and guarding against our passions to have something that we have not yet paid for.

Stay out of debt.

Being in debt is the reverse of accruing interest. It is the other guy earning the gains and you getting the huge bills that seem to never go away, get tired, or ever take a break; they just keep on coming month after month. Avoid going into debt at great cost. Learn to save for your commodity needs instead of charging them.

We think we're being so thrifty and frugal every month by scrimping together enough money to pay a minimum payment, plus a-little extra to knock down the principle on credit card debt. Yet by the fact that we purchased additional items on a card which is carrying an unpaid balance, we also agree to pay 3.9 to 19.9 percent and beyond, extra, depending on our past credit history, for any "need to have now" new purchases. We trade for the privilege of having the possessions now, our agreeing to make someone else richer. No wonder we keep getting offers for new credit cards in the mail; others want to get their hands on our money and put us in financial bondage to them. Now you go and figure that one out. Kind of doesn't make sense does it?

Learn to be frugal and save for your purchases. That way you can start paying without credit for your items. By using cash or a debit card, and never using a charge card which you can not pay off the entire balance each month, you will now have more money to pay down your other cursed existing balances, instead of giving it away in form of finance charges. You will have available more real money to be used in case of an emergency, like the one that started you into the mess of promising tomorrow's, not even obtained, money ...today. Eventually you'll be able to pay off one debt then consolidate your now increased available money and increase the payments to your other depts. Keep this up until you are consumer debt free and can put the whole amount of your previous payments into an interest bearing account to be used when you need it. In the meantime, let it sprout, grow, and get bigger. Teach your children, while they're still young, not to be slaves who make others richer. Teach them to use self control and do not purchase until they have the cash to spend.

A house bought on a thirty year mortgage will end up costing you two to three times more than if you bought it for cash Pay back your house as soon as possible, after your other shorter term and higher interest debts. Yes, going into debt to purchase a home is better than renting and never accruing anything. Remember to be smart about it. Don't place yourself in bondage for a home that is beyond your earning power, should the economy sour in the future. Pay off your less extravagant home early. A quicker fifteen-year mortgage will save you tens to hundreds of thousands of dollars in interest, and put you in position to start enjoying your money many years sooner, instead of giving it away to someone else.

Common Sense lesson: The Wisdom of Discernment

Our whole life we constantly have to make choices based on what is the most logical or efficient option before us. It takes a developed skill to step back and look at the different number of choices that are possible. Discernment is to be combined with wisdom to make that right choice based on essential needs or requirements.

As a teacher it is not our obligation to provide every want for the child, nor is it our responsibility. It is our duty to help our pupils develop the ability to discern the difference between a **want**, a **need**, and a **requirement**. Without the **wisdom** or soberness of experience, a youth is often confused as to what are truly needs, or just wants. As our abilities and situations allow, it is our privilege to assist him in gaining experience to understand the differences and be able to discern what his wisest choices may be.

Any deployment of choices is based on either trying to obtain a want or is directed at the fulfilling of a need. It can also be an attempt towards the satisfying of a requirement. With a want or a need, we still retain our freedom of choice, which is based on the level of compensation we hope to obtain —partial compliance will yield limited satisfaction. But, with a requirement {something we are compelled to do} we must meet the terms or no reparation is obtained; incomplete compliance could leave us high and dry. All choices are base on one of the three.

Let's look at the following examples:

1. John has to make the decision of whether or not to wear a coat today; it is ten degrees below zero. The following is true: John **needs** to wear a coat today because it is bitter cold and if he doesn't he will freeze. He goes through the exposure factors in his mind, in which he will be subjected to the elements. Wisdom then comes into play as he reviews his options. John still has the choice on whether or not to wear his coat; he will suffer if he chooses not to. Of course, any past familiarity from personal experiences or from his exposure to the lessons and teachings taught by others will aid him in his decision.

2. John is a fashionable guy and wishes to be part of the new style that has hit town. To remain popular he **wants** to wear the new trendy coat he saw in the shopping-mall, but it is very expensive and what money he does have should be saved for school. How important is it to purchase and wear this coat? … Should he or shouldn't he? … Is it so important to have this wish? He has a choice to make which will be governed by the priority he places most importance on: school, or being in style? The modern credit card culture has him expanding his debt load in order to do both. He could choose to postpone his obligations to pay until later. Does he choose to become a future slave to his present wants?

3. John has been invited to go to a ritzy restaurant. In order to get in the door he has to obey the posted rule; "**Coat and Tie Required; No Exceptions.**" Tonight, it is a **requirement** that he wear a coat; to make a choice against it would translate into no entrance or no service. His only choice is: "Is it important enough for him to comply with this rule in order that he may reap the benefits the restaurant may offer?" In addition he has an obligation to investigate what standard of coat the establishment deems appropriate, or again access and entrance could be withheld.

The different scenarios of John making a choice to wear a coat each had different compelling factors. He had to use logic and wisdom in making his decisions. He had choices to make based on needs, wants, and requirements. We have already discussed that a want is an emotional desire; it is a wish to be fulfilled. We learned that a need is a lack of something desirable or useful, and is often detrimental if denied. We now discover that a requirement is an essential demand based on an expected ability, or proficiency. In each case, John would have to make his choice according to his perception of what is right, as result he would then be subjected to the consequences of that decision.

OK, this time let's take a look at a more complex example of wants, needs, and requirements and how they govern our rationalization of choices. We will examine them using the act of digging a hole.

How does one dig a hole? ... By moving dirt until there is an empty spot. This can be done with your hands, or with a shovel and a wheelbarrow. For the less physically inclined, the use of machinery like a backhoe, a trackhoe, or a bulldozer can quickly make a noticeable cavity.

Any poor sap that has sweated on the end of a shovel will appreciate power equipment. The toil of labor will lead the inexperienced into believing, "*When I dig a hole, I am going to want to use some type of power equipment; it is much more efficient and so much more modern. That's the way to go.*"

"Or is it?" You must decide using insight and deductive reasoning. The nature of the task determines its requirements.

What to use when digging a hole? ... If you dig a hole in child's sand box you may want to use a backhoe or other equipment, but they are totally not appropriate; with one scoop you will destroy the whole thing.

If your goal was an Olympic sized swimming pool, and you were confined to using a shovel and wheelbarrow, good luck. Remember the Great Wall of China? It was built with a large force working for generations using hand tools and baskets. To do likewise, just be diligent and keep at it and just before you die at age ninety-five you might finish your pool, that is if you worked also on weekends and used all your holidays. If there is no rush, then good old applying one's self and sticking to the task will produce results.

Welcome back to being realistic. —With a shovel and a wheelbarrow it is possible to dig just as deep as a backhoe … it's positively a horrid amount of difficult work. As time is a limiting factor on your pool, a shovel will not meet your needs. Now-a-days a large hole would require a large force in the form of power equipment. However, if a project requires finesse while digging in a very sensitive area, then the shovel is still the tool of choice. Teach your student that they ought to stay in the realms of reality in deciding what choice to make. Each tool has its own limiting factors as to where and when it becomes the proper choice.

When digging close around a hidden a power line, or having to dig that Olympic sized pool the choices are easy to make; we don't have to use much intelligence in coming up with what's the proper pick of tools to use. A little experience does go a long ways.

But what about a harder one where the choice was not as defined? What if when deciding to dig a hole in search of a broken water pipe we chose not to use a shovel because we thought it needed a backhoe. The whole job would have only taken about three hours if we had applied ourselves with a little sweat and toil, yet we wasted days waiting for what we thought would be time efficient power equipment to show up, and then we paid through the nose, much more than the cost of having done it by hand. Here the best judgment would have been realizing that we had the muscle to do it ourselves, and we could have gotten through with the unpleasant task if only we've applied ourselves. Fortitude to keep at a task, even little-by-little, is a trait of great worth. As we gain in skill and ability to rationalize thru harder choices, we discover, even though we might have to get dirty doing a job, sometimes waiting for something or someone else to show up and do it for us —instead of just doing it ourselves, is not our best option.

What if I chose to dig a hole by hand, and then latter realized that my project turned into chiseling through soil almost as hard as solid rock? I then would have to change my thoughts and approach, for now my task requires more. Or I could still be stubborn and try to keep doing it as I started, by wasting my tomorrows because I couldn't recognize, or refused to implement the new requirements that the change in circumstances dictated?

In comparison, a lot of ineffective energy can be spent when you are driven solely by your wants. Wanting to apply for a job that requires, as a minimum, a college degree would be a waste of time if you had nothing else but your good looks and a longing to be employed. Wanting an expensive new car is lofty goal when working at a low paying job; a good used vehicle would suffice just dandy. Discernment will pick the best, in spite of wants.

A loving parent, who is not trying to self-serve in being the world's best friend or provider, will instill in a child's heart the skills and wisdom to limit their wants to what is actually required to accomplish the task. The child's potential as an individual increases when he can rationalize his options and possibilities, then combine common sense to make educated choices. Instead being governed and limited by his immature passions and perceived needs, the child should receive guidance from a respected counselor.

Most goals or tasks can be accomplished by a number of methods or approaches; some just are better than others. An employee is worth more to his employer based on his ability to recognize which methods are more effective. Managers are hired for their abilities of good judgment when making decisions. In any job, educated experience assists performance. All through life, having the wisdom of discernment will help a student save effort and grief. It produces greater rewards through increased proficiency.

Using common sense enough to start thinking of alternatives before one acts, and combining this with the wisdom of discernment are teachable traits, provided a student becomes willing to learn. As a teacher, share with your pupils your advanced knowledge when it comes to decision making. It will aid them so they won't be left on their own having to experiment in order to learn all of life's important lessons. Empower them that they may be able to discover their best choices by utilizing the lessons you have learned. The better you become at disclosing the reasoning which govern your choices, the greater you assist your pupil into developing wisdom for themselves. Help them to develop the capability to assess a situation, define what is wanted and weight that against their true needs. Their choices can be based on their more refined decisions of what are the most correct things to do, if you have taken the time to explain how you would similarly choose. Keep in mind, even with the best of training; it is still the child's choice whether or not he will use judgment. Your job as educator is to expose him to how to use deductive reasoning where he can weigh his desires against the most important true end-objective. Because of your involvement, his vision of possible options has been broadened.

Although it is possible for personal discovery to take place as one remains stubbornly set on learning from experience, or when he chooses the path of lesser pain which utilizes the lessons taught by others. Neither path will yield any awakening unless he has the ability and skill to use reasoning with discernment. Talk with your pupils; share the wisdom which compels you into action. Share why you choose to defer your selfish desires in the quest of higher objectives. Help make others' discoveries easier.

The Trait of keeping one's Personal Commitment:

A far-to-common problem I see youth of today having: is that they are not taught to keep their commitments. They lack the sincerity to live according to their beliefs. In the hold of any moment, their values can be compromised. Many lack personal integrity in their characters.   {As a teacher, how do you teach them otherwise?}

Don't take for granted when a person does keep their commitments. Let them know how much that you appreciate this valuable trait. Treat each new relationship with others as if they were accountable. And when they display a lack of responsibility, hold them to a consequence. Start, as-soon-as they are able to understand expectations. This helps them to see, if they persist in displaying unaccountability, they will be dealt with a lack of trust in the future. Acknowledge their efforts for whatever commitments they do honor, that they may recognize their increased gains whenever they use integrity to keep their obligations and promises.

Common Sense: **To best teach your charges the honoring of personal commitments, let them see this trait in you.**

The best way for a child to learn to honor their personal commitments is to expose them to role models who have shown that they can be counted on. A teaching example is: Let them see you struggling in order to keep a commitment that you have made. They see that, even though life is hard, still one is obligated to fulfill their word. With such a quality being displayed by a role model, it is only natural for the emulating youth to try and experiment with this trait, hoping he might copy it. By viewing others keep their commitments, in spite of being inconvenienced, the youth learns that keeping his can bring a piece of mind, strengthen self-worth, and compel his further actions. He will have a inner-strength he can drawn on whenever he feels his freedoms are being choked as his obligations are becoming too burdensome to bear. If you are in the position to be an influence in a youth's life, become a model of integrity. Be the positive influence in the lives of your pupils. To teach why they should keep their commitments, show them why you keep yours.

Common Sense Lesson: I Will Run.

"Awesome run. I ought-ta to run with you," I pondered for a brief moment before continuing, "Yeah, next year I will run with you!" It was out, I said it. I had finally committed.

"Great, that will be fun; I'll give you a workout schedule," remarked my son Cheston as he slowly walked around striving to cool off his tired muscles. He had just finished the Ogden Marathon "2005" with a time of 2:47.

He loved running, and had committed his free time every day to pursue this passion. In an effort to entice others to share this obsession, Cheston persuaded, in years earlier, his wife and friends into running marathons also. Previously, he had slowed his pace and ran together with his brother Daniel and a close friend, Brady. But this year he was left to run alone; seems he couldn't find any willing victims to share his running fervor.

It was at that finish line, a year before, I had stood cheering them on and also feeling left out of their comradery. In the emotion of the event, a feeble statement of, "I ought to get in shape and run with you guys next year", had been voiced. But, because I actually didn't come outright and commit, I soon let myself off the hook, by rationalizing, "*I don't have the time.*"

Things were different now, I had the time. For I had, since then, given up my previous job in exchange for a new one of only five days a week and just eleven hours a day. As result of today, where I actually audibly mouthed those fateful unshakable words, "I will", I committed myself to run with my son.

Being a true-blue procrastinator, there was no need to start preparing just now. After all, wasn't it a year away? And wouldn't it at best, even with my found free time require me to make sacrifices? In fact, I didn't start giving it a serious thought until two months later when I experienced an injury at work. I fell and smacked a knee. The injury produced a daily swelling with fluid. It caused redness and a constant pain for months. "Now, how will I run?"

Never having been one to go crying to the doctor, I decided to let God heal my knee; I was sure that just given time and prayer this would easily happen. Throughout my life I have had much faith in my ability to heal through God's help with natural means. This was just one of those occasions. I had faith in God and believed He would cause my body to strengthen and be healed; only time and prayer was needed for this to occur. Nevertheless, three months and lots of ointment later, I was still experiencing pain with every step. Yet, in my heart I knew that God would still come through.

November was soon here and I hadn't yet started preparing for my promised marathon in June. My new job was not physical, so I had sprouted a fifteen pound belly doing very little physical exercise; my injured knee was actively "milking it" for all it was worth. Still, never did I forget my words to my son, "I will run with you." It was time to quit procrastinating and start getting into shape. I must invite my injured knee and new found sedentary life style to **"cowboy up"**.

"I hath faith in thee to be healed, Lord; I do need your blessings. I need to be strengthened by you." I started every day with this prayer firmly planted in my head. At this time my injury was not preventing me from walking; only giving me aching soreness with each step. My plan of action was to increase activity, eat right, and trust that God, using time, would heal me. Slowly I increased my distances of walking. Eventually I was covering three miles very other day. As a bonus, I noticed: as I extensively warmed up my knee the pain would go away only to again return as it cooled off. I kept exercising faith.

Another month later, I built up the endurance to jog for fifteen minutes and started on a three-day-a-week running schedule my son sent me. I was feeling better about myself and was actually looking forward to my winter running, utilizing the brief daylight after work. When I was called into a position in my church that required lots of additional time commitment, no longer was I looking forward to the evening runs. There were other responsibilities now. Finding a time to run was becoming a chore. By February, the summer injury to my left knee, which for so many months had caused much pain and concern had finally healed, only to be replaced with a joint pain in both knees. Despite all, I still kept committed to my promise, and, as much as possible, to my running schedule. I was forced to tweak my runs to fit into the ever changing commitments on my time.

On February twentieth, I participated in the Salt Lake City Running Club's 15K Winter Run with Cheston. I was currently running eighteen miles a week. He had become my personal trainer, calling me every week to checkup on my progress. He convinced me that we needed to run this race together, so that I could have the experience of competition prior to our scheduled marathon. It was not to my great surprise that he didn't run with me during the race, but left me in the dust. I guess he couldn't bear to be back with "the old man." I did very respectable with my time and so decided not to give up my running goal. More importantly, I had not finished my original commitment to run a Marathon in June with him.

My training continued, March thru May; by this date I had developed runners' knee. This is where both knees constantly hurt. The only time they didn't hurt is when they were warmed up, this took at least a half mile. I was also experiencing mental anguish in finding the time in my day to run. My odd work schedule and my other commitments caused me to miss numerous critical practice runs. I was questioning myself; for in my pain, I lacked the ability to participate in any running or active games with the youth of my church without warming up for four minutes prior. Other than the actual time I was warmed up and running, anytime I walked, I was hurting at every step. … I thought running was supposed to be fun?

Finally, I had reached the point that I couldn't walk without grimacing pain. My wife encouraged me to quit, she said, "You have finished a run in February with Cheston; therefore, what is the sense in hurting yourself any longer?" The fact that I wasn't enjoying the experience didn't matter to me; I knew that the Lord had healed my previous knee injury, and I'd made a commitment to my son which must be honored; I would just have to man-up and endure the new pain.

There was strength of faith in me, because of another Father who made a commitment to his sons. "Oh Lord my God, I cried unto thee, and thou hast healed me,"…"Thy faith hath made thee whole." {see: Psalm: 30: 2; St. Matt: 9: 22} "But they that wait upon the Lord shall renew their strength; they shall mount with wings as eagles; they shall run, and not be weary; and they shall walk, and not faint." {Isaiah: 40: 31} I had faith in God and knew that these passages were a commitment which He was making; He wouldn't let me down either.

I felt no fear the day of the race, I had honored my church calling, practiced and eaten right. All my life I have tried to take care of my body with exercise and abstinence from harmful substances. I knew that I hadn't let myself down, or my son. I knew that despite my aching knees and short time in preparing the Lord would be with me and strengthen my effort. I had committed to run and had the personal resolve to put in my best effort, this meant to push myself.

I ran and finished the Salt Lake City: 2006, Marathon. I gave it my all, and as I was crossing the finish line I was greeted by two angelic beings wearing red EMT uniforms waiting for me. I had finished with a time of 3:35 and was dehydrated. The Lord's promise of strength withstood the 26.2 mile course and uplifted my fifty-one year old body. I did not faint nor did I slow much from weariness; but the Lord gives no promise that you won't get parched and shaky during your run!

The value of learning to re-commit:

When the overwhelming pressures thrown at you from the tests in life start you to questioning, "Is it worth it … do I have the time?" Or when you start to rationalize, "I have other things I would rather be doing," this is the time to re-commit.

Stop, re-examine what your purpose was to begin with. Re-define your priorities and your personal time line for accomplishing them. Make adjustments. Visualize what the end results of your actions may be; how they can benefit you and what joy may be yours. This will give you the power to re-commit to your goal and finish your test. Remember that even the strongest person needs a break now and then.

Pause, take your break, and then start again.

Common Sense: **You haven't experienced failure until you've given up.**

If you decide to abort your plans, do remember that with time all pain diminishes … except your thoughts of, *"What if I had done things different?"* Don't live your todays to be questioned in your tomorrows.

HONESTY

* * *

Common Horse Sense: Show honesty to others.

Good grief, how often do you think a horse can be tricked into coming to you by shaking a grain bucket that has just gravel in it? How many times will it work to show a lack of integrity and still retain the trust of a charge?

It is easy enough to catch a reluctant horse, if he was previously exposed to eating grain from a bucket. He will change his resistance and sell his freedom for a small tasty reward of a few bites of oats. Why just the noise of the grain being shaken in the bottom of the bucket is tempting enough to make him come a running.

In a pinch, when a knot head horse needs to be caught and no grain is around, a couple handfuls of small rocks will do. Because of prior conditioning, the unsuspecting chow-hound will hear the perception of grain noisily shaking in the bucket, and then come close enough to indulge in a mouthful of ecstasy. You patiently bide for him to put his gullible noggin inside. This allows you to slip your hand hiding a nonthreatening rope around his neck. If the trick works, "BINGO" you have caught your knot head! {Baling twine can be balled up and hidden inside your fist; it's harder to see coming than a large lead rope.}

When he realizes your deception, he'll immediately withdraw. … Too late! The rope is already around his neck. {To a rope trained horse, the baling twine gives the feeling of being caught.} Tricking with gravel and a hidden twine works great —just like the real thing. But, you can't look your horse in the eye for he knows, **you have deceived him.** Your promise of offering a treat to get his consent to being caught is now a lie. You have not kept your pledge. You have lost your integrity. You have lost his trust. …Oh next time he may still come to the sound of the grain or the rocks rattling in the bucket, but he will certainly be more cautious of letting down his guard and sticking his head in your bucket. If the deception is done repeatedly with no additional reinforcement of actual grain, soon he will even refuse to come over to investigate.

It pays to be honest. With actual grain and a hidden rope the resourceful trainer still tricks the animal into putting its head in the bucket; however, after receiving its anticipated reward the horse will view getting caught as a justifiable trade for the few bites of the tasty substance. It will be willing, next time, to once more trade its freedom to partake in a gratifying snack. ...When the horse handler offers gratification, he will be viewed as reliable.

*   *   *

Let's take a moment and individually address our own integrity.

We all error ...

Will I be known as someone whom unashamedly dis-misses his mistakes without thought or feelings as to the negative impact they have on others? Or will I be the honorable individual driven to remain trustworthy?

How would others define my character?

...What behavioral aspect do I want to teach to others in regards to honor?

Question: How does one keep his integrity, as he realizes he's made a mistake and let someone down?

Answer: Seek forgiveness. Not always can one go back and change what has been done. But, one can apologize and seek to make things right as-much-as possible. Asking for forgiveness is not a sign of weakness, but a sign of personal integrity and honesty. It takes strength to rebuild what has been damaged. It should be part of the process of assuming responsibility for our errors.

If you made an error of judgment, own up to your mistake. Apologize for any inconvenience that resulted from your poor choice. You remorsefully state, "I was wrong to for that, and then make amends and repairs where possible. Seek forgiveness for any mistake you made which caused damage to another person or object, and then move on by not readily repeating the same blunder."

Steps to obtaining forgiveness:
1. Admit personal fault.
2. Amend whatever damaged occurred as result of the mistake.
3. Ask for clemency from those affected by the wrong deed.
4. Avoid the repeat of the error.

Tolerating the Pains of Inconvenience:

Common Sense: Life has with it a certain amount of aches and pains. Without pain or inconvenience one can't ascend high enough to enhance his view, nor increase his strength.

A master teacher loves his pupils enough to show interest and compassion in their trials. He is also wise enough not to sanction their self-pity to the extent they' will feel justified enough to quit trying. By him showing besieged learners personal concern for their grievances, he also goes a long ways in displaying an acceptance for them, despite their struggling. From seeing a teacher's caring, they obtain the confidence that they're not standing alone in sorrow. This binds struggler and teacher together, on common ground. Both want some of the same thing. Now, the teacher may show his pupils that by exposure to pain one gets stronger. He doesn't dismiss them from being accountable because of the difficulties that they may be having. Instead, he encourages them to acknowledge their grief, and then continue despite their struggles.

Common Ground is what binds individuals together; it is the starting point of unity from which a relationship can grow. It's the cohesion that keeps two or more souls experiencing a unified happiness or a collective difficulty while they remain engaged in an inter-related battle.

If, as a master teacher, you have established this unity with your pupils, then when they experience a setback in their progression, you could approach them with words like: *"What a horrid mess you've made.* Or, *"You sure screwed up this time …it sucks to be you!"* These comments alone would show a lack of compassion. But if you have previously established a common ground, and you're displaying the body language that's creating light of the misfortune to show that you care, then the afflicted pupil will see it as an effort of concern. He will see that you are interested in him, thereby keeping the door open for your combined relationship to further develop.

Remember the common sense quote: "It is not what you say that matters, but how you say it."

Take the time to develop an interest with your charges as or before you begin teaching. It will help you immensely. In unity, you may make light of their blights in order to assist them without their taking an offense. The fastest way to establish commonality with another is: You embrace or discuss the things which are important to them.

Common Sense: **Common Ground, from a teacher's point of view, is a compulsion of manipulating others to join with him, but it is most easily accomplished as he joins in interest with them.**

For you teachers whom have not developed a common ground, or are thrown into a teaching role without the opportunity to establish a rapport, use the matter at hand to show you care. Your approach could be somewhat like this: *"Look at this problem that you and I must deal with!"* Your words put a hindered student on alert that you are miffed. Yet, at the same time, you release tension by the use of your inflections and body movements to convey, *"Since I care about you, I am concerned with your blight. So will you join me by doing all that you possibly can to help address this grievance?"* With their consent, you are artfully fighting the same battle, which is overcoming the setback of the student. You have not supported their folly, but stand joined ready to teach: *"There is no need to succumb. ...They are not standing alone. ...And you will help them overcome."* With any of their acquiescence, you are free to help them realize more than they might alone.

Common Sense Lesson: Congratulations—You Earned That Blister

While working as a wilderness guide of troubled youth, most every day we hiked several miles while carrying all our gear with us. This moving of camp daily created the opportunity for chores and responsibilities; it forced the youth into opportunities to grow.

One of the certainties of hiking across the wilderness with green-horn hikers is their lack of experience in preventing blistered feet. Each night, as part of a daily personal hygiene time, we would require the students to wash their feet, and then show the clean extremity to an adult staff member. Great would be the concern as the inexperienced youth would point out his or her tired, aching, blistered feet, some hoping to get a sympathetic return, or lack of mileage the next day from the staff. The hindered hikers were hopeful that their problem would become the guide's who would take it upon himself to cure their aliment.

... *{Certainly their compassionate care givers must take it upon themselves to see that this unfortunate suffering never happen again.}* In the new student's mind similar thoughts were often harbored, *"My blisters could mean a reprieve from tomorrow's repetitive duties."*

* * * Side note:* * * **Boy, I saw some hamburgered feet in my stay; the worst were not on the greenhorn first-timers, but on the stubborn multi-day hikers who refused to follow the advice of their instructors. These youths were waiting for the magical "someone else" to solve and whisk away their problems without requiring any effort on their parts.**

My approach was usually the same, "Look at that. You got some mightily fine blisters there. Wow, look at the size of that monster!" I was quick to point out a newly formed bulging pocket of fluid, or a popped deflated specimen. The seasoned kids, who had witnessed this blister oratorical before, would keep quiet as I continued on. "You need to wash them pigs again. This time use soap and water. Don't just wipe 'em with a dirty bandana. Scrub 'em. After that, let them air till morning." I'd look the guilty kid in the eye to see if they got my point, "I'm not going to do a thing for those feet tonight; I'll take another look at 'em in the morning." Latter as if an after-thought I would throw in, "Ya know, you can be real proud of those blisters; they're a badge of honor. They didn't get there by themselves. There is a lot of effort in 'em; you had to hike a long ways to earn those beauties." During the encounter I was showing interest and concern, while seeking a tone of humor to minimize their ailments.

By now any blister infested kids were starting to wonder about me, *"Why wasn't I overreacting to their misfortunes?"* They could see themselves getting no mileage out of their boo-boos, as I was putting the responsibility back on them.

"The way I see it, you only have two options tomorrow. One: you can have me put some tape and moleskin on 'em. Or Two: you can elect to just do nothing and keep-on a-hiking. Either way it is your choice. You can't die from blistered feet, cause they're are a long ways from yer heart. Besides covering 'em won't really make 'em feel any better. They're an inconvenience and not much more. Once you start using 'em, they'll warm up and be less uncomfortable ... not that they'll hurt any less, but yer ability to endure the discomfort will increase as you do something more than just dwell on them." The clients knew I was somewhat engaged in helping them through this dilemma, and that their feet were more their problem, than mine.

* * *Side note* * * If a foot ever had open sores extending below the epidermis into the dermis, I would the next day come up with some other reasons we would not be hiking. I allowed really bad feet time to dry out and heal somewhat to prevent infection. Never did I let the child believe that their feet caused us not to hike.

At this point I would remain silent for a spell to let my words sink in, then inject a thrown-in afterthought, "If you're interested, I can teach you how to prevent blisters from happening in the future?"

Without fail, every new blister infected kid would now ask, "How?"

Now, isn't this the perfect occasion to teach? On one hand, is a teacher having wisdom to impart; he's helping his students' lives become improved. And on the other, are the students willing to listen and learn in the hopes to solve a problem. They truly want to learn some way of getting relief from the pain of tomorrow's blistering feet. *Yes, it's the ideal opportunity; one hoping to teach, and the other wanting to learn.*

At their request, I would continue to teach prevention. "Look at those dirty stinking socks; you haven't changed them in the last how many ... seven days? Your feet are blistering because of the combination of your working muscles, the heat from the ground, and the friction inside your shoes; all are busily producing heat. A blister is a reaction your skin does to protect itself after a burn. Your feet are getting too hot. Always wash or change your socks at least every other day. You are compounding the inability of your feet to get rid of heat with those filthy socks you are wearing; your feet can't breath or keep cool and they are literally burning alive."

"Another preventive action you can take that'll help your feet keep cool is: airing 'em out. Did you air-out your feet with the rest of us during breaks on the hike today?" My asking would boast signs of an, *"I told you so!"* as I recalled their various lame excuses for not participating in the periodic feet airings the group did throughout the day.

Nothing but silence would yell the reluctant reply of the guilty.

To drive home my lesson, I would repeat the previous question, **"Did you, today, air your feet during the rest stops?"**

More revealing quiet would again thunder back. ...Ultimately the response of the injured would almost whisper with a weak, "Ah ... no." This sheepish answer was pried-out by suddenly finding themselves as the center focus of the whole group. This was entertainment at its finest. The other peers would stop their present actions in order to eagerly witness this familiar forced grilling.

"Watch me, tomorrow," I alerted. "While hiking, I take my shoes off at least once every two hours—for five or six minutes. And as I am doing this, I slap my socks on my leg to knock out the sand and salt. By drying out my socks and feet, even for these short intervals, the temperature of my feet goes down. Did you know that I haven't ever had a blister on my feet? I take care of them. When they are hot, they get some attention. If you're paying attention, you can feel a blister coming before it happens too. It starts out as an uncomfortable hotspot, that's your sign—it's time for action. Learn to recognize your hot feet and cool them off before they form blisters, as I do."

There, I unloaded all the information out at once, but it would've been just as beneficial for them if I had stopped after the, *"Wash your socks at least every other day,"* for beyond that, most didn't care to listen any further.   {Most of the kids were stuck back on that one. It required them going out of their way and doing something for themselves.}

Because the whole hiking experience was to create an opportunity for them to take responsibility for their actions, this choice would remain theirs. Most kids will choose not to put forth any effort unless they were forced to. Taking care of their own feet or dealing with the natural consequences was one of those valuable teaching opportunities a teacher is lucky to get. In that circumstance students have to force themselves to assume responsibility, or suffer.

In effort to further help the students see their lame rationalizing, I would ask, "Why didn't you wash your socks?

Their actual spoken replies would state: *"You didn't give me the time,"* or *"I don't have any water available,"* or *"I just want to sit here and relax,"* many different answers would follow. Regardless of the verbalization, their responses would thunder-back, ***"That would be too hard."*** Translated all would mean the same, "No way, that would require effort on my part." All would be nothing more than excuses designed to give some validation to their slothfulness.

I could read their lazy minds which shouted as loud to me as if they had uttered the words, **"I am not going to do anything for my feet that would require any additional effort on my part! Instead, I'll just let you tape them up every day. That way, I don't have to assume any responsibility! These feet become your problem and not mine!"**

It is always amazing to see that even after imparting what you feel is great compelling information, some of your students don't utilize it. Ever notice, that after receiving the power of knowledge, how many refuse when given the choice to be more proactive? They don't want to be bothered; being proactive requires effort. Most stubborn students have to really be uncomfortable, as if in a cave of darkness with no light at all, in order to want to initiate a change.

"They need to be compelled to practice."

As trainers we should do more than merely use our influence to impart useful information, and then just hope when the proper time comes when our students will utilize our instructions. Without previously taking the opportunity to experiment with and work any kinks out of a new idea, at the first sign of trouble they will most likely revert back to doing what has worked in the past. We should, as wise and effective teachers, create situations where in a controlled environment the trainee has an opportunity to practice; where in a safe place, he can attempt to utilize any new knowledge until it becomes the first response of solution. We want our students to be able recall information, and be capable enough to utilize it. This is best accomplished by having experience.

I would, after giving the knowledge of how to prevent blisters, again, remind them on breaks during the next hikes that it would be wise to air out their feet. As an example, I would take off my shoes for a few minutes, while remarking, "I sure don't want to get any of those pesky blisters," Thus, giving opportunity for those students to practice at the ongoing quest of becoming more proactive. However, I let the choice still remain theirs.

I would teach how to use rationalizing to make informed decisions, helping them to envision up coming events. "If you wash and dry out your socks tonight, then tomorrow when your feet start getting too hot and you feel that you need an unscheduled break in order to cool 'em off, I would be more likely to grant it." It was safe for me to phrase it that way because I knew if their socks are clean the over-heating of their feet will not be as much of an issue.

To give you, the reader, an opportunity to practice in your understanding, let's take a look at my use of the Four Teaching Approaches, and again assess my interactions in the blister incidents.

Loving Father:

A child full of self-pity could have felt I was taking delight in making him hike with aching feet; that was not my purpose. It was not me making him hike with blisters; it was him choosing to be slothful, and then paying the price. I simply taught the correct principle, and let him govern himself. No one ever died from sore feet. I knew that once he finally lost his self pity and started to take care of his feet, then he would see that I had only tried to help him learn a better way. Yes, my goal was to teach about feet alright, but, more importantly it was to help the child to learn to take personal responsibility. I was teaching him to take the time to do proper care and preparation so he could save a lot of grief later.

Nurturing Parent:

Nurturing care was offered by doing something for the child whom couldn't do for himself. In addition to this care, I was careful to instill the lessons that his feet were foremost his responsibility. While I would always be there to bandage his wounds if needed, he should primarily seek ways to prevent the blisters in the first place. I was careful not to allow compassion to take over prevention. It was not my goal to baby the injured feet, but to teach accountability and forethought. If needed, I was willing to put the child's needs ahead of my own plans.

Self Entitled:

I would have employed the Self Entitled Approach, if I had made references to my time being wasted, or made it clear how he was slowing down the group because of his unwillingness to take care of himself. I didn't depict this resentment. I have seen peers use shame and blame on a fellow student, but this type of castigation was only effective for the rare someone who actually cared about others. Most of those kids were so into only themselves, that they had no regard for their negative impact on others. I was careful to display only patience in my involvement.

Indifferent Traveler:

At the onset, the characteristics of just letting the child figure things out for himself was used, but only until he showed his desire for a better way. Since I saw myself as a guide on life's paths needing to interact with others, especially persons who are my charges, I therefore had an obligation to offer help and to assist my charges to succeed. As for my duty in teaching blister prevention, I remained apart in the forcing of my agenda, similar to an Indifferent Traveler. I could do so because I was ready when the timing was right. Timing is a key issue in education and often times I choose to put off teaching a lesson because I am waiting for some signs of the child struggling in a cave of darkness; I preferred to wait until he is willing to learn.

Some of the selfish aspects of the Indifferent Traveler Approach may shine forth in me every now-and-then as I sometimes struggle to overcome my own human weaknesses. I am uncomfortable of making mistakes, especially when I'm caught off guard. My fears and delayed reactions may depict me, for the moment, as though I don't want to be bothered, but it doesn't diminish my desires. It only prevents me from immediate action until I have a chance to assess what my correct approach could be. Afterwards, I engage and do it.

In all the blister interactions, I was sure to point out that with this minor set-back, the student was sure to come out the better for having endured it. He was in fact better-off already for having the new experience. Blisters when cared for properly will heal. Extended mileage with proper blister prevention will eventually lead to a hardened and toughing of the foot. This leads to the ability to endure more use. In the beginning their pain was a reminder that things were not quite right yet, and more attention to their cause should be on the mind of each hiker. The pains of inconvenience, likewise shout an alert that more personal growth is needed. An in-touch person will relish a pain that promises an increase of personal potential. He will be aware of the uncomfortable sting, and therefore seek additional information that he may have the opportunity to improve his short-comings.

Teach Courage:

Common Sense: **Face fears instead of running from them.**

* * *

Common Horse Sense: Walk Into The Dog.

A black form streaked out of nowhere and crashed onto the flimsy cedar slat fence. The percussion of the impact caused the barrier to resonate as if it was a flat hand slapping a thin metal sheet. The fence bore the animal's weight by bending outward then inwards with the same catapulting action of a two hundred pound diver launching himself off the city's municipal swimming pool diving board, "Thummp-Whump-whumpa-whumpa-whumpa."

Over the sound of the fence projected a deep, sharp, "**WOOF.**" It opened-up any ear canal blockages, while its base vibrated deep into my chest. My breathing stopped at a gasp. My heart leapt upwards. I was instantly seized with paralyzing force.

Previous to the encounter with the dog, my mount was looking straight down the fence line in the direction of travel. Caught in surprise, at once, she preformed a maneuver unique to a flighty horse—the four-footed launch. This is where the horse startles so fast that it doesn't tense first, or even does it realize what has happened. One moment it's here, the next millisecond there …still looking in the same direction, but now five feet off to the side, supposedly out of reach of danger. Having witnessed or been in the middle of this maneuver many times, I'd have to venture that however impossible it sounds, it seems as though the horse launches simultaneously with four feet in feline fashion. Only after landing does the animal start showing any apparent signs of fear. This maneuver is a reaction so swift that no quick countermove by a rider could defuse or prevented it.

{If the rider was fortunate enough to previously have a good low seat and be set in his balance, then all's well. If not, he might still find himself on the ground at the original launching point.}

"Dag-nab-it!" my training must now take on a new priority before I can continue in my ride. My inexperienced horse's response means I must change my addenda. So I put on hold any of my other desires, and now teach this pupil to face its fears. Otherwise, it will spook at the next time we pass this place again.

Before, I used to simply turn the horse toward the spook and force her to stand until she gave way to being calm. It was a small battle of rider verses animal with a sidestepping dance and a spurring thrown in to entertain anyone watching. This dance was sure to start up again anytime the horse saw a similar spook emerge or latter imagined that one was hiding in the shadows of her mind. In my previous attempts to help her, she hadn't learned to overcome her fears, only to endure them. This meant she also lived in anticipation of them. She was always on the edge.

My old sheepherder friend earlier had given me an answer to training a horse not to shy, or to startle and be afraid. He said, "Walk into the dog." It was time to try it. I have found the extended meaning of this mentor's advice to be:

"Teach the frightened to approach their fears."

During our subsequent rides the next five or six dogs, acting in defense of their territories, got more than they bargained for. As they ran out barking in attempt to scare my in-training horse, their advantage ceased. No longer was I was content to just gain control and have the horse watch in hopes its fear would pass. I would force, spur if necessary, the horse to approach closely as possible right up next to the fence. In the case of no fence at all, we would seize the very ground from the confrontational canine. The effects were amazing. My horse learned quickly. *She was "Bigger and Badder"* than any dog. *"And the dogs—well, they backed down."* An aggressive horse moving into them does wonders at teaching humility.

After two weeks of this approach, she was through being startled by dogs out of nowhere; they just didn't have any affect on her anymore. As an added bonus, all aspects of startling at fears decreased. We now not only stop and re-encounter all spooks, we walk on them. I even go so far as to pester the horse until she touches them, no longer does she endure; she overcomes. Oh, the dag-gum dogs still bark, but their effect is only to booster courage in themselves.

As you are faced with intimidating fears in your own life, or witness children encountering the same, teach being proactive and the use of courage by walking in head-on as I did with my horse. Don't distance yourself, or hide. The cause of the fear will not go away simply because we now choose to change our approach, but it will now transform into something that instead of causing us panic and pain, now simply, becomes another one of life's many problems that can be dealt with in a rational step by step manner. Identify the problem or the cause of the fears, and then set out to find a solution to it. Set a goal to overcome fears by gaining the knowledge to combat them. Apply that knowledge. The end result is: you or your pupils can strengthen in ability and character. Each can become of a greater potential by the conquering of fears.

* * *

Understanding the **Principle of Practice:**

"If something is worth doing at all, then it's worth doing right the first time."

How often in your life have you heard that familiar phrase used? You may, as I have, always thought it a good one and used it for self stimulation to excel at whatever task you endeavor for.

Possibly you are the type who will settle for nothing less than it to do a job correct in the first place. "Congratulations to you." You have a high sense of value, in regards to your abilities. In this area you have a Bomb Proof Character. When you notice a personal shortcoming you're not content until you solve it. You are the driven and goal oriented. You are the exception of most people's thinking.

What about someone else who is not committed into putting forth enough effort in order to do the task the right way? Instead of forcing themselves to do a good job, they'll have none of that challenging stuff. In their minds, they can't or won't do the task right, so therefore they are not even willing to try to do it minimally. They will simply dismiss the opportunity and walk away. In this choice they so miss out on the chance for self-improvement. They forgo the natural highs that come from seeing the progression of a task being mastered, plus they miss out on the chance to learn from mistakes. Don't they understand that every task we learn to master in this life begun with struggling until we got it right?

> **"If something is worth doing right, then it is also worth doing wrong, while you get it right."**   Dave Nelson

In the beginning of a learning curve, how many of us have struggled with using a computer, or at mastering another type of similar challenge where our inabilities and lack of experience quickly turned into a confounding problem? There were times on our own when we exhausted our abilities to work out a solution. We tried to solve it by reading or by trial-and-error, yet continued to come up short. During these perplexing circumstances we were in a teachable state because we lacked the expertise to do our task correctly, and therefore would have taken the advice of any person whom we felt had the credentials to solve our quandary. Additionally, we need to be taught, once more, that practice also gives us the wisdom to be able to improve our short-comings.

The timing of a good coach will also help to empower us, so that we may solve our issues. How great is the lesson-giver who has the talent to see our shortcomings and the wherewith to challenge us to improve? Under the guiding hand of this competent teacher we learn that a most excellent way to practice is to first be exposed to the correct solution. Next, review it over and over again. A good coach will oversee our performance of tasks in a controlled environment before he sends us out in front of the real and sometimes unforgiving pressures of reality, which seem to lurk poised and ready to bounce on the weak.

Outside of a controlled practice-mode environment there will be many critics who will love to point out that our efforts are not up to their standards. Their agenda is not to be helpful or devoted towards enhancing a student's skills. Many may be driven by the competiveness of their motives to tear down our efforts. They will be in opposite contrast to the inspiring coach who critics our efforts, but whose design is to stimulate us to improve and buildup our potentials.

In our thoughts, we can coach ourselves. We can expose our minds to additional experience as we review a task prior to its real implementation. It is here that an active mind gets a chance to re-fine and adjust to the best of its ability. It will weed-out any obvious incorrect approaches and make a mental commitment to use the one that seems to work. Our self-drive to review or to practice becomes our personal coach.

As a teacher, re-enforce to your greenhorn pupils that as they permit themselves to practice, then they begin to develop the skills and abilities to do their tasks more efficiently. Empower them with the idea: **As they keep on learn'n and try'n they'll be closer to get'n things right**. As result, they'll be more skilled when another great opportunity comes.

—You teach them to try again—

Your duty as a teacher is to share information, hold their hands, bend the rules, and inspire action through creating a practice environment. You help with their tasks and buoy up their confidence. You do whatever you can to keep them wanting to try. Do not let them continue in clear conscious to make no effort.

—Teach that continued practice makes perfect.—

A great teacher inspires others by:

• **Being discreet about commanding the participation in new challenging tasks.** In order to teach your students to try new things, which may be tough or appear challenging, it is best if they view an opportunity as a choice to do, and not a declaration of obligation from another.

• *Tactful persuasion.* It is still their choice whether to challenge themselves. Make them aware of any rewards or possible consequences that will motivate their performance.

{*Command only as your last resort.*}

- **Helping them to be prepared.**

Offer training, either in effort to inspire their interest, or in response of being asked to assist. Be aware that a skittish student may have the desire to perform, but also be holding back under the belief that he needs just a little more knowledge.

- **Showing others his witness of The Principle of Practice.**

Let them see your progression and mastery of a weakness. Teach your pupils that with their practice, they too can develop the skills to masterfully succeed.

- **Letting them fail.**

It is by failure that one becomes desperate enough to seek additional help. *Allow them the chance to fail,* that they may become teachable. Instead of taking the easy way out and simply doing a task for your pupil, work with them that they may receive enough motivation to try again.

- **Holding his charges to a level that will raise their abilities.**

If little is expected, then so often, little will be given. To get more out of another, *challenge them.* Most people thrive when presented a challenge. They will give more effort if it is expected, especially if a show of praise and gratitude accompanies their achievements.

The Enjoyment of Life:

Common Sense Lesson: **With Humor, Defuse an Awkward Situation.**

As a farmer, who often employed young unskilled laborers, there were the too often mechanical break-downs of equipment. Some due to wear and tear, but many were because of the lack of experience of the operators. A lot of time and money was lost during the learning curve of these willing, yet judgmentally deficient new guys. Often I would check up on the progress of my young helpers only to meet them perplexed; some still not understanding why that while in their stewardship the swather, or the balewagon, or even the implement behind the tractor, broke down. The more they realized it was from an error on their parts, the further down-trodden and discouraged they became.

Before the onset of a forth-coming investigation, I would start out by laughing at the dilemma; my display of humor would be contagious and defuse their anxiety. They would be compelled to laugh also at their plight. I would even go so far as to rate the severity of the breakdown or the mess-up, "Now that's an eight on the scale of one to ten."… I would always hold my critical comments back until I understood what had happened. First, I would display that I was actually enjoying the predicament.

On one such occasion, I was questioned by the guilty youth. He asked, "Why don't you swear or yell at me, like my dad, instead of just finding it funny?"

Laughter was something that I choose to do; it was how I reacted without displaying negativism. Why did I need to yell and make a fuss over what had already been done? The blameworthy knew that an error had occurred, and for me to attach additional uncensored blame certainly wouldn't help them feel better. And neither would it get the situation solved. *"Besides; it is laughable, that equipment always breaks when you need it most."*

My form of discipline was to begin by explaining what should have been done in the first place to have altogether avoided the break-down. Next it was to require the boy help fix his error to every extent possible, mostly which consisted of him helping me to repair it. It was a great time to chat and bond with the youth as we engaged in the common goal of getting that old piece of equipment and that youth back to work. I never yelled or scolded the blameworthy, for I remember my own misjudgments, and the machinery that I have also broken down in my past. I always ended by making sure that the novice fully understood what had happen, and the proper procedure to avoid any reoccurrence.

Even the worst problems or the most challenging setbacks come with a silver lining. … It could be the newly presented time to join together repairing a common concern. …It may be a bit of wisdom on a strictly laughable aspect, as you realize what didn't work. Laughter helps defuse hurt. Think back on any number of the many times you have viewed a stumble or a dilemma of another and found it humorous, if they can laugh also, healing begins.

In our dilemmas, others are laughing at us. A healthy alterative for not getting uptight and mentally wigging-out is to learn to join them in their comic revelry. So true is the saying: *"A wagging dog receives more petting, than a barking or snarling one."* Why not receive the reward of others still wanting to be around you, instead of them withdrawing because of your poor coping skills.

"Remember that while performing in the role of mentor, others will shun you, or they will feel at ease with their inefficiencies, based on how you choose to handle yourself during a mishap."

Ok, finally the part that most people love; they want to play and have fun. To possess a rounded character, it is important that you know how to let your hair down. Live a little. ... Not only in the rigors of competition, wherein some feel is true excitement, but I am also talking about the fun that comes from doing something just for bringing about pleasure. For me life without playing, or joking or teasing someone else would be like reading a book, "Just Who am I Training Anyway" without any funny parts. It might be possible to be read clear-through a dry self-help book, but what pain and suffering. To enjoy life is to find a peace from its cares and worries. It is, for a period of time, the looking forward to putting back into my emotional savings account a deposit that will grow in interest. I want to increase my sanity reserves in the case I might have to pull out a withdrawal when I am running short. This is the type of enjoyment which I feel when riding through the mountains on a good horse, with friends. Find the thing that your students enjoy doing, and then participate with them, just to have fun. Your reward is piece of mind, a closer connection due to common ground, and a release of pressure in your relationship.

Common Sense Lesson: **Even Dogs Laugh**

My daughter-in-law's parents, Dick and Vickey, yearly invite the Slater Clan to join them in celebrating Christmas Eve. We spend the evening together eating a pot-luck supper, opening white elephant gifts, and participating in group games. One of the highlights of the evening is witnessing the antics of their dog Daisy, a high strung Boston terrier.

Each time I visit, Daisy and I have a friendly game of Tug-of-War with an old sock. To the point of exhaustion, she will play, but as the years have taken their toll on this canine, she now needs more frequent breaks in her rambunctious frolic. Daisy is very competitive for a little dog, so her answer to getting a break from the strenuous game, and at the same time emerge as a winner is to ever increase the pressure of her biting on the sock. If this doesn't yield her victorious, she will go for the greater foe. Never has she slipped and broken skin, but she will, without doubt, push her aggression to its limits with an ever-increasing biting of her nemesis' hands; forcing me to take a break to assess the wisdom of continuing to play this supposedly friendly game.

Later in the evening, after all have eaten and the games have been played, out comes one of the evening's crowning events: watching this canine do battle with a helium balloon. To start the game all that is needed is a wacky competitive dog with a balloon tied to a three foot string and attached to her collar. Everywhere that Daisy goes, there is her shadowing opponent floating above always agitating. It only takes a minute for her to have all of this tantalizing she can stand. Her patience is short, *"That balloon needs to go down!"* She will run, dive, and finally launch herself at the floating archrival.

It is in the spirit of this game that the pooch will wig out; she becomes possessed with her tormentor's down fall. She turns into a maniac. In effort to bite the sphere, she will spring at it. But as she leaps into the air, so does the floating balloon. At first, it hovers a mere three feet over her head, an easy mark ripe for the biting. However as she catapults herself upwards, it moves out of reach. How does it know to move so quickly? Does it read her mind? The ever knowing balloon quickly get her worked-up.

"I must try again, just a little higher this time. ... RATS! There it goes up and out of reach. I'll jump higher next time; I sure will. ... Missed again. ... Maybe faster? ... That's it—I'll go faster, that dumb balloon can't keep up with me!"

She repeatedly jumps, and jumps; and jumps. I'm talking about acrobatic leaps, the ones that are fed with so much adrenaline that

238 JUST WHO AM I TRAINING ANYWAY   DAVE SLATER

the body twists and turns in mid air do to its momentum. Consider this, the string holding the lighter than air balloon to her collar becomes loose as she jumps; it frees the balloon to float up. As she looses altitude, down the balloon is pulled. Only by the repeated attempts does she finally get her timing correct, and she jumps up during the forced descent of balloon. She is eventually rewarded by striking the balloon with her nose.

"Missed the timing of my bite on that one ... must try again!" At this point in the contest, Daisy is laboring from extreme asthmatic breathing. She is bug-eyed and forgets to blink, being so overcome with intensiveness. *"I will keep trying. I know that I can win. ... HUFF, HUFF, HUFF. ... I sure am out of breath, but I'll be damned if I let that cursed balloon prevail!"*

Observing her antics, all onlookers are mesmerized by the attempts of this little dog. Her anger and intensity, combined with her determination has them laughing—the kind of rib hurting convulsions that makes one hold his side in order to get some relief. Emotions swell with a mixture of wanting her to continue putting on her one-doggie-show and secretly wishing she'd stop before you wet your pants. Some of the more sensitive individuals even wish she'd quit before she is overcome with an asthmatic attack or blows a gasket. Whatever their feelings, all still have one commonality; they share unbridled laughter, and she knows it.

I am also an onlooker, and perhaps engaged more than the others as I let my laughter roar. I feel she is getting what she deserves for being too aggressive earlier with my hand. "Get the balloon Daisy. Don't let it treat you like that! ... Ha, Ha, Ha"

By repeated attempts from a never-give-up dog, the balloon is overcome; it is popped. Finally the timing of the balloon's dissention, her jump and her bite all work in unison. Does the little dog succumb to her exhaustion and quit her aggression on her would-be intimidators? ... No, she quickly walks over to me, while I am still caught up in rib hurting laughter at her plight, and politely bites me on the hand. Then she distances herself to go rest and have her laugh.

PART 4

INCREASING EFFECTIVENESS

CHAPTER 12:

AM I AN EFFECTIVE TEACHER?

How effective are you? To determine just where you presently are, ask yourself vocally. Ponder your answer so you may hear your replies to the following highlighted questions:

1. Do I receive the praise of man for my knowledge and presentations?   *If so, then you are learned, but are you effective?*

Being learned means: You are aware of much information. In contrast, being effective means: You influence others toward change. They benefit from your knowledge. As others describe a teacher's ability, how many times have you heard this phrase? "Sure, he knows his stuff, but he can't teach worth a <u>* # ^ 𝕘</u> . In order to have a maximum effect on your pupils, you must bring more into the imparting of knowledge than just the information itself; you need to motivate their desire for improvement.

2.   Do others seek me out?

Do people want to be with you and follow your instructions? Are you sought out because you give the emotional and intellectual awareness people desire? Do, after the fact, people come and seek to get you to continue with an idea you presented? If so, then you were effective.

3. Do I get respect?

Do you command respect? … Do you demand that your charges recognize your importance? If your answer is, "Yes," then know that so does any power-craving taskmaster. They would allow nothing less. Self serving is the master who forces his charges to uphold his greatness or to fear his wrath. Disciples give respect freely; they give it to a leader as they feel inspired by his magnetism. An efficient teacher has earned the honor and admiration of his charges; he doesn't have to worry about commanding respect.

Selfless is a person who takes on a leadership role not in quest of praise or gain, but to inspire others.

4. Do I use consistency?

Consistency in teaching is delivering the same message the same way. It allows the student to develop a confidence in what he can expect from you. Although it may operate from a highly consistent mode, a computer or a machine, when asked the same way, can do little more than give one of a few pre-programmed impersonal responses. These responses can become boring and predictable as the student learns the routine and isn't challenged anymore.

Effectiveness is more than just displaying a consistency. It is also being responsive and caring. It is a willingness to best serve the differing motives of one's charges. To be most effective a teacher will not remain consistent and impersonal. He will, with good judgment and ability, first establish a constancy that his charges can count on, and then adjust his interactions as he understands the motives behind his student's actions. He will have the discernment to adapt his teaching techniques when the need justifies.

Common Sense: **It is much easier to get empathy out of a caring human operator, than from an impersonal, yet consistent, pre-recorded message.**

5. Do I use emotion?

Long after the information has faded and been all but forgotten, the student will remember your enthusiasm for a subject. He'll recall your fervor. Passion is the drive that makes people want more. Your positive emotional display stimulates them with the desire to give up what they were currently doing, and to seriously look at collecting up some new energy.

Emotions are the key to remembering any experience. The greater the level of emotion that can be tied to a learning process, the less likely one is to forget it. The details of the event might be forgotten and the skill that was observed might fade into the un-retrievable realms of the mind, but the emotion felt at the time will long endure as a powerful stimulant, turning a simple lesson into an enduring learning experience. While teaching, if you effectively display such passions as love or concern, guilt or anger; heart-ache or commitment your feelings and excitement will give a powerful resolve for your students to engage and participate also.

6. Do I show compassion?

Do you show compassion and tenderness to your pupils? Do you exhibit that you care for their well beings? As an effective teacher, continue to give support and compassion throughout, even when your pupils don't show appreciation; even when you feel they are not are deserving of another's help.

Beware; as a child becomes aware that someone is listening to his hardships, he will be further inclined to seek sympathy. He will endeavor to manipulate you into feeling sorry for him. Don't fall for his solicited pity. Sympathy doesn't inspire improvement. It only makes the oppressed feel someone cares.

{That in itself isn't bad; in fact, it's a whole lot better that nothing.}

An appropriate response would be to show compassion not pity. A Nurturing Parent, who is determined to meet the child's needs without further empathizing with their trials, would simply state, "I am sorry," or "I too have felt your pain." Then, they would inquire of the troubled, "What are you going to do about it, to overcome your hardships?"

A self-centered reply when your concern is solicited by an injured student is to recall your own personal experiences that had likewise the same disappointments. A self-boasting orator will seek to one-up the other's hardships and tell personal war stories of how he, as a kid, had it much harder than they. *"Look I am still here; it didn't kill me!"* The braggart will recount how he had to walk three miles to school, up-hill both ways, and in the snow. With his captive audience, he'll recite additionally how he was also forced to endure with his brother's worn-out hand-me-down coat and with a hole in the sole of both non-fitting shoes. One-upmanship is acceptable when it teaches a lesson which is beneficial to a charge. It is not appreciated when it is used to boast of the orator's greatness. When trying to inspire the injured, don't use personal war stories in the one-sided attempt to crow of past victories, or as a means of downgrading or belittlement to the listener, for then it is neither wanted nor in good taste.

7. Do I offer high gains?

Do your skills include pointing out all the potential high gains that can come to a student as he engages with your idea? Do you operate from that one-sidedness, as you purposely fail to focus equally on the little he'll have to give up as he joins with you?

"It cuts, it slices, it dices, and it can be used as a spatula, plus it never needs sharpening. You will find this the best tool in your kitchen. Now, be able to prepare those fancy dishes you've only dreamed of. Call in the next five minutes, and we will give you for the amazing low price of $19.95, not one, but two Miracle Knives. Remember that this offer is not sold in stores. To receive this second knife absolutely free, you must act now! Operators are standing by. We accept all major credit cards." {Please include $8.95 shipping and handling for each knife ordered. Also include a sales tax of 5.95%}

This is salesmanship; creating a need for a new product with the starry eyed consumer dreaming of its benefits. It invokes a feeling and pressure to obtain without totally analyzing the true cost.

Being an effective teacher also includes becoming a salesman and much more. Be sure to assist your pupil to analyze his gains, as he uses his freedom of choice to participate in your offer to join your common goal; even allow him to believe it to be his own idea. In order to get him on the road to true improvement, go beyond just selling. Help him see what he must give up in order to obtain, and then retain that benefit.

8. Do I seek help?

A truly selfless teacher will seek-out help to supplement any personal shortcomings as he becomes aware of his lack of ability. It'll be seen as a needful thing. There comes a moment when even an experienced teacher realizes it's time to get help. It's then that he will go out and enlist a more proficient source of knowledge than himself.

Often a busy self-absorbed educationalist may have a problem with his acknowledgement of a self weakness, so much so, that he won't even try to learn and experience new lessons with his charges. He may even excusably think that because he is lacking the skills to teach on a certain topic, then there is no need to be a part of the learning process other than to arrange an opportunity for the child to learn. At the price of his own opportunity for improvement, he will often defer the student with a difficult problem in hopes a specialist may better address the current issue. With any luck, the primary teacher/parent will become inspired to improve his own weaknesses as well.

Circumstance may require that others take an active teaching role of one's charges. Perhaps the appropriate teaching time is also the only time a parent can obtain work, or the lesson to be taught is indeed beyond his present ability. Even as others are employed and filling in as the active tutor, still the primary teacher should remain engaged in also helping to inspire his charges. An effective teacher's motivation is not for personal gain, but is a spinoff from his desires to see his students maximize their potentials and expand their abilities. This noteworthy educator oversees with the intention that the most correct assistance is offered, so that his pupil's current dilemma may be solved.

9. Will I force compliance?

Many assume they're most effective as they force a charge into compliance. Others think: this is taking away a person's freedom of choice, to be forced against one's will. Whatever your feelings about forcing another, you can't deny it's worked throughout the ages. Forcing those who are unwilling themselves does work. Force when necessary: This is whenever the child's safety is at risk, or whenever he has truly given you, by his defiance, no other choice. Be sure to show an increase of love and concern afterwards; thereby, you can use the success of their forced efforts to help them realize their additional gains.

10. Do I inspire others?

Do you inspire others to change their approaches towards solving their problems? By your interaction are others now more able to meet and conquer their difficulties of life? Is your purpose as a teacher and guide to help others see a better approach in obtaining their possibilities?

... Or do you praise mediocrity, showing that you are not concerned with refinement?

A child will need someone to push them into ever higher levels until they can see the wisdom of giving their best efforts. They need a helpful push until they catch the dream of their own potentials, and are able to motivate themselves.

... Do you continually raise the level of proficiently you expect out of your students?

Almost always improvements can be made. You can offer new heights by giving them additional challenges to meet. As a child acquires more refinement, then the level of your intervening can become less frequent and less demanding. Eventually, it is your goal for a child to motivate himself.

... As a concerned teacher, if a student's shortcoming is noticed, is it your obligation to make mention and to point out a better way—just keep in mind your priorities. From a loving standpoint, inspire them in ways which support building them up. Don't just rest on your skill to tear them down. Challenge them with ways to improve. Think... Where would a professional ball player be if all his mentors just praised his childlike efforts and never challenged him to improve?

How about learning to play an instrument? If all his instructors let the child keep producing the wrong sounds, or if they only praised the child's willingness to try and never stated that he could learn to do better, how far would the average child go and learn to play beautiful music without timely positive criticism?

What about an easy test or even no tests in school?   Praising for the wrong answers or letting shoddy work past by as acceptable teaches what to pupils? It teaches them that they are not accountable to learn the correct answers, and it sure teaches that the instructor isn't concerned much about them learning correct principles either.

To inspire... I will stir my charge's embers of desire and oxygenate his self awareness with additional opportunities of acquiring more power and control. To motivate any of his doused curiosity, I must light a spark of understanding that will grow into a burning flame of knowledge seeking. I will fuel his emotions, and fan his craving to perform with positive traits without having to always be told what to do. At any positive success, I'll commend my learner and seek to give him an opportunity to experience the felt warmth of heightened esteem. In addition, I must remain open and truthful by criticizing his lacking efforts—certainly not with the intent to extinguish his radiant glow of energy, but, solely to stoke up his yearning for improvement. I will readily show the reward of acceptance and praise at his intensified efforts to blaze even brighter. ... **I will feed his fires of empowerment.**

Common Sense: **Focus towards offering criticism with the ultimate intent to build up.**

The more involved a student is, the more likely he'll accept criticism when he recognizes it coming from a mentor whose chief concern is for his charge's betterment.

Revise your method of critiquing if it stimulates a kid into inappropriate behavior reactions.

—There's a better way out there than to put out his fire to succeed.

By not going out of his way to inspire, the stand-offish teacher will never receive the second greatest compliment possible from his students. He will never hear, "Look at old So-and-So, just hanging in there trying his best; he sure doesn't know a lot about ___*{canoeing}*___, but it's sure enjoyable being around him; I know he really cares about me."

The highest compliment a teacher can receive is when a student conveys that they're striving to obtain the same qualities as their teacher, **"I want to be just like my teacher; he is such a great role model; he's an expert in his field. I always feel he's really interested in helping me."**

With applied knowledge and proper interaction from an engaged instructor, a pupil has a greater probability of becoming a person worthy of emulation, having acquired proper qualities and positive character traits, like unto his effective teacher.

Now go and teach. ... Just use what you've learned and all will be fine.

Oh, what's that? Am I hearing you say, **'It isn't that easy. You could use more help?'**

Hopefully by reading to this point, you have started trying out some of this guide's ideas. At least you have started role playing in your mind with the different approaches and by now you are starting to question whether or not I have any idea what I am talking about. Your questions are probably similar to this:

"OK, I read your book, and so far some things make sense. But what about ...? "

"I thought I knew what to do, but in real life things are different than in a book. Could you offer more help!"

"I thought that I was doing for the right reasons. Why do I still feel there is more?"

"For some reason or-the-other, things just aren't going as I thought they should?"

"I am still having problems with my pupils, they still won't learn. What now?"

... Do not despair, read on and learn more about how to deal with problem situations.

CHAPTER: 13

GOING BACK TO THE BASICS

Common Sense: **In order to train others, you must lead, or they won't follow.**

* * *

Common Horse Sense: Getting the dog to mind.

We discussed on page 107, how to pick out a good pup; let's look at what happens once we get that pup home:

At first that little feller is going to try to establish a bond with anyone. He wants to fill that void where his mom and littermates were. So it is easy to get that little guy to follow you around; just the thought of being alone will make him whine and howl. He longs for companionship, especially at night. This youthful pup makes a great friend and companion, for it is his choice to join with you. Kids and adults alike enjoy being the center of his attention. He will go anywhere and seems to always want to be your buddy ... until he gets old enough to get distracted.

Upon being distracted by another dog or a cat, another person, or perhaps an interesting smell, your best friend in the world, who's grown a little older and less dependent, will take off. He will, if not properly trained, leave you in the space of a heartbeat, and he won't be coming back until he is good and ready. It doesn't matter how much you yell his name, even to the top of your lungs, the pup will go investigate his distraction.

Which of us hasn't witnessed this spectacle with an undisciplined dog and his caregiver?

{A person standing and yelling for his mutt at the top of his lungs, like he thinks that the dog can't hear and all that is needed for him, the self-appointed master, is to just ask one more time or perhaps just a little louder. You witness the dog acting seemingly deaf to the calls. Good grief, you can hear the doofus yelling at your location two houses down and across the street! I mean like what is that clown thinking? If the mutt isn't going to come back when it's only fifteen feet away, what makes the dupe think that it'll respond way-off at three hundred?}

The dog's disobedience stems from the belief that it can do anything it wants. To its thinking it understands that, *"This person will not enforce his commands with any punishment."* In addition, *"He'll so happy when I finally decide to come back; my infractions will be forgiven and quickly all will be forgotten."*

I'll tell you what that dog needs more than to be yelled at again. **He needs for his person to know how to take the lead role.** This untrained-dog's owner is just that, and nothing else. Which of the two is taking the lead role in this case?

To get what it wanted, before, all the pup had to do was act cute or friendly, sometimes maybe even throw in a little patience with its person. More likely than not, as this dependant escalates his learned controlling behavior, the weak caregiver will eventually come through and provide for its every need.

This pup knows that his person will give in and allow him to get away with whatever improper behavior he desires. His person has lost control, and the dog thinks that he is the one who has retained it. The dog, by remaining disobedient, and then allowed to get away with it, has effectively trained his human to permit him to use inappropriate behavior. As it gets older and cuteness doesn't work so well any more, it will evolve into taking what it wants by defiant or abusive actions. An untrained dog has no respect, no obedience, and no loyalty beyond what it thinks must be done in order to receive its wants. The thing that you can count on is: This untrained dog will stay with you as long as you have food, and/or showing him a better time than he could get on his own. **"If it is your desire to be the leader, take this charge back through the Basics!"**

* * *

In many ways the untaught horse is like this untrained dog. Without a clear leader to follow, the horse is either left confused and bewildered, or it will assume the lead role itself.

Common Sense: **As a trainer, you need to give clear and consistent signals to be followed.**

It is possible to confuse and give false signals to a horse, where the reaction you get is nothing like the one you were after. When it acts contrary to what you want, you may think, **"Bad Horse"...** **"Stupid Animal"**. But really, how can a horse be good or bad? It's just reacting to the stimulus that is presented. In order to get the best response, you need to offer clear and consistent signals with your requests, so that the horse, without confusion, can be conditioned to react with similar reliability.

As I attended a seminar offered by Dennis Reis, he opened my eyes as to how necessary it is to execute the correct steps which lead up to getting a proper response. I learned that it was totally dependent on me, the trainer; "I first had to train myself." I sat for two days and watched Dennis and his wife join completely with their horses as they moved and performed. It was if horse and human had passed through the language barrier; they were together engaged in the same exact purpose.

Even though, I have had much success as a teacher and horse trainer for years, I finally understood why I had not been more successful. Now I was learning how to be more effective. I further discovered from the Reis' the importance of the doing the job of training right and thorough, and of creating with a horse a solid foundation to work from. The equine trainer must always be clear and consistent; he must take the proper leadership role, then the horse can recognize and yield to his trainer's will. I learned that basic fundamental requests and responses are practiced until they are mastered. Always is maintained a good working relationship, where the trainer directs and the trainee follows. Only then are new skills and refinements added. To become more effective, I vowed change, *"I'll not remain of the same past mentality that expected a good teacher/student relationship just because of my own competence and the many dazzling perks I was offering."* ... I finally understood!

I would like to share with you some of the ideas that started to open my eyes. These ideas are the basics of building a relationship when training a horse {or a person}. I will refer to the aids which are presented in the "Universal Horsemanship Mentor Series," offered by Dennis Reis. With my new increased awareness, my intention in this book is to show you the commonalities between training a horse and a person, so that you too may benefit by power of **"The Basics."** You, also, will be able to impact the lives of your charges according to your enhanced desires and new improved abilities.

Common Sense: **Whenever you undertake to effect a behavioral change in another, they and you should be working toward the same end results; there must be the "willing engagement" with both doing whatever is necessary to accomplish the task. Or you must become the leader and take control of the relationship, where they are bound to respond and yield to your requests.**

A novice rider may think that he is causing his mount to travel swiftly when it's headed toward home. The truth is that as his mount gets closer to obtaining what it wants, it refuses to merely walk quicker or with more purpose, and instead takes up a choppy trotting pace trailing towards rest. It remains **reluctant** to submit, and becomes more difficult to manage as it sets in head-strong opposition to the tugging of its rider, whom is also uncomfortable. The rider also wants to get home, but with the smooth rhythm of a faster walk, or held back in the comfort of the slower pace exhibited on the trip from the corral. The interaction that is taking place now it a battle between both trying to take control to get want they want; neither is in total control.

The poorly-checked horse is choosing to increase its speed, so it can get more quickly back to that feed which always accompanies the evening return. Driven by some type of gratification waiting there, it's in anticipation of the freedom to rest, and pushes to get home, end the ride, and be with its other herd mates. This sour horse is in need of additional training. It doesn't need more training to move quickly home. It already does that all too well, and would be in a run if the rider would allow. It has to be trained to respond to its rider when signaled; to know when to shut down and to remain submissively in gait. Too often this one is the most difficult to train.

Training is necessary on the **reluctant**; they require instruction, discipline, drilling, and then guidance to the recognition of pleasure more obedience. They must be handled, so that they will respond to aids and clues, to where they will yield to the authority of another. And as result they receive a freedom from pain, or a pending reward. This **gain** then becomes the driving force that channels the reluctant into compliance. The reluctant are trained to become **willing**.

Why would I go back to the Basics?

Always when working with a horse it is important to start with a good foundation. Therefore; it is advantageous, at times, during future training proceedings to go back again and re-build a crumbling one. When a student refuses to be submissive, then this is a signal that they need a reminder as to their role of being the follower; they need to be taken back to a session in the essentials. The object in any return to "The Basics" is as simple as getting a forward movement out of a reluctant horse at the request of its trainer. The pupil learns and accepts to do the basic fundamentals: to change directions, speeds {walk, trot, and canter}, and then to stop its movements … only to start again at the trainer's signal.

"The Basics" is nothing more than a building and refresher course where proper behavioral training techniques are used by the trainer to cause a change to the trainee. It is a review where both have their roles strengthened.

*   *   *

Common Horse Sense: THE BASICS

Start your training with the horse by going back to the round pen. Here in a small safe area, isolated from all other distractions, both may focus only on each other. Going back to the Basics is: To build a foundation from which all other work and tasks can build on. He is learning to pay attention to you, and you are learning to be clear and consistent. With renewed training, your horse can safely learn his role and confidently count on you to do yours.

Take off the halter, the bridle or any other forms of restraints you have on the animal; he needs to know that he is free to choose his own decisions and actions. You will start working with your horse from the ground during the Basics. This is a new beginning. You haven't earned the trust to ride him. The fact you're both here means, additionally, he hasn't demonstrated his willingness to submit and follow you. Because neither roles has is been applied correctly, both start from an equal standing.

Primarily, you must establish the correct emotional rapport from which to work from. Don't start immediately working or stressing your horse as soon as you get him isolated. What you need is a transition period: a period of common ground. So, spend a little time brushing or rubbing your animal, first. The last thing you want to do is define the round pen or yourself as an inflictor of torture. One on one with you should be the place where your animal wants to go. If at all possible, before you subject your student into the rigors of compliance, allow him to see you as one of the good guys whose company he wants to share. Keep this up for a few minutes.

Next, your horse must understand that as you increase your energy, you expect him to yield to you. This is the basic language that a colt has learned from his youth during his interactions with other horses. It is not foreign. He will recognize it and yield to you as soon as he identifies you in the role of being the leader and himself as intimidated in the role of being the persecuted. Utilize the horse's flight response to fear. Decide which direction you want your horse to move, and then you cause him to move in that direction. You become more energetic and enlarge your impact; you force the horse to correspondingly move with your increase of pressure.

The most basic task is *Forward movement.* This is where you enact a yielding conditioning. You cause your trainee to perform at your bidding. You cause him to move away from you. This is not a flight, of a frightened horse as he decides to run away from you, which you're after. Neither is it the forward movement which the horse decides to do independently as it initially moves forward because it was his choice to do so. The type of forward movement you're after is the movement of the horse which you caused. He must be taught that he is to move, not by his choice, but because you allow him no other choice. He is to move because you commanded him to leave. You are enlisting your horse to pay his attention to you.

While you stand in the center of the pen, you cause the horse to move around you until he tries to stop, and then force him to keep going until it is clear that you're causing him to move, not him calling the shots. He fundamentally learns you are in command.

Secondly, you want to teach that as you decrease your pressure, you are allowing him to decrease his level of response to you also. Diminish your body bubble. The horse can now lessen his moving away, because you as the leader allow him this privilege. If in the beginning as you diminish your pressure and he does not start shutting down, then you restart an escalation of power. You ask, suggest, and promise a punishment until he responds to you, which in this case is him slowing down when you signal him to. For a horse driven with fear and moving unstoppable, your punishment might be you cutting a quarter of the corral's distance in front of him while waving your arms, or flag, or whip. Either way it is you becoming a stopping force to teach this horse: "**You demand he pay attention to you!**" Your student soon recognizes he is to follow your lead, not answer to his desires. You are enlisting your horse's attention; you as the leader control his activity.

At first the key stimulant to signal a change is the swelling of your Body Bubble. After some refinement, it can become as subtle as an expansion of your arms and fingers, a slight notable increase of core size, and/or the focusing of your eyes. In the beginning it may need to be a larger eye-catching whip or a stick with a flag. It is something presented, so that the horse can recognize your display of motivating force. As the horse yields away from this force, you achieve his forward movement. He begins to move away to get relief from your enlarged pressure. To control his movements, you position yourself behind his center line in order to drive him forward, and you put yourself ahead of his center to slow or stop him. As you decrease energy, your horse now aware of your change and will also diminish his desire to move away. With this and each additional new task, you create a beginning and an end to what you are asking the horse to do. You as a horse trainer learn to direct your charge's movements and he learns to yield to your energy. It is so basic yet so important: **You are establishing yourself as being the leader and the horse is submitting into becoming the follower**.

Use a clear Escalation of Aids

Once a leader/follower relationship has been established, then you can move on to requesting other specific tasks. You will want your horse to walk, trot, and canter. You will want to teach your horse to start, and stop. You will want your horse to be able to change directions at your request. You will teach and the horse will follow. You give it a pattern to rely on without getting confused.

Any task you undertake to accomplish with your horse should include the same basic aids. As a show of constancy and reliability, these aids for getting an obedient response ought to remain in their same sequence. This is a language that any student can understand. It is a communication between you and them which brings both together on common ground. Then, and at every request thereafter, you must use the clear escalation of these aids each time you need a **transition:** *A change of present behavior from your horse.*

```
ESCALATION OF AIDS
1. Ask
2. Suggest
3. Promise
4. Reward
```

1. ASK: As the leader, produce a flick of energy to the point that your horse is aware of a slight inflation. The animal is alerted to a recognizable change, and is therefore primed that something is going to be required of it. It becomes aware of this gesture —such-as, you performing a recognizable movement, your use of a recognized sound, or simply you catching its eye. This is similar to calling the name of a child —you are alerting the horse into giving its attention.

You are asking your student to respond by presenting a slight inflation of your body bubble. With the use of mild kissing tones, body language, and/or the interfering with his personal comfort and space, you can ask him to "Please do something." You are causing him to start a task. Because you've just received his attention, you can channel a slight pressure in the direction which you want him to move towards. You push politely and slightly towards that direction. If he doesn't cooperate, then you raise your energy.

2. SUGGEST: By now your horse is aware of your increased energy, and he's starting to get uncomfortable. He may not always recognize what you have asked him to do, but he is aware you require something. It is still his choice as to whether or not to respond. Since he didn't respond to you when you politely asked, go ahead and raise your energy to a command in order to persuade him to commit. Use **clues** like a raised stick, or a louder demanding voice with an additional swelling of your body size. Raise your arms, and with your eyes peer into his, and/or move into his occupied space. Use any combination which equals an enlargement of energy. You are presenting an inflated **Body Bubble**. With this swelling you are applying additional pressure in the direction you wish your horse to move towards. The horse doesn't understand a verbal request to, "Travel left!" But, he does understand that you are getting bigger and more threatening in your energy and it is wise that he should move. So he reacts to your energy change; he gets out of your way, and moves from you. No longer are you merely asking for a response. By this noticeable raising of your force, you are now demanding it. You are actually suggesting the threat: *"If still no cooperation is seen, then I will deliver a punishment!"* and the horse is being intimidated into responding to it.

3. **PROMISE**: Enforce your demand. You deliver, to the stubborn horse, his cost of not responding to your suggestion. You spank the ground using the stick; you jolt him into action. In the future when mounted you can "use your spurs", or you reach back and spank his rump. Always when delivering a promise use only as little of force as necessary to cause a progression of movement in the direction of the original request.

{Remember, it is not the intent to inflict pain to your horse, only to impose the desire for him to do as directed. His perception of your reprimanding actions will translate into the feeling of pain and discomfort. After a few incidents, when you establish a clear delivery of a promise, he will react to your asking and suggesting without the need for you to deliver a punishment each time. It will be his intent to avoid any up coming discomfort.}

4. **REWARD** at the slightest try: As you execute the promise, and then get the correct reaction, back off. Allow the horse its freedom again. {**You are letting the horse feel a release of pressure as a reward.**} This is how a horse learns. Not by the increase of pressure that causes him to react, but by acquiring relief for himself. He learns by the noticing of a decrease of pressure, obtained from you lowering your energy and offering him a rest from compulsory demands. The horse recognizes your backing off as: he must have done something right. This is much better than his instinctual choosing to run away, then being subjected to a consequence of your relentless pressure again. The reward of you offering him a release goes a long ways toward him doing a repeat

of his same actions. He won't feel a need to disobediently run away; he will want to repeat his correct action again.

When you utilize the use of aids, which are **asking, suggesting, promising,** and then **releasing of the pressure** after a proper response is displayed, you are being clear and consistent with the behavioral modifying clues you present. You are offering clues in a transitional order which allows the animal to respond with minimal interaction from you. As result, you are teaching him to repeat his same actions once more. He will strive to duplicate his reward yielding reaction every time he feels those same clues. You are training him to offer a conditioned response to a specific clue.

{The key for you to remember is to give a clue to the animal that a change is coming, and then apply a pressure in order to get a correct response. When the animal displays the slightest **try** to comply, back off enough —so that its try is rewarded.}

Continue to build reassurance:

After you have worked with your animal for a couple of minutes, take a small break. Show him there's more to you than just always requiring him to fulfill your requests. **You make a point to balance with him for a longer period than you caused him to work.** Rub him on the same side or the location where he was being pressured, so that he'll feel he's getting something positive out of being with you. Keep at it until you put him at ease. Show him you are trying to get along, and you appreciate what he's doing for you. You can even verbally tell him what a good job he's done, as he rests. It is not the words that will be understood, but the accepting gestures and tones you offer. Use many short breaks in response to his proper reactions. Offer him a reassurance for a while, and then start again working. As he grows to recognize your signals and clues, he will progress into the routine of moving to your requests. No longer will you have to put great pressure on him to get a response. He will get more proficient. Each requested routine can be broken down into a series of him responding because of a pressure, and then getting a slight release for the correct action. A good training session will be broken-up by many different small breaks as he fulfills a few routines.

Continue training, but don't work him excessively to wear him out. Don't turn his training session into a big blur. One hour is a long time to work on new skills. Always stop the session on a skill or task that he understands; end on a good note that can be rewarded for.

Once you are finally done working for the day, be sure to en-act the most important part of the Basics: **The coveted bonding-time.** You give him something that is enjoyable, possibly a few bites from the grain bucket, but most assuredly see that he gets further gratification, as you teach him by the comforting tones of your voice and the soothing pressure of your touch. Let him know how good he did. This period of time, at the end of a work session, is more than a rapid acknowledgement of his efforts. It is something that he can look forward to. Instead of grooming him completely before, do it now or split it up—some at the beginning before work and some now after he's through. You just don't put him away. He deserves this time of you saying, "Many thanks." He may not understand all your words, but he will understand and feel your body bubble deflate and be drawn in by your request that he join with you. This is when you built rapport. The horse is being gratified, not intimidated as he is with you and part of your herd. You have shown him that you are demanding, but you're also one of the good guys. If all you are is about work, who could blame the animal for not wanting you to catch him next time; what will be his gains? He will learn to look forward to this ending reward period with its bonding and rapport building. You need to offer it each time you finish work.

After a return session of the Basics, a look from the horse's point of view would reveal such thoughts as, "I can **trust** *this guy, because when I do what is asked of me, he gives me a reward or break."* Or *"I understand what my teacher is asking for; I will not be cheated or confused."* As it grows to expect a certain reaction by its trainer, the horse learns to gain confidence.

As a horse trainer, it is your responsibility to get a trust from your horse. With your consistencies to keep demanding cooperation and compliance, your horse will learn what is expected of him. If the horse deviates from his past training, then it is time, once more, to go through the basics again, in-order-to get on a good foundation and rebuild an effective working relationship. It is a common mistake to rush too fast trying to refine an animal into something great —into measuring up to an imposed expectation. Stop trying to get more out of the animal that is struggling. Instead drop-back, once more establish a proper foundation and trust, only then should you attempt to refine.

Any skill or task that you wish to train your horse to do should also be preformed using consistent clues and the proper use of aids. It is also important that with each additional task to be performed, the horse understands what is expected of him, and what he can rely on from you. He increases his ability to listen and respond to your requests by his mastery of the previous lessons. Each task has with it key components which when understood give a more solid foundation on which to build and learn from.

Side note **It is not my purpose in this book to offer all the knowledge needed to fully train or fully experience the joy from proper riding techniques. You can increase your horse training knowledge further by a visit to: resisranch.com.**

Or contact my e-mail horsesense.guide@q.com Share with me your concerns. {As trainers, we're in this together.}

Remember to start out slow. These are the Basics, the foundations from which you build upon later. A return to "The Basics," does no damage; therefore, it can only help an already great relationship. It keeps in check the proper roles where the horse knows what is expected of him. It can also be the turnaround spot; a rebuilding point when roles are strained.

*   *   *

Using "THE BASICS" on a Child

The expectant teacher begs, *"Please, do as I ask,"* but in his mind he knows that'll not always happen. Not all kids are perfect, and none will always do as expected just because they were asked. They have their own agendas.

Like the horse, a child must be conditioned. Only then can a trainee discover why he should or shouldn't. The "Basics" allows him the freedom to see both sides. It puts him in submission to be taught, so he might discover options other than non-compliant behavior. Benefiting by the increase of knowledge his trainer offers, the child can now have his wants more readily accessible. This begins with him showing proper response when asked.

Why would I want to go back to the Basics with a child?

When teaching, it's best to start with a good foundation, and it's advisable during any training process to go-back and re-build a faltering one. Whenever a student refuses to be submissive, such as his trying to retain control by exhibiting an angered freak-out, this is a signal. They need a reminder as to their role of being the follower. They need to be taken back into the groundwork fundamentals of obedient behavior using the "Basics" as a refresher and rebuilding course, where the teacher becomes a trainer and the student submits as a trainee. In such a return, both have their roles strengthened.

Remember, that the kid really wants to have control in his life. And this is accomplished by him being **FREE FROM PAIN,** *and in getting the* **GRATIFICATIONS** *that he desires.* So, in order to properly establish a relationship where the child is willingly following the lead of a competent adult, the kid must feel that he will receive some of that. As he summits with his chosen obedience and follows the lead of his trainer, he additionally becomes free from the consequences of error. He increases his eligibility, because of this participation, for full rewards in support of his actions.

Common Sense: **Kids want you to lead them, not force them. As they make that choice to follow, they gain some control in their lives. They get what you are offering, and have to worry less about decisions. They become freer to experience JOY.**

The first object in any return to the "Basics" is to get voluntary cooperation from the pupil. This is fundamentally the student learning that he should follow the requests of his teacher. He should go, come, and respond politely without wigging-out or using inappropriate behavior. The teacher is obligated to learn effective ways which will stimulate this in his pupil. The objective of any training is to get a programmed response from the student, stimulated from the consistent request of his teacher, whom is assuming the enhanced role of acting as a trainer. In the Basics, proper techniques are displayed by both the trainer and the trainee.

For the same reasons that I would with a horse, I will likewise, create a practice session with the child in an environment free from other distractions. Here training will be much more readily accomplished. The objective is that they also learn when to go forward and when to change speed and directions; they learn when to come and when to stop. They are learning what behavior will be allowed. They learn the meanings of the words **"Yes"**, **"Please"**, **"No"**, and get a taste for earning a heart felt **"Thanks"**. They as students, and I as a teacher, learn our prospective roles: Them to be submissive, and me to give clear signals in order to properly lead.

Common Sense: **When taking the child back to the "Basics" use the same methods as in training a horse, and then add reasoning.**

Question: *Why is it that we, as parents or caregivers, think a child is supposed to perform just because we ask?*
Answer: Because we are assuming that they have been previously trained to do so. Like a conditioned animal, we think that they are supposed to follow without questioning the requests of their instructors.

Most children will have to be shown why they should do as asked; they haven't been trained to be submissive and to yield to an authority figure with just an asking. They haven't had the training of a horse which is forced to comply, and if it doesn't, then it's subjected to endure a negative pressure as it is introduced to pain compliance. Children, who are not regularly held to proper discipline, are probably used to being reasoned with. Their caregivers have tried that approach. ...Much in vain. The ineffectiveness of their past exposures is mostly one-sided. Although they have been reasoned with, sometimes at great length, they have not been forced to use reasoning. They've been given too much freedom of choice without being held to being responsible for their choices. They haven't been subjected to a leader who's actually engaged in exposing them to see ways to improve and become more skilled, and then for the proper reasons he forces them to do so. They probably have lacked being confronted with enough tough love to where they were expected to live up to a challenging standard.

To expect a child to choose to always follow along or make the right choices simply out of reasoning, is to assume they've developed that capability. Additionally, we are assuming, as instructors, we've also developed the skills to always present our ideas, in such a way, to where our students willing embrace them. {see: following Side note.} This is a long shot. It's wishful thinking on our parts. To enhance our ability to persuade, we should deliver our messages in a fashion where our students can understand their gains and benefits.

Working together, in harmony, toward a common goal or objective is the most perfect and desirable way to obtain the unity of cooperation. This utopia only comes with a willing student who has learned to be submissive by being subjected to a tough love. He was held to a standard of compliance, having been taught from a proper foundation when to stop and to change directions. He learns that life becomes easier as he conforms to the desires of his ruler. As result, he becomes willing to go along with his leader in order to avoid being subjected to discipline. **Or,** the student has the capacity to recognize the benefits which may be his, and so, he is willing to make thought-thru choices toward a shared objective.

"How will you obtain cooperation?"

A rational child has the ability to learn easier than a horse. The animal's trainer mostly keeps up a pressure in order to get it to do something different, and then rewards it when this happens. You can let a child know upfront what you expect and what reward you'll give in return for their certain behaviors. You must first obtain his attention, and then verbalize your and his role. You teach alternative behavioral choices before an outbreak. You make your expectations clear and easy for the child to understand, instead of subjecting him to being treated like a horse, which because of its limited understanding of spoken word is left to stumble on what proper behavior you expect. You, as a leader, can present your expectations in such a way that your child will embrace them because he can see how he can benefit, whereas with a horse it learns to recognize a benefit only through the repeated rigor of conditioning.

Side note **Going back to the "Basic" is a two fold quest. It is a careful training to our charges, so that they develop the proper foundation to respond to our requests. They learn to be submissive and to yield to our influence. They, as a result, learn to understand the benefits that can be theirs.**

Before, any of that can happen, additional training needs to take place. It is the training of ourselves. We need to understand how to get the most out of our charges. We need to realize when we're being efficient and equally aware when we're coming across as confusing and causing more harm than good. We should develop the skills to be able to train, before we start, or we will struggle and make mistakes that'll cause a need for ourselves and our charges to be re-trained.

This book is for you to learn the skills necessary to properly train your charges. After, you understand all aspects of your proper role, then, you'll be able to deliver to the child what he requires to help him develop.

The word "NO"

Life is full of rules that must be followed; otherwise we suffer the negative consequence of our actions. By choosing to not follow the rules, we're subjected to losing opportunities, freedoms, and possible gains. We must train our children to obey rules when we ask. It prepares them to have the capacity to receive more. Much of obeying rules has to do with understanding the true meaning of the word "NO". "No" is the predecessor of negative consequences.

"NO" is not a bad word, it is not an inhibitor of action that stifles and causes the shut down of forward movement. It is the opposite; it is the suggestion for a re-evaluation of present actions and the signal to pick a better choice. It allows the child to have control over their lives, before a punishment is delivered. It is the directive that a caring instructor gives in order to get his charges' attention, so that he can alert them into stopping only the unwanted portion of their actions or thinking. "No" is not the authoritarian command to **STOP!** ... It's the notice that a different direction is expected. The student needs to be aware that their present course of action will not be tolerated, so **CHANGE NOW!**

The delivery of a "NO!" is also the signal for the trainer to stay engaged with his charges until they understand what their proper alternative response should have been. For a trainer to withhold telling a charge, "No," is similar to being the owner of an untaught puppy, which is destined to never be trained under the pretense that it's too cruel to do so. As result, the pup/kid is never given the fair chance to reach its highest potential.

Some think that a set law only represents a declaration that connotes a "No!" towards behavior. To come to healthy terms with obeying a rule, the subjected person should respond as if rules represent imposed guidelines which declare what is acceptable. He should be anxiously involved in trying to discover what that is, not stifled into shutting down his momentum because he is fixated on what he is not allowed to do.

"Be wise; offer an alternative which will inspire."

When training a child, it is necessary to establish **who** is the leader, along with, **who** is the follower? Otherwise, on one hand is the teacher expecting to receive attention and compliance from his charge, and on the other hand is the student insisting on main-taining any degree of freedom that he can obtain. The two may be compatible in their choice to enter into a common goal, but yet still are in opposition as to their perspective roles. Both will go merrily along their ways until one wants something which the other chooses not to deliver. They then become contenders opposing each other as to who is subjective to whom. As a teacher, you be the leader, not a contender.

If you wait for a child to willing give you his attention and compliance, then you will only have it when he thinks he can benefit. As a trainer of persons it is, as with horses, equally important that you take the command of the situation; you establish forward movement by an increase of your body bubble and the increase of impact you have on the child. You teach them to pay attention to you. You persuade them to choose to do when you ask, and to change their directions when you say. You maintain your role as a trainer who gives the highest level of opportunity for his charges to improve.

Use the four steps of the Escalation of Aids to also build a proper foundation from which to train a child. Properly executed, they become the steps to teaching a child the Basics. Add to them reasoning behind each step when the child is old enough or able enough to think clearly. The child will see you as wise. You'll become, in his eyes, someone who is fair in your requests, and become a mentor which they would like to follow. You give them control over their lives, as they utilize the ability to reason out their best choice.

Steps to Teaching a Child the Basics
1. Ask
Follow the instructions, starting on page 249, as with a horse. You can substitute the kissing sounds for calling a child by name, and you may now use actual words. Compelling is the use of adding the word, "Please" to your requests for action. Like with a horse, be sure to use pleasant appealing tones and body language. This first step: "Ask" is getting the child to choose to obey. It is not a step of force.

In addition to establishing a foundation of you as the leader and they as the follower, teach more efficient ways than what the child was currently doing. Teach the child to see what gains will be theirs, if they do what you ask or develop the new skills which you offer. Remember that the child wants this freedom of choice. With an understanding of why they should be following your suggestions, comes an increase in their felt supremacy. They will learn to change, and comply, if they can see an appropriate gain.

2. **Suggest**

When the child refuses to do as you asked, or when you are unable to get them to accept your rationalizations of why they should give you their compliance, use the same follow-through as you used for the equine.   {Use caution when using a stick and also when waving of your arms wildly. Even though such usage is very effective when done at home for getting cooperation from a child, those two cues are frowned on out in public. If any stories should leak out, be prepared to deny them fervently. Otherwise, two men in the white coats might be paying you a visit with a tight white coat of your own.}

Add to your suggestion the gains and reasons behind your command. You are trying to talk the child into accepting and into entering into a common goal with you. If he doesn't cooperate, you move into a promise of discipline.

3. **Promise:** {Declaring a Discipline}

To promote self-preservation in believing that he still hasn't been forced to give up his freedom of choice, he may choose not to accept your reasoning and still attempt to place the blame and any lack of his compliance totally back onto you. He will try to justify his unwillingness to obey. This is something that is more difficult for a horse to do. It is something that you ought to be prepared to deal with, if you expect to train an unwilling child. Go back and re-read the use of this step, number three: "Promise". Follow its guidelines. In addition, check out the story of "The Stick" on page 301. You are now dealing with a child, so you, again, may lose the physical stick, but keep in mind its purpose. You must display that you are in control.

You have already taken the occasion, during the previous steps, to make sure that the child understands why he must do as you ask. Don't worry that he doesn't understand your meanings as you deliver his discipline. He knew he had it coming.

Like the horse, if the declared consequence is carried out, after several exposures the child will also become conditioned to respond just with your promise. You will not always have to execute the punishment. He will want to save himself the pain. Proper training is up to you. When you become consistent enough, that he expects your discipline, you will not always have to deliver. His self preservation will kick-in; he will respond just with a reminder and consider himself lucky. Remember, that for the child to have desire for change, as result of a punishment or a consequence, he must recognize the benefit of his castigation, and experience a change of heart; otherwise, it is merrily a form of inflicted revenge.

4. Remember to Reward.

Take time to allow the child to recognize rewards offered by you the trainer, the disciplinary. Offer praises and rewards for his slightest efforts. Similar to a horse, reward comes with the release of pressure. A reward means gratifications and gains that instill the desire to further comply. It is the rubbing that you do before and after the work-out or the round pen session that further bonds the animal to want to be with you. Develop also with a child ways that you may bond with them; show them that you don't have to always be about work.

Give the reward of Time.

An additional word about rewards: Giving a gift, as a reward, to a child is a good gesture; it could be food, money, or the gift of being left alone to do their chosen thing. Giving notice of their achievements is also appreciated. But, the most meaningful and most lasting is the one of time. As time is spent bonding with those in your care, you'll both reap rewards.

Common Sense: **There is no better chance to visit and get friendly than when you are engaged in a satisfying experience with your children. ... Eat a meal with them.**

What could be more satisfying than when you and your family are together enjoying one another's company and partaking in a meal? Mealtime is ideal, especially when no one is feeling the pressure to succeed, to teach or correct another, and all have the same unity of purpose: Stuffing Their Face. This is when the parents can have their children's attention. Physically neither is preoccupied in the rigors of life, and both can have the opportunity to converse by asking questions and listening to others' concerns. After a satisfying meal, everyone is more at ease and sharing ideas or just being together without alternative motives comes more freely.

Minimally once a week the family should spend this time together, free from the outside cares of the world. In this time they are encouraged to talk together, where they can get to know each other's ideas and passions. They get to appreciate one another's company. Preferably they should dine together once a day. In no other time is it easier to build family unity. Children should know that they have access to their parent's undivided attention, no less than once daily; they should not have to always compete with their parent's other interests. Turn off the television.

"With a horse it is so vital to establish proper roles, and then to spend some quality time, free from work, to build rapport and bonding. With this release, the horse will come to view its trainer as being more than someone who is just interested in forcing by putting them in uncomfortable situations."

It is likewise important for a child to view his parents and mentors as someone to be obeyed. But also, more than someone who is just trying to exercise their control. Do not cheat your children out of bonding time with you by being too busy. Don't compromise mealtime with seeking entertainment from the television, spend it discussing ideas and supporting their concerns. Who knows; your kids might learn to value your counsel? Your teenager could again grow to appreciate being with you?

{More information on these **aids** and the **clues** that go with them are found in Chapter Fifteen: "**Graduating Escalation of Involvement**"

There you will find, in more detail and in ways more suitable for the child, additional helps in getting them to submit and change their course of actions.}

CHAPTER 14:

A LESSON OF PRACTICE

Common Sense: **A great guide understands where the true summit is, and how to get there.**

* * *

Common Horse Sense: Trailer loading.
Objective: {Getting the horse into a trailer.}

In most rural horses' lives there comes a time necessary to load that animal into a trailer, this can be exciting for the trainer and the horse. It requires getting the animal to do something new and unfamiliar. There are, on the whole, only two different ways of accomplishing this new challenge. Either by overpowering it and placing it into the trailer, {i.e. doing the task for the horse; no choice was given.} or guiding the animal to choose to engage in some degree in the unified purpose of his moving into the trailer. {I.e. you provide the stimulation and the horse does it for himself.} There are as many methods and ideas of how to do these ways as there are horse trainers. Let me share several methods that I have experienced to help you decide on what your best options are in getting a charge to do something new …possibly something he may not want to do.

1. **Doing most of the task for the horse:** Where it is true that the horse did remain erect, and on four feet most of the time, you still, without obtaining any consent, did physically over-power it and forced it into the trailer. You pushed, pulled, and shoved; you did whatever was necessary to out muscle that being and get him to fulfill your wishes. Congratulations! You got the task done …but only through your efforts. Your horse learned nothing, except to despise you, and that you are toughest. So pat yourself on the back, you'll need it for the next time when you have to go through the same similar approach. Forcing is easy enough to do when dealing with a colt, but without a mechanical device it is almost impossible to do with the older and more powerful. A grown horse is simply too big to place into a trailer without getting some sort of cooperation; its ability to resist is too great.

Direct contrast to pure physical intervention is: **To obtain cooperation without forcing.** This means, in the perfect world, I merely open the door, and the horse walks right in. We've all seen it done before, therefore we think, "That's so easy; no problem." *What is missing, when we witness such voluntary compliance, is the process that was used to teach it to load in the first place.*

Whenever a pupil cooperates, how great the ease, until, for whatever reasons in its one-way mind, the animal decides that, *'Today I am not going to get into the trailer.'* Now the excitement begins. The trainer is left to use any variation of methods to entice the horse to load.

2. **In response to stimulation, the horse decides to cooperate.** Under compulsion, it chooses to enter the trailer: either as result of your promptings, or in effort to obtain some sort of gratification. When getting the resistant to do something against their will, it is better to solicit their involvement.

*** Side note ***   If your goal, in reading this book, is to strengthen child development methods rather than for horse training tips, then just take the lessons and Common Horse Sense ideas and put a human slant to them. These principles easily apply to both. I have used these techniques when addressing new and different challenges with both humans and animals. They will work whenever you need cooperation from others.

Use more force!

About fifteen years ago, I had a three-year-old filly, whose desires seemed solely centered around pleasing her rider. She was just a pleasant animal. As a young colt she would follow her dam into the trailer; it was no big thing for her. Later as she grew up, she still entered freely ... no problems at all.

Once, I borrowed her to a friend to be used together with other horses herding sheep. She loaded easily, and was on her way for a summer of working in the mountains. Four months later he returned with the others. Where was my previously submissive filly?

The next morning after his return, he said, "She just stood there; she didn't want to be led into the trailer. We were in a hurry, so we tried to force the issue by pulling her in with a rope tied to her neck. The working end was looped around a front rack and back again to the rear. We pulled tight, taking up the slack like a pulley. She was half-way in when she decided to hang-back hard! She flung back and peeled the skin off a fore-leg. Now, she freaks-out just getting close to the trailer. I didn't have the time, or know what else to do, so I just took the other, already-loaded horses, and left her up there."

The Problem: *The horse as an independent thinker does not want to engage in the predetermined objective.* {She doesn't want to get in the trailer, even though it is something she was used to doing in the past.}

So there I am. I loaned him a good loading horse, and he turned her into a frenzied nut case in just two loading experiences. I was fuming inside from his lack of responsibility, but I thought, *"He is a friend, so I won't let on."* Instead I said, "I'll go get her day after tomorrow." There was no way I was going to risk him damaging her further. Now, I had an injured horse ...both physically and mentally.

Sure-enough, two days later as I carefully tried to persuade without getting her too excited, her recently learned behavior caused a new freak-out at coming within ten feet of the trailer. During this loading attempt, I didn't tie her solid to the racks. She simply reared back and pulled the rope zinging backwards thru my hands, causing them to seriously heat up. I could see that, indeed, I had a problem. I will have to undo these last three negative experiences.

It did cross my masculine mindset to use a manly response. I could force her into the trailer in order to be done with the problem by using stout ropes and literally over-powered her against her own resistance and strength. I also knew that in her mindset it would be difficult to load her without her getting further hurt. My forcing was an option of having her, at-least, home and off the mountain, but probably scarred further. ...I needed to rethink.

Something had changed in my once submissive and gentle filly. She had chosen for whatever reason not to comply, and then furthered her desires for self-control by completely fighting against the whole idea. She had successfully refused three times and got away with it. {In dealing with a horse, three is the magic number of times that is takes to turn a negative reaction into a bad pattern, or a bad habit.} She had now established a pattern of defiance and would continue to react using an out-of-control behavior when confronted with this loading problem. Unless things changed, she'd continue in this bad habit, because it had worked for her. She had only one thing now on her mind in regards to the trailer, *"I will not go in, and I will defy any attempt to make me."*

Some might feel that the manly response does work, and so be not afraid to use any number of various compelling cowboy methods using ropes and restraints to restrict the animal's freedom of movement. They force the animal to choose its limited options as an alternative to displaying resistance. Although it works in most cases to take away all other choices, leaving only for the animal to load up, these methods still give the animal **something to fight**

against. The trailer and the new pain of the restraints further act to trigger the animal into more resistance—as in the case of my filly.

With fear, the defiant horse wastes itself by fighting, instead of looking for an alternative of confrontational avoidance, such-as remaining calm and following the prompting of the trainer. After learning to resist against a stimulus, the animal will, next time, be more likely to start anxious avoidance just from fear and thought of more discomfort. Fear is a form of pain, and with an animal that is afraid its perception of pain are actually causing and inflating discomfort and grief. The manly response tries to force compliance despite fear.

*** Side note*** **The phrase, "Giving them something to fight against," refers to applying an excess of compelling pressure, instead of persuading compliance. The pressure actually moves the recipient into resisting harder than ever. As with the rider who pulls back too hard on the reins, instead of bumping them lightly, the excessive discomfort signals a horse to resist against pressure itself.**

When time is not of great abundance and an uncooperative horse needs to be loaded quickly, subject it to a greater terror than the trailer. Such a terror is: **Being stuck in a scary situation and also being denied a herd.** This is done by driving a horse, similar to the loading of dumb cattle, into the trailer by means of squeeze gates and chutes. It's the fastest method of loading an untrained animal. This is easy and doesn't take any time commitment to do, just equipment. With a stout, funneled squeeze system the horse has no other choice except getting into the trailer. It is frightened and pressured until it does. It'll quickly realize the dread of being separated from other herd mates as it witnesses them moving into a trailer, and it is being left behind in an uncomfortable situation. So it'll choose to load out of desire to avoid the greater horror.

The questions to be asked when deciding if it is important enough to put in a commitment of time to train the horse to load on its own is: "Will I always be able to use the squeeze method of forcing this horse to load? It is so easy to drive the horse into the trailer, but I haven't taught it a thing —only used its flight response to accomplish my goal."

"Is it advantageous for me to invest the necessary time to teach this horse to load without it having to be driven in as a wild animal?"

Common Sense: **I must change my approach of forcing, for her to change her reaction of fear and resistance.**

Some alternative approaches use a combination of bugging or relentlessly pestering. They don't introduce a great reason to fight, but still they only work because the charge is worn down in their resistance.

Using the "Bug Method"

My alternative plan was put into play. It was formed two days before as I recalled a supposedly proven method I had not used, but had heard about. It is used to get even the rankest knot-head to change its mind about loading. It does take a big block of commitment, about two hours. Having her resist the easiest way of just following me into the trailer and being concerned with making it easier for future loadings, I decided to take the initiative to re-train her right. I would be masterful. I would make her uncomfortable and cause her to embrace the common goal of loading into the trailer; all the while, not giving her something to fight against.

This method involves using a lead rope, two guys, and one six-foot lightweight pole to be used as a poker …

{My son and I spent the next hour and a-half loading that filly into the trailer using the "Bug Method". If you choose to use it on a totally defiant knot head, then you, like-wise, may have to commit that time or longer.}

…the unwilling horse is moved to the trailer, as-close-as she will let you get her before she reacts against it and starts getting nervous. Now stand holding her lead rope, with her looking in the trailer's direction. As long as she is looking that direction, give her the reward of touching or rubbing her forefront together with a calm voice of re-assurance. If she fights against you, then you are rushing it and need to be further away to start with.

The beginning object is to get her to stand facing the trailer calmly. Let her stand until she realizes that she will get no beatings or there will be no forcing to get closer, and she can trust you in that regard.

After she will stand quietly, start putting about two pounds of pressure on her lead rope—pulling her toward the trailer. She has just learned that you are not going to force her into the trailer; furthermore, she hasn't yet had a reason to fight. Time is not an issue. If she senses you are in a hurry and will try to force her, she will have reason to take flight or fight. You must be the master teacher. You mustn't let that happen. Let up before she blows up. Use no more than two pounds pulling force. This method will work in loading the most stubborn defiant animals. The key is that as a trainer you have changed your approach; you are no longer forcing, only coaxing politely.

As you are in the front coaxing, the second guy taps the animal on the rump with the six foot pole, very lightly at first. He continues to bug the animal at different locations on her flanks and rump; she will eventually move forward to relieve the bugging pressure. I believe the proper therapeutic expressions that can used to describe what you are trying to do with this "problem child" are ...

First: ..."**Establish and maintain rapport.**" This is done with your calm manner and actions as you re-assure the animal, and you both look in the direction of the trailer while standing in its close proximity. The horse can see the trailer is not causing you to stress. Your activity is to be together, without either exhibiting or subjecting the other to confrontational behavior.

And Second: ..."**Build insularity.**" This is where you and the horse will address the problem, unified, not as before with you against each other. You and your charge joined together against your common foe.

Now, the new problem is not the trailer or even the fact that she will not get into it, haven't you just spent time building rapport and showing her these are of no more threat? The new problem is that confounded guy with that pole; he never stops. It just keeps tapping and bugging, tapping and bugging.

The solution is to get away from them, the pole and the bugging. Your horse needs to be trained that she is getting relief from her problem as she moves closer to the trailer. Eventually getting into the trailer will become the cure. So encourage your helper to continue to torment the animal. The appropriate response to be looking for from the horse is a flinch, like a reaction to a fly. Don't let your helper tap her too hard at first. She may become desensitized against the light tapping after a while, so the pressure may need to be increased; you are still looking for no more of a reaction than a muscle flinch or a twitch. The purpose is to "Bug" her, not beat her, into the trailer. The smart horse will give up and move into the trailer to relieve herself against this nuisance.

The more stubborn animal may require a bugging of some time. Remember that as the horse moves toward the trailer to get relief from the bugging, you must let up on the two pounds of pressure pulling it in that direction. Your helper must likewise give it a break of ten to fifteen seconds from the previous distinct and separated tapings which had been coming at her every two to four seconds. In addition, you continue to re-assure and calm the animal. At first this moving toward the trailer may be only the simple act of looking in the direction of it. Up the ante of what she has to do to in order to get relief, after she has figured out that it is obtained when she starts directing her attention towards where you want her to go. It doesn't take long before she grasps the idea and chooses to move closer toward the trailer. But it may take some time before the obstinate animal chooses to go inside. No swearing or loud yelling or angry motions. You are seeking to get the animal to react against the pole, not against you. It needs to feel your calmness and keep trust in you, as you continue to pull with two pounds of pressure on the lead rope toward the opening. As forward advance is obtained, release to one-half-pound of pressure for a moment. Keep remembering not to apply too much pull on the lead rope, as this could again give her something to fight against. Even the most obstinate animal will eventually soon give in and try to load; it is better than being tormented by something that can not be beaten.

After getting frustrated enough from being bopped by the pole, the horse it will try to get into the trailer. Help it succeed. I have on many occasions had to place one of the front legs of a young inexperienced animal onto the raised trailer platform. By this time, it is purposely trying to get into the trailer, so this act will be perceived as helping it out and showing what is accepted. As it finally goes into the trailer, reward for proper compliance. Spend several minutes bonding and relaxing together. Only after the horse has been made to feel welcome with its success in the trailer, can you coax the animal to unload. If it is reluctant or unsure, use the same method of bugging. Always use relief and reward as it shows progress.

The whole process is then repeated, five more times, to imprint into the equine brain the rewards of compliance. Each time will get repeatedly easier. Soon it will be ok with the whole trailer loading thing.

You have just taken an animal and used its instincts to your advantage. You had a charge that was fighting you every bit as hard as you fought it. You stopped giving it an obvious reason to fight. You applied a relief of pressure, followed by an "Ask" or a "Solicit for Cooperation". And at the slightest try or positive response you gave a momentary release of pressure. You controlled its reasons for fighting back; you didn't take them away. The release of pressure signaled to the charge's instincts that all was well. It calmed down and diminished its desire to react against your biddings. Then when pressure was again felt, it readily complied further to your requests in order to prevent more discomfort. This method works in dealing with people too. I have used if many times since.

Reward Methods

Common Sense: **The use of a reward is superior to the use of a punishment. It helps the charge maintain their belief that they have some control in their own lives.**

Offering the reluctant a reward instead of a punishment is superior to the "Bugging Method." The horse isn't given the slightest reason to fight back, and a Rewards Method grants to them total freedom of choice in their actions. The disadvantage is that it requires advance preparation that sometimes can not be enacted on the spot. So don't forget the previous method, which for me has always been a proven trailer-loading winner.

For meeting the criteria as a Reward Method of loading—any method where an animal simply walks into the open end gate qualifies. It could be as easy and simple as having an experienced horse inside the trailer, and allowing the novice to walk in behind it or as elaborate as spending hours and days to desensitize the whole loading process by feeding inside.

Once, I discovered an approach that was so easy, it made me feel guilty, like I was doing something wrong: Last year I had five fresh horses in training. Of course trailer loading was put off. I wasn't looking forward to the time involved in "Bugging" each horse into the trailer. Previously, they had been hauled from their birth place by forcing them into a squeeze chute and onto the trailer similar a bunch of wild mustangs—like unto they had become from living in isolation and never having been handled, trimmed, or even touched before. I stumbled onto a great technique of loading, during my preparations to use a modified Bug Method on those fresh horses.

This time, I would use the same bucket of oats, as a reward in trailer training, that I had been offering my fresh horses to help establish rapport. They had grown accustomed to getting a couple of mouthfuls of oats after each training session as a prize. I'd allow them to eat out of a bucket that I was holding. As they chewed, I'd talk calmly and rub or pet them. They looked forward to this reward time, and became quite jealous if another rival horse received training followed by his reward, yet, they didn't get the same opportunity. After putting off this portion of their training, as long as possible, I acquired an assistant in order to man the poking pole. I assigned me, him, and their bucket into teaching these five to load.

Using the "New Reward Method"

"Stand behind this horse and be prepared to poke it with this pole, if I say to," I informed, to prepare my assistant for the worst.

I led the in-training-pupil to the open trailer to look at an experienced "Judas Horse" standing preloaded and tied in the front of the trailer. My trainee accepted, as a token of rapport, a bite of oat. The beginner offered no resistance, and stood its ground peering into the open trailer at the other rival also eating oats inside. I took the occasion to re-assure the new one by rubbing it and talking in a calm nature. I gave it an additional mouthful and acted like what we were doing was old school; everything was calm and normal and the more oats were certainly available. I moved the bucket into the open door and gave a two pound pull on the lead rope. Forward goes my novice up to the open gate. I gave it another bite of oats, then again moved the bucket containing the savory snack deeper into the trailer. The horse showed signs of wanting to follow. One at a time I asked for a front foot and placed it up on the trailer floor. The trainee showed neither fear, nor desire to flee. Again, I tightened the lead rope with two pounds of pull; my trainee loaded right in, then stepped over to the oat bucket and took another bite. As I rubbed her for a couple of minutes, she took in two more mouthfuls. We unloaded and tried it again. Four more times the novice went willingly into the trailer, where I offered a reward and reassurance.

No problems, at all, were encountered. My new horse had a common goal with me: "Get into the trailer and get a reward." My assistant stayed to help with two others, but never had to raise the bugging pole. I never had to force compliance. This method of rewarding, instead of forcing or "Bugging", worked so well, that in the space of forty minutes I had loaded each of the five new animals, five or six times. Gradually, I was able to raise the expectation I placed on them, in order to get their treat. As I finished, they would go into the trailer and their patiently await their reward.

The next two nights I did the same thing again; practicing loading with all five horses. I didn't need to coax, just lead them through the trailer's end gate and give their earned reward. So efficient did this method work, that a week later, as a neighbor girl was passing behind the trailer, while riding one of these green horses, true to its new learned skill, it went in without prompting—carrying the panicking rider. There it stood patiently waiting for a rewarding bite of oats. A squeal from the panic-stricken girl alerted me to the mishap. I had mistakenly left the trailer end gate open, so I can't blame the animal for thinking that this was as open invitation for all passersby, "Free oats are inside and being served." My loud laughter succeeded to defuse the girl's nervousness. There was nothing else I could do except feed the animal its earned reward. Needless to say, after that I kept the trailer's end gate closed. Even a practice ride towing the trailer around the neighborhood with all six horses loaded at once didn't upset any of my new student-horses, they were all trailer broke.

Common Sense: **To keep your charge willing to keep trying, reward longer than you work.**

My charges were responding easier, faster, and with less stress on all concerned. I was still succeeding in the same task of teaching an animal to trailer load. They were receiving gain for their positive efforts, verses a promised punishment for their misdeeds. Since I already had a good relationship with my horses in training, they trusted me. I didn't have to waste time or effort. All that was required was for me to re-valuate, reassess, and refine my own techniques. My own ability as an equine specialist had improved, as result, my training methods became easier and more effective.

* * *

Common Sense: **The inexperienced will charge a hill, lacking the good judgment to conserve.**
The master, in order to keep his momentum, will slow down to match his abilities.

CHAPTER 15:

GRADUATING ESCALATION OF INVOLVEMENT

Common Sense: **To engage another without pain compliance, they and I must share a Common Goal.**

To get another person to change their ways, participate in a new idea, or even to decide to cooperate and address a perplexing problem, I must either by an overwhelming force get them to do as I ask, or bring them to awareness where they anticipate something in return. Just like getting a horse to load into a trailer, forcing will only give the child who is determined to resist an enemy to battle against. Forcing doesn't get either of us what we really want. The best approach is using an alternative other than compelling others by brute force. Their lack of cooperation signals an increasing effort from me to get them to accept a transforming change—first to their behavior, then their desires.

I will not cease in my involvement of getting another to recognize that as they discard current resistance, and substitute it with obedience, they become eligible for rewards for their compliance. These earned gains will further stimulate a joining of this student with me, his trainer; both enter into a common goal for the purpose of conquering the original problem. This brings us closer to **WHAT WE REALLY WANT:** the freedom to personally control our pursuit of Joy.

Graduated Escalation of Involvement:

Be prepared to be Bucked Off

Keep showing Unconditional LOVE

Take away Freedom

Take away something of value
Restore incrementally, relative to positive efforts

{GET BIG}
On
Enforcement of Consequences

Take a break for the slightest try

Declaration of Impending Consequences

Give back control by shortening consequences for positive efforts

Authoritatively Command Compliance

Give back control by offering a choice of compliant terms

Discover Rewards for the
Performance of Positive Behavior

Solicit Cooperation

Ask please...
Reason with and help define positive gains
Offer incentives

Start To Address the
Original Problem

Student and Trainer
Working Together
Solving the Problem
In a **Common Goal**

Freedom to personally control my pursuit of **JOY**
{THIS IS WHAT WE REALLY WANT}

Time for a Re-training

It is a new day, and your horse is acting head-strong and fresh; he is resisting yielding to your signals and commands, even though he was previously conditioned differently. He is choosing to act obnoxious or defiant to get you to quit bothering him. Therefore, something needs to be done or the animal will come to realize that he can get away with this inappropriate behavior. As a trainer, your motive for interaction is to assist your charge to become the best that it can possibly be, therefore you will not let his lack of compliance pass. Whenever you notice a failure of your horse to yield to your of guiding, as though the horse seems to have forgotten just who is riding whom, something needs to be done to restore proper order. You need to re-establish that you are the one in control and he is the subservient.

"How?"

You can for the next two hours of riding either be on edge as he slowly gives up his resistance, after both of you practice again and again. Or you can take him back through the "Basics" where he is quickly put back into submission, until it becomes his goal to work with and please you. Either way, you are in for a period of retraining before the horse again becomes that wonderful animal he was when you put him away wet and worn-out last time.

Similarly, whenever you notice a failure of child to yield to your will, do to their defiant or unbearable behavior, it is your best bet to take him through the "Basics" as well. It gives you, as a trainer, the chance to again establish that you are the leader, and the child is to be the obedient.

Side note **Notice: You only need to re-establish yourself as a trainer when students are acting wrongly in their behavior. You don't need to re-train just because they have a negative attitude. A child's bad attitude is something you can't control or change without them coming into a new discovery. Your intent should focus on their unacceptable behavior. If they choose to cooperate and do it with a less than perfect attitude which doesn't display them as rude or abusive, you should accept this offering. Compensate their obliging service that**

they may discover the type of behavior which brings acceptance from you. With changed behavior, even compelled, eventually a new attitude will follow as your students become aware of their increase of benefits.

A more human oriented version of the "Basics" is the **"Graduating Escalation of Involvement"** {EI}. During the EI, you progressively become more involved with your child by influencing him either with reasoning or by exerting a pressure against him, until he performs a specific positive action of behavior. The performance of your charge's new compelled positive behavior, done as a reaction to avoid a consequence, does momentarily establish the fact that you are in control, yet it yields at best only a temporary change. Only his discovering rewards for positive performance will lead toward a lasting change. He may feel these rewards in his mind as he practices and reviews during calm periods by using rational thinking, or in the heat of a confrontation where he's exercising an opportunity to choose and is pushed into an awakening of translating compelling reasons into benefits of gain. Upon recognizing {discovering} the gains for his new behavior, he now can enhance his position and move down into working with you instead of against you. He can choose to enter into the Common Goal Box. It will become his best interest to do so, that he may receive more gains. In this joining of common interests values, character traits can be experimented with and analyzed by the student as he is no longer acting in defiance or in resistance. Here, he can discover even more additional benefits and further gratifications for the performance of his positive behavior. Here, he may further decide to change additional behavioral patterns when he realizes that these new changes bring with them a reduction of his troubles and offer the freedom to pursue his conquest of **JOY.**

In the "Basics" the horse has no real choice; he performs as result of a **conditioning**. You and it must practice until things become right. In the "EI" process you get the child to yield to your will, also by a conditioning, but thrown into his transformation is giving him the opportunity to use his choice of reasoning. The methods of the trainer are to teach the child to not act out in defiance with unbearable behavioral outbursts. You as a guide, direct him to what his most prudent choice is, and he chooses to perform it. With proper techniques and training the results will allow both the student and his trainer to solve the original problem. With this achievement both get closer to what they want. The dissimilarity between the horse and the child is: the horse is conditioned to respond unquestionably, and the child is taught conditional usage of his wisest choice.

The crescive levels of "EI" get harder and require more involvement the further away they get from **Working Together.** The effort of the trainer has to become more assertive to match the resistance of his pupil against cooperating to address the **Original Problem**. The trainer's objective is to direct a behavioral change and reversal back down towards the **Common Goal Box.** In order to succeed in effecting change with his student, the trainer has to structure a way for his charge to win. Only then will their opposing intensities lessen and permit the two to join together in solving the original problem, that peace may be obtainable.

Solicit Cooperation
Ask please…
Reason with, and help define positive gains.
Offer incentives.

Solicit Cooperation is the first step of "EI" where a teacher is striving to effect change in another's behavior in order to solve the **Original Problem**. In this step, the teacher is asking, "PLEASE." He is begging for the student's help. This is the only step where the student's wishes can be permitted to stop the teacher's commitment of continuing in the involvement process. Only here can the teacher simply drop the question; his lack of affect will have minimal impact on his student who probably is an old-hand at trying to retain a sense of control by refusing to cooperate when asked.

Why burden himself more? After having his petition for cooperation shunned, the self-serving teacher can choose to abandon his original problem by backing off from his appeal. This teacher's purpose for interacting was to ultimately lighten a private burden. He can dismiss his obligation to teach and the student's responsibility to learn. Why stress further; he can probably get the task completed easier by simply doing the task himself? With either backing off, or doing it himself, doesn't there become sort of an ending to the original problem?

However, if it was his design as a teacher to truly affect a change in his student's life, then ending his "EI" by dropping a request for cooperation is not an option. When driven by more than a self-serving motivation, an involved teacher is concerned with more than his selfish counter-part. A greater purpose demands more involvement.

When his student refuses to do his task, the dedicated teacher, who is asking for the student's cooperation so a greater lesson may be discovered, now must act as a guide pointing out a better way. He offers a preferred solution to the problem while keeping the student under obligation to cooperate. To get **obedience without** having to resort back to **pain compliance**, this guide points out the positive benefits the student could be receiving.

If there ain't any good profit to be had; why should the tyke be will'n to oblige?   … To engage their compliance, the guide will convey his understanding of the possible gains available to the student. He has to use additional teaching skills to channel the student into listening and furthermore wanting to adopt a newly aroused desire to change a current behavior.

Some incentives which a guide might point out to get his charges to perform, while still believing that they've retained some control, are:

1. **Appeal to the student's sense of duty.** {Thereby, the student can be gaining more self respect and self esteem.}

2. **Offer a bribe** for the student to comply. In other words, offer some gain for their behavior or conduct. Example: *"If you do this for me, then I will see that you get something you want."* A bribe is an inducement which leaves the presenter under contract to fulfill a commitment or an obligation. The giver has to pay for the service, yet the recipient is still free to choose to comply or not. The presenter has diminished his role as an independent influencer of preferred solutions and become subjected to the student's say-so. A bribe leaves all the choice of compliance up to the recipient.

Common Sense: **The personal gain available from a bribe is only limited by one's ability to hold out for a greater sum.**

Although a bribe is ever-so important in trying to talk a charge into compliance, please consider the fundamental difference between a bribe and a reward. Instead of being offered a bribe, {*i.e. the pointing out of a gain to be received after or before the fulfillment of a task*} which leaves the recipient believing that cooperation is negotiable, he should be left to get an earned reward. {*i.e. a gain given because of a performed effort.*} More end-result oriented are they who respond to tasks because they're compelled out of duty. ... Not from being enticed with a goody.

In contrast, rewards are benefits received as result of a service or an attainment. They are not offered to induce a behavior; they're given after the fact. They are much more spontaneous than a bribe, and don't leave any place for negotiation.

Rewards include, but are not limited to:
   a. Giving a break from stress.
   b. Giving someone something that they'd want.
   c. Displaying to a charge an acceptance of them or their service.
   "Great job!" or *"Keep up the good work!"*
   d. Conveying an appreciation: Saying, *"Thanks, you really helped."*
   e. Boosting an ego. *"You-da' man!"*
   f. Giving a show of affection.

The incentive should fit the person for whom it was intended. Offering a cookie or clapping go a long ways toward showing a three-year-old appreciation, but there are more valuable rewards for the teenager. In the mildest sense it is the release of pressure; the quitting of confrontation. It can be a supporting wink of assurance, a nod of acceptance, or a payment as rich as a genuine heartfelt "Thanks." It can also escalate clear up to the extreme of the Dallas Cowboy Cheerleaders performing at the SuperBowl Half-Time by marching around and highlighting the attributes of the praiseworthy recipient, while the Marine Band is playing, "For He's A Jolly Good Fellow." A reward is any gift that produces a feeling greater than being uncomfortable.

3.   **Show a better approach:** This will work if the student is being non-cooperative because he doesn't recognize a more efficient way. The struggling will appreciate seeing an easier method.

4.   **Appeal to the students:** Enlist their desire to be nurturers. Explain honestly that you are in need of their assistance. Help them to see that they can be of service to you. Indirectly you are offering to the students a self-worth that comes as they realize that others need them and the services they can render.

5.   **Challenge the student.** Allow him to show just how well he can perform the task. The student is led to believe he'll receive an increase of satisfaction, a boost of self-worth, the expanded praise of others, or a chance to show off.

6.   **Offer a relief from pain**: Use logic and explain to the student how their life is going to be better, if they perform the asked task. It will eventually result in less work or less suffering.

Here is one of my favorite: *"Do this, and there will be no need for me to beat you. Therefore, you'll receive less physical pain than if you choose not to comply."*

A parent truly involved in his kid's life could even say, *"Look at all the **emotional stress** you will be saving; you won't be suffering from the guilt of not minding your mom."* You help the child to recognize his gains: both physically and mentally.

As the child acknowledges one of these incentives and then cooperates, receiving a gain as he does well, he enhances a desire to continue receiving gratifications through additional collaboration. Indirectly, he is electing to work with his guide/trainer toward solving the original problem. As result of his new behavior, ultimately he realizes that he's getting the very thing he'd wanted in the first place: **Maintaining more personal control and freedom to seek out his personal quest of happiness.**

When it comes down to getting the child to respond when asked, if you had spent time previously with the child doing things from a common ground, while utilizing the child's interests, a lot of time and effort could be saved. With such common involvement, you take on the role as mentor and companion. In **rapport**, both are free to join in harmony and conformity. No other way is easier or more effortless than simply asking the child to do something, then he without thought or question does it out of a connection of love. He wants to act to further build up additional bonds between you and him. He performs just because you asked.

When the guide has exhausted his ability to point out acceptable corresponding benefits, and he's not able to solicit his student's change toward any tangible signs of cooperation, with that, he should move up to the next level in the Graduating Escalation of Involvement.

Let me state that again, only stronger: *Whereas you are a committed to effect a positive change in the behavior of your charge, and he refuses to do as you ask, even after you have pointed out all the benefits of cooperation, you, then must move up to the next level of involvement in order to apply pressure towards the improvement of his behavior.*

In the next levels of EI the guide becomes more. He becomes as an escalated therapeutic trainer who will use instruction and discipline to affect the behavior of his charge. He, the trainer will not dismiss the lack of obedience as he might have when the request for cooperation was merely an asking of "Please."

<u>Note to remember</u>: **As an effective trainer, never should you start the process of aiming to change someone's behavior unless you are willing to go all the way. Otherwise, you display no creditability to your charge.**

Authoritatively Command Compliance
Give back control by offering a choice of compliant terms

As you command compliance, in this second level, you are now a trainer using assertiveness to get results. Your main purpose is to get the charge back down to the level of a common goal, where-in both choose to work together to solve the problem. You do not re-negotiate with your charge once you have set this parameter, until he has shown his willingness with some compliance in the matter. Then, you can give back some power so-that he may view the change you are requiring of him as still being his choice. As a trainer, you no longer nicely ask for his cooperation; you command compliance with authority.

*** **Attention!** Do you often start to get another to do your will by your issuing all commands, instead of asking them first? Listen to the self-justified; often they skip asking and instead start off with voicing a command. Are you one? Do you say something in the line of, **"YOU NEED TO CLEAN YOUR ROOM!"** instead of saying, "Will you clean your room?"

If you had jumped into this second level of involvement: {**told the charge what to do, without ever asking first**} you may retrace back to soliciting cooperation by using the phrase, "Let me explain my reasons why." This will give the idea of being in control back to the student if he accepts any of your reasons as valid.

By issuing a command for compliance to a charge, the opportunity of controlling one's own personal pursuit of JOY has been denied. It has been replaced with a decree which must be either blamelessly obeyed, or will have to, in some degree, be fought against. Yet, by offering a choice of complaint terms, you are giving the student an opportunity to reclaim some personal control which he doesn't have to fight to keep; he feels it is his choice of how to cooperate. His willing choice of terms has a greater influence to guide him into de-escalation and towards working together than the thought of him just abiding to your command. Many people resent being told what to do, and will, solely for the sake of not loosing their freedom, fight against this control from others. When you are no longer asking, but rather, **"TELLING PEOPLE WHAT TO DO,"** you could get this resentment. *******

The key to success in obtaining compliance is to:

First: **Ask for willing cooperation.**
         ... the agreeable ones will help out.

Second: **Offer a choice of compliant terms ...** *to the **reluctant**.*

Third: If no success is obtained, **A direct statement of what is expected is presented** ... *to the **obstinate child**.*

At this third level, there is no arguing or trying to talk that person into a type of conformity. You, as an authority figure, simply state what is expected, and move on. You hold them accountable where they are obligated to perform.

If you had to move into this level in an effort to get compliance from a child that is acting out in defiance, or from one that is displaying abusive behavior problems, then your foremost objective is to regain control. In order to have any success you must strip this warrior of the control that he is obtaining by his inappropriate behavior. You have to out-power this combatant by doing whatever is needed to train him again to use an alternative behavior. You the leader, in an as-simple-as-possible way, tell him what you expect him to do. There is no discussion of his feelings or allowing him to defend his reasoning, until he is in a de-escalated emotional state and can control his outbursts of behavioral displays. In other words, you distance him from his problem until he displays a calm teachable demeanor. Either you leave and dismiss yourself of the argument by your declaring an end of the conversation, or you separate him for a period of time from his emotional stimulation to

294 JUST WHO AM I TRAINING ANYWAY   DAVE SLATER

take a few minutes to think of his situation. Your initiation of this separation causes in him a **forward movement**; you have caused a decrease in his defiance.} Before you allow him your audience in order to continue to defend himself, you must establish yourself as the leader once more. { see: Chapter 13: Going Back to the Basics}.

Quit giving an opportunity for arguing. Arguing is a method of communication with each individual waiting for an opportunity to voice his opinion to the other; each focuses mainly on personal emphasis without any attempt to understand the other's point of view. As long as the child has a chance to argue, he has an opportunity to display his controlling influence. By you not continuing to engage in an exchange of will, your child has lost some of his power and you have obtained more.

First, he is cut off from his argumentative heat-of-the-moment combativeness, and subsequently not allowed to express his views or position until he can calmly show some sort of compliance. To be able to regain a portion of his feelings of control back, he must again appear teachable; he'll have to de-escalate again into some sort of submissive state. Power is what he wants, and you have just stripped him of his. So, yielding to your influence is what he temporarily does.

Once partial compliance has been obtained by the de-escalation of his fight or flight mode, and he is actually starting to except the idea of conforming to the original request, then you may offer terms that let the student feel he has not totally lost all his freedom of personal choice. In regards to your purpose of getting his further cooperation, you can now offer a partial relief of the controlling power which you have displayed. Because now he will see you as in control and as himself as choosing to obey, he will be able to more clearly define his role of working with you, as he is de-throned in his struggling attempt of having to be the leader. Even though, he may choose to obey your commands only to eliminate a pending disciplinary action, no matter; he will see it as still his choice, and as him working together with you, instead of working for you.

Change can now occur. The combination of retaining some of his freedom of choice, the gratification of receiving a reward, and his continuing desire for more possible benefits will convince him into working with you further, as he develops the ability to see beyond the moment of his need to act out inappropriately. He once more feels in control of his destiny when he exercises his choice of how to cooperate. Even though he is doing something that someone else demanded, the fact that he was able to have some choice in the matter has erased most of the sting of conforming. **By keeping his ability to somehow win,** he becomes open to change.

Getting Cooperation from the Non-combative Child:

When any child lets me know they choose not to comply, and they can do it without resorting to insolent or intolerable behavior, then I can treat them differently than I would treat their rude or disruptive counterparts. When they can calmly communicate, *"No, I don't want to {clean my room},"* this gives me the freedom to set the problem off to the side, to isolate it, and to address it as not being a part of the student or myself. For with them, there is more readily a hope, as they haven't totally removed themselves from a teachable state.

The way I do this is to ask without any form of malice, *"What is the reason which prevents you from doing this?"* Then, I wait for their reply. This means I must stop what I was doing, make eye contact, and listen to their response. It requires using good listening skills, and asking the child to cooperate in telling me their apprehensions.

Learn to restate their concerns: Treat others' concerns as valid, by making sure they see you as acknowledging their points of view. You verify another's concerns by stating it back to him, as you understand it. *"Yes, I know that it is late and you are so very tired."* Ask him *"Is that correct?"* Call it reciprocation, feed back, or even back-tracking, what you are doing is stating again their concerns, and taking away any further need for their combativeness. You restate their emotion and the theoretical reasons for it. At this moment, your opponent feels somewhat understood as he receives validation.

{The safest place to start instituting **change in others** is when they have enough trust to recognize that you are listening to their concerns. Therein they have the confidence to share what their hopes for themselves are, and of what their expectations of others, and especially of you, may be. This is the **depth of listening** which you should obtain whenever you present yourself as audience to another. You offer them empowerment, as they place themselves in the vulnerable position of self-evaluation, from where they might recognize a need for self change, or perhaps be more receptive to the non-judgmental suggestions of others.}

Now you can safely throw-in things that perhaps your child hasn't considered. You have gained his audience to introduce what else you expect him to comprehend, because he knows that you, in-part, identify with him. You have displayed courtesy, and in some measure joined with him against the problem. What's more, your compassionate leadership position demands that he considers your views also.

Everyone wants to be understood; all want to win. Whenever they perceive that you understand their position, then you may safely add, *"And you know that your room needs to be cleaned. Right?"* In order to get your charges to invest further, let them win, *"Can I give you a choice of when to do it, or are you going to do it now?"* Or, very similar, you inquire, *"So just how were you planning to get that filthy room cleaned?"*

...Awesome, now you're joining with the child against the problem, not pointing it out as being them.

Give a willing child a choice of compliant terms:

Whether or not to clean the room is not up for discussion, you have long since pasted that state by you commanding that it be cleaned. Only because they are still in a teachable state are you giving them a choice of terms in which to do it. Unless you are a power seeking tyrant, their latitude of when or just why they do it shouldn't matter. The fact is you are still getting their cooperation, and you'll get it easier if you give them a choice of compliant terms—especially if you word it to where they have power in choosing one of their alternatives. You also improve any mileage of their obedient service by pointing out benefits which they may not have thought of, or any of the following possible negotiable terms involving the fulfillment of their task:

1. Choice of Time Frame:

"Would it be easier for you to clean your room now, or in the morning before you go to school?" ...The choice to clean his room was not offered, but a differing time was, by your allowing the student some choice of when.

Personal Benefit: He feels he's following his own decision.

2. The Choice of Additional Perks:

"When you clean your room in the morning, if you put your dirty clothes in the washroom, then I'll wash 'em." ...No choice to clean their room was offered. However, a choice of whether or not they wanted fresh clothes was given, and it was supposed that they would tidy their room. They certainly want unsoiled clothes, so the masterful way you worded it ties one in with the other.

Personal Benefit: Cleaning the room offers a feeling that he's helping himself.

3. Accepting Help:

"How can we make cleaning your room easier to do for you?"

His response: "You can't, because what I really want to do is to go to my friend's house."

Your possible comeback: "I can make these choices easier for you. Go ahead and go to your friend's for an hour, then come back and clean up your room. I'll even get the vacuum out for you. Be back by five o'clock so you can get your room done before supper. You can do that, right?"

...The child who is generally cooperative might need help occasionally. Allow for some latitude. Although the above conversation does meet the standard of offering a bribe, it also gets him to buy into cleaning his room without a fight. It is easier for the child when he sees that you are willing to help lighten his burdens. Two helping with a task make it more bearable, even if your part is only offering a suggestion of a way to make the labor more efficient or less burdensome.

This child has earned your trust in the past, so give him some slack; you probably won't get burned. . . .

Personal Benefit: The burden of missing the chance to have fun was lifted, now he'll not view his task with as much disgust, plus his chore has just become easier.

. . .Follow-up; check that he does clean his room. If not, he eliminates himself from any negotiation next time.

4. Seeing Beyond the Task:

"What will you be spending the rest of your day doing, once your room is clean?"

Personal Benefit: This approach empowers the child to see beyond the hardship of the task and strengthens your statement that they must clean their room prior to having free time. It also introduces a reward that is possibly theirs, if they choose to comply.

5. Using an Existing Level of Self Esteem:

"I appreciate how hard it is to clean up your room, especially when you would rather be doing something else. Still, I know you'll feel better about yourself once you've done a good job."

Here, you are showing compassion without bailing them out of the task; furthermore, you are giving them a taste of a personal reward to dwell on instead of the hardship at hand.

Personal Benefit: Answering to their sense of worth becomes more of a compelling force than wasting time rebelling against you, for in it, they can see a better way to win.

6. Receiving a Reward, Based on an Expected Level of Effort:

"After you have cleaned your room really good, help me decide on a weekend outing for just you and me, since I'm undecided on what we can do together?" . . .If worded correctly, his choice of this compliant term can cause the child to fall all over himself and do a splendid job at the very thing that he was refusing to do, in the first place.

Personal Benefit: Once the child has agreed to the task, he has now moved into the Common Goal Box and therefore can allow himself to see some wisdom in what you're telling him to do. Even he can see that his room does look better, and now he's free from the burden of that task.

Beware of the partial compliance.

... It is a complicated thing when a child lets you know they're done, and then you find out latter the job was completed far below the level of excellence you envisioned. Certainly you don't want to destroy what little progress that was made.
YOU MUST REWARD FOR THE SLIGHEST TRY!

They made some effort which must be acknowledged. So, get out of your comfort zone and point out something that was done right. Use that as a basis for a likewise weak reward. If the child was playing you for a sucker by undertaking to get you to pass off the task as being completed, then by your making the effort to check on it, you show that you care. Because you stay involved, you can have an opportunity to teach again the level of expectation you deem as satisfactory. Although you may call their bluff, still you need to acknowledge their labors. So *match their efforts* and let them know that you're purposely rewarding slightly. Go ahead, give a much lesser reward than was anticipated, and then use this as a teaching opportunity to point out that their efforts were much lower than you expected, also. Ask them to come up with what could be a preferred solution. They will be watching and see your level of involvement. They may even feel guilty if, in fact, they had tried to pass off a knowingly poor job. Help them to see that they have the power to win greater, next time, if they can boost their level of participation closer to what you expect.

They perform, you reward. It's that simple. Failure to do so will impact the child toward feeling, *"Why do I even try, when you don't give me credit for what I do?"* or even them stating, *"You always just point out the bad things, never any of the good."* You don't want their complete shut down, so go ahead and give that weak reward. It's important that you show a consistency and thank them for their efforts spent. As they accept any reward you offer, you're both joined on a particle of common ground, and for that moment, you are no longer telling them what to do, you're giving a rest. Everyone knows: "**A change is as good as a Rest.**"

Their future efforts towards cooperation are in your hands. You and they can joke about their poor performance, you may offer sarcastic suggestions, or even take the time to properly train them in their duties. You have all the power, use it to get what you want. ...Use your advanced abilities to help them win.

Common Sense: **When you stop being so uptight about the poor effort given, the child will become more at ease and comfortable, and you will be building rapport.**
...**OFFER A SUSPENSION FROM TENSION.**

Lighten up your reprove: "Great job putting your new coat on a hanger in the closet, and I also noticed that your school books made it on a shelf instead of being dumped on the floor. See if you can help the rest of your stuff find their proper places, also. I'm sure if they could talk they'd complain about the poor treatment they've been receiving." After a moment of humor, it will be easier to instruct how to do things better; tell them what your level of acceptance is, and until that level of completion is reached they are required to keep doing the task ... so get with it! For them to try again to past off a less than qualifying effort will earn for them next to nothing, unless, it was more attention that they were craving. Let them know that when the expected level is reached, then they are done. "Go back and finish the job, this time, do as great of job as you did last Thursday, and then you can spend some free time as you'd like. Oh and thanks for the better effort you will be giving."

Go beyond forcing them to comply. Think, *"How can I set things up so my charge can really win?"*

All types of behavior are forms of communication. Negative behavior shows resistance. By their verbal refusal to comply, or with their defiance shown in rebellious actions, or even by their silent completely-do-nothing ignoring of the situation—your charge's message is clear. He wants little part of being told what to do, unless he can recognize a personal benefit. If he, despite your best efforts, still sends the message: *"For whatever reason, I continue to refuse to obey,"* he moves both himself and you into the next level.

Declaration of Impending Consequences

Give back control by shortening consequences for positive effort.

Study this Common Horse Sense example, "The Stick". It helps explain just how a declaration of imminent consequences can work:

* * *

Common Horse Sense: The Stick

One of the favorite horses, which the neighborhood kids often use three days a week, is Hotlips. She is a ten-year-old mare, and "Bless Her Heart," she has in the last three years started over forty kids riding. I don't have to worry if the kids are safe; never has she offered to hurt any of them. Because of her proven patterns, she has become the beginning rider's choice.

In dealing with her many riders, she can be counted on simply enduring the confusing types of reining and signals which green riders do for just so long, until she gets balky. She gets insensitive to their signals, as she endures their inconsistencies and lack of ability to establish themselves as in control. She is very predictable in this. I only have to check that she's still moving to be able to know how her riders are doing. If they don't remain in control, Hotlips will make ever decreasing slow circles in the corral by getting tighter and tighter until she has reached its center. She comes to a stand still by shunning their poorly presented demands, and simply caters to her own agenda of doing nothing. She displays no real meanness. And, true to form, is smooth and safe with her protests as she endures, yet ignores, just another inexperienced rider.

Her beginning riders' hopes fall short of their being able to experience a ride where she will maneuver to their every whim and expectation. What they don't realize is they don't know how to obtain it. Often a fearful youth will be clinging to the mane or the saddle horn in a death grip because her slow calculated movements caused them to feel unsafe when they realized they had no control. Other adventurous ones will be tugging or struggling in vain to enforce their weak and confusing intentions on this kid-wise horse.

From the latter, I hear the pleading words, "She will not go where I want," as they expect me to solve their dilemmas.

Hotlips will rein great for someone with a little experience; she will perform smoothly to a rider that knows about pressure and its release. What she balks against mostly are the riders who will not release pressure; they keep tugging and pulling to stop, then yanking to go. She will desensitize herself to the confusing **clues** given by such an indecisive rider. And in protest she will attempt to fight against those signals by stealing control of the reins from that kid, and then leisurely moving, as-she-pleases, to the center of the corral. The braver or more willing to learn riders will have caught on before they ended in the middle of the corral. They would have followed my reining directions by getting BIG, if she should start to sour.

As for the less assertive ones, after sitting unproductive in the middle of the corral, it is easy to know which ones still want to learn how to ride, verses those who just enjoying sitting on a horse. I will help the ones who ask for it; the others I just let enjoy the moment.

To the kids that ask for help, I will say, "You have to take back control." Or, "By the look of things she is riding you." At this point, I'll show them, again, how to rein properly; the first time they probably weren't really paying attention. They must have thought they already knew how. {**Very rare are the kids that admit they don't know how to ride, to start with.**} The problems they encounter are because, as of yet, they haven't learned properly how to ask, suggest, and promise a discipline. They are still using too many inconsistencies. They still don't have an inkling of the necessity to enter into an Escalation of Involvement, in order, to force her back into a submissive state where she might yield to their desires. Even after learning the skills to re-enforce their intentions, still they are too timid to show enough force to win back control. So for these less brave "CHICKENS" out comes the "Stick." What a great tool for taking control when all else fails.

I don't know who invented the stick, perhaps the first cave woman needing to enforce her will on a burley mate. When exerted correctly, it is a great equalizer to inform another of your wishes. Hotlips respects it. It will get her going again when timid kids can not. Whenever she becomes insensitive to their confusing signals, she remains callous unless they increase their demands by backing them up with a recognizable force.

The Stick represents a clear and consistent Declaration of Imminent Consequences. I show the kids how to raise the stick to the striking position near her rump, symbolizing the promise of a reproof. With the stick promising a chastisement, she will respond immediately with forward movement again. The stick is so effective at promising consequences, it doesn't have to be used every time, in fact, very rarely. Hotlips has no doubt to its meaning when properly presented. The stick is shown, so she cooperates. She lets her anticipation of pain motivate her. She remembers what the stick can do.   {Sometimes a mere display can cause more suffering than the actual use of enforcement.}

When deploying an impending consequence, it is important to keep creditability. If Hotlips comes to realize that the young rider won't really use the punishment, then she becomes conditioned to ignore it. But at first she doesn't know, so she moves forward. It is funny to watch; she will step out forward so instantly the beginner will be caught unawares and will loose his balance.

Terrified beginners will often drop the stick and flounder to grab onto the horn. Or they could panic and pull back on the reins with their hands raised up to their own chins and their elbows pointing outward past their ears like horns on a buffalo. All the while, they scream as a banshee, "Whoa!" in an attempt to stop her just as she starts to move. As they no longer posses the stick, she will again stop because now it's no longer a threat. She senses their confusion. Again, there they sit on this horse, her not moving, and them not wanting her to move. By the time they build up enough courage to try again, she won't move in response to their weak displays of promising a punishment. She has figured out that no meaningful discipline will happen if she fails to cooperate; she knows that they will not follow through and enforce. Plus, she also recognizes that no meaningful reward is being presented by this novice trainer, even when she does cooperate.

With a poor presentation of their demands and a weak follow thru of what will happen if she fails to perform, Hotlips is like so many other students whom are stuck unable to further their behavioral modification experiences. She recognizes neither pain nor gain if she cooperates; there are neither benefits nor losses that are sufficient to cause her to mind. Even though she's somewhat aware of the commands from her riders, she also realizes that they lack the ability to enforce them. She dis-engages with their prodding and clearly displays back this message: **"I can't change because you haven't been powerful enough to cause me to deviate from what I want."**

The responsibility first lays with the trainer to be clear and consistent, and then be powerful enough to carryout the promise. *… How is your creditability as a parent or a teacher, do you follow through and enforce?* Or do you display a comical appearance and simply howl as a mythical figure to be once again ignored?

Common Sense: **As a trainer, it is very important to understand that when you state a pending discipline and it produces no results, then you have no choice but to follow through and enforce it. Establish your creditability even on the small things, and your charge will be more prone to obey your declarations on the big ones.**

You must condition your charges to know that you will not allow them to get away with improper behavior. Their believing this will act as an additional deterrent in their decision making process of deciding when to act out. They will feel that if a small violation brings to them a punitive consequence, then they will be surely be less willing to risk the corrective actions which a large infraction will demand. They will become conditioned, that if they don't display the right behavior, then they are in trouble. They know that their punishment will happen.

An effective way to do this is to review, during a calm moment of rapport with the child, your future expectations and the coinciding disciplines which will be enforced if the child doesn't comply. Do this when you have your student's attention and his willingness to do the right thing—prior to the fact. You pre-state the rules that will apply and the consequences which will be imposed for any failure to follow them. It will save you having to issue them in the form of a threat, which will probably be met with defiance if declared during the heat of a confrontation. It is easier to get a student to agree when they are thinking calm and rational and feel inclined to work on a deficiency, then when they are in the middle of an outbreak and are being threatened with an ultimatum.

Example: *"Mike, be aware that in order to be allowed to have your friends come over and visit, you must also agree that if you behave mean or defiant, they will be sent home. Do you agree to remain respectful while they are here? … You can do it, Mike."* Next time his friends are over, if Mike gets belligerent, you sent them home.

Oh! ...I forgot about those kids, who may be at a standstill sitting on Hotlips in the middle of the corral. *I will help them if they still want to learn* to ride, at this point, *most don't.* The skills they have developed to manipulate their human mentors do not work with a horse. Some resign and give the appearance they are happy just sitting on and being with the animal. Others have allowed themselves to get scared when the horse doesn't behave to their every whim, so they're thru. Most now choose to end their riding experience. They believe that getting the horse to cooperate takes too much effort; it causes them too much discomfort.

* * *

A declaration of impending consequences is an imminent penalty. It is a statement promising a disciplinary action if no cooperation is received. It is uttered in a language simple enough to understand. If it's important enough for you, as a trainer, to move beyond the asking level, then stay focused until you receive compliant behavior. By you consistently following through with your declared consequences, you establish a history of your charge knowing he's got one coming should he choose not to cooperate.

Keep the Consequences Relevant:
Remember that for the child to have desire for change, as result of a discipline or a consequence, they must recognize the benefit of their castigation; otherwise it is merely a form of revenge inflicted on them. To be most effective in inspiring a desire for change, the consequence should be pertinent to the lesson which you're seeking to teach. Notice how much more effective threatening with a relevant discipline is, verses declaring a pending consequential punishment just for penalty's sake:

"If you don't do a good job in cleaning your room today, then you can just stay home and practice your cleaning skills on the rest of the house this weekend." {More forced cleaning chores are the last thing a kid wants.} As regards to, *"If you don't clean your room, then you will be grounded."* If the child is having trouble doing a thorough job, certainly more practice is a relevant sentencing.

If the problem is that a child is chronically late coming home, then an appropriate consequence would be to declare that the time to come home will become earlier, until he can show for two weeks that he can meet a schedule. To avoid any miss-communication, workout a doable hour to come home, before hand, then hold him to it. Be strong on this one. When the kid tests you and comes in one minute late, you enact his consequence. You state, *"You knew the rules, you could have come home earlier instead of pushing the limit."*

Common Sense: **If you declare a consequence, you'd better be prepared to enact it.**

Here are some more things that could be used to help the child in his decision making process, as you declare an impending consequence.

- **Give a choice of the lesser of two evils:**

"You must clean your room. Clean it now or you won't get to go to the party on Friday." The choice is not whether or not to clean their room, it is a choice on whether or not to go to the party, and they still have to clean their room. Besides you have just given them a way to feel a personal gain; if they follow your demands precisely, they score an additional win.

You are asking your child to question in their own minds: "Which is worst; having to clean my room now, or not being able to go to the party? …What horrid thing will I be subjected to endure by spending a hard hour working on my room now? …Is that thing as vile as missing an activity I have been planning for weeks?" Choosing the lesser of two evils will keep the child feeling that they are still in control.

- **Be specific in your consequence:**

Avoid saying, *"If you don't clean your room, then you can't go to the party."* When presented that way, you are letting the child keep the option to clean his room or not. All he has to do is decide against going to the party, and then he becomes liberated from having to clean his room. Be specific; take the guess work out of what the child thinks he can get away with. {This child really didn't want to go to the party anyway.}

- **Never threaten, and then not follow thru.**

Promising a consequence is a commitment with your word on the line. To remain effectual, you need to maintain credibility. Like the raising of a stick into the striking position prior to using; if you have a track record of nearly always following thru with consequences, then just the declaration of one should get results. Avoid establishing a pattern that your promised threats aren't important enough for you to follow through with. Don't let the child believe that you can be ignored, and then nothing will happen. As results, your future threats will not be taken seriously; they will not be recognized as important enough for the child to comply with. After promising a consequence, if your charge is not driven into action, you must enact the decree.

- **Be believable or be a joke; suggest realistic consequences.**

When a threat of a discipline is declared, be careful to make it one that you can actually carry out. Think of all the times you have heard a child being issued a pending punishment, and you knew that there was no way for the trainer {parent/teacher} to carry out that particular threat. As in the looming choice of words, "I am going to kill you!" When it is uttered, does it motivate with an equal, "Risk all at any cost!" desire to comply? Or do the words lose their meaning because of the many times they have been uttered and the child's life was not taken? At the very least, deliver some form of punishment, or find yourself chasing after a three-year-old who is laughing and running away after receiving such a hollow threat.

In the case of the trainer who isn't always believable or creditable, the charge soon learns to recognize the tone of delivery, instead of the meaning of the actual words used. When the tone used denotes rage or at least an above normal sense of urgency, the castigated will be on the alert to perhaps listen closer because, at least, **anger** commands attention. Even an accelerated Declaration of Consequences will lose its threat as the child becomes desensitized to non-backed-up words, especially, if the inept trainer doesn't have a past history of enforcement. This undisciplined child gets to the point where even harsh words of his trainer do not send a threat that must be obeyed. If a punishment was actually enforced on such a desensitized child, it would be an offending shock because the thing the kid was clueing on mostly was a display of anger, not particularly to what was being said.

Dealing with Anger

Common Sense: **When a tutor gets mad and loses his control, he's sending a message: He hasn't any other skills to use.**

Getting angry is a natural emotion, as result, of things not going the way they were suppose to. Whenever an instructor acts in wrath, it teaches to his charges that getting angry is an acceptable emotional response which they too can use for causing others to take greater notice. Quickly the students learn that with practice, a large emotional display can be used for driving others away. Whenever, you allow yourself to get angry, and then act in that anger, you risk becoming as the drunk who has to apologize for his actions the next day as he sobers up. Anger only offers to its author a crutch to hide a weakness with. The weakness is: they lack the ability to verbalize their feelings and possible choice of options, without escalating into an aggressive display manipulating others by reverting to name-calling, threats, sarcasm, and acts designed to intimidate others into assuming blame. Leave acting in anger only to those whom don't possess the skills necessary to appropriately deal with themselves or their circumstances.

When a person allows himself to act in anger, as in the case of experiencing too much pressure to deal with, he often rationalizes that outside forces have caused his reaction. He may feel aggressively combative so that he blames others for his feelings. He acts in rage to force his control onto others. He is in need of a teacher who can help him discover: How one acts in anger is always a personal choice; it can be controlled.

It's not always a choice whether or not to feel angry as one experiences a flaring up of emotions, but it's always in one's power to make a controlled choice on how to act in that emotional state.

When confronted with hostile feelings, the recipient does have a choice to fight back or not. He may choose to take the withdrawn position of a timid receiver of wrath by displaying the unhealthy position to cower and become a victim, where he cowardly shields himself from all further confrontations by distancing himself from the perceived source of his distress. On the other hand, he may also stand firm with knowledge that he has the power to confront his dislikes without either becoming a victim, or without himself also becoming aggressive and assaultive. He might develop the skills to transform the energy of his anger emotion into constructive action.

He can assertively place himself into the role where he communicates his thoughts and feelings to others. With accountability using a new arsenal of personal actions, he stands in powerful self-control to deal responsibly to whatever set-back he is confronted with. He doesn't have to sink back into the helpless victim, nor revert into the out-of-control tyrant who will not take accountability and must blame others for his troubles.

The choice is always to confront his problem by making others aware of his feelings and of his responsible desires of personal change. He can further take responsibility by sharing his outlook of hope, in which he appropriately verbalizes expectations of change from others. The key to dealing with a personal display of anger is to have usable tools other than ones of destruction. Knowing that others do understand him is a key alternative to coping with his anger, without him feeling the need to lash out.

To help them break the emotional rut of reverting to acting-out with a display of assaultive temper when things don't go their way, you must implement a change of course for a kid who is acting like a raging idiot. You must obtain a stop to his uncontrolled behavior, before you can ever attempt to teach him any alternative behavior or effectively instruct him how to deal more appropriately with his feelings.

Lead a student's behavior where you want. If you blowup, then by your example they will receive a validation for their outbursts also. Keep your emotions cool, don't bestow on anyone so much power that they cause you to consider acting in anger; you're trying to help others, not to satisfy your revenge.

Common Sense: **Applying too much pressure as a solution only gives the learner, something to resist. A soft approach teaches the subject to yield to pressure.**

* * *

Common Horse Sense: Something to fight against

"Giving them something to fight against," refers to the person who doesn't understand that a horse learns from the release of pressure. When too much pressure is applied to a horse, in reciprocation it gets angry; it fights against that excess, instead of yielding to its proper minimal use. It reacts without thinking. As it is kept under pressure, it will negatively apply as much resistance as possible in an effort to obtain relief.

After becoming escalated, horses can cause great disasters by pushing, or moving from too much stimulation. In an effort to defend against an excessive pressure, they forget what conditioning they have previously learned. This is often the very opposite that the inexperienced trainer wants, more resistance from his trainee.

Next chance you get, watch an animal demonstrate his displeasure of too much pressure before he blows-up; he will show classic signs of anger. He will display laid back ears and fire in his eyes. He'll even start to snorting and blowing as he arches up his head in combination with an overall tensing of his body and movements. Evaluate what stimulus you are presenting that's causing this over-excited behavior, and then do away with that trigger. Unless you want the animal to blow-up, quit giving so much pressure. A relief of some pressure will produce a decline in the behavioral pattern of the animal much faster than insisting on forcing until it blows up, and then having to take a much greater amount of time afterward to calm the beast down.

*   *   *

"What about the child that has an anger problem?"
Answer: There needs to be a re-training.

By you giving him something to fight about, you also strengthen his resolve to use anger as his coping mechanism for resisting the setbacks he is experiencing. In your effort to control him, do not engage back with the child by using equal or greater displays of harsh words or threatening language. Do not argue with an arguer. When a child sees a pattern of using anger to confront difficulties, he or she becomes conditioned to use it. Train yourself to stop using displays of wrath to show the child how one wins. Winning this way only teaches the use of a quickly expended explosive power, and usually winds up with somebody getting hurt.

First: **Stop his assumption that the anger which he is seeing in others is a sign of them establishing control.** As long as the child believes that a display of anger will yield to him benefits, he will use it. Acting-out in anger does not eliminate a problem beyond causing others to not seek further interactions. It is a poor means of dealing with a situation, wherein, it only produces a temporarily feeling of control to the user as he shifts his blame to something else. Its only attribute is possibly awaking the emotions of the user and motivating him towards maladaptive actions. The angered soul, when faced with daunting burdens, aggressively tries to harm or belittle others as his stormy solution. He tries to intimidate his foe and place himself as superior. **The angered must see it is not the use of anger that causes things to happen; solutions come when the proper steps to problem solving are envisioned, implemented and re-fined.**

Second: **Stop caving in and giving them what they want.** The angered want to argue. They want to make it so you lose and they win. To have a chance to help the angry, you should work with the child to develop his anger as a problem, and you enter with him in an effort to overcome and beat it by progressing up the Graduating Escalation of Involvement. On the onset, it will not work if you meet his aggressiveness with passiveness. Neither will the act of sitting down and rationally discussing his anger issue, if you try to do it during the time of an emotionally fueled out-break. You can only obtain success by pointing out positive behavior based benefits when you have the student calm enough to be willing to consider a change. Until this happens, you use your training skills to cause a transformation in his unwanted behavior. Don't give into his displays of anger. **Remain calm and to the point, state what will or will not happen, and cause a separation with him and additional emotional fulfillment.**

Third: **Once his behavior has calmed down and will allow him to process information in a rational manner, then together discuss alternatives and address the reasons for the anger in the first place.** With help, the child will be able to recognize and have the tools to properly choose other actions, instead of acting out. You train him toward other behavioral skills. When he becomes aware that other coping mechanisms can bring greater personal gratification, he will begin experimenting. **In order to use differing reactions, other then anger, he has to learn them from somewhere.**

A trainer's role is to assist the enraged into bettering themselves through means other than the intimidation of others. He teaches additional outlets for the child's anger. He models how to act, not in wrath, but to assertively declare a personal hurt. He teaches it is ok to share a personal vulnerability of powerlessness, by letting others know why there is anger, and what the factors were which triggered a renewed onset. The student is taught skills which inspire an introspection of change, instead of a defensive reaction driven by combative aggression.

As an alternative to just getting angry, the angered or hurt should be taught healthy communicational skills to inform their offenders of alleged shortcomings. Demonstrate, it is best to use discernment when pointing out another's inadequacies. Only suggestions are given, so that the offenders can be inspired to self-improvement, not forced to yield, or to return battle as a means of self-defense.

You cause a reason for change in the angry. As the angered learns to express himself in assertive terms, you a trainer, develop a culture of repeating back his appropriate desires, as you understand them. Instead of giving accreditation to his old patterns of being held captive by his victim blaming or locked in old statements of announcing only aggressive intimidation, support him when he acknowledges his emotions and in what he thinks can be done that will produce a superior outcome. Oh what communicational power a child receives as he learns to assertively express himself by objectively giving reasons for his feelings, by declaring what hopes he will aspire to in the future, and by communicating the suggestions he has to others which will make further interaction with them less of a burden. He will quickly see that with this new way of expressing himself, he is understood more clearly, and others are aware of alternatives.

You can give the gift of confidence. Instead of remaining controlled by his emotional upsets, he can become the controller, as he learns to channel his emotional anger to declare and overcome his problems. He receives emotional fulfillment as he practices non-combative ways to express the desires he has for others to re-fine their interactions with him. He also gains self-assurance by inviting others to join with him, helping him to identity, and then defeat his shortcomings. You, the trainer, orchestrate this renewal of confidence.

{Alternatively, you can beat the kid into submission, with-in an inch of his life, so that the last thing he ever thinks about is displaying more anger.}

"No?"

"Why not?" Many think that this works and it is the best way to train a horse, or a dog!" {Or even a child.}

Once you have declared an impending consequence, then there are no more negotiations, unless the child starts to collaborate with your first solicitation of cooperation. He has to begin doing what you say. When a child chooses to perform the task, even as result of the punishment levied against him, "How sweet it is." That's what you wanted to begin with, the student working with you to solve the problem. To further build rapport and as a reward for the positive behavior he now displays, you can lessen the consequence after this show of cooperation.

On the other hand, if no cooperation is given by the student in this Impending Consequence Level, then it is time to rise up and move to the next intensity.

Side note* Your show of good faith will be much appreciated by your pupil when you can lessen their discipline for a display of good behavior. It doesn't mean you are weak, or that you have given in. It means that you are rewarding for an exceptional change of behavior from your pupil. {*If none was noticed, offer no lessening of their fates.*}

"You catch more flies with honey, than with vinegar," [Author Unknown]

Common Sense: Offering a ***conditional kindness*** to an offender for his proper repentant behavior will have the same rewarding effect as giving it to anyone else. Even more so for him, because it will be a chance for you to be seen from his eyes, as having compassion, and as being an administrator of justice.

By repeated displays of kindness you will be seen as less-threatening in their eyes. They will seek you out and want to experience what you have to offer. As with any behavior you want to re-enforce, drop focusing on the negative; develop a pattern of offering affirmations for positive behavior, and others will move closer to becoming teachable at your hands.

Ok, now what if you are in a situation which warrants having to impose a set consequence for a child who has a track record of being willing and compliant to his duties? When this child has out-of-character messed up, what do you do? **You are still under the obligation to do your part to enforce the rules: Like putting into effect a pre-discussed consequence that was promised earlier. You must remain consistent and give some form of castigation.** Yet what is wrong if you let the kid know that justifiably he could be held to that stricter standard with his present consequence, but, since you trust that he didn't intentionally or defiantly disobey, then this time, you're giving him a bit of a break? For this kid, after you have gained his consent to not fall short in his duties in the future, you can withhold a reasonably lesser privilege, and then move on. By him agreeing to perform differently in the future, aren't you getting his pledge of a change of behavior? What else do you want? You are showing that the consequence is important, and so is he. Allow the freedom to start fresh.

Tomorrow is a new day, in which the bad performance of today can be forgotten and not be brought up again.

Thru-out the Escalation of Involvement process, your number one objective should be to assist in the changing of your child's behavior, so that he will be the position to ultimately receive more joy in his life. Your demanding of compliance and then seeking to impose a consequence should be to that end also. Your actions are governed by you wanting to do the best for your child, not for an obtainment of your selfish desires.

CHAPTER 16:

HOW TO DELIVER AN EFFECTIVE PUNISHMENT

{GET BIG}
On
Enforcement of Consequences
Take a break for the slightest try

Common Sense: **As a trainer, you should deploy whatever energy is necessary to motivate your charge. Each child is distinctly different; all are not motivated in the same way.**

The purpose of this step is to see that the charge who remains resistant to your commands does receive his promised consequence. You deliver what has been declared. His penalty has been earned as result of his refusal to carry out your order for compliance, now you must be consistent also in your delivery. If your pupil will accept this penalty on his own, then it will not be necessary to "**GET BIG**" just remain loving and caring, and deliver it.

The following situations all contain reasons that would influence a student to accept a punishment as a correctional consequence:

1. The punishment was agreed upon earlier, when the student was in a frame of mind striving toward a common goal.

2. A student is, as result of a new increase of understanding, willing to do the consequence because he views it as a chance to receive some additional benefits, such as more practice or additional recognition from others. The learner is in hopes of receiving some form of gain.

3. The new consequence comes as result of a perceived natural process; it becomes an additional burden or dilemma which was not the result of a trainer's doing.

When the effect of his first refusal to comply causes a new dilemma, it is often called a "**Natural Consequence.**" It comes as result of not doing the right thing to begin with. This is the easiest form of punishment to get a defiant student to swallow. It comes directly as result of their error. It is such a additional, logical, burden that it is accepted as being caused mostly from personal fault, and will give only the most exasperated student something to fight against.

A natural consequence is a great teacher; it engraves an impression not to make the same mistake twice. Who wants to do double the work anyway?

EXAMPLE: As result of not picking up her school books and homework, Sue's assignment was destroyed as her little brother rifled through her things which were left abandoned on the kitchen chair. It doesn't matter how peeved she becomes, Sue's natural consequence will not diminish; she must redo her homework, after, she finds and picks up her books.

4. A sufferer feels they had no choice but to comply, because they were pressured by the influence of another. They feel that they were completely victimized and had their choices taken away.

For one person to obey a consequence under those premises, testifies of another's supremacy. Being forced does cause resentment, and does little, at first, toward getting the acceptance of a change from the victim. If it is done repeatedly with a meaningful reward attached when a proper response is obtained, it'll eventually lead the sufferer into realizing that even though he is being pressured against his will, he's also a recipient of benefits. As rewards are acknowledged then embraced by the previously forced, a transformation starts to take place; behavior then attitude changes in an effort to obtain more, when the benefits are great enough.

If you can not get your student to accept a consequence, then it is necessary that you "**GET BIG**," and **BIGGER,** and impose more energy towards them than they have resistance towards you. Don't be confused into believing that this means you are now to get all mean and angry and seek to strike fear into the hearts of your charges. This is not the case; "**Get Big**" refers to you acting in confidence and strength while delivering an all out involvement if needed. You will not quit or be deterred from your efforts of getting them to do as you commanded; their cooperation is still needed, and now they have added a penalty for their failure to comply. You will now deliver their consequence, which is the cost of their refusal to address the original problem. You do not show anger, only firmness. Be prepared as needed to engage in more effort than they. You use whatever resources you can put at your disposal. You are teaching your charge that you'll not stop short your goal of their cooperation. You get them to understand that you are not fooling around anymore.

Side note **By your example, as you Get Big, you are also teaching them how to become powerful when they want to get something out of you. So do not become abusive, disrespectful, obnoxious, or inappropriate, for your child will not have the wisdom of discernment, and any offensive performance by you will be modeling to them an unwanted behavior which they might adopt.**

5. The student resigns to do the consequence out of fear. They're afraid if they don't, then a greater punishment will follow.

Remember that the desire of youth is to be in control of their lives. Having someone add burdens to them is not what they want. Their self-preservation will dictate they must choose to do that which offers the least amount of pain. Your firmness on enforcement is vital. They must see that by your bigness you will do whatever it takes to get their compliance. In order for them to refuse you, they need to get bigger and more confident than you. Most will not choose this. The desire to be in control of their lives will begin to decree, *"Just do the requested tasks, so that, additional burdens will not be forthcoming."*

If, as a parent, you do not have the ability to enforce control on your children for their inappropriate behaviors, use a larger spouse, the school system, the police, or the courts to do it for you. If the child does not like you because of your display of power, then that is something that they'll have to deal with. Their despise will pass as they come into an understanding that you permitted their punishment, not from the stand-point of whether or not they will continue to like you, but for its hopeful positive long-term affects.

Whenever the moment is, in-which it finally sinks in that they must endure additionally because of their failure to comply, some will try to negotiate. They will want to just attend to the original problem and fulfill the first requested task so that you dismiss their most recent earned penalty. This is great, and as they do be sure to genuinely thank them for their efforts. Rapport is being established between the trainer and the student as you reward their efforts and give them a break from your constant pressure; further benefits can now be talked about and envisioned. Together you are working toward a common goal. However, now they must also do more than the first requested task; they gave up that option by not complying before.

Lighten the Sentence

As they exhibit a willingness to work with you, it's a profitable thing for you to think of a way for them to fulfill their punishment and also get a lessening of their sentence. Have fun with their consequence; do it with them, or make it a race with a reduced penalty if they perform with an exceptional speed or manner. Laugh with them about the pickle they caused themselves. Your involvement will enhance their desires to endure, and you'll be showing your willingness to work together in the same cause. In addition to rewarding for positive behavior, always point out the benefits of working with you further to solve the original problem.

Be certain, they see you as offering them a chance, because of their responsive deeds, to only to lighten their punishment, not that you are offering a chance to eliminate it. It is of utmost importance to somehow enforce their sentence. Never, all-together, dismiss it. This will strengthen your role as a behavioral trainer and leave an undeniable impression on your charges as to the level of commitment you'll hold them to in the future. With enforcement and a lightening of the penalty, you show that you are fair. You display that you're capable of some mercy for their good behavior. Your charges will, as result, see you as just and forgiving. Plus you'll have their admiration for upholding them to a high level. To completely dismiss the declared consequence will create more harm than good—especially the next time you ask them to do something.

After asking, commanding, threatening, and punishing a child there will be those who still refuse to cooperate with your original request. {**Don't be discouraged, you didn't do all the things which your trainers asked from you either.**} It is still their choice to listen to instructions and to decide whether or not to follow. It is because of their choices that new consequences are heaped upon them. If they still don't give any cooperation, then enact their consequence to its fullest and move on. It is still your hope to get a change in their behavior. Don't get disheartened. You can do it. You've got two other steps which haven't yet been used.

Take away Freedom
Take away something of value
Restore incrementally, relative to positive efforts

Freedom is the most valuable thing that any child may possess. It is the lack of restrictions which enables one's choice of actions. The accumulative results of non-cooperation will be the hardest felt if any additional freedoms are lost. Personal freedom is the very thing they are striving to preserve. Make it clear that even though they had a punishment levied for their choice of non-compliance, they are still required to comply with the task you asked for in the first place. They need to address the *Original Problem.* For them to continue to refuse will result in addition loses of their freedoms; they will be having more restrictions placed upon them, and be losing more things of value. The non-compliant child must feel his freedoms slip away further.

Trainers, do you understand? By their continuation in refusing to meet your first request, you are far from being through yet; you are still under obligation to act Big.   ☆ ☆

Another story of Common Horse Sense will help you to understand this principle.

* * *

Common Horse Sense: Crossing the Kolob River

I recall a trail ride with eight boys and three leaders. As part of our trip, we had chosen to go up thru the Kolob Canyon in Zion National Park located in Southern Utah. Prior to getting there our group had ridden for two days and traveled sixty-five miles. We were in good spirits and had a great time enjoying the five shear fingers of ornamentally eroded cliffs along the Kolob drainage; a more beautiful place on God's earth is hard to imagine.

While following single file up along a river of about two and a half feet deep and about fifty feet wide, we ran out of passable options. The cliff banks cut off our west-side passage. So, it became necessary to cross this fast moving frigid steam. It was the Third of June, and this drainage was swollen being fed by resent snow melt.

The river's bottom was covered with melon-size rocks and the water white with froth, enough that it made any footing difficult at best. No passage was better than the next. As I urged him into the chilly stream, my stallion's hoofs sent dis-lodged rocks rolling and clanking with each step; his footholds were not stable, yet he forged across because he was being asked to. Upon entering, he gasped and snorted, blowing air with each step in response to the bite of the bitter cold as he floundered to gain footing. Coming up the far bank,

I insisted he stay close to the water's edge, to help make sure that each boy was able to persuade his horse to cross.

There were other animals that resisted the entry into the cold and frightening flow. I watched as each boy approached the bank. Some had to merely ask their mount to follow the previous horse in front of it. Some had to "Get Big" and demand that their ponies cross the unfamiliar waters. They did by first approaching the bank riding in normal fashion. As their mounts refused to go into the water, a touch of both heels to the flanks of the resistant delivered a consequence that some responded to. Other horses, after being given every opportunity to cross on their own, had to be whipped to make it more painful to resist. Finally all had crossed, except one.

The last boy had been trying every trick in the book in hopes that his mount would commit and plunge into the uncertain menace. Instead it wheeled around even though the boy was applying as much pressure and discomfort as he could. It would not cross; it would not even allow itself to enter. We, on the far bank, rode on out of sight and waited for his animal to get nervous and think it was being left by the others; still it refused to address the original problem of crossing this stream. I instructed the others to remain on the far side and re-crossed in hope that the reluctant would find a renewal of courage and follow shortly behind my horse as we re-entered the water again, for a third crossing. No success. Again I went back across the torrent for the fourth time, after all else had failed, to take away more freedom from this non-compliant. At present, we had probably spent an extra forty minutes persuading this animal. Even time was spent allowing this reluctant to stand facing the waters to take away its reason to fight. Still, he wouldn't do it. Soon it refused to even get close to the water's edge. Kicking, spurring, and the stick only escalated this animal's resistance mode. This defiant animal needed to be restricted further in its freedoms; it needed more options taken away.

Since we had been traveling for miles along this stream, I knew no other superior passage options were available; this horse must be forced to cross here. I slipped a rope around the neck of the sweating beast and had the boy hang on. I dallied around my horn and my stud put all his weight into it. He obligingly fought his way across again, battling both the river's bottom and his hanging-back cargo. He keelhauled that obstinate horse across the stream taking away all its freedom, other than to just lie-down and be choked. The disobedient horse had known what was being asked of him, but as long as it was his choice in the matter —he was in the mind set to continue to refuse. He had to have all his options taken away before he submitted. He wasn't aware that true freedom was in compliance.

Shortly afterwards, as we continued on our journey, we had to cross back once more, then multiple times thereafter to follow a passable trail. Progressively the horses and particularly this hold-out became more compliant and less reluctant to take additional precarious plunges. All learned to accept their fates and cross when asked. I was amused, yet still sympathetic, each time as I listened to them snort air from their noses and saw them tense up as they reentered the frigid and scary waters; I was aware of the discomfort they were enduring.

* * *

Common Sense: **Take away just enough to get the student to comply.**

Don't get in a big hurry to take everything away. Some students, who feel they've lost all freedom, will often quit, or turn around and make deliberate negative choices of aggressive behavior just to feel some sort of control in their life. They're trying to show that they don't have to obey if they don't want to. Remember, when all else fails they may resort to violence, stealing, lying, or other assaultive behaviors in order to keep their presumption of having retained some power or control. So, in the beginning, unless you have the ability to micro-manage and oversee constantly twenty-four hours a day and seven days a week when working with a problematic child, it is wise not to undertake a fight on every issue. Pick the few that do matter, and let the child feel that they have retained their freedom on some of their other choices. As refinement takes place, the proper moment to work on the other issues will come.

324   JUST WHO AM I TRAINING ANYWAY   DAVE SLATER

You gave it to them, you can take it away. Personal effects can be lost and life still goes on, although sometimes less pleasant. Free-time, games, cars, toys, clothes, phones; even soft beds can be taken away for a period. They can be taken from the defiant child and easily put in a prominent place where they can be seen or referred back to. Yes, even enjoyed for a brief period, if compliance so warrants. The items that are taken away from view, or placed completely out of possible restoration soon will be replaced by something else and forgotten. They lose their worth as any type of penalty, if they are thought of by the pupil as not obtainable in the future. Withholding some items requires the trainer to be even more involved. If a yummy food is withheld, then it should be replaced with something as nutritional, but less desirable. The objective is to take away just enough to arouse their compliance.

"It is mine, not yours," will be the reply from the deprived.

Have the guts to stand on your own two hind feet; you just got "Big" in the last step. **REMAIN BIG NOW!** Give a rationalized reason for the withholding of the item, then stick to it. A reluctant child will use all of their energy endeavoring to shame you into questioning your own motives, or into talking you into restoring their lost privileges. Don't give in. Stay firm and calmly repeat this worded response, "Yes it is yours, and again you may earn back its use and benefits. However, first, there are some changes that need to be done around here." Remember to state what you expect them to do.

Don't be afraid to give back something in increments. This works superbly parallel with the incremental cooperation that you are likely to get.

A Loss of Trust

Trust is a valuable thing in a child's life, they want it from you. It represents not having to explain or be micro-managed in every aspect of their lives. Back in the "Basics" they learned that when they lose another's trust, they receive in return an increase of imposed limitations. {*This is BAD NEWS for a seeker of freedom.*} Be clear in informing to your unyielding child of the lack of trust that goes with their present poor behaviors. Include the future restrictions that will be imposed until that loss can be regained. Be fair and also let them know how difficult it will be for them to regain the lost trust, and how now they'll be judged with less leniency than before. More limitations are not what the child had in mind and should cause introspection. An honest self-evaluation will yield questioning, followed possibly by a change in some of their present actions.

It is a good tool for altering another's behavior when they can discover how their poor behavior affects others. Help them to be able to see beyond themselves. Let them realize that their lack of trust puts additional burdens on others, as well as back on themselves.

Grounding

A common tool which parents like to use in the taking away of a child's freedom is "**Grounding**". Parents feel that they are making a big difference by taking away something that the child wants to do. When done right, it is very persuasive in getting the youngster to comply. Let's look at two opposite spectrum approaches of utilizing grounding as a punishment and a loss of freedom.

1. *"You are grounded for two weeks, for fighting with your sister, young man!"* This declaration gives no way for either the parent, or the child to feel that they are in control. Let me explain:

Since a time frame was attached to the punishment, the parent can't now lessen the duration as a reward for good behavior without losing creditability. When a parent only gives a statement of time to a punishment, what he is really meaning to imply is, "I hereby wash my hands of any further involvement regarding this matter for that length of time."

The child hears the specified time, and feels, "*I am sentenced to suffer for a mandated sentencing without a chance of parole.*" His reformation process is minimal as he consigns himself to fulfilling his stretch, only thinking of when it is over. Even in the criminal justice system, a convicted felon knows that he could get time off for good conduct.

2. *"Johnny, you are grounded until I start to see your change.* — *It will be you getting along with your sister by refraining from fighting or calling names for a period of twenty-four hours."* Here both the parent and the child are engaged in a **flexible punishment.** It promotes the child into wanting to change, and also gives him a time-frame that can be lessened or lengthened according to his ongoing behavior. Johnny will be inclined to do the necessary things to lessen the duration, and the parent will be looking for the slightest effort in order to reward him. A *"Win, Win"* situation for both is in place. **A new common goal is quickly established**: "Getting the child off being grounded." Whenever the child finally conforms for the period of a full day, he can be paroled. If he still acts inappropriate, his time of punishment is lengthened. Each day, or if needed each hour, can be processed with Johnny to review his compliance.

Consider if you'd just used, *"You're grounded until I see a change."* This is a declared, yet flexible punishment, but it could be more effective. What is the change you are looking for? Is it a two day display of yucky fastidious behavior to a sibling? Or is it a day where Johnny avoids all contact with his rival, so he won't be tempted to break-down. What were you wishing Johnny to learn?

Can the child just assume that all he has to do is display a desire, and that becomes a change? When he verbalizes, "OK, I've changed … I won't fight anymore," is this enough?

Merely *i*mposing a punishment without declaring a specified change is lacking in direction. The expected behavior was not defined. Give the kid a chance to win, define what you are looking for.

Restricting Freedom in the Workplace

The previous grounding declarations could be used in withholding freedom in the workplace or in a formal training situation. Whenever a **supervisor** undertakes to make a point about a mistake his apprentice made, he can also use either of those opposite spectrum approaches to take way liberty from his charge:

"What a stupid error you made. You are hereby band from using that piece of equipment. Don't ever touch it again!" barks the superior in response to the novice's mistake. The apprentice is left questioning himself and wondering what exactly to do. The superior has made it clear that he is distancing himself and does not want to be involved in helping his trainee. The trainee hears, "I am not trusted," and so is not inspired to improve.

From the opposite side: *"What a mistake! Sure looks like you need help; so don't use that piece of equipment again until you can be properly trained."* Here the supervisor is conveying that he will not distance himself from future involvement. He is conveying that trust could again be restored and it is possible for his apprentice to develop additional skills. The apprentice has the freedom to seek for help to improve his own ability.

Both differing approaches will covey to the trainee that he is losing some freedom. One has him wanting to quit making an effort. The other makes him want to try even more.

An even more empowering chance at recovery for the apprentice, as-well-as defining the supervisor as one who appreciates the initiative of his apprentice is displayed by the supervisor adding something close to the following: "I will arrange more training for you starting Monday of next week."

Don't make the mistake as a parent, trainer, or a supervisor to solely declare a loss of freedom for a set period of time. Such a statement is a declaration of sentencing, not an invitation to do whatever it takes to improve. Neither is it a challenge to cooperate in order to lessen the punishment.   Instead: **A. State the nature of the lost of freedom.   B. Announce what it is being withheld until it can be earned back.   C. Inform him that you expect to see striving for improvement throughout the interim.   D. Declare the type of behavior you expect to see before you lift the sentence.   E. Ask if he understands?** This promotes a discussion from which both can understand the other's concerns. Now together you can discuss yours and his expectations and come to some common understanding. By doing so, your child can start making proper plans to fulfill his sentence to his utmost, rather than to his least.

Common Sense Lesson: **The Perpetual Grounding**

"Thank you for giving me something I can use to punish my kid with," a neighbor said, without any other explanation.

"Huh?" I replied as I was caught way-off my guard.

"The horse riding," she replied seemingly so proud of herself.

"Uh, ok. ..." I stammered back, while raising a puzzled eyebrow. She certainly had succeeded in getting my attention.

"Before," she continued, "nothing worked which I could use to ground Amanda; she didn't care about anything. Since she has been going over and riding with you and those other kids, she loves it and looks forward to it, like none other. So, when she misbehaves, I grounded her from horse riding and does she ever suffer. It's great."

I can kick myself for my next choice of action. Self-importance got to me; I foolishly took her words as a compliment; I interpreted them as: '*I was doing a good job, and keep it up.*' I continued thinking while patting my own back, "*Well, now your daughter will surly cooperate with you, cause she does love to ride. **Oh-yah, riding horses has done it again!**"*

When I finally let my pride vanish enough to digest what I should have done, I started having another small prompting in my gut. It was to say, "Quit-it! You're screwing it all up." But, I didn't act on it. After knowing I should have said something else, I let Amanda's mother get away from me.

The reasons, at the time, for not speaking out, I can't remember for sure. I was probably very busy, or the timing wasn't right to go into that issue with others of her family present. My words left unsaid permitted a virus of sequential affects brought on by Amanda's open-ended punishment.

Plagued to my mind were these things that I should have said, yet did not. "*While spending all this time with your daughter, I am building rapport with her,*" I should have started off with that one. "*And because we now have a relationship with things in common, she and I talk.*" Or, "*I am making great headway in helping her to see that most of her problems can be lessened or even done away with by a change in her actions and abilities. The horses do a lot of that teaching for me."* There were any number of responses I missed.

Continuing, I could have said, *"Your daughter notices that the horses give her a hard time when she demands that they mind."* ... *"She isn't very effective in asking them the right way to do things because she gets so angry and has no patience.* ... *"She doesn't want to put herself in uncomfortable situations."* ... *"She is starting to see herself in some of the horse's responses, as she tries to lord over them; they give anger back to her when she displays it to them."* ... *"She questions when things go amiss,* **'Why are they acting like that?'"** And I missed my chance to say, *"There are perfect opportunities for her and me to discuss the fighting with her brothers, and her disagreements with you, her parents. Her interactions with the horses bring up many discussions about short-comings."*

I saw Amanda a week later passing in the hall at church, "Missed-yah riding last week. Your mare was so sad when she had to stay back at the corral while all the others went out for a ride."

"I got grounded for fighting with my brothers," was Amanda's slow quiet reply. "My horse really missed me?" she queried, her eyes opened wider breaking-off her slump of self pity.

"It sure did. It acted cheated standing there alone with a long face as the others rode off. It seemed to say, 'Why don't I get to go?' ...How long did you get grounded for?" I questioned.

"A week," she readily replied. Thoughts of a new opportunity, next week, finalized her flip-flop. She was bubbling with anticipation, "Then, I can come over and ride. On Monday, that's when I'll get off."

"Great," I said, "See yah then. And try not to fight any more with Sam."

"Oh there is no way that I'll do that again," she chirped back as she fluttered away down the corridor.

The next week at church, I again saw Amanda in the hall; she hadn't come over to ride the last Monday. "How is it going? We sure missed you, again. " I fished for her interaction.

"Well, I got grounded for not cleaning my room," she relinquished.

"Oh, so how long did you get grounded for?" I solemnly inquired, while mirroring her gloomy countenance.

"Two weeks, I can come over not tomorrow, but the following Monday," she replied. There was no happiness shining on her face.

"Did you clean your room yet?"

"I cleaned it the next day. Guess they are trying to make a point," she said, while pretending to be interested in a hall poster.

"It is important that you do as they ask; make sure you clean it extra well," I offered what I thought was good additional advice.

"I did that already. It seems like they love to punish me," her face was depicting a general state of disgust, as she turned from fingering the invite to an upcoming youth dance.

"Try extra hard," I said. I was thinking of the foregone opportunity her parents missed to reward her for cleaning her room extra well, even if it was a day late. They could have gotten much more mileage if she could seen a reward for what effort she did do, instead of them sticking to a decreed length of sentencing for a crime which was paid back in full.

Two weeks later, I opened with, "Amanda, how are yah?" I was endeavoring to break the ice as we, once again, crossed paths in the hallway. She had a cold and stiff look of total displeasure; she was obviously seeking to exhibit resentment to all who would dare to gaze upon her.

"I got grounded again, for talking back," she stiffly replied, while purposely forcing her eyes to not deviate from their frozen trance.

"Bummer." I knew that no charm could speedily thaw her, so I quickly added, "How long for this time?"

"Who knows, maybe until … I … a … start minding? Anyway who cares?" Then she popped-off, "I can't stand my parents, they make me so angry!"

I departed with some cheap comment like: "Sometimes all you can do is hang in there until things get better."

I knew that I needed to talk to her parents and see if they understood that my progress with their daughter was being stifled. I couldn't just walk up and tell them this, as I had missed my chance weeks before. So I prayed that they would want some pointers on teenagers. In answer, they did approach me later, in a round about way, that very day. As results, Amanda again started coming over and riding. As she did, she again saw ways and reasons to refine her own conduct. She continued to realize the need to improve her angry interactions with her family, as brought out by her experiences with the horses. She developed more control over her emotions, plus things started to improve greatly in her relationships with her family.

Her mom and dad have since learned some new ideas on teaching, and still like most of us, they have a long ways yet to go. They have learned to reward for the slightest try. Additionally, they have learned that it is possible to take away freedom for so long that a child learns to live without it. They have witnessed that gone can be the desire to comply in order to get an elapsed freedom restored when the child views it as being impossible to get back. "*It will not be worth the effort anymore,*" as he or she learns to accept the lost of what was once enjoyed. Yes, her parents still discipline, but withholding as dear of passion from their daughter as riding is no longer the punishment used. They instead have learned to use it as a means of inspiring more compliance.

Use grounding as a tool so the kid wants to go through the changing process with you. The wanting to change does the magic, not the grounding. What good does withholding a freedom do, unless you get them to introspect and verbally state why, they acted so? Get them to realize the trigger that caused their outburst, and what they'll do next time instead of using that inappropriate behavior which gets them in trouble. You get them to think about alternatives, and then you can work towards that end. With such an interaction, they are held accountable. If a punishment is nothing but an attempt to force the guilty to make recompense, then as it is enforced, the only success is them harboring bad feelings.

As said before: When delivering a punishment stay clear of the flat statement of a consequence which you require the guilty to endure, so their suffering makes things right. **A punishment in its** best scenario is enforcing a carefully crafted lesson of disciplinary practice, until the disciplined get things right. As they do, be sure you make the effort to give some feedback of what great things they're accomplishing. You guide their behavior. With a child being handled in the best scenario, how can their attitude do anything besides start changing for the positive; haven't they just discovered a new way they might win?

Common Sense: **Seeing the end objective, thru the clouds, inspires one to ascend toward that goal.**

* * *

Common Horse Sense: To inflict a physical punishment on another is to take away their freedom from pain.

"I will just kick 'em in the gut. That'll make 'em behave!"
Joe Marshal

The Author, an old-style cowboy was commenting on how to get the defiant to behave. His advice does work with a mean soured, non-submissive horse which is trying to over-power any opposing foe.

Becoming the recipient of a retaliatory pain does go a long ways towards changing the mindset of a disobedient animal which is forcing you to bend to its will. In order to get this brute's attention, you must act more powerful than it. But, your objective as a trainer is to join with your charges and in unison work together toward a common goal—it is not just to force them to comply. Physically forcing does have its place, and when necessary is often the most efficient and least damaging approach. It gets the attention of your pupil fast, and with that awareness it is noticeably easier to channel their efforts with yours. However, when using a physical force as a discipline, it should be only as little as possible to get the non-cooperative to consider an alternative behavior.

Giving a physical punishment should never be a way or means of just getting even, nor should it be for the purpose of inflicting an injury or a lasting pain in order that you somehow receive a satisfaction from another's misery. It should be used mainly for the purpose of halting a currently unwanted activity, and of obtaining the attention of the recipient offender—that a change of their heart may be allowed. A good kick in the ribs of a non-cooperative knot-head does well to get the attention of a soured or spoiled horse, which is so busily trying to enforce its desires on you that it blows off any acknowledgment of your authority. It is also very therapeutic for the deliverer. However, the same results can be accomplished with a sharp tightening of the lead rope, or an intruding poking of the animal with a finger, as either is combined with a swelling of your body bubble and displays of you getting larger. The key to all is that the horse recognizes you as being the dominant lead-mare. It identifies you as taking away its freedom to experience life without pain.

Handing-out a corporal punishment will not force all receivers into obedience. It only causes a pause in their present actions, that the previously conditioned may hopefully see an error in their ways and therefore diminish their improper behavior. It accomplishes nothing to the young or naïve animal that a good scolding wouldn't have done, except maybe make its farrier momentarily feel better. After resorting to a hard swat or a kick, the emotionally riled horse handler now has to deal additionally with a reactive and fearful animal whose attention he's just gotten. The same success could have been achieved with a loud slap or swift spank, even with a noise producing stimuli that wouldn't have caused a mental scarring or permanent injury, just an awakening remembrance.

When handing out a physical punishment, in order to achieve a behavioral modifying response, the receiver has to be able to understand what you wanted done. Giving an excessive walloping does get you their undivided attention, but without the previous steps of involvement, you could have the recipient wondering, *"What the heck was that for?* It also could launch you, instead of being someone who is respected and obeyed, into someone to be feared.

For the irrationally defiant, consider using restraints of freedom which deliver a hurt when the trainee fights against them. They also help to isolate the punishment as not being your fault; making it appear as not being caused by you. Restraints that limit freedom, such as ropes and pain delivering tack offer the delivery of pain for specific acts of disobedience. When the horse remains cooperative, the restrains only offer a minimum of discomfort. However, when the resistive animal moves against them, their inflated severity is felt. All the while, the trainer is free to move about and is not seen as having to get "Big" so the pains of the restraint will not be attached to him. The cause of the pain will be to the particular restraining device, or more specifically, to the last preformed action. If the captive quits its defiant reaction the pain diminishes. A new behavior is learned to eliminate the pain, allowing the trainer to be seen as the one who assists in the lessening of the restriction after a preferred response is obtained.

Restraining devices are the quickest, yet often most highly abused tools in halting the unwanted behavioral problems of a horse. For in the hands of an unskilled trainer, they can be poorly timed or improperly delivered.

Being subjected to restraints puts the recipient in a frame of mind where they are searching for an action they can do to eliminate their present unwanted misery. The behavior modifying effectiveness of the restraint is only felt as a discovery of an alternative movement is tried and less pain is the result. The educational trainer helps his charge to figure out these alternatives. If an awakening occurs in the thinking of the controlled, they will now perform a previously refused option as their new choice in an effort to obtain relief. They will utilize a new problem solving technique in effort to minimize the pains of their restraint.

*   *   *

Giving a quick discipline verses a long lasting punishment:

After declaring an impending consequence, how much easier is it to deliver a quick punishment, instead of sentencing the perpetrator to a lengthy disciplinary internment, and then trying to enforce their participation? **The quick reprimand assists the child to alter their** performance **NOW**. Thereafter, you can get on with giving a reward. With a long drawn out stretch, the convicted are spending time striving to get out of it, and you are locked into insisting that they fulfill their obligation to repay all debts for any infractions. Enforcing any drawn-out punishment can seemly go on forever, while delivering a effective quick discipline allows the changing process to begin much sooner. It gets their chastisement over and done with, and allows their searching to begin to discover what possible different course of action they might use next time.

An Alternative Corrective Action

A possible alternative to just delivering a corporal punishment is constructing the wording of a punitive declaration to separate the problem from the charge and his trainer. It is a properly worded statement which establishes the perimeters of a penal restriction, so that it limits the child's freedom to pursue Joy until an acceptable requirement is reached. It is best when it is done in a way where both the trainer and the trainee are working on the problem without having to focus on the child's poor behavior. This places the lack of obtaining the predetermined goal as recipient of all attached blame, which becomes the enemy to be overcome, not the child or his law-enforcer.

EXAMPLE: *"When you can raise your score in spelling up from a "D", then you may have use of your videos back. Show me your next two assignments."*

The parent can now help his child overcome the problem which is the bad grade, not the student. Both can unite working on corrective actions, although one's driving force is getting the freedom to get his video back, and the other's is the improvement of the child's ability to spell. *The parent shouldn't have to force him to do the right thing. It should be the child's objective also.*

Throughout this consequence the parent is freed from the obligation to help the kid, who is assuming the responsibility to overcome his deficiency. When the child gets his schoolwork into the hands of his parent, then the parent takes some co-ownership of the problem as well. If the child chooses to not address the problem, then the parent is absolved from helping. The child is left in his state of decreased freedom. The continuation of the consequence is the acceptance of this child when he or she doesn't focus on any corrective actions.

Rules

Another alternative to physical punishment is the use of rules and regulations which have already been established. To a previously aware person, they are devices of restraint which halt most of the need for the trainer to have to get BIG {aggressive}. They act as restraints to limit the freedom of one person to abuse another; they should be obeyed, so that all can have equal opportunity, not just a few free to express themselves at another's expense. With rules the student knows beforehand what is expected of him so will attach little blame on his trainer should enforcement become necessary.

EXAMPLES:

- *Rule Number Two* is: **Use respectful language in class.**
—Any person caught talking discourteous will be required to write five alternative ways which they could have communicated without using rude comments or foul language. In addition, they must sit on the front row until the end of the class period, and until they write the new possible choices.

The rule is posted in such a way that every class attendee knows what Rule Number Two is. Before any infractions, all understand what the ramifications will be.

- *Classroom Regulation*: **"In order not to have a pre-assigned seat, a student must show proper classroom behavior for two consecutive days."**
—The reward is earned when the student feels that the likely gratifications from sitting were he wants warrant his controlling himself. He alone is responsible for where he gets to sit.

In the above examples, breaking the rule and not following the regulation, infer the punishment of improper manners as being caused by the actions of the defiant, not by reciprocation of the trainer. For the use of improper language the student knows before hand there will be a preset unwanted punishment. It will not be a total surprise when it is enforced. The enforcement of pre-set rules, which limit freedom, is the quickest and most effective tool in decreasing future unwanted behavioral problems of a child. {**Should the student refuse his punishment, his is removed from any other stimulation until he fulfills it.**}

"When it is appropriate to use physical force?"

Common Sense: **There will be times when it is necessary to physically overpower a defiant charge.** —If he or she is injuring themselves, others, or destroying property and no other intervention works, you must bring them back down to a stand still before any other means of interaction can be effective; this includes the showing of love. Overpower the out-of-control child to bring them back again to a safe state, and then start pouring on the love.

"Does the child being in an unsafe environment warrant the need for his overseer to use physical force against him?"

Most defiantly! It is used in its proper sequence in the EI process, after all verbal intervention has failed. **Physical Force** is the hands-on restraint of freedom done to limit the movement of a charge. When a mom grabs her totter by the hand and leads him against his will away from a potential disaster, this is using physical force. Any time a loving caregiver holds on to rambunctious child to limit their action, this constitutes physical force. All delivery of physical force should be controlled as not wantonly designed to cause lasting injury to the receiver. All should be as little as possible, to get and obtain the attention of the child, in order, to stop his unacceptable movements. It is only wrong according to the intent of the deliverer.

* * *

Common Horse Sense: Discipline, but don't get angry or loose your own control.

You don't negotiate with a defiant horse which is causing damage to itself or to something else. To discipline the horse that is wigging-out, you need to "Get Big." Be assertive. Use sharpness to establish control over it, but, use the least amount possible. When you need to discipline, keep cool, calm, and to the point. This will lead your charge into a de-escalation mode much sooner. Displaying anger will prolong the time needed to bring yourself and them back to a stand still.

With both a kid and a horse, after you have gotten their attention, get them back again where they can be reassured and calmed. Bring them to a point where they are willing and submissive, then ask again for their cooperation. Use effective controls for as short of time as possible, and then let off the pressures by loosing the restraints, the quirk, or the punishments. Don't continue to be as large and aggressive. Let them breathe and think of what they have done. During this break from the previous stress is the time to attempt to reassure them that everything is ok. You send the message that there won't be further inflicted punishments, as long as they remain calm and collected.

Remember that a horse does, and the student can, *learn not from pressure, but on the reassuring release of it.* ... **IN ORDER FOR IT TO BE RELEASED, IT MUST FIRST HAVE BEEN APPLIED.**

In the hands of a knowledgeable trainer, the trainee's focus is switched from the reactive behavior, preformed as defiance, flight, or fight. Their resistance towards pain and restrain is turned into wise and willing actions done because of the properly timed release of pressure and the offering of rewards for correct behavior. The charge's new goal will become behavior that will bring a freedom from discomfort. In that choice he joins with his trainer, working together in a common goal, instead of just against his restraints.

If a teacher chooses to govern passively by being patient in order to get a standstill, a change in his charge's resistant behavior might eventually happen. Eventually the most out-of-control body will tire out. But, during that time a lot of damage could occur.

You are limiting your prowess, when your principal disciplinary action is to exhibit patience; you are subjecting him and you to a more involved process of restoration. In no sense of the word are you being a trainer by hoping that child would change from some other stimulus other than you. You may still have your child's best interest in your heart, but you have chosen a long path for him and you to travel.

Common Sense: **To engage others without pain compliance, they and I must have a <u>Common Goal</u>. Therefore; my objective is always to get them to join with me instead of remain against me.**

After a punishment has been levied, don't continue to castigate the child with constant reminders of their bad choices. Forget about it and start tomorrow as a new day. Relate to: If you had just come to an understanding and were in the process of making amends, you wouldn't want someone continually bringing up your past mistakes. ...Neither would anyone else. In fact, that does damage. If you continue to bring up their past blunders, they will seek ways to avoid your company. ...Drop it!

...{Unless, of course, you are so insecure with your own abilities that you need to keep reminding others of their past imperfections in order to make yourself feel better.}

While attempting to form a common goal is not the best timing for repeated reminders of others' infractions. They had their reasons. Keeping a common goal alive is an occasion for additional support in what they are trying to do; it is the stage for an increased showing of love from you.

Great is your joy when you see a change in the behavior of your charge. Yes, it would have been a less painful experience for all, if they would have out of guilt embraced a reason to change without you having to resort to delivering a punishment for their failure to comply. Even still, your skills as a trainer have taken their resistance and guided them into wanting to join with you in their effort to receive a reduction of pressure. With less pressure the child is free to continue on his pursuit of happiness.

Beware of the strong-willed or irrational youths who can not see the benefits of a common goal with their trainers. This is where these child may breakaway from all that has been taught in the past, and do something stupid, irrational, or out of past character just to preserve a feeling of some **retention of personal power** in their lives. They may even do things that will knowingly bring hurt, or be of the mindset to endure or accept any pressure you place against them, if in their minds it helps them retain some personal control of power.

If your charge has moved up to that level of resistance to where they are set on defying at all costs. If even the affect of your physical consequences for their poor behavior has yielded no change of heart, least-ways a noticeable change of behavior. Then, you are left with no alternative except to move into the highest level of the Graduating Escalation of Involvement. This intensity will bring the most heartache as you must witness your loved-one maintain defiance. Still, the possibility of their turnaround is achievable, and whenever any success is obtained you will experience great Joy. In this final level of involvement, you should never give up. You must never give in. You keep engaged at all costs ... even though you see no end in sight!

CHAPTER 17:

NOW IS NOT TIME TO QUIT

In an effort to retain some sort of personal control, the continually non-cooperative student may move up to a higher level of defiance. This is the time when they will act out against and figuratively "Buck Off" all forms of power or control over them. They will toss you!

Be prepared to be Bucked Off
Keep showing Unconditional LOVE

"Ouch, that hurts; it doesn't feel good. It certainly makes you feel that you need to do something about it!" ...What must be done is: to somehow get control of this out-of-control situation! ...Even though they're not being allowed to have their way, they're still defiantly taking it. ... Something will have to be done, but what? ... Resorting to killing them is not really a credible option." These are your real emotional feelings and thoughts as you've just been just left lying on your hinnie. You may wish to be able to do something drastic that would eliminate a charge's defiance forever, but be realistic, who really wants to deal with that old dead stinking carcass anyway?

There is a way for you to deal with your rebellious charge. As nothing has worked, you now must move into the highest level of involvement in order to remain somewhat effective. As you get ready for the worst, you prepare to be Bucked Off.

*   *   *

Common Horse Sense: Bucked Off

Next time you want some thrills in your life, go to a Rodeo. See a cowboy pit his will against that of a mean, ornery, and cantankerous critter. The animal is fighting at all costs not to be controlled and the rider is attempting to do just that, establish his dominion over the beast.

{Why this is like standing outside in the hallway and watching the battle that goes on between two siblings, after you just offered a younger brother five bucks if he will go in early on a Saturday morning and succeed in causing his seventeen-year-old sister to get up, so she may get an early jump on her weekend chores. The beast is committed to fight, its nostrils flare, and a snorting ensues. Its anger evolves until it erupts into a mad fury hell-bent on seeking to dislodge the small brave soul who's attempting to defy her! As she pitches the lesser well from her presence, you can only resound, "Well done, young man," as he does the brave things we only wish we could do, but haven't the guts! Witnessing the exhilarating performance as the two engage in a contest of will was well worth the cost of your admission.}

The fun begins when the rodeo rider climbs onto the animal as it is contained in the confinement chute, and therefore, can do very little against the restrains put upon it. A bucking strap is cinched tight onto its flanks in order to give it more to fight against. When all is ready the cowboy signals and the gate opens. The animals, from being previously trained, will give all they can against this stimulus. They are conditioned to fight against this form of control. They'll frantically resist in order to retain what they feel is their freedom. They will spin, dodge, run and buck in order to get the cowboy and his restraints off their backs. Most of the animals feel an adrenaline rush and delight in the event. The brave cowboy has committed himself into taking whatever the beast can dish out. In fact he's scored on his ability to give to the animal more stimulation to "Keep-on-Buckin'." A time limit of eight seconds constitutes a completed ride. For the rider, this can seem like an eternity when he and the animal are not in synch with each other. Barring no one gets hurt, this is entertainment at its best.

Now consider this: What if things were different?

… If it were possible for the cowboys to stay on longer than eight seconds, would the animals eventually wear themselves out?

… If additional restraints were placed on to the animal, it would be easier for the rider to stay on?

… What if no bucking cinch was used at all, and the cowboy sat calmly on the brute without further stimulating it? Given less to fight against, would the bucking horse soon lose interest in acting up?

… Finally, consider if the cowboy had spent a lot of time prior to the rodeo where he and the horse developed a working rapport, wherein their interactions were mutual and positive?

With each of these considerations, when the chute opens, how much bucking will the animal do? These "what if," things happen all the time; they happen in every-day life when someone is anticipating a possible buckin'-off, and so, takes steps to prevent against it. A prior positive relationship with the cowboy and the animal probably would mean less people would go to the rodeo. There certainly would be fewer reasons for the horse to buck.

Most horses when suitably stimulated will buck. If a horse has nowhere else to flee, or it feels that it has lost more freedom than can be dealt with, it could buck. Even the seasoned horse, often left for long periods without use, may resist. Now I don't know exactly why they do it, perhaps they have lost their conditioning to yield to others; it does seem they have lost their good reason. Maybe they buck cause they're havin' a great time seein' if their rider is serious about his commitment to ride?

Every horse person who is committed to helping an animal reach its highest potential knows that if bucked, he must then stay with the horse at all cost. This means if possible: get back up on the saddle. Of course it's hard to get on a horse that's running back towards home at top speed; especially when you're still sprawled-out laying in the dirt a-cussing that mangy inconsiderate critter. So you let him run. You couldn't have gotten on for a minute anyway, even if that knot-head had stayed around to bask in his glory. You're still too dazed to realize which way is up, not to mention you have no immediate desire, nor ability to move. So you lay there in order to clear your head. After the stars dim and you recuperate for a moment, you start the long walk home extremely frustrated for being so naïve as to not seeing it coming.

Thanks to your gone astray horse, you have just acquired some A-1 perfect thinking time. You summons a smile as you endure the sneers from your buddies, whom after witnessing a rider-less horse go by at a neck breaking speed, stop whatever it was that they were doing and now wait around aiming to see what fool hit the deck. When you get home, you can chose to get back on and attempt riding by rationalizing that if you just try harder, then things will work out for themselves. Or, get realistic and admit that you do need additional help from a visit back to the Basics … again. Really it doesn't matter at that moment; the horse got away with it and will probably again attempt defiance. Only, next time, you'll want to be prepared to be "Bucked Off."

"Just how is it done, to prepare oneself to experience a totally defiant attempt by a charge to eliminate your control in their lives?" Well, since you can't always control the horse when he bucks, you'll want to give him less to buck about when you are controlling. And you want to establish a good foundation of constancy, trust and reward before any bucking takes place.

Even after all your timely efforts and training there's still a possibility that your mount will pitch you. In the event that you get thrown, you will want to, again, revert back to the fundamentals of ground training where you control your horse in a familiar environment and at slower speeds. You'll want to re-establish the relationship of being the trainer and the horse as being the submissive, before you again attempt to check it at high speeds or in any other situation when it thinks it's been given a free head. Experience has now taught you to be aware where your horse is at any given time, and, as you need, lean to stabilize your position.

As the possible recipient of defiant behavior, you need to learn to keep your balance, so that any rank display doesn't unseat you and put you in the situation where you are powerless to further control your animal. You learn of your duties and responsibilities in your relationship, that you may be prepared for an outburst of resistive behavior.

Pay attention to detail. There was a point prior to him pitching you off, when the horse decided that it was not going to submit to your will. He may have prolonged his eruption and decided to endure until a good opportunity for expression presented itself, but if you were paying attention at all—you knew something was up.

Most horses will not buck every time when ridden. But, all will in some way check out your commitment to see if it is stronger than theirs. If so, they'll choose to descend into trying to work with you. The one that does not yield to your prompting signals is the one harboring its own feelings of resistance; it is getting ready for an explosion of self expression. Have a good deep seat and keep both two hands on the reins, and if possible look for a good place to land. You might be going for a different type of ride than you had in mind.

Addressing the Repetitively Defiant

I must say, that every good cowboy knows that he doesn't give in to a defiant horse. You ride them, scold them, or turn them in circles until they ask for your forgiveness by showing signs of submission. Because, if you did nothing it would be allowing your animal, just as the rodeo stock, to become conditioned to give an all out effort of defiance when they feel an overwhelming amount of control is placed upon them. The repeatedly resistive have learned if they oppose hard enough, and for long enough, then the irritant will leave and go away. As a cowboy, you get ready, and then give an all out effort to stay in control. You remain responsively adaptive so as your charge alters their behaviors, you likewise adjust your efforts in order to still stay on top of the game.

*"**What to do with the rogue**?"—The one that never is reformed by the restraints placed upon him?"*

Since you asked, I'll answer the only way that I can: **It depends entirely on how much involvement you are willing to invest.**

That you can **over-power** a horse by training techniques, and establish the **fear** of you as a herd leader, and as the **giver of pain** is true. And that you may be able to finally **wear it down** or **force** it to quit fighting against you is likewise correct. Many have learned successful ways to **break a horse**; they have developed dominion over the equine and have achieved a forced compliance.

To have any **positive effect** on a rogue, to where it experiences a **change of heart**, you must win them over with love. With an out-of-control horse this means an out-of-control amount of time spent with the animal, either in the form of forcing them to behave, or allowing them to **feel of your love**, so that they may sequentially learn first to endure, later to accept, and then finally to esteem you.

The rogue horse should feel that you want to be with it, not that you are spending time together just to be lord. It has expressed unyielding resistance to all of your insufficient efforts to persuade compliance. If you still have as your goal to positively affect this hold-out, then you need to give-up having an object or a lesson you are force feeding. Its unyielding past dictates that you change your style of teaching techniques, not your desires or energy as a trainer. Because you are committed, take another style of less demanding. You will have to present yourself as a fellow traveler who is developing a friendship before you can guide. Out of last resort, only focus on trying to show this defiant some form of reduction of your controlling requests forced upon it.

You are not waiting for this rebel to give up; you are creating an interaction where they don't have to focus on more resistance. You are offering a relief of pressure, followed by acceptance of them as they currently are, in the hopes that they may, thereafter, be attracted towards your love. Your do not abandon your goal of addressing the **Original Problem**; you put it on hold and go after just remaining able to stay in a teaching role. You increase your commitment to do whatever it takes to remain involved.

To the defiant horse, the fact that you are offering your acceptance is not of much importance. Because of your past confrontations, it only wants two things from you now, rest and food. —All else means very little.

1. Rest. They want to be left alone without your interventions. Of course you can't give that to a dependent, you still have to maintain control over them. They are still in your care, but you can make it a point to not always be pushing your control on them. It is not so hard to do if you think about it. Pick something that they are doing, that you may also do. Join them in something that requires no intervention, so that nothing is expected of you or your charge, and then just be there with them in that. In this starting point activity don't push yourself on them too much. They may even perceive you as having minimal interest, but they will also see you as not a threat. {Like silently watching a video with a child, then when it is over you politely say, "Good night," and excuse yourself to bed. Or in the case of a horse, you work with another compliant animal while in the presence of the defiant.}

What is the point? There was no interaction as each was seeking gain for themselves while having next to nothing to do with the other. ... The point was that something else was happening. It was that: EACH WAS GETTING NO FURTHER CONFRONTATION FROM THE OTHER. Some common ground and rapport, even if it was only a minuscule amount, was being laid. In concurrence with your commitment and goal to positively affect your charge, you have done it. You have shared some time with them and it was not negative. They have endured you, and aren't worse off because of it. Now, work at showing that you are enjoying the time you spend in their presence. Increase your efforts to show that you are enjoying doing things for them. You are showing them love and they are learning to accept you. Now you can start again slowly; you have something to build on. You as a mentor/trainer have to maintain that you are willing to do what the horse/charge wants, just be there as he rests. If you don't display any alternative agendas that will cause their withdrawal, they will grow to look forward to your interaction and even hold in esteem the time spent together.

2. Food. Your dependent charge still looks at you as the provider of the necessities of life. They view your obligation is to give them what they want, and theirs is to take it. Unless you have turned it loose, this horse still looks to you as the provider of a meal and a good drink. So, use this to your advantage, like I did with Charlie and the water. As your rogue eats beyond the necessities of life, you require that at least he receives it in your presence. You may want to start with bucket feeding oats. It works miracles in giving an opportunity for the horse to want to be with you without strings attached. If your rogue's behavior is so far gone that even offering oats doesn't work, you may need to bring another bomb proof horse along to show by example, so that your rogue's fears don't get out of proportion and he freaks out. Allow him the freedom to eat in your presence without anything else happening.

When you can, you'll want to get some forward movement; to start making progress. At first progression may be as little as the eating of the oats with you watching. After this becomes something which they accept, then you'll be able to move a small step towards refinement. This would be the eating of oats with you holding the bucket, then talking to them as they eat, add to this touching them, and eventually rubbing them if possible. On the onset, each is done without asking for anything in return. Start out slowly. Patiently you move closer when they show acceptance. It means at this time you are only concerned with the smallest step toward compliance. The horse must feel he gives to you freely, not that it was it forced from him. Take your time; you are building a new relationship. The rogue has chosen to act out in defiance before, either out of fear or because of his overwhelming desire to be the one in control. The object now is to spend enough time with them to gain rapport and thereby allow them to desensitize. They are the ones to move forward in effort to dismiss their fears, having faced the dog and not been bitten. {see: page 229, "Walk Into The Dog"} You are building another foundation of trust to build upon.

*   *   *

By now as you read this book, you've seen that it is my purpose to correlate the similarities between training a horse and a child. As you read how to have an effect on a horse, your mind is also racing and making notes on the same results as being possible with a child. For the purpose of more firmly implanting in you the correct knowledge, we will also address the same question, only directed towards a child.

"What to you do with the person who is rebelliously defiant?"

...This depends entirely on you. Are you willing to continue to be involved? How much more are you are ready to invest!

If you still have it in your mind to get this individual to behave, to conform, or to change you must become even more committed in your involvement in-order-to cause them to abandon their inappropriate behavior. At first, you tried to rationalize with them in order to solicit their change. They didn't buy in. Next, you tried policing a halt to their unwanted actions. And yes, if you remained "Big" enough you caused a lock-down of their deeds, but still had no lasting change of attitude. If you were manipulative enough, you may have been able to coherence them into passing through your imposed hoop. And when it happened, didn't you even go so far as to give a cookie? But, why isn't this kid now jumping to change his attitude?

Aren't you with your new learned methods and techniques being tougher than he? Certainly you are showing him that you're the boss, as you've been now, for some time, masterfully forcing him to do your will by efficiently taking away all his various reasons to refuse. You have abandoned setting back and allowing him to freely get away with his inappropriate behavior. So, how is possible with all your interactions, that he can be anything below a saint? Aren't you are always pointing out that you're right, then bringing up his errors by letting him know that you disapprove when he messes up? You are remarkably, intently, engaged using much time and energy trying to get him to change. You're constantly coming up with new ideas and methods that could work. Why you are—

"STOP RIGHT THERE!" <u>You must also come at this from not always having to **FORCE** him to change.</u>

If you are desirous enough to invest in a reluctant charge to cause their change, then you must be willing to put in additional non-intrusive time with them. You have forgotten the fourth step in the Basics. You are doing the forcing part well already, now you must go beyond that. You have forgotten all about the break-time, and that your student learns more when you release the pressure. Your task now is to be with them without trying to argue with, belittle, or alter them. With this unchangeable kid, it is time for you to change; you show them only that you care. ...

{If your motive is more than this they will see right through you.}

... As you spend time with them, without your motive of forcing your desire to make them change, this will open the door for you to show your approval for things that they are doing well. It might come hard because you've been so busy seeing just the bad. You haven't dwelt on the good that they do have. Spend time with them, serve them, and get to know them again.

Until now you have been forcing change. Has it been effective? Is your relationship with them improving so that they willing except the suggestions you offer? So far you have tried all else, and you are getting only an increase of resistance. You must re-enter with them again into the basics of relationships. You must seek in a place where neither is inclined to justify past behavior. Find a neutral place with you not coming down on them and they are not stuck hell-bent on avoiding you. {Sharing a meal, quickly establishes common ground. It is a safe way for all to be together without a contest of will. Don't turn mealtime into a reprimand session.}

To further build your shaky relationship, try building on their desires, not enforcing yours on them. Why do we keep trying the same old things that weren't working in the past? Only after you recognize something genuine about them, and then extend a valid reward of acceptances, praise, or acknowledgement will they let down their guard. If your compliments are honestly enough, you'll give 'em a desire to want to further seek your approval and companionship.

Common Sense: **Have you seen the vision yet? First you sepa-rate your charge from the superficial cause of their rebellious behavior, then you give them needed relief.**

*   *   *

Again, let's refer back to the problem horse: Step back and think of what you needed to solve your original problem? ... *"It is you and your horse working together in a common goal."* Moreover, what you need is a horse conditioned to want to be with you. You need one that wants to be part of your herd, and therefore willing submits to your promptings in order to engage with you. This will take extra time for the rogue; you will have to restructure your approach to get it to want to join with you.

Be advised; there are those extremely rare cases where the animal goes against all nature and doesn't want to be part of your herd. It chooses to act out in opposition, and may not ever submit to your kindness, for its motives always remain the same—It is continuing to acting out of fear or anger, or the failure to see another way. Even as said before, this defiant may be overcome and out-powered with ropes, and bits, and by the trainer acting more defiant and aggressive than it. This horse may never reach the place of freely cooperating in a common goal with his trainer and may always require the escalated efforts of his mentor. Are you willing as a teacher, in this case, to always give and never receive?

In the beginning; you asked yourself, "Why do I want to teach?" After you have had no success with this resistive animal, ask yourself, "Why, again?" If your answer is no longer to provide a safe environment and to do whatever it takes to help this animal reach its highest potential, then get rid of him. Sell him off. This rogue won't have the desire to change if you are not willing to give unconditional love.

*   *   *

Common Sense: **Change starts to transpire when the subject wakens to pain, and then aspires towards easing its discomforts. Transformation continues with a discovery of wanted benefits.** New gains inspire a hankering for more.

—To get a change from a reluctant hold-out, you must inspire his awakening, that things can be better than they presently are.

Common Sense: **"It is not how hard you get bucked off that makes the man. It is what you do once you get back up."**

Those are words that every person, teacher, trainer, and yes, even every student should live by. In our quest for change, we all make mistakes ... even teachers. Although these blunders are not sought after, they are indeed a part of life; they are part of the great learning curve that all travel through. We become aware of their existence when we notice our balance is no longer adequate and we're heading for a fall because of our actions. We sense we're losing our way. In the case of dealing with an out-of-control charge, sometimes we get "Bucked Off" because we never really had control in the first place. Our being bucked off occurs as we realize, "We've lost all chance of control, and our charges aren't going to give in as long as they have something to fight against." If we can't train them, then we must re-train ourselves. We must quit making the same mistakes, and undertake to change what is in our control to do. Either we have it in our power to get back up on and once again confront our opponent with an additional exchange of physical strength, or we desist and show the strength of will and ability by showing **Unconditional LOVE.**

"We must be willing to keep showing unconditional love as long as we have no control."   Let me rephrase that:

"Because at this point, in this the final and most difficult step in the 'EI' process, **no amount of control will cause the defiant to give in,** we are therefore obliged to do **the only thing that will truly cause them to want to change;** we must be willing to show an **unconditional love** toward our offenders."

Very few have the emotional strength to keep fighting a one sided battle forever. As we, without accusations or underlying desires to effect change, interact with our past foes, we give them nothing else to fight about. Because our actions from this time forward will be of love and acceptance, they will soon see and feel the change in us, and eventually take upon themselves the desire to perpetuate further contact. Carefully after building a foundation of rapport and a mutual closeness, we have a chance to raise what we expect out of them to keep this newly salvaged relationship intact. We carefully with patience and love, combined with the use of increased skills, motivate our charges back into working with us, where the original problem can be solved. With no more to fight against, why should they keep on acting defiant?

Unconditional love is not giving in or giving everything to the child. It still requires you to uphold your expectations of them. You still hold them to accountability for their infractions. You don't go about enacting enforcement with a vengeance; you become an enforcer who uses finesse and tact.

"**Foremost your intention is to show that it is them you love, no matter what they are doing. It is not that you love whatever they are doing.**"

This is why the highest level of involvement has this sort of love attached. It takes much effort and engagement to do it right. At this time in your relationship nothing else would make a difference.

Earlier we gave a reward for the slightest effort, now we are giving love without bounds, for defiance. {**Wait ... that's not correct.**} We are giving love without bounds to the defiant.

Giving unconditional love is very tricky, if done with too much sweetness and frosting, the charge may soon learn to run over his sugary mentor. Soon the new goal of this child will become seeing how much he can obtain from his new benefactor; he becomes entitled and spends effort in trying to keep things slanting toward his end of the table. He doesn't grasp the vision of doing what he can to solve his own problems. He may grow to take advantage of his overly zealous caregiver's liberties to where he expects to be saved and taken care of by his easy mark. All may happen before the sugary loving mentor has a chance to move with the child into the common goal box.

Be sure you are using the right motives, then you'll know the most correct actions to take. You have already punished. You have taken away freedoms. You have used the rod. It is now time to show that increase of love to end their resistance. … *"Of course, you can always abandon all and sell your kids to the Gypsies."*

In trying to effect a change on a child while upholding your use of unconditional love, you still use the sequential steps of the EI plan; you do so carefully to ensure that your charge is not constrained to fight against you. Your level of expertise has improved to the point where you are keeping the child willing to communicate with you.

As you discipline for their wrongs, you do so while presenting that only is your intention to get them to learn appropriate alternative methods. You convey that they are accountable for their actions; yet will be completely forgiven of their errors, as they make amends. In the meantime, before they make restitution, they can expect to be deprived of pertinent things that are directly associated to their follies. Use words like: *"As result of that mistake, you can expect the following consequences."* Never deprive them of your readiness to help them to see a better way of doing things. You are committed to force their compliance just enough to alter their attention toward seeing a better way.

Maybe they never will really conform, but there will be an occasion when they have quit acting out in defiance, it is during this pause for breath that you slip in a loving break. You quit delivering additional punishments and lessen your pressure against them. Let them know there is a lessened trust of them, yet you will continue to serve them; you still want what's best for them. This takes a great deal of maturity on your part to pull off. The personal letdown of them not obeying will have you wanting to disengage your level of activity and make them pay additionally for their crimes. Don't do this. You have tried punishing them thinking that it would help. Now what they do need from you is additional love and support: "lest he esteem thee to be his enemy." {see: Doctrine and Covenants: 121:43} To the level of your ability show love throughout the entire ordeal, it'll cement in the perpetrator's mind that still you care for them, despite their choices.

Common Sense Lesson: **Using Unconditional Love**
She was consistently an intelligent individual. She would study things out for herself, and was very motivated to do her best at whatever she tried. Her good work habits, learned in part during the many hours cleaning the farrowing barn on the family pig farm, helped her all throughout her life. Using her work ethics together with her music involvements gained her two scholarships to universities where she studied to earn a major in music. Books and tuition were covered as long as she kept up her grades, so she regimented herself to study and practice. In addition, her necessities required that she work to get the money for personal food and lodging. By applying herself she obtained her goals. I am proud of her accomplishments.

There was a point in her life where she chose to rebel against our family's religious and political beliefs. She, in her adolescence, questioned our methods of teachings. By the time she became a senior in high school, she yearned for freedom as an adult. A free-thinking boy friend and other liberal adults supported her perceived persecutions of being a victim of overbearing parents. These new distractions were offering a chance to feel increased personal freedoms and less parental control in her life. They led her down other side-roads. She started openly defying curfews and questioned other forms of perceived restraints. While under her parents' roof, she did summit to levied consequences for her actions, yet made it clear that she didn't condone being limited in her choices. As-soon-as possible, she abandoned past religious beliefs and morals, and distanced herself from all our parental regulations.

How can such a lovely daughter, who used to believe anything that her parent said, have turned on them so? I often questioned myself in the process. The other family members could see her road to rebellion and thought her wrong in her decisions. I felt that it was my duty to confront her on her new beliefs and undertook to discredit them. This only brought a more distancing of our relationship.

At eighteen, immediately after high school, she moved out of the house and onto a path where she could now control her quest for happiness as she saw fit. Mistakes were made; her choices didn't always turn out to be the wisest. But, she was learning and delighting in her new freedoms. She clearly stated that, "I will never again be controlled by the ideas of someone else." During the time, I felt that was exactly what she was doing; she was letting the view points of others outside her family influence hers.

In order to awaken her senses and cause her to abandon her new ideals, plus, embrace our religion and family standards, once again, my parental involvement was to point out all the things that she was doing wrong. I made that my personal goal every time I saw her. The opposite happened. My involvement with her would bring uncomfortable feelings. I searched for what to do as a father to make my child see the errors of her ways. Deep inside, although I tried to change her, I knew that I couldn't make her do anything. She had made her choices. I'd have to live with her new choices or without her; I didn't want either.

Later as I matured, I started to see the things I was doing wrong in not accepting her for who she was. I realized that in order for her to appreciate her family and its methods of teachings, I would have to just love her —*not as I expected her to be, but as she was.* ...even with her new lifestyle. I wanted to once again help her to see the true Joy and peace of mind in following the Ultimate Loving Father. Even though I didn't condone or agree with all she was doing, I knew I must slack off on making it my constant personal goal to change her.

As I modified my approach, our relationship did improve; she started to realize that her family was her greatest asset. We started having conversations about her life as it was. With my new involvement I was able to offer solicited advice and assist in her decisions and personal problems, instead of following my own tunnel-vision agenda to change her. She again saw the benefits of understanding and support from her family and felt love being extended without any control being imposed. She once more embraced her family and sought to perpetuate our relationship. Together we experienced an increase of peace by focusing on the things she was doing well, and as I mentioned before, they were many. I learned to show unconditional love. What I got back was a thoughtful and family oriented daughter. Heather has many talents and is still working to improve herself.

Now, wasn't that what we wanted in the beginning?

Unconditional love is accepting a child, whatever they are doing, while not always condoning the specific action it may be doing. Such a love is also not abandoning the belief that the child should be responsible for his/or her actions. If you keep a child from paying for the cost of his consequences, then really, what does that teach him; where is his improvement and growth? This is a love so overshadowing that you relinquish what you wanted to do as a concerned parent, and hold him accountable, regardless of your sympathy. It is a commitment to the child so strong that you set a limit and make it clear you don't agree to the crossing of the line. Yet, you will continue to work with this child until he sees and institutes change. It never faileth. It enables the both to enter into a relationship where changing solutions happen.

Student and Trainer
Working Together
Solving the Problem
In a **Common Goal**

The work of solving the original problem is not ended with the first specific compliance of the pupil with his trainer. Each step in the "EI" process had a longer term goal, not merely the completion of its specifically requested task. It was the getting the pupil to work together in a greater common goal with his trainer until the child's current unwanted behavioral deficit finally becomes solved. In the **Common Goal Box**, rules are set and their expectations followed. A freedom from the burden of confrontation is obtained. An emerging liberty comes from fewer nuisances from the original problem because intensity diminishes as solutions are enacted.

Working with the Obedient

The willingly compliant child will enter submissively into this Common Goal Box. He is teachable to the idea of further working together with his trainer. He, upon noticing the rewards which come his way, will want to stay here in obedience, because he is experiencing meaningful Joy.

Working with the Not-So-Obedient

Within the young or the unengaged, is a child who is seeking gains which will fulfill personal wants of time, substance, or feelings. To say to this novice, *"You will feel better, if you comply more with this "BETTER" appropriate choice,"* is of little value to this person who was acting previously for just that reason. His actions, whatever they may have been, were already his best attempts to feel better. He hasn't developed the ability to see beyond his own immediate selfish desires. It might be that for this kid, no one has taken the time to teach him in such a way that he understands. He hasn't discovered that his behavior is lacking and an improved way does exist. The truth of the matter is: If compelled to comply this child may feel worse off than ever, for as of yet, he can identify no benefits.

So, whose fault is this child's behavior when he has not met up with somebody confident enough with discipline to force him to quit acting out? This child will have to experience discomfort in order to change. So, let him retain his discomfort; don't deny him his right to experience the very thing which promotes change. His having to constantly feeling good is not your main concern. The choice to fight or flee, to cower, or to learn in order to do things different is always his to make. Let uneasiness be his alone for a period of time. Feeling good promotes no change; it sends the signal that things are just fine the way they currently are. You inspire no change by your treating someone as though they can not handle controversy.

As the young child matures in his ability to see beyond the moment, he questions why things aren't going so well for him. Experiencing an emotional low expedites his seeking possible alternative solutions. His lack of self-deserved happiness will thrust him into exploring other ways of coping. In his lack of contentment, he considers other ways of dealing with his losses beyond the defense tactics he previously was addicted to. He steadily becomes aware of increasing, lasting, and meaningful gratifications because you are there, with good timing, to point them out.

With his wellbeing in mind, force this kid to behave in-order-to help him. *Take the responsibility for letting him know what he was doing is not his only alternative.* Teach him a better way, and then reward him as he does right. As he accepts his reward he will start to recognize new gains beyond the uncomfortable moment. He will notice his worth to self and to others increasing. After a while, doing things to keep his new positive feelings will become priority.

Optional Responses for the Blatantly Disobedient

In contrast to the willing and those who can notice a better way when led into an uncomfortable situation, is the obnoxiously, disrespectful, and defiant child. This holdout kid has been subjected to some type of uncomfortable situation, perhaps by you, and he is resisting with his non-malleable will against it. Do consider, he is simply using defense mechanisms that have worked, in the past, to give him some relief from similar situations. This is what he knows. He is uncomfortable so he defends against that feeling. For any change he requires the corrective involvement of his trainer. His disobedient behavior patterns are locked in because he lacks the

360 JUST WHO AM I TRAINING ANYWAY

ability to see beyond his immediate skills; he lacks the ability to efficiently problem solve. All his exertion is to demand freedom from present discomforts. In his thought process of rationalizing what his best coping options are, he chooses to react rebellious, rude, or abusive, because this inappropriate behavior works for him by partially supplying the gratifications he's seeking. In his out-of-control state, he will not be willing to consider a rationalized change.

When you have acted powerful, and have applied superior force against this kid, you may have temporarily gotten a different response do to your pressing involvement. It will not continue once you diminish your control. He still remains in need of an involved effective trainer.

Your commitment dictates establishing a foundational rapport with him. You must offer to him something he wants. To change in any lasting way, he will have to feel he's getting some sort of freedom from pain. You only have two basic methods of changing this resistant charge.

1. **Get him to an obedient state where he is willing to learn.**

With your masterful knowledge and your a established relationship of rapport, you present to him an alternative to his negative behavior. He accepts it because he somehow recognizes that he's hit an uncomfortable bottom place that hurts. He recognizes he needs help, so he willingly tries something different.

You remained the teacher.   **The timing was right.**

2. **You have to overcome him.**
You became a trainer, like a "Lead Mare."   {*see: page 168*}

He must be compelled to obey enough times so he finally realizes: persisting in his past behavior will bring him more trouble then it is worth. Simultaneously, after his try for compliance, you will lessen his resistance with rewards offered for correct behavior. With that, he will eventually become ready to join with you in a different approach.

Remember forcing a child that can't recognize his need for help doesn't usually produce a lasting change in behavior. In the beginning of a forced changing process, once the pressure of the trainer is relinquished, the castigated will revert back to his previous manner of doing things; he understands no other way. He hasn't awakened to a new personal discovery that he has alternatives to his current behavior. He hasn't been forced to use other choices, or been trained to consider them when he's in a non-combative mindset. He continues to feel that only his uncivil behavior will force others to back off.

For a moment, look outside your box to his way of thinking—it is to some degree working for him. It is only inappropriate for you. It's only **your goal** that he needs to develop optional responses to deal with his problems which abuse and dis-respect others. The ultimate goal with this hard-nut case is to get him to recognize the gratifications that can be his because of proper conduct.

And how is your goal to be accomplished?

...By first disengaging him from his unacceptable behavior.

The child who uses inappropriate behavior must be dealt with in such a way that he no longer is getting power and control from this conduct. Distorted perceptions by both trainer and trainee have led to a less than effective past relationship. A compulsory change of behavior is more likely when directed by a competent trainer, who is taking the lead role by not accepting inappropriate behavior, and he holds the child accountable. This process of change is an escalation of the involvement by the trainer, whom no longer allows the child power by caving in to his charge; he directs a new action.

Tools are available to help the trainer with this blatant child.

- Start out with confronting the specific issue at hand: It is the issue to be dealt with first.
- Point out the unacceptable behavior or the poor choice which was made. This is the enemy, not the person.

{Given another circumstance, and a different behavior, you would probably readily accept the child and his antics.} So, make war on the specific issue, not the kid in general.

Example: **"Kathy, quit talking disrespectful!"** *This approach singles out the child as having a problem, and that she is at fault.*
Better alternative: **"Kathy do you think that language is appropriate right now?"** *As you have stated, Kathy is given an opportunity to view the behavior as the enemy, not herself.*

- Don't brand the kid as being "Bad." With such a declaration, you are most likely to get a continued wall of resistance, either displayed as additional defiance, or as a justification for avoidance of future interactions. Such a mark of disgrace inspires the kid not to improve, but to continue to live up to his label.
- Don't go into battle finger pointing and making blank statements, like, **"You always ... "** or, **"You never ... "** or even, **You can't. ... "**

{Such statements tend to stereotype the person into a set behavior. They attach a label of being nothing more than bad or at fault.}

- Be specific, state clearly what behavior will not longer be allowed.
- Realize that helping the child to feel good is not the goal of a trainer. His emphasis is holding the child to an appropriate behavior. As behavior is changed, feeling different about oneself will follow.
- Hold him accountable for his action; teach him that excuses and shifting the blame do not justify the use of unsuitable behavior.
- During a period of serenity, discuss your expectations to which you will hold the child. This should be during a peaceful time where neither of you are cruising for a fight. It is then when a child is most likely to buy into his need for a more appropriate behavior. It's in his calm introspection of his last outrageous performances that he realizes, what he got was not what he was really after.

{A child who is still getting benefits from inappropriate behavior will see little need to curb himself. You must somehow eliminate those benefits.}

- Clear rules are established with the child. He is led to help set his own consequences for any inappropriate conduct in the future. If he has a hard time coming-up with consequences, then suggest to him possibilities. **There must be some retribution for not following the rules.**

A good deterrent for an escalating behavior is to have pre-recognized warning sign that the trainer can give a child. It will indicate to them that it is time to take a break from their present course of action. Kids love secret signals and most will halt their activities when they realize their errors, especially if the signal is given before they freak-out completely. Have the child help you come up the signal which will say to them, "You are starting to act out inappropriately."

- For the older child, help them to realize a pattern of time or events which seems to set them off. Teach ways to break that pattern through avoidance, or a better choice of actions.
- When trying to halt an unwanted behavior don't just blurt-out, "**No**" or "**Stop**" or even, "**Don't do that.**" Be creative enough to replace the unwanted action with one which the child can do. It will give him something to focus on instead of what he can't do.
- Use a "STOP GAP." As the child's attention starts to deteriorate, call his attention to something else. *"Hey, Look at this … Show me your new toy … Let's play a game …* or something similar to the old catch phrase used with adults, *"So what about them Dodgers?"*
- Disconnect the child from the source of his irritation. Ask him to leave for five minutes, or you leave, that he may have the chance to reconsider his actions. In non-combative intro-spection, both are free to plot a new course.
- The best way to distinguish the heat of an argument is: refuse to engage in it. Don't stay where you are getting further upset. You, be proactive and take the steps to diminish the potential for an increase in the negative escalation of behavior.

After the child has acted out inappropriately, he needs to be held accountable to make his error right. Part of making it right is: for his ability, hold him accountable to mend any damage that he caused. A young child can't pay monetarily for damage, but he can understand to some degree loss and error. He must be held responsible to do some service to pay recompense for the damaged he caused. Because of his having to make a form of restitution for damage, he learns new perspectives. He learns he is answerable for any similar responses in the future, and he receives a closure to his present screw up. He may even feel good about his efforts and his sacrifice to right his wrong, especially when you make a positive production out of it. Get him to clean up his mess, or to fulfill additional unwanted chores to make up for his wrong.

There are additional measures which promote hopeful avoidance in the future. These measures empower the child into changing his future responses.

- Ask him what he was thinking that led up to his action?
- Identify the trigger that caused the outbreak, and then make it clear that this still doesn't give him the right to use inappropriate behavior. Help him discover things that he can do to avoid these influences in the future.
- **Get him to obligate himself to specifically what he will do next time as an alternative**. —Instead of him being punished and then turned free again to commit his same error,

For the child to just say, *"Next time things will be different, because I will change,"* is not a liable answer where his actions can be evaluated, re-adjusted, or even defined. It has to be more specific. He must hold himself accountable for a commitment of compliance which can be checked up on and/or measured. For him to realize and then verbalize, *"Next time my brother makes me so mad that I need to hit him, I'll first stop and go to my room five minutes for some personal thinking time. Then I will come back and deal with him without hitting. I will instead____(the child fills in this blank)__."* This is an answer that shows a pre-planned alternative to an inappropriate behavior. It identifies the trigger that caused it. It gives him the responsibility to be aware of what is happening. He now is empowered to act differently. Your goal is to get him to this awareness.

- By listening to discover what it is that he doesn't like, you can become aware of his preferred solution. Now you and he can join together in the goal of problem solving his dilemma.

- Help him identify what's really bothering him. Lead him to understand that he has the ability to initiate change. He may not always be able to eliminate that which is troubling, but can learn to redirect how he lets himself be affected by it.

- He is helped to discover what his best options are to manage the situation.

You might help him practice by reviewing possible different alternatives and then envisioning what responses he is likely to get by delivering them.

- Point out any possible rewards for correct behavior. So, next time, in his rationalizing attempts, he'll know he's got something to gain, as well as to lose.

- He is taught that only his behavior is what matters, not the reasons for it. Rules still apply even though things did not go his way. He is held to the standard to use acceptable responses first. If he can not oblige, that still does not give justification to abuse another.

- Impose consequences for his badly chosen actions that are time and task oriented.

A freedom is withheld from the child for a compliant time period. You say something to the effect of, *"Billy, you will not have the privilege of any electronic devises for three hours. I want you to have the uninterrupted time to think of your actions, and what you might do differently next time —only then, come back and discuss with me what you have thought about."*

Upon returning, if he still answers with a hollow, "I don't know," he's still displaying that he is not engaged in the changing process. Avoid eliminating his duty to, at least, try to come up with some alternatives. You aren't doing him any favors if you quickly fill in the blanks by giving him an answer before he seeks an awakening.

366   JUST WHO AM I TRAINING ANYWAY   DAVE SLATER

Your obligation is to continue to lead him in a direction toward where he may help himself. You do so by saying something like: *"I don't feel you used your time wisely in reviewing your poor behavioral choices. Try again for another hour without any electronic distractions. ... Really think what other options you may have, and then comeback and tell me. Your privileges can be restored once we discuss different things you could have done ... those things will have to be more appropriate than the hitting that you did do."*

- For the young, make their consequence age and ability suitable.

"You can not play with the rest of the kids until you can go ten minutes without an outburst." ... Or, *"You now get a timeout. Go sit by yourself and think of different things you can do instead of hitting or getting mad and throwing your toys. After you have been there quietly for ten minutes, come back, and tell me how you will act better."*

- Start with something that the child can actually do, then remember to acknowledge with a reward of value when he does properly comply.

"You did it; you stopped crying! Can you, now, play with the other kids without getting angry when you don't get your way? ... *"How will you do that?"* ... *"Great, if you'd like, you may go back and play nicely with the other kids. ... This time don't throw a tantrum or chuck things when someone else has a turn, or you will have another timeout."*

Following the imposing of any time-oriented consequence, there ought to be an important discussion between the trainer and his charge. The purpose is to identify new behavior options.

- The child is led into vocalizing the actions he will take the next time instead of simply reacting to his difficulty with an outburst of inappropriate behavior.

The possibility of new actions may be his, but only after his mind opens to an alternative role-play depicting a different end result: *Him being able to continue playing with the other children in a way that all enjoy themselves.* This process is much more involved than merely wishing for things to happen. The child must come up with an alternative plan.

{You, the trainer, may rest assured your reprimand was appropriately on the road to your charge's success, if he is able to state alternative changes for his behavior which will lead to a common goal based ending.}

- If he is stumped and has no answers as to what different actions he might take, then you lead him to seek the answer to the following questions:

  … *"What will I see you doing differently that will show a change?*

  … *How will you know if your new behavior is working?*

Remember, the purpose for a consequence is more than the enforcement of a punishment. It is also a chance for the reproved to **take a secluded break from his or her past behavior** in hopes to discover that what they did could be improve on, and that to continue in similar behavior would not be to their and other's best interest.

Wishful thinking on the part of the enforcer has the perpetrator also developing a compelling desire to make restitution for the previous error, in effort to make things right, once more. To assist the perpetrator, it's the obligation of the enforcer to go beyond conveying: "Next time, do a better job." The enforcer, additionally, has a duty to present an opportunity for making retribution.

- The penalized must fulfill his obligation to make things right, before his reinstatement to full privileges.

  To assist him you may ask the following question:

  …*"How will you amend for the wrongs you have done to others?"*

Your role of involvement is to assist the child in creating a practice session where he is:

1. **Visualizing his new performance.**
2. **Seeing additional benefits.**
3. **Committing to make restitution for right his wrongs.**
4. **Choosing to use better behavior the next time.**

- You work with him to put a plan in place that will implement his new correct choices.

To keep the behaviorally challenged child wanting to keep using appropriate actions, start with a level that they are currently on. See that they are aware of enough reasons that they will want to keep showing proper behavior. Praise is good, as-well-as a continued manifest of their freedom. Give gain for the proper behavior you want to continue. As the child builds up the skills of maturity sufficiently enough to want to comply longer, then expectations levied against him should also increase.

- As he now uses his new behavioral options, be sure to praise his attempts and evaluate with him any results. Help him to know when it is necessary to make adjustments.

The child becomes eligible for real earned gratifications as he acts in compliance with the rules and structure; he is now **Working Together** with his teacher, so additional returns will be his. If his rewards are appropriate for his needs, he will upon repeated practice sessions learn to recognize these gains as desirable. His attitude will change into one which promotes his obtaining of these increases. This is the process of change. It is best enhanced as the child encounters love and concern from an *engaged trainer* using a selfless teaching approach.

CHAPTER 18:

PUTTING IT ALL TOGETHER

Beyond Common Sense: Obtaining a change from another takes work. It takes an increase of involvement from an educated trainer who is committed to do whatever is in his command to make a difference. This educator wants change from his charge, so he'll first modify, as needed, his own interacting.

In this chapter we will examine two true hard-nut cases. First, will be where a correction is needed out of a horse. And the second will reflect a need for a behavioral change out of a child. In both cases, their trainers are in need of enhanced abilities as well.

* * *

Common Horse Sense: What to do?

I have a beautiful little paint mare, whom I have been working with for a year on the same problem. She does something that I don't like, and I want it changed. Other than this problem she is a pleasure to have and be around. I have struggled many times with getting her to see the error of her ways, but still I come up short. I don't share my distress on this subject from the muffled and diluted recollections of the past, but from the sharp clear sting of the present. According to all that I understand and have experienced as a trainer, I should be able to solve this problem, but haven't as yet seemed to come up with anything that really makes a difference in her performance. So I'm left with a choice of what to do? Do I continue to do the same things and hope that she will improve? Or do I raise my level of understanding and interactions, in the hope, that I can come up with a combination that will affect her to have a desire to change her actions?

At times, because of my inability to govern her behavior so it fits into my criterion, I allow myself to display a frustration to the goings on. This is lacking, because my annoyance transfers directly to my horse, and as result, I get nowhere fast in solving my problem. What I want to display is a consistent confidence, wherein, my charge can be encouraged by my demeanor, not be pushed away by my aggravation.

Coming up with an effective solution is on-going; I haven't as yet cured the problem, neither have I given up. Every now and then I feel that a measure of success has happen, that she is displaying a behavioral change. It is then when I feel she understands my intentions, and I can deliver praise for her actions. She accepts this praise and I think, "All is well; today finally a difference has been made… my problem is on a direct road to being solved. Beware, life is not always that easy. For although, this time, a difference was seen, cruel reality reveals under identical circumstances I get the same old problem back again the next time, or the time after that. A lasting impression has not happened where my hoped for change has become a habit or a programmed conditioning for my horse, Maple.

Under close supervision with narrowly controlled allowances, she will obey all my wishes. So much so, she's a joy to ride and to be around, and shows a genuine return of love and respect. But when it comes to speeds above a slow canter together with the absence of barriers to limit her freedom of expression, she will go after an exhibition of speed. With anything more than minuscule freedom, she forgets her past lessons learned in an effort to fulfill her passions.

She will push all controls and signals aside. She becomes fixated with continuing in her speed and will not yield, slow, or waver from her efforts to satisfy her obsession; she becomes almost uncontrollable as she gratifies her feelings of power and unrestraint. As she experiences the exhilaration of being able to self-express by exhibiting a little speed, this triggers her to where she demands a huge show of force in order to get her to deviate from the **all-out sprint she desires to experience**. It takes over two minutes once I start asking her to "Slow down" in where I struggle to get her to properly respond. She seems to interpret my efforts as even more stimulation to keep on going. ... She sure can cover a lot of ground in a two-minute period.

Freedom of expression involving speed is offered to her rarely, because she lacks the ability to keep her passions under control. She won't shut down at the proper time. She has, during her displays of fervor, *"Too Much Go and Not Enough Whoa!"* Whenever I know it'll be difficult to shut her down, I dread going fast.

My choices

... Do I try to change her to fit my predetermined mold as to what I feel she should be doing? In reality, isn't it I who has the problem? For in my mind, don't I cling to a pre-conceived notion of what an ideal horse should act like? She is not meeting this standard. Should I hold her accountable to what my ideals are?

... Or do I take her strong points and use them in such a way that she can continue to give 110% efforts in what she does best? I could change my own thinking to appreciate her as she is. I could look for a way use or rationalize her behavior so it's no longer a problem or a concern. Instead, it can become a desirable attribute and a strong point. {**This way she never needs to know she has a problem that her rider can't stand.**}

If I do that, then I have decided to endure her weakness, in order to enjoy her strengths.

... I certainly would like to be able to show her the error of her ways so she understands that her actions could be improved, while, still retaining her freedom, her self-worth, and her desires in all other aspects to remain submissive and teachable.

... I really can't say she takes ownership of her problem. She can't, as yet, see her error. Therefore, is it my duty to keep still and endure her inappropriate behavior? Do I cling to the hope that somehow she will recognize she can improve her overall worth to herself and to me, by a change in her actions? Or should I assertively do something to show her the error of her ways, by revealing her uncontrollable desire for speed is not acceptable?

Where to start: How can I make a decision on what choice I will take, before I really have defined what my objective is? This is my starting point: **Am I doing it for her**, or **I doing it for me**?

...If I come to the realization that I want her to be able to reach her highest potential, I also see her actions are something that must be overcome.

The **Difficulty** is not that I don't want her to exhibit speed. I enjoy a willing horse which will burst into whatever gate I ask. With her, I always get that. The problem is when she in running, she doesn't respond to what I am doing to shut her down ... without much effort on my part. It is then that I feel she is displaying disobedient behavior; it is then that I feel like I have limited control.

The Cause: She enjoys the high of being on the fly.

When given the go-ahead to run, this horse is obsessed to keep going; she gets so wound up. She forgets all about her previous lessons learned. It matters not if she is alone or in competition with another horse. She loves to run; it creates excitement. It stimulates her natural endorphins. Yet, to also have control of this gratifying sensation—**this horse needs more training**.

... {*Is there something I could be doing different?*}

So I made plans and implemented them to obtain a solution:

1. I became bigger and more forceful than she, in an effort, to coerce her behavior. {*This is the only thing that seems to work, but inefficiently.*}

2. We went back for some round pen retraining: {Consisting of re-establishing a strong basic foundation between the trainer and the pupil.}

3. I developed, again, a consistency for issuing punishments for improper behavior.

4. I let her, again, feel rewards for proper performance, by releasing my control at her correct responses.

As result; what I did do had effect on her; she did measurably better. Yet she didn't exhibit a lasting change, only temporary corrections that were the direct result of my accelerated efforts. This is my reality, despite my efforts to change her, she basically remains the same.

When all else failed, I even tried turning aside and abandoning any effort to correct this pupil, and instead just accepted her as she was. But that is not my end goal; I want my horse to be the best that she can be.

Because, I am not pleased with my end results, I resort to **E.R.R.R.** I evaluate, re-adjust, re-fine, and repeat. In my increased efforts to obtain additional insight, I grasp where a portion of the problem might be. I, as a rider, am not giving properly recognized signals which are **MEANINGFUL ENOUGH** to keep this horse in check. Although she is motivated by the exhilaration of displaying speed, I mustn't rule out the possibility she's also stimulated because of some triggers of which I am mistakenly presenting. If I want something different than I have presently, then I must re-adjust my involvement in order to obtain that change.

Shazaam!!! I come to the conclusion I have a duel problem. Now I must re-define a solution.

Apparently I must train myself to a new level in order to deliver in a more refined fashion. I must present none of the false signals which stimulate her unwanted behavior. I must abandon the perpetual clues which keep her disobedience going, even-though I want it to stop. In order that I obtain a different behavior from her, I vow to start again.

I evaluate the previously tried attempts to train this horse to respond to the slowing of her speed without a great deal of effort from the rider. The results were giving small success, not the lasting one I was hoping for. What I want is an obedient and calm horse, who will also give speed and remain in control all of the time. I do not have this now. I have one or the other. If I do not ask her for anything beyond a canter in the controlled space of an arena or large pen, then I retain my submissive horse. When in the open country, along a back road, or in an open field, I retain my submissive and calm horse only until she is subjected to the trigger of speed. Not being the type to give up, I return again to additional steps to be tried to continue striving towards reaching a lasting solution:

1. **Review fundamentals**. Return again to the round pen for ground work of getting the horse to shut down when the rider deflates his bubble. She needs to follow my lead—for she presently does not get as much gratification from deceleration as she does with speed.

2. **Read, study, and learn new ways**—so that I, as a **trainer,** will be able to convey the correct message to my pupil. I will continue to re-fine myself, and be open to new ideas, and suggestions.

3. **Control Freedom.** I will insist on establishing a foundation of her remaining controllable, before letting her experience any grandiose liberty. She must be conditioned that her speed increases are something which I am allowing her to do, not something she is taking from me. She has to react positively to my re-fined signals for a decrease in her gates. Because it is the open country that provides the additional stimulation, it must be I who teaches her to shut down, always, when asked. I will practice until I always receive a shut down of speed in a small area, and then increase the extensions of her freedoms, while retaining her submissiveness. I will give ever meaningful rewards when she properly shuts down so she recognizes the benefits which I offer outweigh the gratifications she desires. As she shows her compliance, I will gradually increase her level of freedom.

4. **Keep striving for success.** Possibly the most important step, in this case, is to give an opportunity for my horse to practice and then practice again, until the lesson get ingrained in her mind.

- I want my charge to experience the joys of refinement. {That is: her discovering the same exhilaration she finds in an unrestricted sprint, but for her to get it while performing as one with her rider.}
- I want for her to look forward with anticipation and excitement at doing her best.
- I want her to perform at utmost efforts, while still remaining submissive and responsive.
- I must be willing to be patient, and to still able to correct subtly.
- I will hold my charge to a higher standard.

... She must be able to distinguish that when she chooses again to not be submissive—a new restriction is placed upon her.

- I make a point to continue to show an unconditional love and acceptance for my charge, while not condoning her unacceptable actions.

5. **I remain positive.** Before each success, I will treat my pupil as though the end results have already happened, by starting fresh each new practice phase with no held-back animosity. I will harbor no repercussion of yesterday's performances. I allow her the freedom from previous encumbrance, so that she may learn to recognize the joy of working with me. Although she will come to view me as someone to be obeyed, she foremost must view me as someone she is comfortable with. I continue to reflect that I enjoy working with her. If I keep learning and improving, she can also.

Enticing change is my ongoing quest.

When dealing with a person, who has a difficult problem which I feel needs to be addressed, I have the same options as with my horse.

Join with me to review my choices, when I insist on a change.

- A role play is started in my mind, *"I totally believe they are worth saving; it's how that produces my quandary."*

- As I struggled with my options of what to do, I must look at my problem from the stand point of doing the right thing. *For whom do I do it?*

Once again I must look inside at my motives. *Just whom am I trying to help by addressing this problem?*

- If it's me, then the solution is easy. All I have to do is confront my charge and say something to the fact that, *"I have a problem with something you are doing. I can't stand it any longer! Therefore, I need you to quit messing up. You need to change in order to make things right!"*

By using this selfish feel-good approach, I accelerated my own entitlement. I receive a form of satisfaction by expressing, "It is not your choice!" I express my concerns with malevolence similar to the re-known words of the famous Count Dracula, "I will force you … to do … my will."

So, what are the likelihoods of this particular approach inspiring any charge to want to improve? …

Don't get defensive; this is a **GOOD** approach when both the student and trainer are interested in solving the problem in question. However if the charge was doing what they thought was their uppermost, then this confrontation will leave them a tad-bit frustrated and confused —to say the least. They probably won't be overjoyed in changing just to make someone else feel good.

- If after an inter-examination of just whom my motives are trying to help, it is revealed my motives are to assist another, then I must consider these other options:

… I can allow them freedom to continue in doing as they may. Therefore for anything to be different in our relationship, it must be I who must change. So, I enact a change in myself, or in the pertinent circumstances surrounding my problem.

… Really, just how can I expect another person to, in every way, measure up to my ideals of them? I must consider compromising my expectations.

… Is it possible that my standards are too high?

- I can keep quiet and let the problem remain without causing change in my charge.
- I can consign myself just to try to look at my student's good attributes instead of dwelling on their negative side.

WOW! I have discovered an answer to my impasse. I will rationalize in order to control my dilemma.

"This is a **BETTER** approach at solving my problem. Others are not expected to change, only expected to keep doing as they did before. After all, I can much easier change myself, than I can change others. Possibly my problem isn't as bad as I thought. I can surely receive some satisfaction, if I adjust a few personal things here and there."

...{In this approach, when I have done all that I could do and my difficulty still remains, I'll most likely get frustrated. Furthermore, my charge probably won't be better off for my efforts other than their self esteem will not be injured.}

The **BEST** approach I could take in solving my problem, involving others, is to create a win-win situation. I engage with them, and we together refine what we are both doing, so that the best possible turnout occurs.

- I start with making sure that they know that I appreciate their efforts; I want them to be willing to continue giving me their support.
- I must become much more involved with them, so they view change as something we are doing together; instead of just me coming down on their case.
- I listen to their ideas and reasoning, while being open to learn or gain.

Yes, before I point out to them any differing knowledge that I have gained, or subject them to being exposed to my new superior insights, {*which, of course, I think are right and they will be extremely foolish not to give heed to and likewise utilize*} I must demonstrate I'm willing to hear them. I use the "Art of Listening". Whereas I reflect on their proposed ideas involving me, they're more prone to consider working with me.

- Together we'll create an advanced unison of ideas and practices, which is stronger and comes closer to meeting both our needs than what may be done singularly or in opposition.

In this approach if properly done, neither will get too frustrated and both receive an increase of Joy.

The Art of Listening:

One of the surest ways to get a troubled soul to feel of his importance is for you to show interest in what he's going through; you engage in just listening. As another person has a concern or a dilemma, stop what you where doing; and what you were going to say, and allow them to share their issues with you. It takes courage to confide in another, so don't blow off their attempt by you not appearing interested or by trying to inject your own ideas and values to them just as they were trying to get you to understand theirs. As time is spent allowing them the freedom to share their concerns with you, an improved answer of what they need to do in order to solve their problem frequently comes to mind. You validate their problem and slightly lead them to seeing things in that different light. In listening, you do not tell them an answer —that would be teaching. You show interest and concern, and patience. As they get closer to your proposed yet still un-revealed solution, you give additional guidance to assist them toward that direction; lead them to except it as their own. By your art of listening, you give them the confidence to continue. They come up with a solution without you every having to spell out the answer. You establish communicational rapport where they are free to feel of your understanding and support, and they get closer to a more defined answer toward solving their problem. {see: **depth of listening**: *page 296*}

In the following story, attempts of a trainer to affect a child are in question; only the names have been changed.

Common Sense Lesson: **When Do I Give Up**

A while back, as I was walking down the hall in church, I saw a family of six together just standing there killing time with their backs to the wall. Having met the Kerchiefs previously, they recognized me as I politely made eye contact and said, "Hi."

I couldn't bridle my curiosity so I asked, "How is it going," the standard invitation for: *"Tell me more if you would like?"*

"Oh," says Mom, "Nick's be'n impossible; he won't mind or sit still in the chapel." Pointing to a now closed door she continued, "We felt like if he wouldn't behave in there, we had-ta take him out in the hall where he can't bother anyone with his act'n out. He's gitting worse. We can't control him a-tall; we don't know what'ta do."

I gazed down at this five-year-old; he didn't look like a kid who had just gotten into trouble for causing such a ruckus that his entire family had to seek seclusion. He was grinning from ear to ear. He was enjoying himself. On him there was no remorse or hint of anything wrong.

He had previously been labeled as an "out-of-control kid" by most everyone who knew him. His activities most often included continually running around defiantly with no regard or sense of discipline. I have witnessed, before, his parents struggling to keep him under control. *{Surprisingly today standing in the hall with everyone staring at him, he was not acting out.}* Normally his conduct seemed to be going from one display of purposeful unruliness to another.

Earlier, he on different occasions had been caught by the neighbors for taking bikes and toys from their yards, as result, he's now in trouble with the police, who more than once have said, "He is not to be allowed outside alone ... even to walk to school. He must be accompanied always by a parent!" Nick doesn't mind his

380 JUST WHO AM I TRAINING ANYWAY

parents, and has no sense of duty regarding the use of good behavior.

Within the same family, in direct contrast to Nick, is an older brother Hank. He is the perfect model of behavior. He is polite; he communicates well; he is meek and submissive. In this, he is so very much like his mother. He is the exact opposite of Nick.

I have been to the Kerchief Family's home on several occasions and observed Nick in action. When he is in the spotlight and positive attention is given to him singularly, he will engage and seems to stop his resistant behavior. However, when he has lost his individuality, and becomes just a part of a group of children, he will soon be totally beyond control by doing things to draw attention to himself. {*See the pattern? He is asking for individual attention, and will do whatever it takes to get it.*} He probably, in his young mind, doesn't even know why or what he does.}

So, as I see these folks standing alone in desperation, my mind asks itself, *"Just who is in control in this family anyway?"*

"Can ya help us?" the mother asks, as she interrupts my reflections. Then, as if an after-thought she adds, **"Ta make Nick behave?"** ...

Again I reflected, *"If it isn't possible for you to control your kid in the privacy of your own home; what makes you think it would have been any easier out in public? Expecting a five-year-old to behave simply because he is in church, bares no weight on a young mind. 'HOW CAN YOU BE SO BLIND?'* " I wanted to blurt-out, *"It couldn't be any clearer. Yes, you have a problem. Your son will not be-have, but the problem is not his alone. Together you and he must go back to the Basics!'*

My plan of action in review :*** { **What this boy needs is for his parents to become better at parenting. Without this, he has no chance of changing at his young age. His behavior is an attempt at maintaining a personal control in life, no matter how distorted it may look to anyone else. Nick is shouting for wanted attention. And he is receiving it by his incorrigibleness. Presently, the only personal** attention he receives that separates him as an individual from his brothers and sister is obtained as he acts out defiantly. His parents are stuck in the rut of ignoring him, when he is good. They give him attention when he is bad, really bad; otherwise, he is regarded as just one of the kids.

Perhaps they could be taught that their giving to him attention, in some other form besides a punishment, will lead him toward wanting more of those good feelings of gratification. In this, he would start to look for ways of getting more positive interaction from others without his having to go through the efforts and consequences of his improper behavior. He would be retaining more of a sense of fulfillment. If I could help his parents see the strength of proper parenting, this would be a start. They'd then ever-so-greatly be increasing their effectiveness as trainers on this young boy.

A pre-starting place would include more engaged effort by Dad. He could further develop his relationship by following a plan to give more one-on-one interest to Nick, without the other three siblings present—especially his perfect older brother. This would be difficult and take planning on both parents' parts, given their small house and opposite work schedules {Almost always is the second parent out working. The only exception is on Tuesdays and Sundays, when Jeff has a day off.} Yet it could be done.

This plan would require advanced coordination and sacrifice. It would not be the easy cure-all, "*Someone else fix my problem for me solution,*" that they are looking for. It would include Jeff learning better parenting skills, and then with his son going back to the "Basics" where both could be schooled properly to learn the meanings of "Yes", "No", "Stop", "Don't do that", and "Now you are in trouble because you didn't mind, young man." This would be establishing a positive forward movement, the starting point from which all other training would be useless without. To be more effective, both parents will have to learn how to carry out a promise of discipline and follow through. Then, they would have a chance of young Nick learning respect and proper behavior. All these fundamentals are better when taught in a controlled environment such as the home, without other forms of distractions. But, in their case with always the constant barrage of other stimulations going on, learning this lesson out in the secluded quiet of my horse pen would have to do. Dad needed to understand such a plan, and then have the desire to implement it.

These things I considered when I first was approached two months before to offer assistance to this family. We met on numerous occasions for observation of family dynamics and to make plans to start a formal training relationship. In their home there existed such chaos, with the kids clamoring for attention and the parents each stuck in their ineffective parenting roles, that it was most difficult to create an environment of teaching —where there was freedom to learn. I felt it would be best if we separated Nick from his triggers, and could start teaching in an environment where he would be willing to be taught.

Both parents had before accepted my invitation for starting an equine assisted therapeutic experience, where Nick might be taught in an effective way to behave differently. Together we made arrangements on three separate occasions to start. I knew that, if they could witness the proper role of a horse trainer in action, it would awaken their discover process of them implementing those basic practices within their family... especially with Nick. I felt I could then take Jeff aside and appeal to his sense of duty as a father and get him to where he understood his proper role also. I knew that little Nick would respond to listening, if he was receiving one-on-one attention in something which kept his interest. They agreed, three times before, to rearrange their schedules and attend these horse assisted therapy sessions. They didn't show up.

During the planning of our sessions, I envisioned Nick's parents seeing carefully constructed tasks with the horses which would exhibit the same type of dynamics as existed in their family. As they witnessed what was happening, I would be able to bring up the following points:

1. What the Problem Is: Nick acts undisciplined.

His behavior can be addressed simple enough. The specifics can be lumped together; they will be dealt with individually during the refinement process. Let's just say, for now, all his different infractions are a problem of Nick's. {*Wait, that isn't fair to say, remember, that Nick is displaying his behavior in order to get what he wants, so he isn't aware he's got a problem.*} Nick's behavior is a problem to others. It makes them uncomfortable and so they want to change him, to force him to stop what he is doing. But, this just gives him something to fight against. His open rebellion is the reason that his parents are seeking help from others, and at this time, from me. The problem of Nick is only, at present, of a true concern for his parents, his neighbors, and the police. I knew I could help with Nick's problem, by allowing Jeff to discover: a horse responds differently after its trainer presents the right signals. The horse doesn't really become teachable until its trainer can offer some consistency in what he expects. Such was the case with Nick also.

2. The Cause: He is a difficult to control five-year-old kid.

But, at that young age, can't he be easily taught new skills and ways? Both his parents, and now his neighbors, as he ventures outside of his previously small environment, have been so far dealing with just the symptoms of Nick's problem; they have been seeking cures for the parts they can't stand. They haven't as yet dealt with the true causes. Little Nick hasn't had that much exposure to outside influence which could have formed him into what he is now. He had to have learned his behavior from the result of something he has been exposed to in the home. This is the true problem and the cause of Nick's behavior:

Nick watches his dad. He sees how this adult gets what he wants. He sees the influence that Dad has over Mom, and Nick likewise wants that. He has learned from watching dear old dad's control, that Mom will allow anything if a pressure is put against her. He sees his perfect brother's manners getting nothing but praise from his mom. He receives no such praises for his, from either mom or dad, only plenty of excuses that are being offered in his behalf. He is not being dealt with on the same level. He is not being held to any level of accountability, only being overlooked at a high level of permissibility by an unengaged father, and a non-confrontational mother. He sees his perfect brother and his mother as getting controlled by dad. Nick wants more; he wants the power he sees from his perceptions of reality, in regards to his father. He attempts to follow his dad's example and wants to also be in control also.

"Is Nick's behavior of concern?
Yes, but it is minimal in comparison to its cause:
His dad!"

As a parent, Jeff has a problem. He has a past history of being irresponsible. For years he has kept his family just one step ahead of the creditors and the rent collectors. His has difficulty holding a job; others are always at fault when he losses it. Somehow he always manages to shift the blame from himself when he doesn't show up. Instead of him admitting his need to improve, he will blame anything else for his being a slacker at home and in the work place. He has an inability to force himself to deal with uncomfortable situations without getting angry. His disrespect of his wife has been a non-shinning example for his second son to follow. By example, he teaches his son that it is appropriate to insult mom with the lowest and most foul language possible, whenever she gets on your nerves. As result Nick also uses filthy and abusive language to get a reaction from others. However, in his youth, he still hasn't learned the true meaning of his words. *{Nick hasn't totally learned when to turn it off, and when it's beneficial to act sweet, at times, like his dad.}* In order to teach his son to change, Jeff needs to change himself.

Mom has a problem, although not with her nurturing wants and desires; that she does extremely well. In fact she has taken up for the shortcomings of her husband. In spite of having four young kids at home, she has taken on a fulltime job in the attempt to provide for her family; she fills the void for Jeff. Her problem is her lack of self-esteem, and because of it she does everything for her family to the point where she lets her husband, and now her son run her down. She is to the point where she expects it. She accepts her plight in life, by controlling it with acting so sweet and nice in her interactions with others. Her perception is that they are all victims and if she just tries harder she can make it up to them. She has adopted the trait, of being a "True-Blue Butt-Kisser" when it comes to anyone who tries to inflict their will against her.

3. How to Fix It:

Individually these three have problems. I felt the most effective and vital step to addressing them was to get the father off to the side and to help him to discover: *What his proper role of a Father and Husband is.* {*see: page: 22*} And to help him see*: His lacking is causing problems in his family, and in his life.* Once this is established, where Dad accepts his own refinement as a new goal in order to help his family, where he sees his potential as a father, and has a desire to improve it, then the other family's shortcomings will be easier to deal with. In fact Jeff will mostly cause their cure when he properly changes his teaching approach.

As far as dealing with Mom: I would try to get her some free-time around women who understood their proper roles as wives and mothers. I'd enlist them to help in ways that I might not have the best skills. But I am jumping the gun. First as I see it, I need to train the father, so that he'll be supportive in the future reinforcement of his wife's self-esteem and coping techniques, beyond her being a passive victim of circumstances.

My purpose in getting Jeff and Nick together for some horse therapy was to create an environment where Jeff may understand his proper role, and to allow him to experience and feel some success in positive dealing with his problem child. He would see a healthier relationship develop quickly as he does the right things and for the right reasons. With a recognized success, Jeff would be fueled towards wanting to continue in personal reformation. He would start to see his gains and increases; this would hopefully cause him to except additional responsibility and to allow me, to help him even more.

Nick's changes would come, a portion, from the results of seeing his own errors. Even as a five-year-old he has some capability to understand new ideas when they are pointed out or shown to him. The majority of his change would be as result of his being exposed to engaged parents acting as teachers and trainers using knowledge with consistency and skill. His could grow from being taken through the Basics, where he would become aware that he gets more out of life when he cooperates, than if he is defiant. After Nick has achieved proper forward movement, his trainers would then be able to expose him to proper character traits as refinements, helping him become the best he can be. Nick's changes would be a product of the good parenting skills and his learning better coping skills to retain his freedoms and control.

...This, I was in hopes to help his parents understand.

4. Wish For and See Great End Results.
...As If They Had Already Happened:

I have seen many people and animals benefit from trainers whom became more successful, as they refined their own skills first. I had experienced my Uncle and witnessed how he masterfully dealt and trained others to reach their highest potentials. I have, as I matured and gained knowledge, seen the effectiveness of both the masculine and feminine teaching roles. I have personally grown my abilities, and now I wanted to share them with the Kerchief Family. I knew they could benefit from my experiences; I wanted to help them achieve the peace and Joy that I have.

That's why I wanted to help the Kerchiefs—I could see this family finding more JOY.

a. With the proper exposure, I could see his parents understanding why Nick is really acting undisciplined.

b. I believed, I could help them explore new options, other than just using harder punishments or more restraints on Nick.

c. I envisioned the greater possibilities when Jeff could recognize his potential for improvement. I fully believed that he and his whole family could benefit.

d. I felt I could orchestrate a healthier relationship between Jeff and Nick as we together sought to develop more meaningful one-on-one/father-son time. } ***

5. Implement a Solution: *"I decided to start again to answer their plea. I needed to set in motion the previously unfilled steps in order to help this family. This was vital—without these no other effective lessons could follow."*

■■■ So I answered mom back as she and her family stood in that hallway, **"Yes I can help."** And for the fourth time, I tried an attempt to make arrangements for a session at my place, to start working on a plan of action with my behavioral mirroring horses.

"Come over, Tuesday starting at 4:00p.m. for some equine assisted therapy." I was clear this time and specifically stated, "I need, Jeff and Nick." I was most interested in getting the father first, without his son present, so I could help him recognize what he will have to do to become better at parenting. Afterwards I wanted Nick and his dad, so the boy could get some much needed one-on-one nonjudgmental attention from his father. I was willing to try once more.

"That will be great," says Mom, "I'll be there."

"No, it will work best if it is first Jeff, and then he and Nick," I responded back quickly, knowing the key to this whole solution was to engage the father.

"Fine then, I'll come," he said, just a tad-bit put out.

"I think he said this just to defuse the situation," my thoughts injected silently to my mind.

Tuesday came, and again I waited for the fourth time. Nothing happened once more. I planned, prepared, and set time aside in order that I could assist this family; Jeff didn't show up or call, nor was he even home. I checked. He made no attempt to reschedule; he was still under the impression there was no need for **him** to do things different.

"You can lead a horse to water, but you can't make him drink."

There was nothing else I could do. Dad will have to put forth some effort. He is noticeably operating using the personal motivation of the *"I-Can't-Be-Bothered"* mentality. He was hoping things would cure themselves. His approach was that of the Self Entitled and Indifferent Traveler. Mom was good at using the Nurturing Parent Approach, but she was stuck in her unique slant to the Good Mother side of things. Oh, she was trying to do the right thing, but going overboard at the same time. She was stuck being overly protective; she was dismissing others shortcomings as she was trapped in her *"You're-a-Victim-and-I-Am-So-Sorry"* mentality. Once again, with this family, I was not given the right opportunity to help.

Dad didn't get it. In order to effect change on his son, he has to be trying harder than his sought after child behavioral problem-solving teacher. The teacher couldn't do this one without his engagement. Dad must be willing to put forth effort to change himself and then offer a change to his son.

In order for me to be effective in helping Nick adopt other forms of behavior; I need Jeff to embrace becoming more engaged at becoming a better father. He needs to recognize his lack of parenting skills and want to learn to improve. If I could affect Jeff, then Nick would be an ease. Little Nick is still hunting for ways to help himself, but unfortunately with his distortion of how personnel power is obtained, he just can't recognize socially excepted methods. Jeff needs to assist with Nick.

Presently Dad doesn't have enough desire to put himself out in order to help his son. So, until Dad sees the light and becomes more pro-active, my hands would remain tied. I couldn't do anything more. Except wait until he gets more thirsty.

"Do I give up and quit?   No ... but I had been "Bucked Off." I had hit the dirt. And after this many times, I was looking at nothing but more of the same, if I tried once more. Now, I must do the only thing that would possibly help, I increase my own efforts and show an Unconditional Love.

Now, you can see why I wrote this book. I pray that Jeff reads it when I give it to him. I hope that he may have the desire to improve, that he may gain from the power of knowledge and grow to understand effective implementation. I have faith he will willingly allow his training of himself, and then correctly train his charges. Additionally, I hope all others who spend the time within these pages will recognize ways that they may improve their methods of teaching others. It is my hope that all may see clearly their own responsibilities as teachers, which includes training themselves to become the most effective they can be.

Side note Let us analyze further that last true story to help us practice using common sense principles; that we too may learn.

Question: Is Nick's unruly behavior a problem that he wants to change, or is it just a problem and an uncomfortable situation for his parents and neighbors?

Answer: If Nick could receive some equally appealing gratifications for a different conduct, then he'd change his behavior. He's a five-year old kid; he's going do the easiest thing to get the feedback he wants. His dad has to evaluate for himself the reasons that he wants this problem solved, because his son sure doesn't have a need or desire to change at this point. Nick is getting what he wants ... attention. His defiant conduct has been so far productive. Yes, he does at times experience minimal punishments, but those have been a small price to pay for the much sought-after special treatment that they conjure. His disobedience eventually demands that his parents to give him one-on-one time. And since he is often hollowly threatened, but rarely punished, all he has to do is keep moving and out of grasp of his folks, then he gets away with anything he desires. With a system like that, why mess it up with compliance and risk becoming like Hank?

Question: What controlling methods would be best for Nick?

Answer: None at first, the thing he needs more that anything is to have a break. He needs to be able to recognized unconditional love first. Jeff and he should spend enough time together that he will desire additional praise from his father; right now he probably can't even recognize any positive benefits from being with dad.

Question: What teaching approach would work best for Nick?

Answer: All teaching approaches, when used by an engaged teacher will work to some degree; however, an engaged teacher wanting for Nick to become his best would be the preferred. Until Jeff can see more clearly his motives for wanting to solve the original problem, then the best approach will not be used. Jeff must want to help Nick become a better person, because of his love for his son, not just merely force that kid to mind to eliminate a bother.

Remember, that Nick is acting this way encouraged by his pursuit of Joy. From reasons that are valid in his mind; they are his perception of reality. The engaged teacher is obligated to show him that any acts of defiance will from this day forward cause him suffering and discomfort, and any acts of compliance will result in new freedom along with new recognized control. He must be held to a standard of making wise choices to cooperate with others. A successful teacher must create an inquisitive learning environment to show a different reality; he must teach new skills to help a child get what it desires.

* * * * * * * * *

You have just read an entire book on some of my experiences. I know that now your eyes are opened a bit more clearly. You are empowered with basics that can be expounded on. I am sure, as you have read this book, you have thought many times, *"I can do that."*

"Yes, you can!" As you need help in following the ideas of this book, re-read the different chapters and stories. See the correlation between how to train a horse and a real live person; they're very much the same.

Perhaps you have started implementing changes already. It is mind boggling how things so basic could be so effective.

Why it is as though they had come to have from a divine master-trainer, teacher, and guide. … They have!

Look back at what you now realize and understand; you are gaining the power to be in control as a teacher; you are increasing in skills and gaining in knowledge. In the next chapter you will learn from the Supreme Good Parenting Examples; you will learn from the best. The parenting and teaching skills discussed in this book are divine. They come from examining and then copying the very methods used by God.

When you are ready, please read on.

PART 5
THE ULTIMATE TEACHERS

EPILOG

CHAPTER 19:

RECEIVING GUIDENCE FROM THE

ULTIMATE TEACHERS

In respect to the many similarities between a learning horse and an inquisitive human, one difference stands out as being the foremost defining factor which allows advanced discovery by a student. This is the ability to question, plan and ponder events. Both the horse and the child have the ability to make choices based on a conditioning that has occurred in the past. Both can choose to do the thing which will lead to the most gain. Yet the human can also think ahead beyond its present desire to react to eliminate its pain. The human child has the ability to rationalize as it weighs the factors of possible outcomes. The child can look back on past events and go over in its mind the wisdom of its own actions. It can problem solve, then can pre-plan its decisions based on a desired out-come. The child has the ability to ponder the unseen; it can seek a discovery of what is beyond the present moment in time.

This ability to seek answers can lead the child to ponder its choices and its very existence. First come the primary wants to fulfill basic survival needs of a person, and then can come the desire for answers which will satisfy deeper questions. Guidance to finding such answers has forever been the deepest role of many teachers. Such teachers strive to provide answer to deeper questions of wonderment.

A pondering mind will ask: Are we here on this earth purely by chance to live out our lives in some sort of unorganized progression? —As some would have us believe? ...Did we come to be only as a product of nature's selective evolution of the right genetics? ...Do we only exist by chance on this un-governed sphere of solids and gases which somehow evolved into a receptive host, and now miraculously contains everything we need for our continuation? Have you asked yourself, "What is beyond that which I can see?"

We started out as infants having no skills, no memory of our past, and no goals of our future. Our only desires were to be free from pains. We continued developing as babes gaining experiences and increasing in our wants. As toddlers and then as young children we learned new skills, step-by-step, working toward mastering them as we pursued what we thought would bring us happiness and personal gratifications. As we sought to have control in our lives, we experimented with different ways and ideas. Emotions gave us fuel to continue to seek personal gratifications. We developed new responsibilities as we matured; these came with new definitions of what we wanted.

At present, we will continue spending our lives figuring out how to succeed to further obtain what we feel will give us additional joy and happiness. And for what end or purpose—that we may just get old and die? ...Is there anything beyond our eighty-plus-or-minus years that we have on this earth? We can't just be here today and then gone tomorrow. There must be something else.

The Answer is: "Yes! ... There is nothing that just appeared, and nothing that just vanishes." All matter has a continuance. It all came from somewhere and continues to exist even when its present form is changed. The very intricacies of all creation demand that all life is under the orchestration of an all knowing Being who combined the laws of nature in a divine pre-determined purpose.

Even the tiniest seed from the peskiest weed that has ever grown, had to have come from somewhere; it didn't just appear. As this seed first sprouts, then grows, and finally matures into a plant it only continues in an environment that induces survival. And it will pass on to its posterity a chance to grow and prosper also. In life it reaches down and takes in nutrients from deep within the earth, then places these where they are later available for its offspring, to help fertilize and give them a chance for a better life. It produces offspring to take advantage from where it has evolved. Likewise in our existence we have the same opportunity because of a loving God. We didn't just appear—we were also created.

God, the Supreme Being, is the Father of our spirits, and under his direction did creation happen and does it continue. He is the orchestrator of these chance happenings, which were controlled and governed, so that we might be given the opportunity to be born and to obtain experience. He has caused that this earth be organized as a safe environment where we, his children, can grow and develop. It is his purpose that we started out our lives on this planet without memory of our past existence in order that we learn to live by faith.

Faith is a confidence, a belief in something which remains un-provable. Faith is an assurance of things hoped for, the evidence of things not seen. {see: Hebrews: 11:1} Faith is more than a passive belief or a learned knowledge; it is a driver of actions. Faith is the power to excel. Only by using faith do we set goals for improvement and then work toward their fulfillment. It is faith that gives us strength to continue when logic demands that we quit. We, his children, have been given a chance by him, our Father, to come to this earth to learn to live by faith, for the purpose that we are able to progress and reach our highest potentials.

In order to really learn and progress it must be by our choice. We must have our **free agency** to decide what direction our earthly existence will lead. God is the Ultimate Loving Father who possesses all knowledge and supremacy. He has provided this earth as part of his plan, that we may show willingness by our faith to prove ourselves responsible with our proper decisions and actions. God loved us enough that he provided this learning opportunity for us to experience adversity, so that we may grow and develop our worth as individuals. As we take on and develop more of the values and character traits of God, we also experience an increase of our Joy. God will reward us for our actions. Part of the uppermost reward he has for us is to return and dwell with him in the next life; it is based on our choosing correct choices.

Our Heavenly Father is perfect and lives in a perfected state. He has a resurrected body of flesh and bones. As the literal father of our spirits and it is his desire that we, his spirit children, experience for ourselves a fullness of Joy and return to dwell again with him for eternity. For this purpose we have been given the opportunity to come to this earth to receive a body, to be tried and tested, and then judged to see if we are found worthy to return and live with him; ourselves also, approaching a perfected state.

God the Father is the ideal trainer who rewards us for our slightest tries and gives us consequences for our wrong choices. He wants us working with him toward the common goal of us obtaining our highest potential joy by living again with him. Therefore, he has given us laws and commandments to live by, that we may become refined. Since he is perfect, he must adhere to eternal laws; one of which is the Law of Justice. Justice demands that when a sin is committed, a punishment be given. Our Heavenly Father must adhere to this law. In it, he is bound to punish us for our sins. Sins are our failures to comply.

God the Father, is perfected and sinless, and can't dwell with or abide sin. He demands that, in order, to come and dwell back in his presence, we also must become sinless and perfected. When we sin, we become less than perfect; we experience a spiritual death, a separation which causes us to be denied being in the presence of God. In sin, we forfeit our chance to dwell again with our perfect Father.

Reality is that we have all sinned and would never again be able to return to the presence of our Father in Heaven, unless there is a redemption made. Our Ultimate Loving Father must punish when there is sin. He is also merciful, and provided a savior to teach us how to strive for perfection, and additionally to restore us from our spiritual death. This savior offered himself in our behalf to make restitution for our sins, which we could never fully pay for ourselves because of our imperfections. With the intervention of a savior, we could be eligible for forgiveness, and then be given the chance to return and live, once more, in God's presence.

In discussing his plan for all his children, during our pre-earth life, God asked his gathered multitude, "Who shall I send?" Of the two volunteers that replied, the second wanted to force us to comply with all of our Father's commandments, in order, that everyone would be eligible to live again in God's presence. To do this, he would have to take away our freedom of choice, our free agency, which was granted to us by virtue of our creation. It must have sounded like a good idea, reasonable enough that many of our spiritual siblings embraced it. These joined a fight on the side of this would-be savior, Lucifer, and fought against the angels of God; they fought against the very plan of God in order that they force others to except Lucifer's idea also. These rebellious and defiant were cast out from heaven and will never be eligible to return into God's presence. {see; Abraham: 3: 25-28, Revelations: 12: 7-9}

Lucifer, also called Satan or the Devil, was a good teacher, so good in fact, he led one third of all God's spirit children to rebel against their Father. They, in turn, lost their chance to fully experience earth life; they will no longer be able to receive a fullness of Joy, and will never again be able to dwell in the presence of God. Satan had convinced those who followed him: none would be lost in sin. They were willing to trade their freedom of choice on this earth for what they thought was a guaranteed free ride, an easy assurance of returning back again with their Heavenly Father. They feared their own ability to choose for themselves, and therefore were unwilling to risk a wrong choice or action. {*If Satan's plan would have been implemented, then we would have been not much different than a chained dog or a corralled horse that is forced to doing its master's will, never really being given the freedom of choice.*} They were deceived; they thought that all they had to do to get back into Gods presents was to not sin. They didn't realize their role in order to live again in God's presence was: **They must reach a state of perfection.** All have to be proven in the face of having choices, to obey or not to obey; to follow good instead of evil. Satan convinced them wrongly in the false assurance they could return and live with God. As this could have never happened without the proving of themselves first, they were deceived into following a false idea.

As result of their previous poor choice, Satan and his followers have lost their chance to receive earthy bodies; they will never be allowed to return and reside with their Father in Heaven. And presently, it is their purpose to tempt us so we'll not be found worthy, also; thereby, losing our chance to return and live with God. They know that if we sin and don't repent, we will, like them, experience unquenchable sufferings and torments for past conduct. Additionally, we become ineligible for our highest reward, and they will not be alone in their sufferings of what they have given up.

"Misery loves company." [Author unknown}

Satan voluntarily agreed to go down and assist all to return again to God, but his motives were wrong. His motives for teaching are the prime example of the Self Entitled Approach; he was acting in the disguise of a Nurturing Parent. Satan wasn't concerned with our well beings as much as he was in getting gain from us, as his charges. He wanted for himself the very glory and honor of God. He said, "Here am I send me… and I will redeem all mankind that one soul shall not be lost, and surely I will do it; wherefore give me thine honor." {see; Moses: 4:1}

God allows Satan to tempt us in this life, so that we may learn the difference between good and evil. Satan entices us to sin, to break the commandments of God; he guides us into believing that we are gaining control over our own lives by gratifying our own desires. The fact is: When we gratify our own desires, to the extent that we break the commandments of God, we are losing control, because we are losing the ability to return again with Him. We also become subjected to the cravings of our desires, so-much-so, it often causes us to feel we must perform unwise choices; we feel inclined to participate in unhealthy practices in order to maintain our addictions. Even though it sometimes takes great personal control and a command of high mortal character, it is still our choice to not concede to the evil tempting of Satan by succumbing to the cravings of our earthly bodies and following after the unrighteous desires and passions of our hearts.

When we refuse to succumb to the tempting of Satan, we start to show our willingness to follow the commandments of God. Now is when we can start to receive rewards from God for our actions. Without our adherence to His commandments, any benefits we receive from our contrary behaviors are solely the earthly results of the natural consequences we have earned; they're earthly delights with very little lasting pleasure. We have to choose to submit to follow Christ's teachings, and not to our own selfish desires in order to be eligible for our greatest rewards.

When we have this change of heart and enter into the Common Goal Box with God, we join our desires in a unified purpose to do his will. We forsake ungodly paths. We have the new desire to honor his commandments and do as he bids. It is here that we manifest our greatest worth in sight of our Lord.

In contrast to Satan's self-seeking desires, was another who also agreed to volunteer; in fact he was the first who did. He said, "Here am I sent me." He offered to do the will of the Father, seeking to do the right things—not for his personal gain. {see; Moses 4: 2 and Abraham: 3: 27} God chose to send the first, Jesus Christ as his immortal son, to come into this earthly world and to guide us in the paths we should follow in order to be eligible to once more return again unto Him.

Jesus Christ became our savior. As result of his giving up of his immortal life, he was able to redeem us from the grasp of our physical death. He then offers this gift, a re-uniting of body and spirit after death, to all of God's children. With his gift of resurrection, we can also have an immoral and perfected body like unto God's.

Christ lived a perfect life while here in the flesh, in this, only he could suffer for our sins to appease the Law of Justice. By his atonement, we can be released of being subjected to eternal consequences for our transgressions. He has the power to make us whole, once again, before God. By his suffering he atoned for our sins before the Father—if we would but repent and follow his teachings.

Those gifts Jesus Christ gave us. He didn't want personal reward; he did this out of his love for us and his desire to follow the will of his Father. He also did volunteer, but, he did all in charity, not in search of any personal gain.

A rich owner of an exceptionally fine horse, whose blood lines and conformation have given it the potential to be a note worthy champion, desires such. This lord wants so much for his charge to reach its highest potential that he spares no expense in its training. Our Heavenly Father also spares neither expense nor training to get the most out of His children. God has seen that His children are given the best opportunities to improve and excel. He wants for us to become like the bomb proof horse that has proven itself, having been subjected to all manner of choices, and still it remains trustworthy and submissive. He sent His son as a guide and example for us to follow that we may become such champions. God has also inspired other great men to instruct us in the ways of becoming the best we can become.

*   *   *

Common Horse Sense: The Right Choices

The horse which makes the right choices and executes all the desires of his trainer, while keeping its freedom of spirit, is the one of greatest worth. It doesn't force its trainer to have to move very far up the Escalation of Involvement incline to punish or limit its behavior. Witnessing such a horse that seemingly moves freely with its rider is like watching perfection.

Having seen Dennis Reese ride a well trained horse without bit or rein is a breath taking experience. You can't think of how this animal could be better. Dennis solicits cooperation without the horse needing to be forced to comply; he does this with just a series of asking and then reinforcing when his horse is doing the right thing. Both the horse and trainer have a common goal. Because the horse chooses to make all the right choices in following the will of his lord, it could be said: as to its worth, **"There is a perfected champion."**

* * *

Jesus Christ became our guide pointing out the best paths, and continues instructing us as to our best choices. He does ask for us to acknowledge what he has done for us, not that he gain in glory for himself, but that we glorify God, who sent him to assist us. Christ's purpose is to implement God's plan. Under the direction of God, he formed and created this world, in which we live. He didn't want to force us to return to live with God the Father. He wanted us to be able to choose this for ourselves; he allowed us to keep our free agency. Christ understood the nature of man. He knew that man would often choose to rebel against and not to comply with the teachings and practices of an unseen God. Christ understood that without guidance, mankind would lack the personal discipline to put off the immediate gratifications which untrained natural passions yearn for.

He has always offered an unconditional love towards every being, for those who are defiant; as-well-as those who willingly choose to follow all his teachings. He hopes that all may perpetuate their desires for contact by seeking out him, through prayer and faith. He always stands ready to up-lift us, to comfort us, and to love us no matter how resistive we become. He has made it clear it's us he loves, and not our defiant ways of sin exhibited in our choices to go against his commandments. Eternally it is his hope that we choose the correct paths and make right choices; he taught us so we might join with him and develop character traits of great worth.

It is for this purpose that we were created: that we can grow and sink our roots ever deeper into fertile ground. As we obtain wisdom and traits of value, we can offer to our offspring assistance. We have been given the opportunity to develop into something greater than we currently are. We, because of a Loving Father, will be exposed to adversity in order to refine ourselves as we learn to overcome setbacks. We will experience the joys of pleasure and the sufferings of pain, as we try to learn lessons, as we make wrong choices, and as we experience all the good which life has in store. Throughout all, we in the hands of our Ultimate Teachers can even become perfected champions.

Christ because of his love for us became the supreme example of the Nurturing Parent. He agreed to come to this earth and to spend his life for us. When we call on his name, he protects us from being overwhelmed by Satan and his misdirected followers. He sends his spirit to nurture us when we need his help. He paid the price of our sins to appease the Law of Justice. He, by spending his whole life in service to others, teaches us the meaning of charity.

Jesus said unto the rich young ruler in answer for his question of, 'What shall I do to inherit eternal life?' "Thou knowest the commandments … yet lackest thou one thing; sell all that thou hast, and distribute unto the poor; and thou shalt have treasures in heaven: and come follow me. {see: St. Luke: 18: 18-22}

He becomes our light when we are in the cave of darkness and have nowhere to turn. "… I am the light of the world: he that followeth me shall not walk in darkness, but shall have the light of life." {see: St. John: 8:12} Like a child striving to learn from a teacher, we must likewise put forth effort to learn from him. The light of Christ will be with us to the extent we let him into our lives.

Christ will intervene with justice in order that we can stand without the consequences of sin before our Father in Heaven. He will arbitrate in our behalf, just as an earthly mother invokes her husband to show mercy toward his child. He atoned for our sins and paid for our infractions before the Father. We can utilize his atonement in our own lives, by being of service to our fellow beings, then accepting Christ as our savior and repenting of our sins. {This is our slightest try.} Because of the Atonement of Christ, and our efforts to obey his teachings, we may stand sinless before God to see if we can be found worthy in our good works and refinement as eligible to dwell again with God.

In the Lord's Prayer we are able to see the different roles of God, his Son, and the great tempter, Satan. We see the well meaning Provider, the Merciful and Nurturing, as well as the entitled and self-serving. Here it is as being worded by Christ:

"Pray ye...Our Father which art in heaven, hallowed be thy name. Thy kingdom come thy will be done in earth as it is in heaven. Give us this day our daily bread. And forgive us our debts, as we forgive our debtors. And lead us not into temptation, but deliver us from evil: For thine is the kingdom and the power, and the glory, for ever. Amen. {St. Mathew 6: 9-13}

In this prayer is a model of the plan of life; it also displays all four teachings approaches:

1. God and his Son, Jesus Christ, together want us to receive the best possible they have to offer. So they teach us the way of the returning again to their presence, all the while expecting us to make choices of good verses evil. As we refine to know God's will, they encourage us to transform our good intentions into our best performances. They offer us the reward of living eternally in Joy. It can only be gained when we follow and summit to their will—proving our worth.

2. In Christ's love we find the power to resist evil temptations; we also can have the reassurance that he will intervene for us by his atonement. We have no need to feel depressed and alone, for Christ will see that we are properly led if we utilize faith, he will always be there to comfort and assist us.

3. Satan in his evil role as the world's foremost entitled being, deceives us to believe we should be able *to gain from another's pain*. It is in his interest that we are not eligible to partake in the blessings that are in store for us when we cooperate with the Father.

4. We need no teacher's example of the Indifferent Traveler, for it is displayed by us so wanting to not engage and forgo our personal desires that we deny our compassion and service to others. Behavior of this fashion is certainly not of god. In Christ's prayer we learn that we will receive the same pardons and leniencies from God, which we willing give to others.

As well as showing us these teaching roles, Christ also made it clear our role was to receive assistance. We are to be lead into becoming grateful and submissive recipients.

God desires for us to succeed as **parents** and as **teachers**. He wants us to develop teaching skills that uplift and help our charges to become more able to return, again, to live with him. He has not left us alone in this task and has provided, for our help, many good books and teachings; he has provided books of scripture and prophets that direct us. Each time you undertake to correct another, or to discuss an idea, or even decide to withhold information, take a moment, and be aware of what your motives for doing so are. Think, "Who is most likely to benefit from your actions?" As you examine your motives for teaching, with God's help choose one that benefits others, that their and your Joy may be full.

God also has instilled in each one of us the light of Christ, which will help us throughout our lives to follow him. This spirit will help us to make proper decisions when it comes to the following of good verses evil. To recognize these prompting we must be earnestly striving ourselves to become the best we may be in following after the teachings of our Savior, Jesus Christ. If our intentions are pure and for the right reasons of wanting the best for our children, to the extent that we are engaged in providing an opportunity for them to reach their highest potentials, then we can receive inspirational promptings from God to assist us in teaching them. He extends to each of us that if we will seek him with quiet reflecting and the study of his word, joined with pondering solutions to our problems based on the implementation of his will, then we will receive thoughts and impressions within our minds where he can teach us as willing and supple students. We then have claim that he will nurture us, and lead us in all our honorable journeys through life. Christ taught us to pray to God for this guidance.

Charity

Charity: It is the highest level of motivation and purpose that one can act from. Charity is the pure love of Christ, as exemplified by his life and death. He would that we too will act from this highest form of motivation. It never fails or quits; it never gets tired or wants to just give up. Its whole purpose is to benefit others. It is the unconditional love that allows the unruly to be forgiven, and start anew and refreshed, after their penitence.

Charity is manifested as we put into our actions the belief we have in others, and the hope we posses that they will perform to our expectations. Yet, it is also the absolution we offer for them to re-adjust, re-fine and re-peat until they get it right. Charity is the highest level of the Loving Father and the Nurturing Mother Teaching Approaches combined. It is a character trait, modeled by both God the Father and his son Jesus Christ.

We too can develop charity, with it being a driving force in our teaching, our training, and in our interacting with others. While acting in charity, we are using unconditional love and we are serving others. It is then, that our motivation is: **They are able to have the opportunity to reach their highest potentials.** This brings us more joy and pleasure when we put others ahead of ourselves and our selfish desires. As their needs become important, just as our own, we are likewise meeting our very purpose and duty.

The Parent's Duty is to provide an atmosphere where children can be reared in love and righteousness. Parents aid in their children's refinement by providing physical needs and assisting with their intellectual growth. They teach by words and examples, that their children may learn to respect and serve others. A parent trains his children to observe the commandments of God and to be productive members of society.

A Teacher's Duty is to give service and be a guide towards the exposure of knowledge, that their charges may have the information available to enable the most correct and meaningful choices as they travel on the road of life.

THIS IS NOW YOUR BEGINNING.

GO AND TRAVEL WELL

Index

A

Aggression 95, 132
Aids 166, 252, 255, 266, 270
Anger.......131, 132, 308, 309, 311, 331
Anguish............................... 131
Apologize............................219, 309
Arguing................................. 294
Attention getter...................... 49, 93
Attitude.................117, 285, 332, 349

B

Back to the Basics
    See Basics.................................. 13
Bad... 141, 250, 274, 300, 336, 350, 362
Basics........................... 250, 253, 261
Behavior 144, 249, 251, 261, 285
Blow a nose 159
Body language ... 38, 40, 162, 174, 220
Bomb Proof 190, 231, 348, 401
Bribe 47, 56, 200, 289
Bucked Off 341

C

Candy ....See Reward
Cave of Darkness...................89, 149
Changing others 76, 292, 296, 373
Character Traits 190
Charge............................... 17
Charity 406
Child 17
Clues...........................44, 252, 256, 270
Colt................................ 44, 140, 166
Commitment........................105, 212
Common goal..........47, 149, 243, 265,
    283, 317, 339, 358, 397
Common ground 15, 220, 291, 300,
    347
Compassion 200, 242, 314
Competition 109

Conditioning 286
Consistency 241
Cowboy Up 115, 215
Criticism 57
Cry Baby............................. 107, 152

D

Debt..206
Defiance.............. 293, 339, 341, 345
Denise Reis 250
Depression...................................131
De-sensitize 166, 171
Deviant 97
Discipline............... 302, 333, 359, 382
Discouragement 131
Disobedience 360
Dream.......................43, 68, 90, 245
Drugs 129, 133

E

E.I. 286
Emotion 75, 144, 241
Employer
    See Supervisor............................34
Example......................................132

F

Failure.............................. 29, 91, 234
Faith 193, 396
Father's Duty.........See Father's Role
Father's Role...............................22
Fear 114, 126, 131, 161, 228, 230
Feminine Role...............................22
Flag Method 167
Force 32, 225, 244, 257, 273, 303
Forgiveness........................... 219, 404
Forward movement252, 254, 262, 382
Freaking-out 162, 261
    See Anger..............................165
Free agency.................................396

Friend.............................. 62, 269, 355

G

Gains *31*, 124, 243, 252, 267, 288
Goals.. 47, 71
God.............................. 190, 198, 214
Golden Rule 34
GPS.. 65
Graduating Escalation of
    Involvement............................ 286
Greeting Levels............................. 39
Grief... 131
Grounding.................................... 325
Guide ... 16, 43, 64, 148, 165, 227, 271,
    291, 400, 407

H

Habit 274, 370
Help.. 244
Honesty..............................82, 218
Hoof Trimming........................... 94
Humor.. 234

I

Instinct.....................66, 108, 140, 279
Instructor 16
Insularity.................................... 277
Integrity........................ 190, 212, 219

J

Jealousy....................................... 131
Joy.... 124, 138, 283, 361, 395, 404, 406
Joy... 261

L

Laughter...................................... 236
Law of Justice............................. 397
Lazy....................57, 99, 136, 199, 225
Lead Mare 168, 361

Learn...................... 104, 136, 140, 392
Learning..158
Liberty................................. 113, 122
Listening............. 41, 98, 156, 295, 378
Loneliness....................................131
Love 21, 34, 49, 193, 220, 263, 291,
    337, 346, 354, 357, 397, 404, 406

M

Mad..76
Manipulate 99, 148, 305
Masculine Role...................... 22, 274
Master..... 16, 36, 46, 98, 220, 277, 282
Mealtime................................ 269, 350
Mentor...... 16, 106, 159, 163, 202, 291
Micro-manage 116
Mistake 81
Money.................. 113, 136, 203, 268
Mother's Role 22

N

Natural consequence...................317
Natural Instinct 111, 132
Need................................. 43, 72, 212
Negativism 84
NO 265, 363, 382
Nothing to Fight Against............110

O

Out-of-control..18, 148, 165, 198, 274,
    337, 346, 379
Over-Nurturing Parent.................29

P

Pain ...49, 124, 138, 166, 217, 257, 275,
    283, 319, 332, 339, 352, 395
Pain compliance 142, 262, 283, 288
Parent..... 16, 45, 58, 76, 111, 138, 158,
    187, 262, 304, 357, 381, 392, 405
Parent's Duty...............................407
Passion.............. 76, 92, 242, 371, 400

Patience.......... 137, 227, 329, 339, 353
Peer pressure............................63, 134
Perception of pain.................168, 275
Perception of reality 163, 391
Perseverance 78
Personal discovery........ 158, 212, 361
Physical Discomfort..................... 131
Physical Force 337
Physical Punishment 332
Potty Training................................ 45
Power ...41, 67, 90, 108, 123, 125, 132,
    148, 182, 192, 202, 217, 225, 246,
    251, 292, 318, 361, 371, 389, 396
Practice79, 93, 185, 189, 226, 231, 262,
    285, 365
Prayer 191, 201, 402, 404
Problem Solving 70
Productivity 34
Punishment... 131, 143, 254, 268, 279,
    304, 306, 317, 332, 381, 397

R

Rapport34, 63, 107, 221, 269, 277, 305,
    347
Rationalization.........35, 144, 209, 267
Rebellious.................96, 110, 301, 349
Red Cliff Ascent............................ 64
Refine.....41, 48, 79, 189, 245, 324, 377,
    397, 407
Release of pressure .96, 111, 236, 268,
    290
Relief of pressure 111, 279, 346
Repetition..................................... 79
Requirement................................ 208
Respect 194, 197, 241
Reward.................18, 47, 56, 64, 169,
    233, 257, 268, 279, 289, 298, 314,
    351, 365, 397, 404
Rogue 345
Rules 146, 233, 264, 265, 305, 336, 363

S

Sarcasm 40
Self confidence............................. 202
Self esteem 200, 288, 298

Self-reliant 122
Service..................... 22, 290, 364, 407
Sin 397, 399
Single parent.................................27
Sleep...128
Spank 49, 107, 143, 257
Spooks.................. 165, 230, See Fear
Spurs...257
Strength ... 75, 106, 127, 201, 216, 220,
    352, 381, 396
Student...104
Supervisor 17, 34, 327

T

Tantrum.......................................113
Teacher...17
Teacher's Duty 407
Teaching Approaches 25, 226, 391
    Engaged...................................144
    Good Mother 27, 389
    Indifferent Traveler..... 35, 57, 227
    Loving Father25, 53, 226, 397, 406
    Nurturing Parent. 27, 55, 181, 227,
        389, 403
    Self Entitled 29, 56, 227, 389
Teaching Techniques
    Adventurer 54
    Bug...276
    Critic 57
    Dictator 59
    Engaged 54
    Fellow Traveler 64
    Friendship.................................63
    Guide 64
    Managerial.................................55
    Overly Protective 55
    Sneaky......................................53
    Unengaged 57
    Victim's.....................................56
Timing 92, 98, 133, 200, 228, 328,
    360
Tough love...................................263
Trailer loading.............................271
Trainer.17, 49, 111, 250, 283, 287, 292,
    304, 316, 321, 334, 336, 358, 369,
    382
Trigger 113, 331, 364, 382

Trust..........................82, 167, 325, 355
Try............................78, 105, 257, 282

U

Unconditional Love..............352, 357
Uneasiness 131

V

Values.............101, 188, 189, 378, 397
Violence.......................................165

W

Want.... 27, 43, 211, 240, 283, 304, 327
Wigging-out 96, 129, 236, 262, 338
Wisdom 17, 43, 123, 133, 189, 207, 223